SITAR AND SAROD IN THE 18th AND 19th CENTURIES

PERFORMING ARTS SERIES

General Editor

FARLEY P. RICHMOND

VOLUME VII

Allyn Miner

Sitar and Sarod in the 18th and 19th Centuries

MOTILAL BANARSIDASS PUBLISHERS
PRIVATE LIMITED • DELHI

First Indian Edition: Delhi,1997

ISBN:81-208-1299-9

MOTILAL BANARSIDASS

41 U.A. Bungalow Road, Jawahar Nagar, Delhi 110 007
8 Mahalaxmi Chamber, Warden Road, Mumbai 400 026
120 Royapettah High Road, Mylapore, Chennai 600 004
Sanas Plaza, Subhash Nagar, Pune 411 002
16 St. Mark's Road, Bangalore 560 001
8 Camac Street, Calcutta 700 017
Ashok Rajpath, Patna 800 004
Chowk, Varanasi 221 001

For Sale in India only

PRINTED IN INDIA

BY JAINENDRA PRAKASH JAIN AT SHRI JAINENDRA PRESS,
A-45 NARAINA, PHASE I, NEW DELHI 110028
AND PUBLISHED BY NARENDRA PRAKASH JAIN FOR
MOTILAL BANARSIDASS PUBLISHERS PRIVATE LIMITED
BUNGALOW ROAD, DELHI 110 007

Foreword by Series Editor

India is one of the great repositories of performing arts, particularly those of the classical, folk/popular, devotional and modern traditions. The sheer enormity and diversity of its cultural expressions in music, dance, dance/drama and theatre are the envy of many nations around the world. This series intends to assemble some of the best books now available on these subjects.

Without exaggeration, a series such as this would not have been possible twenty years ago when I first began writing about Indian theatre. At that time little more than a few dozen books comprised the entire field of scholarship in the English language, not to mention the paucity of materials in regional Indian languages. Today that picture has radically changed. Numerous publishers have devoted precious press time to volumes of well-illustrated, detailed and, yes, sometimes even esoteric works on the multiple aspects of this fascinating subject. Comb any bookshop in Delhi or Madras, Bombay or Calcutta and you will regularly find new works appearing on the shelves. This represents a real area of growth! It is to the credit of Motilal Banarsidass Publishers Private Limited that there is now the potential of assembling numerous volumes together under one umbrella.

The sitar and sarod occupy a place of honor on the stages of the world as well as in India but little is known about the origins and development of these classical instruments at an important stage in Indian history. This welcome book sets out to fill that gap. Like so many other works of late that flesh out details of important topics related to Indian performing arts, this book offers new insights.

FARLEY P. RICHMOND

Table of Contents

PART TWO: CENTERS, FORMS AND INNOVATORS

PART THREE: TECHNIQUES AND COMPOSITIONS

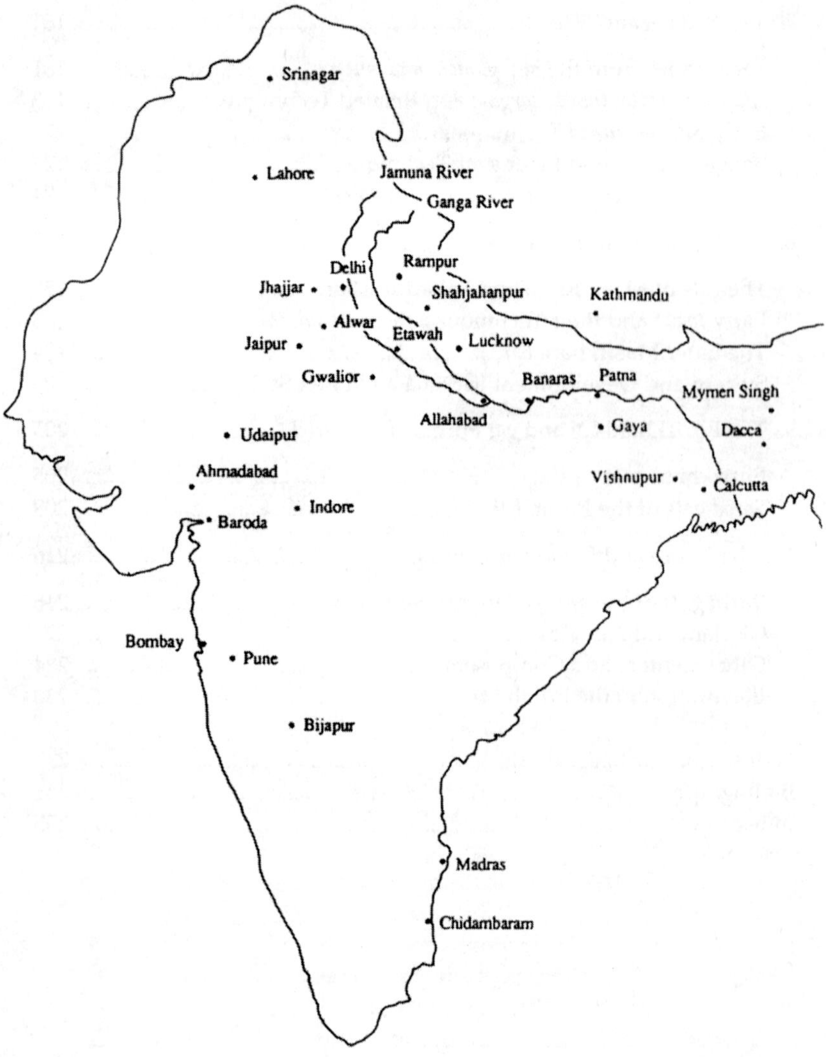
Srinagar
Lahore
Jamuna River
Ganga River
Rampur
Delhi
Jhajjar
Shahjahanpur
Kathmandu
Alwar
Etawah
Jaipur
Lucknow
Gwalior
Banaras
Patna
Mymen Singh
Allahabad
Gaya
Udaipur
Dacca
Ahmadabad
Vishnupur
Calcutta
Indore
Baroda
Bombay
Pune
Bijapur
Madras
Chidambaram

Preface

Despite the prominence of the *sitār* and the *sarod* in North Indian music and their renown throughout the world, little written information is available on the pre-20th-century history of these instruments. Accounts of early players and their music lie hidden in the oral histories of professional family lines, and in 19th-century books, largely inaccessible even to serious students. This study is an attempt to help fill this gap in the history of North Indian music. It uses oral, written and pictorial material to trace the changing instruments, the players and the music from the time of their earliest appearance in India to the end of the 19th century. The 20th century offers very different sources for its study and has been reserved for a separate work.

This project was originally done between 1976 and 1981 and submitted as a doctoral dissertation to the Department of Musicology at Banaras Hindu University. Its background dates to 1971, the year I arrived in Banaras on the Wisconsin Year in India Program and began my study of the *sitār* under my principal teacher, Thakur Raj Bhan Singh. During intense years of performance study, my interest in the history of performance was aroused by the stories about early players and the glimpses of older styles that I heard. Here was a subject that deserved immediate attention, since a large body of information was clearly in danger of being lost.

The oral histories of instrumentalists who traced their traditions into the 19th century were a major source of information for this study. I was delighted by the responsiveness of the musicians whom I approached, and the openness with which they shared with me the histories of their families. Their accounts provided details on personalities and vanished styles that were not only substantive but full of spirit. When these musicians demonstrated or performed, they exemplified the high professional standards that notations in published collections could not touch. I wish to note that there are a great many musicians with whom I was unable to meet, and that there is a good deal of material on this period which escaped my searches. I also wish to apologize in advance for any errors, or for statements in this study that might seem to offend or misrepresent members of any family lines.

Sadly, in the years since I worked with them, many of these artists have passed away, and despite my efforts, I fear that this documentation does not come near to doing justice to their profound knowledge. It is my strong hope that students and family members will pay increased attention to collecting information from the living masters.

Library collections in India, Europe and the United States provided Urdu, Hindi and Bengali handbooks dating from the last quarter of the 19th century, which made up the second main source for this study. Written, notated and illustrated in delightfully individualistic styles, these books presented the rudiments of music to literate amateurs of the late 19th and early 20th centuries. They now offer a vital source for our understanding of the music and atmosphere of the time.

General histories, miscellaneous accounts and travelogues by Europeans formed another source. They complemented the oral and handbook sources, and helped to set the larger context for this study. The illustrations were gathered from India, the United States and London in 1988 and 1989. They have proven to be a valuable source in their own right, and one worthy of more comprehensive collection and separate examination.

This work is divided into three parts. Part One deals with the physical history of the instruments. Here the questions of origin are discussed in detail, and the structural changes in the instruments are traced as closely as possible over time and space. Part Two focuses on the courts and cities where significant musical activity took place, and on the leading instrumentalists of the times. The cultural and political environment of each center is examined here as it relates to musical life. Details on the family and teaching lines of individuals who represented specific styles fill some sections. Part Three deals with the music itself. It is based on notations from 19th-century books, and compositions from oral traditions. The intention is to discover, in so far as it is possible, aspects of form, style and technique from the oral and written remnants of performance practice. Each of the three parts is internally ordered by chronology and region, and each begins with a brief background to the 18th century.

A number of books on the modern *sitār* have been written in the last twenty years.[1] Some of these can be useful as learning primers: Ravi Shankar's classic "My Music, My Life" (Shankar 1968) and Manfred Junius' "The Sitar: the Instrument and its Technique" (Junius 1974) stand out in this regard. Sen's "The String Instruments (Plucked Variety) of North India" (Ghosh 1988) is a significant effort at presenting instrumental history *based on some oral traditions. Slawek's "Sitār Technique in Nibaddh Forms"* (Slawek 1987) is a recent attempt at more specialized writing on performance technique. The "New Grove Dictionary of Musical Instruments" (Sadie 1984) contains substantial entries on Indian musical instruments. Those on *sitār* and other stringed instruments (Dick 1984) represent good modern scholarship. Besides these, new works on specific Indian musical instruments have added to a growing literature in the field. Joep Bor's "The Voice of the Sarangi" (Bor 1986-87) is an excellent presentation of written, oral and pictorial sources pertaining to the history of Indian bowed instruments. James Kippen's "The Tabla of Lucknow" (Kippen 1988) is a welcome addition to literature on this important instrument. A stress on documentation and attention to performance practice that recent works show is a notable trend in writings on Indian music.

Note on Transliteration

Transliteration and notation are mildly problematic but essential aspects of this study. Every attempt is made to define and clarify terms as they are presented, but a basic familiarity with musical, cultural and geographical terms and names will be helpful to the reader, as their regular use here is unavoidable. The transliterations of Urdu and Persian try to follow the guidelines set up by the United States Library of Congress. Transliteration of Sanskrit follows the standard system of diacritics for that language. The transliteration of Hindi follows the Sanskrit system here, but drops the "a" following final and some medial consonants to reflect Hindi pronunciation. The Sanskrit transliteration of *rāga* and *tāla* has been retained to conform to normal usage, despite their colloquial pronunciation, which normally drops the last vowel sound. The choice of transliteration has in many cases been complicated by the exchange of the same terms among Persian, Urdu, Sanskrit and Hindi sources. The language or pronunciation of the immediate source has been the criterion for the transliteration choice for each occurrence of a term, with the result that a term may appear in different spellings to reflect different language contexts.

Diacritical marks have been dispensed with altogether for proper names and for place names to reduce the complications that arise in transliterating modern names, and to allow the use of conventional city name spellings, which should allow for easier reading. Exceptions are the use of diacritics for authors of Sanskrit texts, and for the Persian-Arabic *'ain*, which has no English equivalent, as in "*Na'mat.*"

The terminology used in the classification of musical instruments is that of Hornbostel and Sachs, now considered standard in most musicological literature. A simple Bhatkhande-style Hindustani musical notation is used in Part Three. This is an efficient system for conveying the relatively simple melodic information given here, and is nearly self explanatory. The chromatic twelve-tone Hindustani octave is notated here as S $\underline{\text{R}}$ R $\underline{\text{G}}$ G M 'M P $\underline{\text{D}}$ D $\underline{\text{N}}$ N. Notes in the lower and lowest octaves have one dot and two dots below them respectively; notes in the upper octave have a dot above. In the sixteen-beat rhythmic cycle *tīntāla* in which most of the notations are set, each of the four sections is divided by a vertical line and each section contains four beats. Each note or set of notes receives the instrumental stroke or strokes notated below it.

Acknowledgements

I would like to acknowledge the individuals and institutions who helped make this work possible. To Ustād Ali Akbar Khan Sahab, my teacher since 1986, and with whom I had the privilege of tying the thread of discipleship in 1991, I owe my continued inspiration for performance and study in this field. The profundity of his musical personality is beyond words, and I can only attempt to be worthy of his teaching. Thakur Dr. Raj Bhan Singh of Varanasi, my Guru from 1971 to 1982, gave me intense, devoted and solid training in *sitār* performance. From him I received the view of both the music and the culture that inspired me to devote my career to this field. I am indebted to him for life. My revered Dada Guru, Pandit Shivram Ramchandra Mavlankar of Allahabad, initiated me into his illustrious Gwalior *sitār* tradition over the same years. Between 1980 and 1982, Pandit Jyotish Chandra Chaudhury introduced me to the teachings of the great *ustāds* of early 20th-century Bengal. Ustād Ilyas Khan Sahab thrilled me with his Purab style *gats*, and taught me generously before his death in 1989. I owe my knowledge and interest in musicology to Professor Prem Lata Sharma, former Chair of the Department of Musicology of Banaras Hindu University (B.H.U.). She coached me through the doctoral program at B.H.U., and continues to be my advisor and mentor in ongoing musicological projects.

Many other artists and scholar-musicians whom I approached for information were open and generous. Pandit D. T. Joshi gave of his vast store of knowledge and experience over many meetings. Ustad Umar Khan Sahab was generous with his time and provided a number of *gats* and a detailed history of his family's *sarod* line. Ustad Mushtaq Ali Khan met with me in a number of sessions, and provided valuable information on the Senia line of *sitār* players and their music. Pandit Radhika Mohan Maitra, in his generous and scholarly manner, gave me a great deal of material on his *sarod* line, and demonstrated some extraordinarily beautiful Firozkhani *gats*. Sri Satya Kinkar Banerji, who played *sitār* in the delicate style of traditional Vishnupur, kindly provided me with details of that illustrious tradition. Ustad Asad Ali Khan and Ustad Zia Moiuddin Dagar Sahab were very kind in speaking with me of their *bīn* traditions. Other musicians with whom I met and talked were generous, and I remember their warmhearted cooperation.

My colleague Dr. Joep Bor has been a valued collaborator and critic and I am grateful for his sharing with me the results of his years of research and his marvelous collection of illustrations. I would like to acknowledge George Ruckert, Michael Rosse and Jerome Bauer. I also wish to thank Dr. Bonnie Wade for her encouragement. The Fulbright Foundation and the Asian Cultural Council supported me throughout the vital years of performance study and research in India. I especially wish to acknowledge the Department of South Asia Regional Studies at the University of Pennsylvania for its support since 1984.

Part One

THE INSTRUMENTS

1

The Origin of the *sitār*

The age and origin of the *sitār* have been the subjects of a good deal of controversy in modern India, some of it exciting a passion that is indicative of popular concerns about North Indian social history. Here the main opinions, popular and scholarly, are first presented in overview and then examined in detail.

Ideas on the origin of the *sitār* fall into a few groups. The view predominating by far, especially in popular accounts, involves the Central Asian-Indian poet and musician Amir Khusrau who lived in the court of early 14th-century Delhi. Amir Khusrau, it is generally said, created an instrument on the model of an existing Indian stringed instrument, and gave it a Persian name, *seh-tār* "three-stringed."[2] Popular books on music nearly all recount this story. Amir Khusrau's role in the creation of the *sitār* in India has gradually been discredited by historians, but social motivations and the tenacity of tradition cause the idea to persist, and it seems that it will continue to be a popular belief for generations to come. In defense of this belief, however, the Amir Khusrau connection has a traceable origin. It is now fairly clear that a 19th-century error led to the mistaken identification of the famous Amir Khusrau with a later figure, possibly named Khusrau Khan, who lived in the 18th century. Written sources support oral accounts that speak of a musician by this name at the court of Emperor Muhammad Shah. When reinterpreted in an 18th-century context, then, the Amir Khusrau theory takes on a new significance.

One of India's great modern *sitār* players, Ravi Shankar, brings up a second view on the origin of the *sitār*:

> Many scholars believe that the sitar was in existence long before Amir Khusru's time, in diverse shapes in different regions of India. It was variously called *tritantri veena* ... , *chitra veena* ... or *parivadini* ... (Shankar 1968:46).

A number of writers have argued, with or without the mention of Amir Khusrau, that the *sitār* was a modification of or a later name for a stringed instrument (all of which were called *vīṇās*) existing in India and listed in the Sanskrit music texts. The *tritantrī*, "three-stringed," *vīṇā* is found in the 13th-century *"Saṅgītaratnākara,"* and the *citrā vīṇā* is described in the earlier *"Nāṭyaśāstra"* of Bharata. This group of theories deserves examination, first, for bringing up the issue of continuity in Indian musical history, and second, for representing a prominent late 19th-century idea, that many of India's modern cultural innovations are actually products of pre-Muslim Sanskritic traditions.

A third idea on the origin of the *sitār* refers to the appearance of long-necked lutes in 9th- and 10th-century Indian temple sculpture, and suggests that the *sitār* was in existence from this early time in India. No specific author or *vīṇā* name is suggested. The appearance of long-necked lutes in medieval temple reliefs and the question of their relation to the *sitār* are valid topics in the study of Indian musical instruments and will receive some attention here.

Finally, most current musicologists are convinced of a Central or West Asian influence in the origin of the *sitār*. One writer speculates that the *sitār* developed from the Persian instrument of that name but that the Persian *setār* had earlier evolved from the Indian *citrā vīṇā* (Roy Choudhury 1957:72). Most, however, trace the *sitār* directly to some long-necked lute of Persia, Turkey or Central Asia that had come into use in Northwestern India or the Mughal courts. The Persian *setār*, the *tambūr* and in one case the Uzbek *dutār*, have been suggested by different writers as the *sitār*'s immediate ancestors.[3] Pictorial and written evidence shows a possible historical relationship between the Indian *sitār* and more than one of these instruments. The melody *tambūr*, its modification the drone instrument which we will call here the *tambūrā*,[4] and the Indian *sitār* clearly appear related, but evidence will point to the Persian or Kashmiri *setār* as the mainstream *sitār*'s most likely immediate predecessor.

A more detailed look at each of the theories follows. The cultural complexity of North India at the time of the earliest record of the *sitār* and the lack of specific source material prevents many details on the origin of the instrument from coming to light. But while some speculation is unavoidable, a generally satisfactory picture emerges from the available oral, written and pictorial material.

Amir Khusrau and the sitār

An outstanding figure in medieval Indian cultural history, Hazrat (an honorific) Amir Khusrau was born in 1253 in Patiali, a Braj[5] speaking area in what is now Uttar Pradesh, to a Turkic Central Asian father and an Indian mother. Based in Delhi, he served in a succession of courts, one of which was that of Allauddin Khilji, powerful ruler of the Delhi Sultanate (1296-1316). Of Allauddin Khilji's rule, a contemporary writer said:

> The most wonderful thing ... which people beheld in his reign was the throng of great men of all nationalities, masters of every science and experts in every art. The capital of Delhi, by the presence of these peerless men of extraordinary talents, had become the envy of Baghdad, the rival of Cairo and the equal of Constantinople (Mirza 1962:107).

Amir Khusrau, among Delhi's prized artists, was especially enamoured of the art and culture of India, and travelled the width and breadth of the country recording in his prose and poetry events and observations on the culture of the time. His works provide one of the most important sources of information on his period. Khusrau died in 1325, a few months after the death of his famous Sufi mentor Khwaja Nizamuddin Auliya (cf. Ansari 1975, Mirza 1962).

Besides for his numerous *ghazals, mathnavis,* prose and Hindi *(hindavī)* poetry, Amir Khusrau is famous for his activity in the field of music. His writings indicate competence and sensitivity in both Persian and Indian music theory and in vocal and instrumental practice. It was his strong expressed interest in Indian music that led later writers to credit him for the introduction into Indian music of a number of melodic forms and instruments synthesized from Persian sources. While he may have had an influence on the music of the time, the extent of his innovations is often clearly exaggerated. The *"Tuḥfāt al-Hind"* and the *"Rāg darpan,"* 17th-century Persian works on music, list a number of composite *rāgas* said to be introduced by Amir Khusrau, including the famous *rāga yaman*, but most of these *rāgas* are not mentioned in Amir Khusrau's own works.[6] The same texts, along with popular tradition, also credit him with the invention of *qavvālī*, a vocal form associated with Indian Sufism. Khusrau was certainly a Sufi devotee and an important composer of *qavvālī* lyrics, many of which are still sung today (cf. Qureshi 1986) but his role in introducing the musical form is unclear. His alleged invention of *tarānā* is also questionable.[7] Most importantly, he is often credited with the introduction of *khyāl*, the genre now dominating modern Hindustani vocal music. However, Persian scholar Shahab Sarmadee thinks that Khusrau used the term in the normal Persian sense of a figure of speech, not for a song form.[8]

Khusrau's works give a significant amount of information on musical instruments. The *chang*, a sixteen-stringed harp, appears as one of the most prominent instruments of the time. Khusrau has high praise for its leading player, Muhammad Shah. He frequently mentions the *rubāb* which he describes as having two strings, *bamm* and *zīr*, and he speaks of the *barbat*, also referred to as *rud*, which had four strings over a hollow body and was played with a plectrum called a *zakhma*. He describes the *tambūr*, which will be discussed presently in some detail, as having four strings, two silk and two metal. He also mentions two Indian *vīṇās*: the four-stringed *alāvan*,[9] and the *kingra*, which he mentions as a folk instrument (Sanskrit: *kinnarī*). Among drums he speaks of the *daff*, a Persian frame drum, and the *duhl* (Sanskrit: *ḍhaula*, Hindi: *ḍhol*, a barrel drum) (Sarmadee 1975a:255-8). Although the invention of both *sitār* and *tablā* are popularly credited to him, there is no mention of either in his writings. But we can still look to other sources for additional information on the instruments and forms of Amir Khusrau's period.

Some Sanskrit treatises and Persian sources are informative for the field of music in the 13th and 14th centuries. Among the Sanskrit works, the first half of the 13th century saw the appearance of the most important of all medieval musicological texts, the "*Saṅgītaratnākara*" of Śārṅgadeva. Śārṅgadeva lived in Daulatabad, Maharashtra, and his ancestors had come from Kashmir (Śārṅgadeva 1978:xiii). The primary *vīṇā* described here is the *ekatantrī*, a stick zither, which Śārṅgadeva hints is the predominant *vīṇā* type of the time.[10] 14th-century Sanskrit musicological literature following the "*Saṅgītaratnākara*" includes the "*Saṅgītopaniṣatsāroddhāra*" of Sudhākalaśa, a work from Gujarat, notable for its indication of new trends in the classification and visualization of *rāgas* (Sudhākalaśa 1961). The "*Saṅgītopaniṣatsāroddhāra*" lists thirteen *vīṇās*. Among the listed instruments there is no *sitār*. Nor is there mention of *khyāl*.[11]

The inventions and practices of Persian court poets and musicians might not be expected to appear contemporaneously in Sanskrit works. Two Persian writings, then, might represent more closely the Muslim court music and culture of the time. The "*Ghunyat al-munya*" of the 14th century and the "*Lahjāt-i Sikandar Shāhī*" of the late 15th century, are prominent Persian sources on Indian music (cf. Ahmad 1984:17, Sarmadee 1971). Neither mentions *sitār* or *khyāl*. The pictorial sources, available from the early Mughal period, show some of the Persian instruments mentioned by Amir Khusrau. The harp which must be the *chang*, the skin-covered lute that must be the *rabāb*, and the long, thin-necked *tambūr* are the stringed instruments found in 16th-century and later paintings (cf. Figures 5-6). On the basis of the available material, it must be concluded that claims for the existence of the *sitār*, and the sung *khyāl*, near the time of Amir Khusrau are unfounded. This is not a new conclusion and was put forth as early as 1935.[12] It now deserves general acceptance.

What remains of the Amir Khusrau theory then? It is clear that some oral histories and the literature that emerged from them lie at the source of the story. While Amir Khusrau is often credited with the origin of the *sitār* in these sources, actual performance practice is traced only to the time of Masit Khan, a figure of late 18th-century Delhi. A few traditions speak of a performance history extending to a generation before Masit Khan. Vague ideas of an earlier association with Sufi music are sometimes expressed, but details are not known. There are some oral accounts, however, that speak clearly of a figure named Amir Khusrau or Khusrau Khan of Delhi. A careful search among written sources reveals scattered 19th-century references in Urdu, Hindi and even English that seem to link these accounts to earlier oral traditions. Finally a few references in 18th-century Persian sources indicate that there indeed existed in 18th-century Delhi someone who had a role in the earliest appearance of the *sitār* there.

The 18th-Century Amir Khusrau

Credit should go to K. C. Brhaspati for pioneering studies of the Persian and Urdu sources relating to music in the Raza library at Rampur and the presentation of material from them in his works. Brhaspati states repeatedly that Khusrau Khan was the actual originator of the *sitār* (Brhaspati 1976:241-2, 1974:14, 79). While the specific origins of some of Brhaspati's statements remain elusive and are possibly a mix of oral and written sources, his ideas are easily substantiated, and the written history of the mix-up is not very difficult to trace.

In 1834 an ambiguous statement appears in the important work by Captain N. Augustus Willard (Willard 1965 [1834]).[13] Following a description of the *"tamboora,"* he says of the *sitār*: "This is likewise a modern instrument, and was invented by Umeer Khosro of Delhi" (*ibid*.:84). What does he mean by "modern?" It is intriguing that later in the same work Willard speaks specifically of the 14th-century Khusrau using a different spelling for the name: "Umeer Khusrow of Dehli" (*ibid*.:121). Was he referring to a different, later man in connection with the *sitār*? 19th-century writer F.-J. Fétis thought Willard's Amir Khusrau lived sometime after the 15th century:

> Willard, qui a recueilli ses renseignements chez les musiciens indiens, dit que le *sitar*, instrument à six ou à sept cordes pincées, a été inventé par un Mongol de Dehli, nommé *Oumir Khosro*. Il n'indique pas l'époque de l'invention; mais elle ne peut être antérieure au quinzième siècle de l'ère chrétienne, dans lequel fut fondé le royaume mongol de Delhi (Fétis 1869-II:288).

In 1874, however, the prominent Calcutta music scholar and writer Sourindro Mohun Tagore interprets Willard's statement in his own way, saying "It was, according to Captain Willard, invented by Ameer Khusroo in the beginning of the 12th century" (Tagore 1965:348). Tagore's idea reflects his overzealous campaign for the early dating of modern phenomena. We cannot say what Willard knew about the inventor of the *sitār*. Very likely he was simply recording what he had heard from contemporary musicians, an admirable characteristic of his work. His ambiguous statement, however, became a source of confusion for Tagore and others. Tagore alone, however, cannot be faulted for the introduction of the theory linking the early Amir Khusrau with *sitār*. Muhammad Karam Imam Khan of Lucknow, in his 1856 *"Ma'dan al-mūsīqī"* states that Amir Khusrau invented the *sitār*, along with other instruments and vocal forms (Khan, M. K. I. 1925:23, 58, 227). It is likely that Karam Imam's statements are expansions of the ideas expressed in the earlier *"Rāg darpan"* and the *"Tuḥfāt al-Hind"* where Amir Khusrau is credited with numerous modern innovations.

Despite the strong multilingual influences of Karam Imam and Tagore who propagated the story of the early Amir Khusrau and the *sitār*, a written tradition survived that remembered the later Khusrau. A number of sources speak of an Amir Khusrau who was not the 14th-century figure. A 19th-century example appears in a paper presented before the Poona Gayan Samaj in 1884. The speaker, one Mr. Natekar, states that the *bīn*, the North Indian *rudra vīṇā*, was introduced during the time of Akbar and that "Satar was subsequently introduced on the model of Bin by Amir Khusru."[14] Two early 20th-century works representing regionally separate traditions add details on the lineage of the 18th-century Amir Khusrau. *"Saṅgīt sudarśan,"* written in 1916 by Sudarsanacarya Sastri, a disciple of the Jaipur *sitār* player Amrtsen, speaks of the *sitār*'s inventor as Amir Khusrau *"faqīr,"* a descendant of Miyan Tansen[15] through his daughter's line. According to Sudarsanacarya, Khusrau was the father of Firoz Khan and the grandfather of Masit Khan (Sastri 1916:26). A similar account is found in a 1934 Pune collection of anecdotes and histories of musicians by L. D. Josi. Josi speaks of Amir Khusrau as father of both Firoz Khan and Masit Khan (Josi 1935: 250). Firoz Khan (known to modern musicians as Adarang from the signatures in his *khyāl* compositions) was a musician in the court of Muhammad Shah (1719-1748). Masit Khan, also famous in Delhi, was the creator of the *sitār gat* (composition) form bearing his name. Firoz Khan and Masit Khan are by all accounts leading figures in the early history of the *sitār*. It is not surprising if we hear that the later Amir Khusrau was related to them.

Some oral accounts, despite the strength of the wider popular belief, continue today to speak of the later Amir Khusrau. Here the name Khusrau Khan replaces Amir Khusrau. *Sarod* player Umar Khan, on the basis of his learned tradition, spoke of Khusrau Khan as Firoz Khan's father.[16] Muneshwar Dayal of Gaya spoke of him as Firoz Khan's father and younger brother of Na'mat Khan.[17] Brhaspati makes the same statement on the basis of unspecified sources (Brhaspati 1976:242). Na'mat Khan, the most prominent musician of Emperor Muhammad Shah's Delhi, will presently be discussed at length. Undoubtedly other accounts of the later Amir Khusrau, oral and written, will continue to turn up.

For more conclusive information on the 18th-century Amir Khusrau and his family we finally look to the available literature of the time. At least six contemporary and near contemporary Persian texts speak of Na'mat Khan, where he appears as the leading musician of Muhammad Shah's court. Those texts are the *"Jahāndār Shāh nāmah,"* the *"Tārīkh-i Muhammad Shāhī"*, the *"Muntakhāb al-lubāb"* (all 18th century), the *"Risāla-i ẓikr-i mughanniān-i Hindustān"* of 1734-35, the *"Mir'āt-i āftāb numā,"* compiled in 1803-04, and the *"Muraqqa'-i Dehlī,"* written in 1738. The *"Jahāndār Shāh nāmah,"* the *"Tārīkh-i Muhammad Shāhī"* and the *"Muntakhāb al-lubāb"* are historical works that briefly refer to Na'mat Khan's family and position in the court in Delhi. The *"Risāla-i ẓikr-i mughanniān-i Hindustān"* contains a short biography of Na'mat Khan as does the *"Mir'āt-i āftāb numā."* From these two texts we learn the name of Na'mat Khan's father and the list of his teachers and his royal patrons in the Delhi court. The *"Mir'āt-i āftāb numā"* speaks of Firoz Khan as Na'mat Khan's son-in-law and disciple.

The most outstanding picture of the musical state of Muhammad Shah's Delhi court is to be found in the *"Muraqqa'-i Dehlī"* (cf. Khan, D. Q. B. 1933, 1982, 1989). This wonderful work contains an enthusiastic first hand description of nearly sixty musicians and performers at the Delhi court. The leading musician of the time is Na'mat Khan. His brother and a nephew are described as noted instrumentalists:[18]

> [Na'mat Khan's] brother has an amazing skill at playing various instruments. For four hours at a time he can play various types of

> tunes *(dhun)* but his art is such that there is no repetition. Seeing his artistry many good musicians are awestruck. God did not give this mastery and accomplishment to everyone. He is also skilled in singing.
>
> Na'mat Khan's nephew is very expert at playing the *sitār*. He has created various new methods. Whatever tunes are played on all the well known instruments, this man can play on the *sitār*.[19]

It is notable that the author does not speak of the *sitār* as a new instrument in the hands of Na'mat Khan's nephew. Some oral accounts, as already cited, give the credit for the introduction of the instrument to the brother. If we rely further on these traditions, the brother was Khusrau Khan, later known as Amir Khusrau, and the nephew was Firoz Khan. Given the corroboration of oral accounts and contemporary written records, it seems fairly conclusive that Na'mat Khan's brother and nephew were responsible for the introduction of the *sitār* in Delhi. Part Two contains a full discussion of this family.

Sitār *and the* vīṇās *of the Sanskrit Texts*

The mention of a *vīṇā* whose name means "three-stringed" in the important 13th-century Sanskrit treatise the *"Saṅgītaratnākara"* inspired some writers on music to formulate theories relating the *sitār* to it. Sourindro Mohun Tagore, reflecting the so-called Hindu renaissance of 19th-century Bengal and the fervent interest in Indian cultural history that it stirred, makes what is apparently the original claim for such a relationship. In the *"Yantra Kshetra Dipika"* of 1872 and the *"Yantra Kosha"* of 1875 he claims that Amir Khusrau gave the name *sitār* to such *vīṇās* as the *tritantrī* and the *kacchapī*.[20]

Sourindro Mohun, a prominent member of the erudite Tagore family of 19th-century Calcutta, took it as his mission to promote an improved understanding and respect toward Indian music among Europeans and urban educated Indians. His numerous works in English, Bengali and Hindi and his school of music in Calcutta, the first of its kind, were significant in helping create the tremendous popular interest in music seen in Calcutta in the late 19th century (cf. Rosse 1980:525-6). In his enthusiasm for proving the antiquity of the music, however, one of his actions was to impose Sanskrit *vīṇā* names on instruments of his time. He carried this one step farther and went so far as to create a number of new instruments to carry the names of *vīṇās*. His examples of the *kinnarī, vipañcī, nādeśvar* and *bharat vīṇās* are fanciful combinations of modern Indian and even Western instruments. The instruments are listed and described in his *"Yantra Kosha,"* and collections of them which he presented to a number of museums around the world can still be seen (cf. Figure 36).[21] One wonders at his intentions in this endeavor.

Tagore's enthusiasm in proving the antiquity of Indian music found resonance among some Indian thinkers even in post-independence India. Establishing Sanskritic origins for modern instruments was a way of stating that Western, and especially Muslim, influence on modern Indian culture was minimal. Lalmani Mishra in his *"Bhāratīyā saṅgīt vādya"* exemplifies this thinking in his attempt to trace the *sitār* to the *tritantrī vīṇā* through the *jantar*. According to his argument, based on references in the *"Saṅgītaratnākara"* and the *"Ain-i Akbarī," tritantrī vīṇā* was later called the *jantar*, and *jantar* was an early name for the *sitār* (Mishra 1973:45). The *tritantrī vīṇā* is mentioned in Śārṅgadeva's 13th-century *"Saṅgītaratnākara,"* although no description is given. In his 15th-century commentary on the *"Saṅgītaratnākara,"* Kallinātha states that the popular name for the *tritantrī vīṇā* is *jantra*.[22] The *tritantrī* was evidently disappearing at that time, at least as a name, as it is not mentioned after the time of Kallinātha. The *jantar* on the other hand is found in the 16th-century *"Ain-i Akbarī"* of Abul Fazl, the great chronicle of the court and times of Akbar, where it is one of the most prominent instruments of the time. Here it is described as having five strings, a hollow wooden neck with sixteen frets, and a half gourd fastened at each end.[23] Akbar's *jantar* may well be the same instrument as Kallinātha's *jantra* and may also be related to Śārṅgadeva's *tritantrī*, an interesting fact in itself. But it is clear that the *jantar* of the *"Ain-i Akbarī"* was a stick zither, the predominant North Indian *vīṇā* of the time. Frequently seen in miniature paintings and structurally unrelated to the *sitār*, this *vīṇā* is often pictured in paintings with half gourds rather than the full gourds of the later *bīn*. The similarity of the *bīn* and the *jantar* is clear from the *"Ain-i Akbarī"* which lists the two side by side and states only that the *bīn* has fewer strings. Later the positions of the *jantar* and the *bīn* were to reverse, as the *bīn* became the larger and predominant *vīṇā* of North India. The *jantar* is still found as a folk instrument in Rajasthan and is a small *bīn*.[24] The term *jantra* later came to be used, mainly in Bengali works, in its Sanskrit form *yantra*, "device" or "instrument," where it was modified by other specifying terms. Thus we have *yantra kośa*, "dictionary of instruments," *sitār yantra*, and *yantra saṅgīt*, "instrumental music." The *jantra* has no direct relationship to the *sitār*, nor does the *tritantrī vīṇā*.

Another proposed progenitor of the *sitār* is the *citrā vīṇā* found mentioned in the earliest Indian musicological text the "*Nāṭyaśāstra*" of Bharata (c.400 B.C.- 400 A.D.). Swami Prajnanananda says:

> The origin of the *sitār* or *setār* can be traced back to the *chitrā veenā* possessed of seven strings. The *gātrā veenā* is also possessed of seven strings, and the *gātrā veenā* is more ancient. Narada mentioned the name of the *gātrā veenā* in the *Śikṣā*. So both *gātrā veenā* and *chitrā veenā* can be considered to be the fore-runners of the modern *sitār* (Prajnanananda 1973:468).

The *citrā vīṇā* is specified in Bharata's "*Nāṭyaśāstra*" as having seven strings (Bharata 1964-IV:124), but its structure can only be surmised from related information. It is normally accepted on the basis of Bharata's descriptions of *vīṇā* techniques, *dhātu,* and supported by the temple art of the time, that most *vīṇās* of the time were harps (cf. Coomaraswamy 1930:248-9). Several types of short lutes are also seen in paintings and temple reliefs dating to the first few centuries A.D. and Mishra has tried to identify the short lute as the *citrā vīṇā* (Mishra 1973:41-2), but the evidence is far too weak for any conclusions. A relationship of *citrā* to *sitār* and both to the Greek *kithara* or *cithara* on the basis of a perceived etymological basis[25] is also not supportable, but the area of ancient Greek and Indian musical interchange is overdue for a careful study.

Long Lutes in Medieval India

The appearance of long-necked lutes in some South Indian temple reliefs has been the basis for the suggestion that *sitār* existed in India from pre-Muslim times (Tarlekar 1972:88-9; Deva 1981:54). The long lutes as seen in medieval temple reliefs are problematic in regards to both their identity and their place in musical history. They appear in South India in the 10th-century Calukyan period at Pattadakal (Marcel-Dubois 1941:89) and at Cidambaram in the 12th century (Figure 1) but are rare in comparison to stick zithers. They vary considerably in shape, but allowing for the possibilities of artistic license, it must be assumed that the basic type did exist in the contemporary society.

The stick zither takes prominence over the harp in Indian iconography after the 6th century. It is the only *vīṇā* type explicitly described in musical literature until the late 17th century when Ahobala describes the *taumburam* in his "*Saṅgītapārijāta*" (Ahobala 1982:82). This is not to say that no *vīṇā* listed in the earlier texts is a lute, but there is no clear evidence at this point by which any *vīṇā* name from among those listed can definitively be applied to the long-necked temple lutes. While no evidence exists in India that would indicate the name of the long-necked lutes, a tempting source of identification is found in Southeast Asia, where long lutes exist whose names derive from the term *kacchapī* (cf. Marcuse 1964:268; Kunst 1968:15-16). The *kacchapī*, "tortoise,"[26] is one of the *vīṇā*s listed in Sanskrit texts from the early time of Bharata. It is not described, but the 10th-century commentator on the "*Nāṭyaśāstra*," Abhinavagupta, distinguished three categories of *vīṇās*: *vakra*, "crooked," *kūrmī*, "tortoise," and *alābū*, "gourd."[27] The categories seem to hint at harps, lutes and stick zithers respectively. The *kacchapī* might have been a lute. Much later, in the 18th-century "*Saṅgītanārāyaṇa*," the author assigns the name *kacchapī* to the Indian or *dhrupad rabāb*. The Hindi *kachuā* is used to describe the flat-cut gourd of a *sitār* type called the *kachuā sitār*.

The long lute, whether named *kacchapī* or not, is given little prominence in the Sanskrit texts and in temple art. It appears to have been a lesser used instrument than the predominating stick zither *vīṇās*. Its regional occurrence in temple sculpture indicates that it was isolated to the south of India. Outside of India, the history of the long lute is traced to the Arab world. According to Farmer, it was first seen by the Arabs in Mesopotamia, and came to Arabia as early as the 5th century A.D. (Farmer 1929:4-7). It probably existed in its fretted form in Persia by the late 10th century, and not long after became one of the predominant instruments of Persia and Central Asia (Farmer 1964:180). It may be more than coincidental that it is also found in India from the 10th century. Sea routes from the southwest coast of India to and from the Arab world were functioning from very ancient times and were early passages of cultural exchange. It is possible that the temple long lutes had their source in the Arab world.

These instruments disappear from temple sculptures by the end of the 12th century and the long lute seen next in Indian history is the fretted *tambūr*, prominently depicted and reported throughout the art and literature of the Muslim courts of North India. There is no doubt that the *tambūr*'s immediate source was Arab-Persian culture. What happened to the long lutes of the temple sculptures? It is possible that in South India they continued in a minor or regional role, finally re-emerging as the Karnatak *vīṇā*. The origin of the Karnatak *vīṇā* is a problem deserving of more attention. For the present, however, it can be said that there exists no continuity between the lutes depicted on the medieval temples and the *sitār* to indicate any sort of relationship there.

The tambūr

The early waves of Muslim invasion in Northwest India and the 12th-century establishment of the Delhi Sultanate by Turkish Muslims introduced profound change into North Indian culture. Over the next six centuries the art, literature, religion and customs of Turkish, Persian and Central Asian cultures came to India with the artists and scholars of the Muslim courts. Historical records hint that for some time the Persian music of the courts thrived without any influence of India's musical culture (cf. Askari 1972:102). Eventually, however, the presence of Indians in the courts became a force for change and synthesis. This is known to have begun significantly during the time of Amir Khusrau, and to have culminated under the Great Mughals in the 16th and 17th centuries. The result was a dynamic music unique to the courts and urban centers of North India.

Among the instruments that appeared in North Indian history from the early period of Muslim occupation was the *tambūr* (also transliterated *tanbūr* or *tunbūr*), a fretted long lute. Farmer found the earliest descriptions of the fretted *tambūr* in Arabic manuscripts dating to the 9th and 10th centuries and traced its origins to the 8th century when texts spoke of the "measured *tunbūr*" and called it an instrument of Baghdad. Farmer found that by the mid-10th century the *tambūr* had become a dominant instrument throughout the Middle East (Farmer 1926:26-8; 1929:15).

In India as early as 1076, during the occupation of the Panjab by the Ghaznavids of modern Afghanistan, one of the first Indo-Persian poets, Masud-i Sa'ad-i Salman, spoke of the *tambūr* among the Arab and Persian instruments at the court in Lahore.[28] One of the earliest Persian chroniclers in Delhi, Hasan Nizami, made references to it in about 1200 (Askari 1972:102). Amir Khusrau described the *tambūr* of the late 13th-century Delhi court in some detail. After his time references increase in frequency and continue into the 19th century.

The features of the early court *tambūr* as depicted in the earliest miniature paintings are consistent. It had a small pear shaped body with a flat face, and a long, narrow tapering neck (Figure 2). The tuning pegs, usually four, were in lateral positions on both sides of the pegbox at the end of the neck. We know that the bridge was thin, an important distinction from the later *sitār*, and that the frets were gut wrapped around the neck. The instrument was made entirely of wood. Amir Khusrau describes the *tambūr* as having two strings of silk and two of metal, and producing notes that were "precise and piercing like arrows" (Sarmadee 1975a:258).

The *tambūr* figured with some prominence among court instruments in Delhi after Amir Khusrau's time. An account of the reign of Sikandar Lodi of the late 15th century just preceding Mughal rule mentions a *tambūr* player, along with a *vīṇā* player, among four instrumentalists employed at court.[29] In the 16th-century *"Ain-i Akbarī"* four *tambūr* players are included among the thirty-six listed musicians of the Mughal emperor Akbar's court, the largest number of players mentioned for any one instrument, including the important *bīn* (Blochmann 1965:214-6). An outstanding miniature of the Jahangir period (1605-1627) shows a solo *tambūr* player performing in a rural setting (Figure 3).

The 'Adil Shahi dynasty in the Deccan court of Bijapur was an important center for Urdu language and literature and Muslim court culture, including music. This was especially so under Ibrahim 'Adil Shah who ruled 1580-1627, contemporaneously to Akbar and Jahangir. Ibrahim 'Adil Shah himself is reported to have been an expert *tambūr* player. He named his *tambūr* "Moti Khan" and was very fond of it, alluding to it in a number of songs. His courtiers and the public knew of his devotion to it. One poet reports in a poem

> that when the Sultan took the guitar and sat in a posture of playing on it, his courtiers bowed down before it, made obeisance and paid a respectful homage to it (Adil Shah 1956:53).

A chronicler of his reign tells us that

> when the king wished to take it from one place to another, it was placed on a throne followed by the royal flag and the trumpet etc. and the accompanying nobles paid respectful homage by bowing down before it *(ibid.)*.

Ibrahim 'Adil Shah was fascinated with the music and religion of his Hindu subjects and is known to have been a composer of *dhrupads*. The *"Kitāb-i nauras"* is a collection of his songs to be sung in Indian *rāgas*. We do not know the character of the music that he played on "Moti Khan," but we can guess that his was a style that blended elements of Persian and Indian forms and melodies. It may be significant that from around this time the instrument began to be called *tambūrah* or *tambūrā*, a detail that may reflect the Indianization that music literature and cultural history indicate.[30]

The *tambūr* of Ibrahim 'Adil Shah presents an interesting problem, however, and exemplifies the difficulties one runs into in dealing with this period. A painting of Sultan holding an instrument, presumably

"Moti Khan," was done from life by a court artist, Farukh Beg in 1610-11. The instrument depicted is a fretless lute shaped like a Persian *rabāb*. Unlike the *rabāb* it has a wooden face.[31] If this was indeed a *tambūr*, then the definition of *tambūr* for that time period or for the region must be expanded to include wooden-faced instruments other than the pear-shaped fretted long lute. The instrument will remain problematic until a thorough study of the period is done.

By the 17th century the culture and music of the Mughal and provincial courts was a fascinating mix of Indian and Persian elements. The *"Tuḥfāt al-Hind"* of this time speaks of the notes of the *tambūr* in terms of their *śruti*, the Sanskrit theoretical tradition's microtonal division of the octave. A line drawing in a manuscript of the *"Tuḥfāt al-Hind"* shows a *tambūr* with its *śruti* positions designated alongside the neck (Figure 4) (Khan, Mirza [17th cent.]:chapter 5, folio 125). Around 1665 Amir Faqirullah, a native of Kashmir and a courtier under the Mughal emperor Aurangzeb, wrote his important *"Rāg darpan,"* which he stated was partly a translation of a Sanskrit work, the *"Mānakutuhala,"* written about a hundred and fifty years before.[32] Faqirullah reports that the *tambūr* had two strings of metal and two of gut, or five strings made of iron or copper (Faqirullah 1953; Ahmad 1984:30). He includes three players of the instrument in his list of the most famous musicians of the time, and he says that the foremost *tambūr* player, Shauqi, "was well versed in Persian and Hindi melodies."[33] An indication of the degree to which the *tambūr* had become accepted in 17th-century India is the fact that one disciple of Shauqi was Tara Chand Kalāvant, a Hindu. Figures 5, 6 and 7 show the *tambūr* in court settings grouped among instruments of Indian and Persian background.

A related occurrence in the indigenization of the *tambūr* is its appearance as a drone accompaniment to voice. This version of the instrument, which will be called *tambūrā* here, appears in paintings beginning in the 16th and 17th centuries under Emperors Akbar and Jahangir (Figures 8 and 9). These *tambūrās* clearly have a flat-surface bridge, a bridge that is unique to Indian string instruments and dates to a very early period.[34] The addition of this bridge type to the *tambūr*, clearly an adaptation from the *bīn*, and the use of the instrument by vocalists seem to mark a step in the adaptation of the *tambūr* to its Indian environment. The drone *tambūrā* becomes omnipresent in paintings depicting music from the late 17th century, and in later paintings is usually seen in a large size that clearly differentiates it from its ancestor the melody *tambūr*.

The full indigenization of the melody *tambūr* by the time of the last powerful Mughal emperor Aurangzeb is confirmed by its appearance in

Fig. 1. A long lute, Chidambaram temple, 10th century. Courtesy Joep Bor.

Fig. 2. A tāmbur *player. "Akbar Nāmah." Mughal, Akbar period, 1556-1605. Victoria and Albert Museum. I.S. 2-1896, 117/117.*

Fig. 3. *"Visit to Holy Men by Prince Salem." A* tāmbur *player. Mughal, probably Jahangir period, 1605-1627. The Metropolitan Museum of Art, Gift of Alexander Smith Cochran, 1913. 13.228.39*

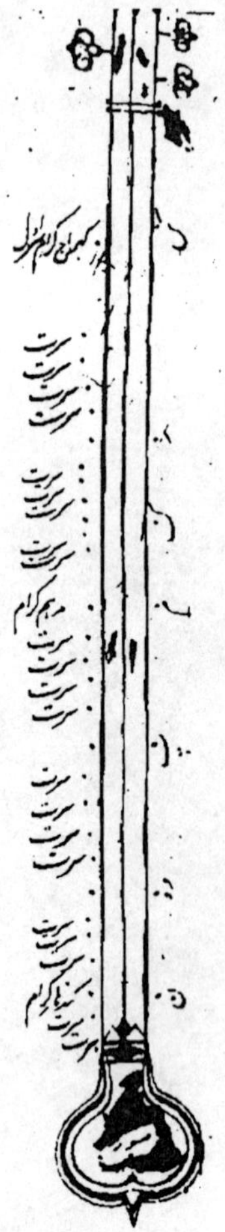

Fig. 4. A tāmbur *with* śrutis *marked alongside the neck.* "Tuḥfāt al-Hind," *17th century. University of Pennsylvania Libraries. Microfilm 2948.*

Fig. 5. *Twelve musicians playing Indian and Persian instruments. "Sāqī Nāmah" of Zuhuri. Deccan, 1685. By permission of the British Library. BL Or. 338, f. 54 b.*

Fig. 6. Khusrau Parviz listening to music. Panjab, 1719. By permission of the British Library. BL Add. 18804 f. 325 b.

Fig. 7. A group of women in a garden with musicians. Deccan, early 18th century. The Freer Gallery of Art. 07.263 ID 21.

Fig. 8. Abul Fazl, Faizi Birbal and Tansen. Mughal, late 17th century. National Museum, New Delhi. 57.116/12

Fig. 9. Prince Sultan Parviz with courtiers and musicians. Mughal, Jahangir period, 1605-1627. The Metropolitan Museum of Art, The Theodore M. Davis Collection. Bequest of Theodore M. Davis, 1915..30.95.174

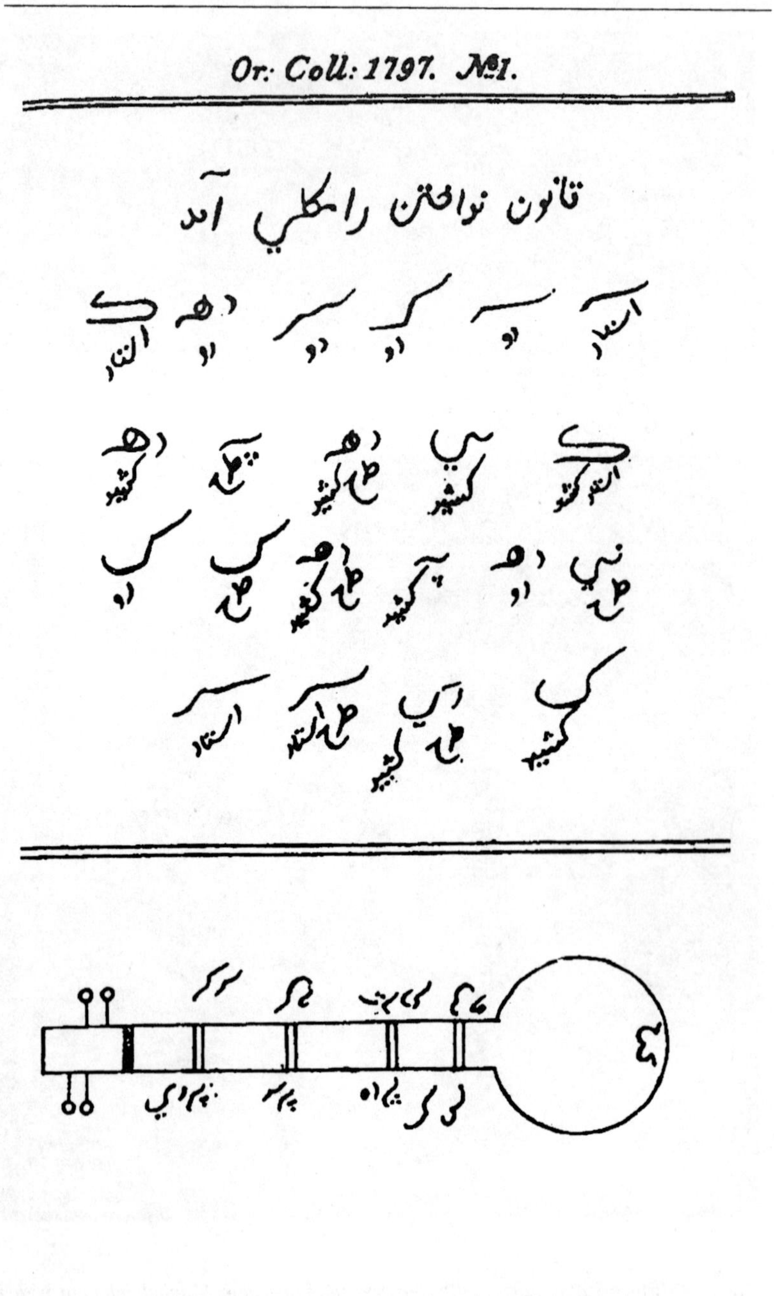

Fig. 10. A page copied from a manuscript of the Parijatak (18th century), showing a nibaddh tambūrā. *Ouseley 1965:170-1.*

Fig. 11. Tambūr *and* daff *players. Mughal, c1780. By permission of the British Library. IOL Johnson Album / no. 23 (drawing).*

Fig. 12. A lady listening to a female tambūr *player. Mughal, Farrukhsiyar period, c1715. Victoria and Albert Museum. IM 294A-1914.*

Fig. 13. A woman playing a tambūr. *Mughal, early 18th century. By permission of the British Library. BM 1920-9-17 012.*

Fig. 14. Rāginī Todi (a female tambūr *player). Pahadi, early 19th century. Bharat Kala Bhavan, 328 P.*

Fig. 15. Balwant Singh of Jammu listening to musicians. Panjab, 19th century. By permission of the British Library. BM 1948 10-9 0130.

Fig. 16. A Bhand. North India, c1820. Private Collection.

a Sanskrit text, the *"Saṅgītapārijāta"* of Ahobala written in 1665, about the same time as Faqirullah's *"Rāg darpan."* This text describes both an unfretted, *anibaddha,* and a fretted, *nibaddha, "taumburam."* Both are described as made entirely of wood. The *nibaddha taumburam* has string *(tantrī)* wrapped at the note positions. It has four strings and is played with two fingers. Unfortunately, verses describing the bridge are missing in the available editions. A Persian translation of the *"Saṅgītapārijāta"* called the *"Pārijātak"* was made by one Pandit Dinanath in 1724. An intriguing drawing of the fretted *taumburam* from a manuscript of Dinanath's *"Pārijātak"* was copied and published by Sir William Ouseley in his late 18th-century article "Anecdotes of Indian Music" (cf. Figure 10).[35] The instrument is drawn so as to indicate the fret positions for playing the *rāga rāmkalī.* An intriguing aspect of the illustration is the strikingly short, wide neck shown on this *tambūr.* Maharaja Sawai Pratap Singh of Jaipur follows the *"Saṅgītapārijāta"* closely in his *"Saṅgīt sār"* of 1790. He comments that the *nibaddh tambūr,* which he says is popularly called *tambūrā,* is in fact another name for the *sitār* (Singh, S. P. 1910-II:7). It is clear, however, that Pratap Singh's identification of the instrument described in the *"Saṅgītapārijāta"* as the *sitār* is his own idea. He makes several changes to the description of the *nibaddh tambūr* to fit the *sitār* that existed at his time. The instrument in Dinanath's manuscript, on the other hand, must be assumed to be a diagrammatic representation of the *tambūr,* since no mention of the *sitār* occurs in that or any other contemporary text.

Reference to the *tambūr* in late Mughal Delhi occurs in the *"Muraqqa'-i Dehlī"* of 1738 where a player named Baqar Tambūrcī, of Emperor Muhammad Shah's court, is highly praised. In the *"Nādirāt-i Shāhī"* of 1797, a collection of songs attributed to the Emperor Shah Alam, there is separate mention of both *tambūr* and *tambūrā,* providing a possible indication that the two terms denoted different instruments.[36] The melody *tambūr* maintained a widespread presence not only in Delhi but in Panjab and the northern hills in a variety of settings throughout the 18th and into the 19th century (Figures 11-16). As late as the mid-19th century, Muhammad Karam Imam mentions an unusual *"tambūrah"* having five strings and gut frets. *Ālāp,* he says, was to be played on this instrument as on the *bīn.* The instrument was rare, however, as he had seen only one player, Tulsi Ram Kalāvant, who belonged to the Nauhār *dhrupad* style (Khan, M. K. I. 1925:57).

The Appearance of the sitār

While references to the *tambūr* continue to the end of the 18th century, *sitār* makes its first written appearance in 1739. The *"Muraqqa'-i Dehlī"* gives the earliest reference to the name in the course of its description of Na'mat Khan's nephew. No written occurrence in India from an earlier time has yet been found, and claims to that effect are so far unsupported.[37] By the third quarter of the century the name appears in Hindi poetry, such as in the *"Nādirāt-i Shāhī"* of Shah Alam and the *"Hammīr rāso"* of Kavi Jodhraj, and in European travelogues, the earliest European reference found so far being a 1777 letter, to be cited later.

The exact circumstances of the *sitār*'s appearance in India are difficult to determine. 18th-century paintings show a number of thin-necked long lutes, but these can be characterized as *tambūrs* by at least three features: the lateral positions of the tuning pegs, the tapering neck, and the thin bridge, where visible. What is labeled the *sitār* first appears in European and Company style art only in the late 18th and early 19th centuries. Since no mid-18th-century visual representations are available, we must go by later examples to determine the characteristics of the earlier *sitārs*. The earliest dates to about 1790. Maharaja Sawai Pratap Singh's fretless *tambūrā* is beautifully preserved in the Maharaja Sawai Man Singh II Museum in Jaipur.[38] In his *"Saṅgīt sār"* Pratap Singh describes the *nibaddh tambūrā*, the *sitār*, as exactly like the *anibaddh tambūrā*, the drone, except for the presence of frets. Its small size makes it closely resemble the *tambūrs* of the 18th-century paintings, but its frontal as well as lateral pegs (one on each side of the neck in this case), a neck that does not taper toward the end, a gourd body and a flat-surface bridge are features that set this instrument apart from the *tambūr*. It might be reasonably assumed that playing position, stroke technique and tuning were added elements distinguishing the *sitār* from the melody *tambūr*.

Small *sitārs* closely resembling Pratap Singh's are seen in the art of the early 19th century, and these appear to represent the mainstream *sitārs* of the time. A watercolor by a Patna artist around 1820 and two portraits done in Delhi in 1827 show such *sitārs* (Figures 17-19). The wonderful portraits of *sitār* players Sukir Khan and Jangi Khan, employees of Colonel James Skinner (Archer 1960:608-15), show every detail of player and instrument. Here the frets are flat, and apparently made of metal, as they are depicted in gold paint. Especially noteworthy is the position of the melody string which is near the center of the instrument's neck, allowing for lateral pulling with the left hand, a technique whose beginnings in *sitār* are closely associated with Delhi. Even Sukir Khan's hand position seems to indicate a pulling action.

Since these early *sitārs* resemble so closely in size and shape the melody *tambūrs* depicted in the 18th-century miniature paintings, can it be said that the *sitār* was a direct modification of the *tambūr*? There is reason not to think so. In the *"Muraqqa'-i Dehlī,"* *tambūr* and *sitār* are both mentioned separately and no association is noted between them. Neither in the oral tradition is there mention of the *tambūr* in connection with the history of the *sitār*. Shah Alam in his *"Nādirāt-i Shāhī"* mentions three terms, *tambūrā*, *sitār* and *tambūr* in his poetry, further suggesting that the *sitār* and the *tambūr* existed side by side.[39] If they existed contemporaneously without noted association it is unlikely that one was descended from the other. Despite the similarities then, there may have been another instrument behind the inspiration for the earliest *sitār* of Delhi.

The Kashmiri *setār* (the Persian pronunciation is usually retained for this instrument) exists today as one of the most prominent of the regional *sitār* types in India. In Kashmir the instrument is said to come directly from the Persian *setār*. It is especially associated with *sufiāna kalām*, the Sufi music of Kashmir, thought to date to at least the 15th century, an intriguing mixture of Persian and Indian influences (cf. Pacholczyk 1978, During & Dick 1984:354). The Kashmiri *setār* has a wooden body, gut frets and seven to nine strings. Six of the strings are tuned in unison and are strummed as drones. A double course (a pair of strings set close together) is used for the main melody (During & Dick 1984: 355). It may have a narrow or a wide neck, depending on the number of strings used. The original Kashmiri *setārs* can be assumed to have had the narrow necks of Persian *setārs*. Some oral histories in India speak of early associations between the *sitār* and Kashmir. The tradition represented by Umar Khan tells of the originator of the *sitār*, Khusrau Khan, visiting or residing for some time in Kashmir and bringing the idea for the *sitār* back to Delhi.[40] Considering the location and history of Kashmir, it is very likely that the Persian-derived *setār* existed there prior to the *sitār*'s appearance in the plains of North India. So far, no 18th-century art of Kashmir has turned up examples of the early instrument, but as a part of non-court or rural culture it would have remained unrepresented in mainstream art. A probable scenario is that the Persian *setār* in Kashmir found its way into courts and regional use in North India. In Delhi it kept the small and narrow-necked form exemplified in Pratap Singh's and Sukir Khan's *sitārs*.

Outside of the court, the *sitār* took on different modifications. The small thin-necked *sitār* is not the only type to be seen in drawings of the late 18th century. A Belgian writer and artist F. Baltazard Solvyns, who lived in Calcutta for fifteen years, produced a large work entitled "A Collection of Two Hundred and Fifty Coloured Etchings Descriptive of the Manners, Customs and Dresses of the Hindoos." It first came out in Calcutta in 1799, and was redone twice and published in London and Paris (Solvyns 1799, 1804, 1808-10). His etching of the "*sittar*" shows an instrument with a wide neck and six strings (cf. Figures 20 and 21). Aside from the larger size and number of strings, a noticeable feature of Solvyns' instrument is the distribution of the strings from edge to edge of the neck, a feature that would prevent any lateral pulling of the melody string. This appears to represent a *sitār* type significantly different from the Delhi *sitār* of Sukir and Jangi Khan. It is striking to find characteristics of the Solvyns *sitār* in some present day folk *sitārs*. The *deśī*, "indigenous," *sitār* of Gujarat has a wide neck and a doubled melody string. Six to eight other strings are tuned in unison and strummed as drone background to the simple melody. The pair of melody strings is positioned along the left edge of the neck, and no pulling is possible. A wide neck on this instrument is suited to the accommodation of a large number of drone strings, while that of modern mainstream *sitārs* is necessary for a capacity to pull laterally on the melody string. Whether regional types such as the *deśī sitār* were descended from early non-court instruments such as Solvyns' *sitār* or were later adaptations of modern instruments is a subject that deserves investigation.

In Afghanistan and Pakistan, long lutes of Turkish and Central Asian origin other than the *sitār* are still in use today and reflect the variety of instrument types that must have existed in Northwest India throughout the earlier periods. The large *dutār*, "two-string," the fretless *dambura* and a number of other instruments are broadly related to the *sitār* as fretted long lutes. It is not impossible that some of these might have had an influence on the Delhi *sitār*, as suggested by Dick, but a historical necessity and a regional connection have yet to be demonstrated.[41]

2

The Changing *sitār*

Oral and written sources indicate that the *sitār* appeared in the Delhi court shortly before 1740. Paintings and drawings show that more than one version of the instrument already existed by the end of the 18th century. The shape of the bridge, the material of the frets, the position of the tuning pegs, the width of the neck, the position and tuning of the strings, and the right hand playing position help us in determining *sitār* types and in tracing the progress of change. In this chapter, information is sorted out to determine the changing structural characteristics of *sitārs* and instruments related to the *sitār* in the 18th and 19th centuries.

The Earliest sitārs

The earliest mention of the *sitār* in the "*Muraqqa'-i Dehlī*" provides the information that in the hands of Na'mat Khan's nephew it could produce anything that could be played on any of the well known instruments. Another early reference has quite a different account of its musical usage. A British traveller, Mrs. J. Kindersley, describes a "*nautch*" dance performance in a letter dated 1777 from an unknown location:

> The girl sings, while she is dancing, some Persian or Hindostán song; some of them are really pleasing to the ear, but are almost entirely drowned by the accompaniments: several black fellows stand behind, who likewise sing with all the strength of voice they are masters of, making, at the same time, the most ridiculous grimaces; some of them playing upon a *sitar*, which is something like a guitar, but greatly inferior even to that trifling instrument; ... but all this, loud as it is, is drowned by those who play with two pieces of bell-metal, which they work between their fingers, and make the same noise as braziers at work upon a large copper.[42]

A European drawing of 1832 shows a *nautch* scene with what seem to be imaginatively rendered *sitārs* (Figure 22). That the *sitār* was used as an accompanying instrument to dance is clear from written and visual sources throughout the 19th century (Figure 23) and into the 20th century (cf. Figure 81). The adaptability of the *sitār* to a wide spectrum of musical contexts was a characteristic that was to remain with it throughout its history.

In the last quarter of the 18th century, as already mentioned, one of the earliest descriptions of the *sitār* is provided by Maharaja Pratap Singh of Jaipur in his "*Saṅgīt sār.*" The "*Saṅgīt sār*" was a Hindi compilation and interpretation of musical information from Sanskrit sources, mainly the "*Saṅgītaratnākara*" and the "*Saṅgītapārijāta.*" The description of the *sitār* is a modified version of that of the *nibaddha taumburam* found in the "*Saṅgītapārijāta.*" Pratap Singh's version says:

> Now the *tambūr*, the *vīṇā* played by the Gandharva named Tumbar, is described. This is popularly called *tambūrā*. Make the *tambūrā* of wood. On one end attach a half gourd and cover it with a thin wooden board. Attach three or four metal strings *(tār)* to it. Use one string for help, tune the others to one note and sing to the sound of this. The *tambūrā* is of two types, one tied *(nibaddh)* and the other untied *(anibaddh)*. On the *tambūrā* on which *rāgas* are to be played, tie wire *(tār)* at the note positions and play *rāgas* on the tied wires. This is the *nibaddh tambūrā*, which is popularly called *sitār*. The one on which gut *(tānti)* is not tied is the *anibaddh*, to the sound of which you can sing *rāgas*. The *tambūravīṇā* is like the *rudravīṇā* in length. At the note positions, tie frets *(tāt)* on the neck, and, two fists toward the neck on the board covering the gourd *(tumbā)*, put a bridge *(ghoḍac)* in the middle to support the strings. Place the bridge so that the strings take on a good sound when played. This is the *nibaddh tambūrā*. And where there would be seven or five or four strings *(tār)* at the note positions on the neck, there is no string *(tānti)* tied, but in all other ways it is like the *nibaddh tambūrā*, and supports the notes in singing, that is the *anibaddh tambūrā*.[43]

His ambiguous language makes interpretation of the fret number and material difficult. He seems to be describing an option of four, five or seven gut frets. His term for the bridge, *ghoḍac*, means "horse" and is a typical pre-20th-century term for the bridges of both *sitār* and *sarod*. He says "*ghoḍacī*" is the popular term for *meru*, the bridge on the *rudra vīṇā* (Singh, S. P. 1910-II:3). From Pratap Singh's description and his *tambūrā* in the Jaipur museum we note a few differences from the *tambūrs* of the earlier paintings. The flat-surface bridge here, the gourd body, the front and lateral peg positions and the non-tapering neck stand as the features distinguishing his instruments from earlier *tambūrs*. The two or three strings to be tuned to one note, if we take the evidence of later usage, are the tonic S, while the first string is Ṁ for the *sitār* and P for the *tambūrā*. Tuning will be discussed more presently.

In 1799, F. Baltazard Solvyns published the first edition of his large work featuring a collection of his own etchings portraying Hindu dress and customs. Among his drawings, Solvyns shows a peculiarly large, multi-stringed *sitār* (Figures 20 and 21). Its bridge, though relatively thin, seems to have a flat upper surface. The material of the frets is not determinable. The strings are positioned on the bridge to cover the width of the neck, reaching to the very left edge (or the right edge in the earliest rendition, which is reversed). In his cynical description, Solvyns refers to the low status of the *sitār* at this time:

> The *Sittar* is now seldom used in India; perhaps the better sort of Hindoos have taken it in aversion since the *Loutchias*, or people of dissolute manners, have taken to playing it for money, and have chosen this music to accompany their obscene songs and other immoral practices. At their feasts, the *Nautch*, a dance ... is sometimes performed to the sound of the *Sittar*, and some tolerable musicians, or rather meer players upon it, may be heard (Solvyns 1808-II:2).

He speaks cynically of the playing style and mentions a strange use of iron rings on the strings:

> An European would make much more of this instrument than the Hindoo musicians, who are satisfied with touching the chords meerly from time to time; and as they are much more charmed with the noise than with the melody of their music they frequently, to create a variety in their dull and monotonous sounds, place an iron ring in each chord of the *Sittar*, which being put in motion by the vibration, and striking against each other, produces a singular noise which delights the ear of the Hindoos and appears to them the supreme degree of perfection (*ibid.*: Plate 2).

The rings are seen as tiny in his drawing, placed on the strings behind the bridge in the modern position of fine tuning beads. His comments indicate a metallic buzzing effect not unlike that of a pronounced *javārī* sound.[44] The *sitār* he describes appears to be a type distinct from the solo instrument of the Delhi court. It was not structurally set up to participate in the *gat-toḍā*, a solo *sitār* music that required precise strokes and lateral pulling of a single melody string.

Performance tradition points to the systematic beginning of a classicizing influence of the *bīn* at the time of Masit Khan whom we can place in late 18th-century Delhi (cf. the later discussion). The "*Sarmāya-i 'ishrat*" (1875), for example, speaks of the Delhi *bāj* (school or style of playing) of Masit Khan as being imitative of the *bīn*, played complete with "*mīḍ-māḍ, ṭhonk* and *jhārā*."[45] *Mīḍ, ṭhonk* and *jhālā* are techniques involving deflection of the main string and particular *bīn* patterns of right hand strokes. Sudarsanacarya in his "*Saṅgīt sudarśan*" states that Masit Khan "purified" the *sitār* after he had learned it from his father (Sastri 1916:26), implying movement toward the regulated style of *dhrupad* music and the *bīn*. The *sitārs* of Sukir and Jangi Khan are probably the closest we can come to an idea of the *sitār* used by Masit Khan. Their metal frets and capacity for a degree of pulling make it possible for the mentioned *bīn* techniques to have been rendered in some form. There is no evidence for the presence of *cikārī* (drone) strings on any 18th-century *sitār*.

Early 19th-Century sitārs

Captain Robert Smith, in an account of a journey in India between 1828 and 1833, speaks of the *sitār* accompanying dancers:

> these nautch girls accompany the recitative with slow and graceful movements, beating time with their feet, on which little silver bells are hung to the music of the saringee and sitar.

Smith saw a separate instrumental performance as well as a dance:

> On the same night of the nautch ... we were entertained with a concert ... . At the concert ... there were five performers; the principal one and he was considered first rate played on the sitar an instrument resembling the guitar but strung entirely with wire, in which respect it may with more propriety be likened to that Italian instrument the mandolin; it was played upon principally with the forefinger armed with a piece of wire passing over the top and round a little above the first joint ... . [One] beat time with his fingers on a small soft toned drum ... there were two other performers in the rear all sitting on the carpet who seemed to take very subordinate parts. The first musician displayed uncommon execution and had he possessed an instrument of greater power and more harmonious tone, would have effectually removed the prejudices of the company; as it was several of us were delighted with the performance the airs being wild and plaintive and forcibly reminding us of the Scotch and Irish; ... (Smith 1915 [c.1833]:n.p.).

Captain Smith's pencil drawing of the concert ensemble shows a distinctly wide-necked *sitār* with five pegs all crowded into the pegbox in

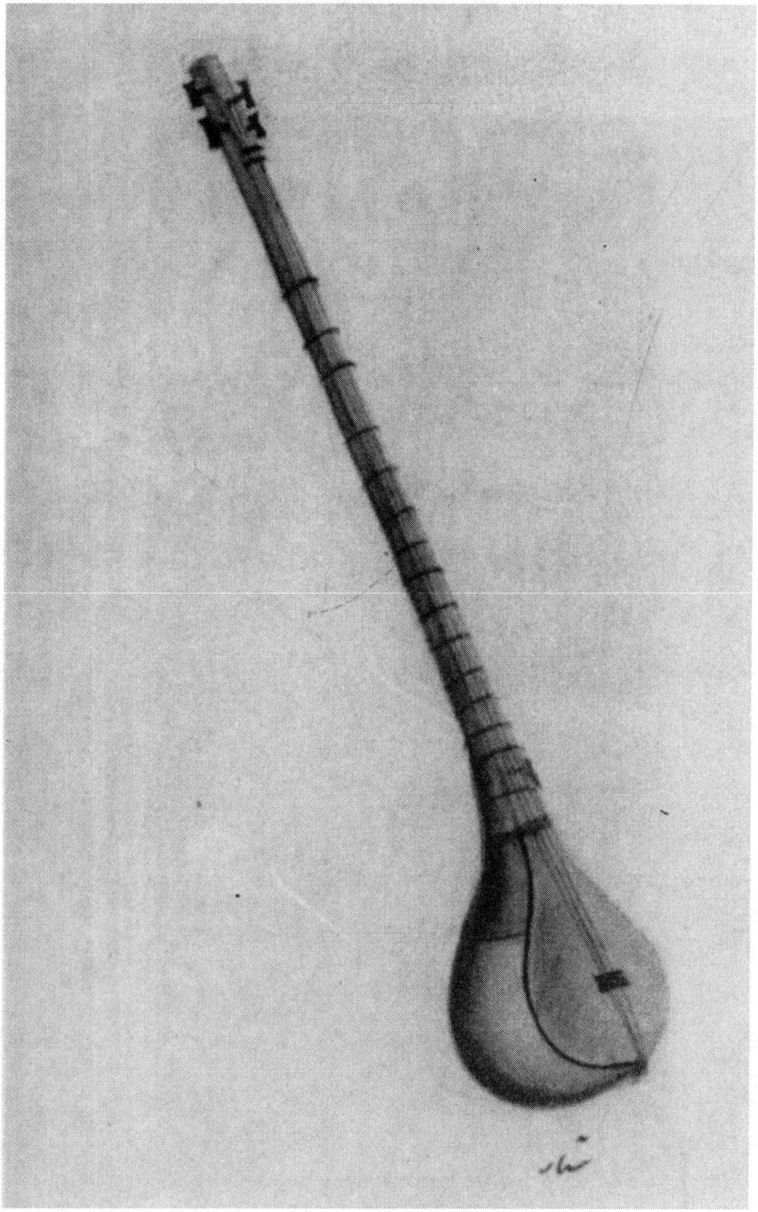

Fig. 17. A sitār. *Patna, c1820. One of 23 drawings of musical instruments. By permission of the British Library. IOL Add. Or. 2624.*

Fig. 18. Sitār *player Sukir or Faqir Khan. One of Colonel James Skinner's retained musicians (Archer 1969: 198). Delhi, 1815-27. By permission of the British Library. IOL Add. Or. 1279.*

Fig. 19. Sitār *player Jangi Khan. One of Colonel James Skinner's retained musicians (Archer 1969:198). Delhi, 1815-27. By permission of the British Library. IOL Add. Or. 1280.*

Fig. 20. "A Sittar." Solvyns 1799:Section II, No. 4. By permission of the British Library. BL 149.i.16.

Fig. 21. *"A Sittara or Guittar." Solvyns 1804:Plate 48. By Permission of the British Library. BL 455.e.8.*

Fig. 22. A nautch *scene. Belnos 1832:Plate 18. By permission of the British Library. BL 1781 b 18.*

Fig. 23. Karva *dance. Seventy-two paitings depicting trades and crafts in* Cutch, *1856. By permission of the British Library. IOL Add. Or. 1520.*

Fig. 24. A concert ensemble in Kampur. Smith, R. [c1833-I]:316. Victoria and Albert Museum, I.M. 15-1915.

Fig. 25. An ensemble of women musicians. Company style painting, 19th century. Victoria and Albert Museum, I.S. 02198.

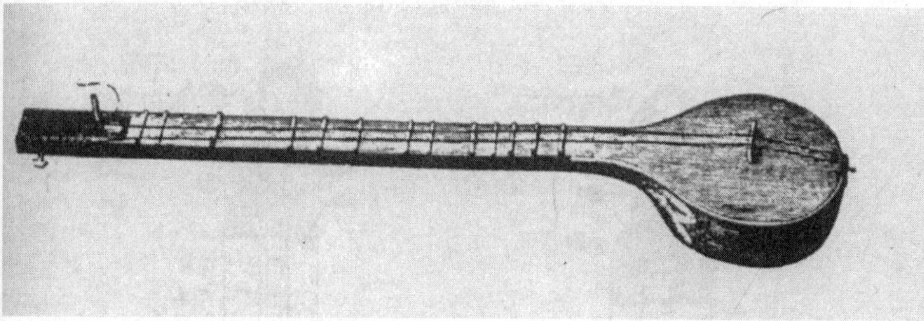

Fig. 26. A sitār. *Fétis 1869-II:286.*

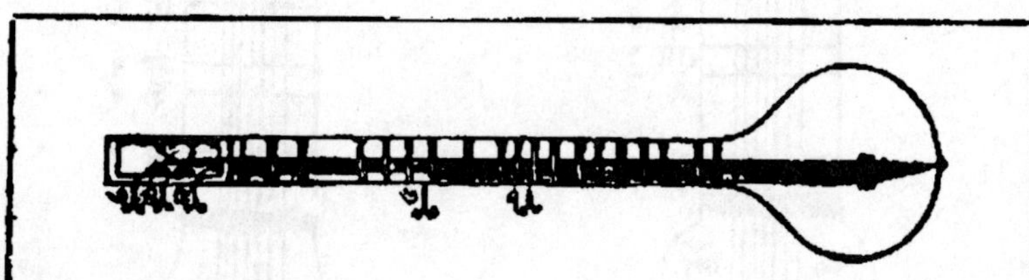

Fig. 27. A sitār *and its tuning. Tagore 1976:18.*

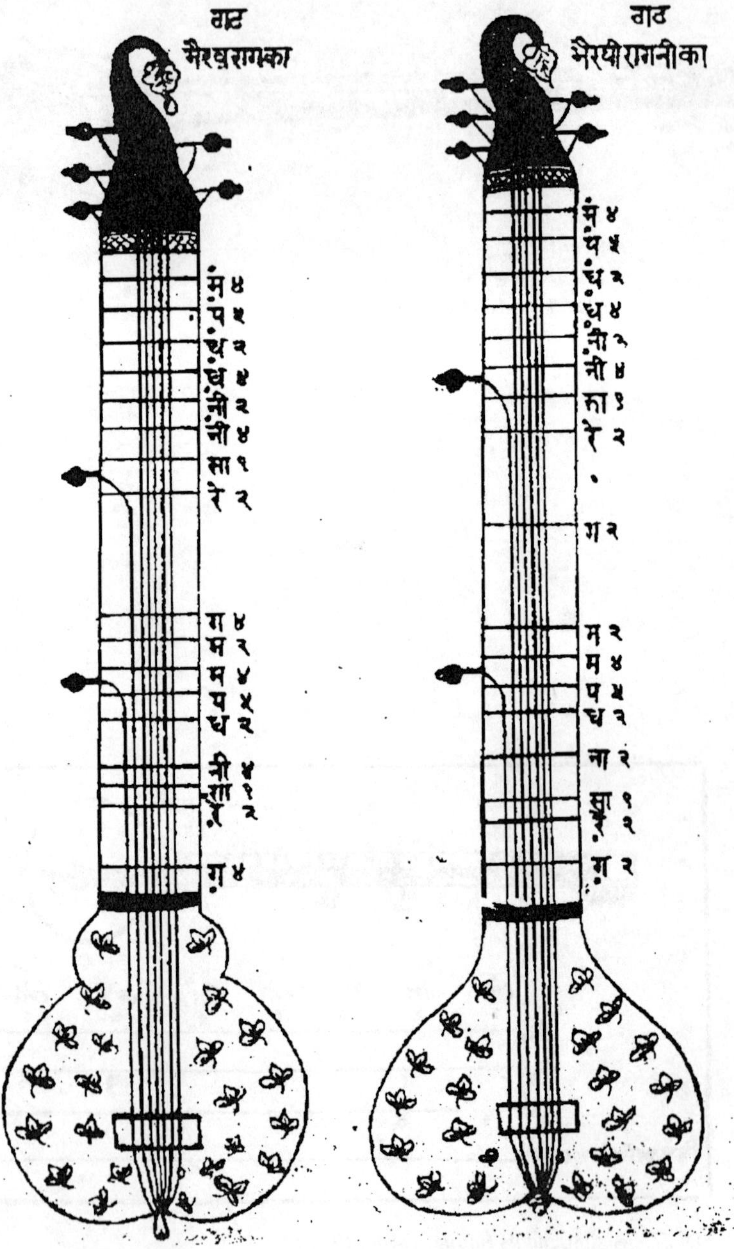

Fig. 28. *The* ṭhāṭs *of* rāgas bhairav *and* bhairavī. *Munib 1925:n.p.*

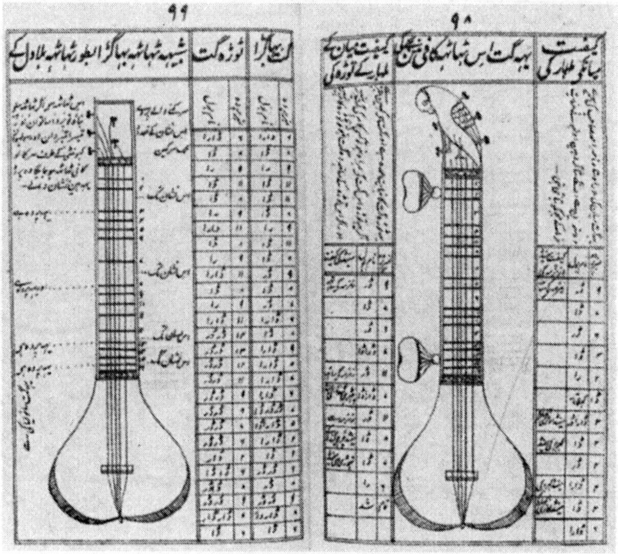

*Fig. 29. A three-*tumbā sitār *and notations. Beg 1876:98-9.*

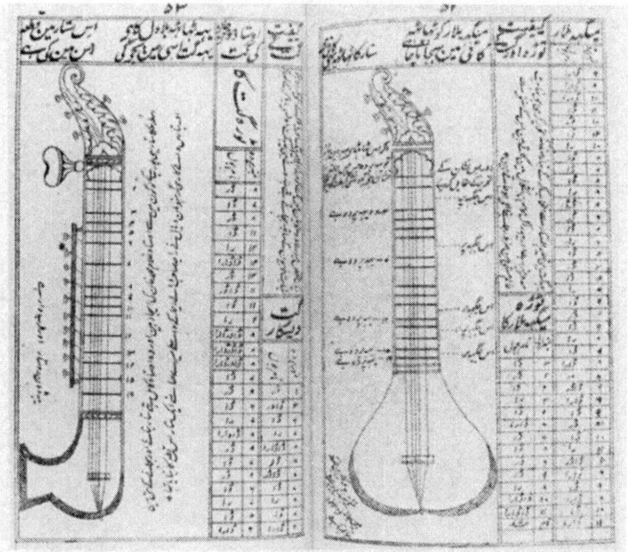

Fig. 30. Ghulam Muhammad's sitār. *Beg 1876:53. By permission of the British Library. IOL 767 VT.*

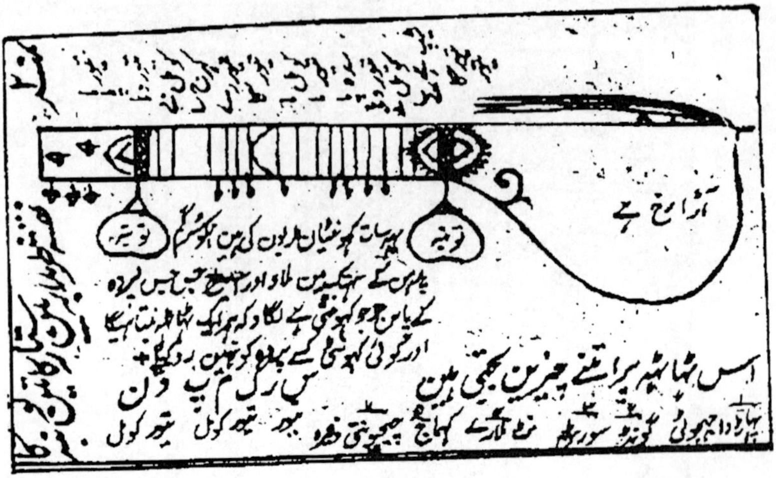

*Fig. 31. A three-*tumbā sitār. *Khan, S. A. 1884:190*

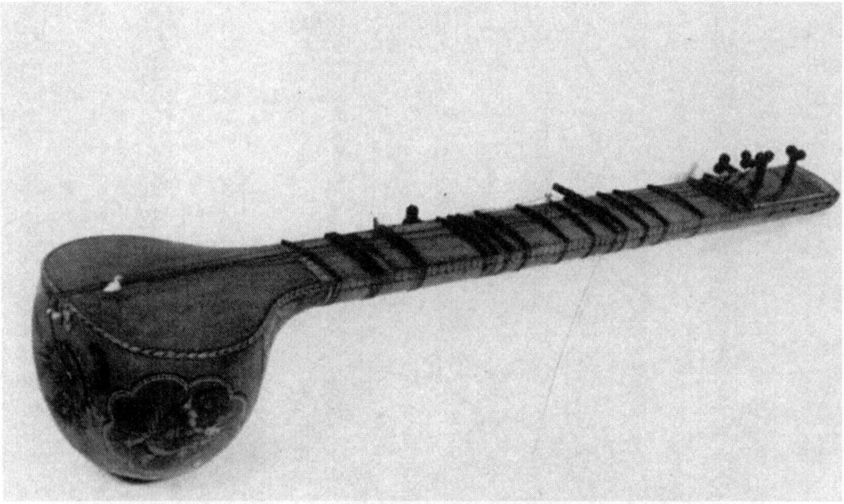

Fig. 32. Sitār *with a painted gourd. Loan from Day, 19th century. Victoria and Albert Museum, Gx 4414.*

Fig. 33. Sadhu playing a sitār, *Company style painting by Kehar Singh, labeled* "Mehmai shahi Sadhu Nirtkar Lahore Anarkali Samvat 1929." *Panjab, 19th Century. Bharat Kala Bhavan, 1848 C.*

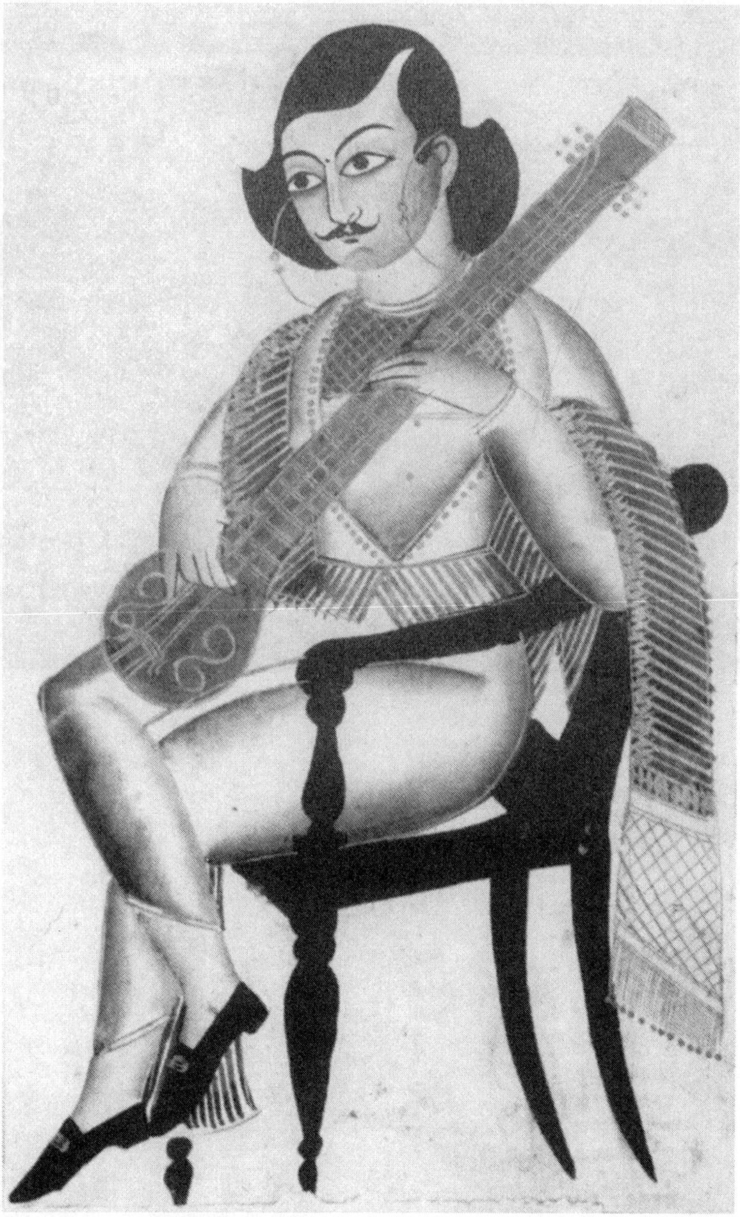

Fig. 34. *A* sitār *player seated on a chair. Kalighat, Calcutta, 19th century. Victoria and Albert Museum, I.S. 08144 a.*

Fig. 35. A gentleman entertaining a lady. Calcutta woodcut, 19th century. Victoria and Albert Museum, GD 2353.

frontal positions (Figure 24). The right hand and general upright positioning of the instrument over the left shoulder resembles that of the earlier Solvyns' player. Despite the use of the wire plectrum, the *mizrāb*, the right hand had evidently not yet found its position fixed by the thumb at the base of the neck, so essential to later *sitār* players. A very large *sitār*-like instrument in Smith's drawing is a fascinating predecessor to the *surbahār*, to be discussed in a later section.

At about the same period Mrs. Meer Hassan Ali saw three-stringed *sitārs* being played by professional female musicians:

> the Domenie ... are women of good character, and their songs are of the most chaste description, chiefly in the Hindoostaunie tongue. They are instructed in native music and play on the instruments in common use with some taste, - as the saattarah (guitar), with three wire strings; the surringhee (rude-shaped violin); the dhome or dholle (drum) .... The harmony produced is melancholy and not unpleasing, but at best all who form the several classes of professors in Native societies are indifferent musicians (Ali, M. H. 1832-I:195-6).

The Company style painting in Figure 25 shows an ensemble such as Mrs. Hassan Ali might have seen.

One of the most informative descriptions of the early 19th-century *sitār* is given by Captain Willard in "A Treatise on the Music of Hindoostan," published in 1834. Willard speaks of metal frets and the use of the *mizrāb*, and gives a few specifics of string tuning:

> It resembles the last mentioned instrument [the "tumboora"], but is made a good deal smaller, and has movable frets of silver, brass, or other material, which are fastened with catgut or silk. Seventeen frets are generally used, and as they are movable, they answer every purpose required. The shifting of these to their proper places requires a delicate ear .... This instrument derives its name from si ... signifying in Persian *three*, and tar ... *a string*, as that number is commonly used. More modern players have made several additions .... Of the three wires, one is steel, and the others brass. These last are tuned in unison, and are called Khuruj from their sound, and the other is a perfect fourth to it. The fingers of the left hand slide over the frets on the fingerboard, and stop the notes in the same manner as on the guitar, and the wires are struck with the forefinger of the right, to which is fitted a kind of plectrum or instrument called a *Mizrab*, made of a piece of wire curiously twisted, to facilitate the various motions of the finger .... The Sitar is very much admired, is used by both professional men and amateurs, and is really a very pleasing toned instrument in the hands of an expert performer (Willard 1965 [1834]:98).

The word *"kharaj"* is a corruption of *ṣaḍja*, the full name of the tonic note S. It is a typical early term for the second and third strings, both tuned to S and later called *joḍī*, "pair." Today the term is sometimes used for the lowest S string of the *sitār*.

Traveller Fanny Parks in her journal entry of November 1832 speaks of a four-stringed *sitār*. Parks says "I have received a present that pleases me greatly, a sitar ... an instrument in general use all over India." This one was made at Lucknow and is "very beautifully put together." The first string is steel, the second and third brass, and the "fourth and smallest" steel (Parks 1850-I:250). We already know the tuning of the first three from Willard's description. The fourth, if assumed to have followed the tuning described in later accounts, was a Ṗ. Fanny Parks' liking for the *sitār* contrasts the attitude of Mrs. Kindersley. However Parks was an exception among her compatriots. She says

> I ... favoured the party with some Hindustani airs on the sitar, which I could not persuade them to admire; to silence my sitar a dital harp was presented to me; nevertheless, I retained a secret fondness for the instrument, which recalled the time when the happy slave girls figured before me.[46]

The mizrāb

The wire plectrum fixed on the right index finger seems to have been an invention of Indian *vīṇā* players. It was used during the Mughal period, as we find in a 17th-century account by an Italian traveller, Pietro Della Valle:

> ... he touch'd [the frets] with the left Hand, to diversify the sounds, and the strings with the right, not with his Fingers or Nails, but with certain iron wires fastened to his Fingers by certain rings like thimbles ... .[47]

The early name for this plectrum was possibly *nakha*, "fingernail."

An Arabic word derived from the root *ẓarb*, "to strike," the term *mizrāb* was used as the name for the flat wood or eagle's talon plectrum of the Arabic and Persian *rabāb* from an early time.[48] It was later the term for the plectrum of certain Persian *tambūr*s (Farmer 1964:180) and probably came into India with that instrument. One of Ibrahim 'Adil Shah's poems says:

> The instrument [*tambūr*] is the heart containing secrets of hundred mines. It should be taken as an ocean and its strings the rolling waves. The plectrum [*mizrāb*] is the pen with which he writes a letter demanding the tribute from the mines of the pearls in form of Moti Khan [sic!] (Adil Shah 1956:54).

The *mizrāb* for the *tambūr* was a flat hand-held plectrum, but a second usage of the term refers to the stroking technique of the Persian *setār*, in which the index finger without a plectrum stroked in quick back-and-forth rhythmic patterns (During & Dick 1984:353-4). This is probably the immediate source of the term in regards to the *sitār*.

The two-sided wire *mizrāb* extending over the end of the finger from front to back contributed an essential feature to mainstream *sitār* playing: the capability to produce precise single notes with a versatile back and forth movement. This movement contrasted that of both the free hand technique of the *tambūr* and the brushing stroke of the Persian *setār*. It must have been marked by a new clarity of sound and capability for speed. It became the basis for the structure of the *gat-toḍā* solo genre, and allowed for an imitation of both *bīn* techniques and patterns of free-hand instruments such as the *rabāb*.

By the 1830s the *sitār* was known for solo performance as well as dance accompaniment. It had three to five strings and flat metal frets and was played with a *mizrāb*. It was capable of producing some *bīn*-derived techniques, notably those involving deflection of the main string. But still to be added were several of the basic features known on the modern *sitār*, including *cikārī* and *tarab* strings.

Sitār *at Mid-Century*

If the late 18th and the early 19th centuries had been formative for the *sitār*, by mid-century the instrument was fast becoming a phenomenon. The *gat-toḍā* had developed into a sophisticated solo genre and *sitār* players were tackling many of the techniques of the *bīn*. In urban India *sitār* had begun to capture the popular imagination with its versatility and easy access, and was being adopted by more and more amateur players. The physical history of the *sitār* from mid-century is a record of the various shapes and sizes and the number and tuning of strings that it took on at the hands of the growing number of professional and amateur performers.

A detailed description of a mid-19th-century *sitār* accompanied by a drawing is found in Francois Joseph Fétis's *"Histoire générale de la mu-*

sique: depuis les temps les plus anciens jusqu'a nos jours," where he meticulously decribes an instrument he saw at the International Exhibition of 1855 in Paris (Fétis 1869-II:285-6). He calls it not *sitār* but the "chikara of Benares." It is 1m 12cm long, its gourd 26cm in diameter across the face, and its neck 7cm wide. It has five principal strings which pass to the tuning pegs across two ivory bridges at the top of the neck, and two other strings that attach to tuning pegs much lower on the left side of the neck. These two "harmonize in unison with the notes produced by the progression of the fingers on the principal strings." Fétis has made here the earliest reference to *cikārī* strings without using the name. There are twelve movable frets, made of brass or silver, which "determine the intonation of the strings under the pressure of the fingers." Willard, we remember, had mentioned seventeen frets in his earlier description (Willard 1965 [1834]:98). The instrument is beautifully ornamented, Fetis notes, as are all the musical instruments made in Banaras. Its tuning pegs are ivory and carved in the shape of double elephant heads. Where the gourd joins the neck there are "leaves in wood sculpted with great delicacy." A long strip of ivory extends around the perimeter of the entire gourd (Fétis 1869-II:285-6). Fétis' drawing seems to show a simpler instrument than he describes (Figure 26). The frets of the instrument are flat. The bridge appears fairly thin. The gourd is cut in a style later known as *kachuā*, "tortoise."

Another informative description is provided by Muhammad Karam Imam Khan in his "*Ma'dan al-mūsīqī*" of 1856 (Khan, M. K. I. 1925). The *sitār* has six strings, the first of which is steel and is called *bāj*, "play" or "playing." *Bāj* is the term for the main playing string generally used from this time except in the Bengali language tradition. The second and third strings are brass and named *kharaj*, as in Willard's account. The *bāj* and the *kharaj* are to be tuned to M and S. The fourth is a steel string called *pañcam*, the fifth is a brass string which Karam Imam calls *gandah* (probably the note *gāndhār*), and the sixth is a steel string which is called *cikārī*, the earliest reference to the word found so far. The *cikārī*, Imam says, should be tuned to M or to any note one wishes, but he notes that it is useful only in the second or third octave *(sabtak)* not in the first (Khan, M. K. I. 1925:227). The *cikārī* string's relationship to octave is notable here.

Sitār frets are called *pardā* and *sundarī* by Karam Imam, terms that seem to specifically signify the tied metal frets of the *sitār*, in contrast to gut frets or the fixed metal frets of the *bīn*. *Vīṇā* frets are called *sārikā* or *sārī* in the Sanskrit texts and *sār* by Karam Imam (Khan, M. K. I. 1925: 57). *Pardah* or *pardā* became a standard term throughout the 19th and 20th centuries for the moveable *sitār* fret. This word, meaning "veil," came allegorically to mean "division," "note" or "scale" in Persian poetry in medieval times. The Persian term for frets was ordinarily *dastān*, "hand." Whether *pardah* was also used for gut frets or came into use with metal frets is not clear. Karam Imam, in speaking of gut frets for a rare type of *tambūrah* calls them *tasma charmī*, "leather straps" (Khan, M. K. I. 1925:57). In Hindi the term *sundarī* was also used for *sitār* frets to the end of the 19th century, and *sārikā* or *sār* was sometimes used.

In the portrait of Sukir Khan it is not possible to see exactly how the small metal frets were tied to the neck of his early *sitār*. In later 19th-century examples, the metal frets are shaped with a lengthwise groove on each side of the rounded fret. The string that ties the fret to the neck lies alongside the fret in the side grooves, alternating sides at each circling of the neck.

Drone strings were present on the *bīn* from at least the 17th century. Called the *pārśvatantrī*, "side string," in Sanskrit texts, one was made of brass, strung low along the player's left hand side of the instrument, and probably tuned to a low pitched S or P. The "*Saṅgītapārijāta*" describes three strings on the right side of the *daṇḍa* (neck, "stick") as well. They are called *śruti* and used for "accomplishing note consonance" *(svarasaṃvādī siddhi)* (Ahobala 1982:79).

Although the name *cikārī* is presently used for the drone strings of the *bīn*, it seems to have first come into usage for the *sitār*. Karam Imam speaks of the techniques *ṭhonk* and *jhālā* for the *bīn* but specifically mentions *cikārī* only in connection with the *sitār*. The word is Hindi for a gnat or mosquito, from *cikārnā*, to squeak or cry (Platts 1960:434). The term seems to apply specifically, as in Karam Imam's reference, to drone strings tuned to a pitch at the mid or higher octave. The addition of *cikārī* strings followed the wide bridge, metal frets and the use of the *mizrāb* as elements of the *bīn*, but it continued to be optional on *sitārs* throughout the 19th century, as indicated in many of the drawings in the *sitār* handbooks. It is notable that at this period the *cikārī* strings were apparently not essential to the playing of *jhālā*, a technique from which *cikārī* is inseparable today.[49] One modern writer expresses the opinion that *cikārī* strings were added to the *sitār* after their appearance on the *surbahār* (Roy Chaudhury 1975:137). *Cikārī* strings were apparently a part of the *surbahār* from the time of its origin, which Tagore places at about 1825. But Tagore describes the *surbahār* as having the same strings as the *kachuā sitār*, implying the *kachuā*'s earlier existence and its earlier use of *cikārī* (Tagore 1976:34-5).

Sitārs *in the Later 19th Century: Bengal*

Bengal, and especially Calcutta, became increasingly important for instrumental music in the second half of the 19th century. The earliest and most detailed of the Bengali language books on *sitār* are the 1866 "*Sitār śikṣā*" of Krishnadhan Bandyopadhyaya and the 1872 "*Yantra Kshetra Dipika*" of Sourindro Mohun Tagore. Products of the cultural and educational renaissance of 19th-century Bengal, the works are meticulously detailed and influenced by English style. "*Sitār śikṣā*" uses staff notation throughout. Both works are fairly similar in their descriptions of *sitārs*.

Tagore's attempt to link the *sitār* with the medieval *vīṇās* takes the form here of his assigning to each part of the *sitār* an alternative name from the Sanskrit tradition. The first of each pair of terms is the Bengali colloquial, the second the Sanskrit. The gourd is the *khol (dhvanikośa)*; the face is the *tablī (dhvani paṭuka)*; the neck is the *dāndā (daṇḍa)*; the flat face of the neck is the *paṭarī (angulī paṭuka)*; the pegs are the *kāṇ (kīlaka)*; the strings are *tār (tantra)*; the string holder is the *panthi (śālāyanī)*; the bridge is the *sauyārī (tantrāsana)*; the beads are *mankā (mānikā)*; the frets are the *pardā (sārikā)*; the string tying the frets is *tānt (tantava sūtra)*; and the upper bridges are *āḍi (setu)* (Tagore 1879:2-3).

The *sitārs* described have five main strings, and *cikārīs* of varying number. The first main string is named *nāyakī*, "heroine," a term used frequently in the Bengali texts replacing the term *bāj*. The second is the *kharaj*. In "*Sitār śikṣā*" we see for the first time a single *kharaj* instead of the usual pair. In the place of the second *kharaj* is a brass P̣ string. This is found on standard *sitārs* of the present day. The fourth string in both descriptions, is a steel P, normal on *sitārs* of the period. The fifth string, and this is a notable feature of the Bengali descriptions, is a thick brass string tuned to a Ṣ an octave below the *kharaj* (Figure 27) (Bandyopadhyaya, K. 1866:21-2; Tagore 1879:5-6). An alternate tuning described in "*Sitār śikṣā*" calls for double *kharaj* strings and the fifth string tuned to low P̣ instead of low Ṣ. This is a tuning specified as appropriate for small *sitārs* (Bandyopadhyaya, K. 1866:22).

In the "*Yantra Kshetra Dipika*" the *sitār* has double *kharaj* strings, called *joḍī*, "pair," the first reference to this term. The term *joḍī* came into general use and has remained so to the present day despite the absence of the original pair of strings in the second and third positions on standard modern *sitārs*. In the "*Yantra Kshetra Dipika*" the fifth string is a brass S tuned to an octave below the *joḍī* and simply called "*ṣaḍaj*" (Tagore 1879:5-6). The presence of the low *ṣaḍaj* string on the Bengali *sitārs* is striking, as it is often heard that it is a recent addition to the *sitār*. The presence of this string may be related to the strong influence of the *surbahār* in Bengal at this time. 19th-century performance use of the lower strings differed from modern practice, as will be discussed later.

According to the *"Sitār śikṣā," cikārī* strings, which are to be put on larger size *sitārs*, are tuned to P (its peg is near the P fret), and S (its peg is near the S fret). If this follows modern tuning, they are in the lower and middle octaves respectively. The *"Sitār śikṣā"* has an intriguing reference to "other strings" besides these, which have their pegs in the neck of the instrument and are to be tuned to the predominant notes of the *rāga* played (Bandyopadhyaya, K. 1866:22). Although the short reference sounds very much as though it is describing sympathetic strings, Tagore speaks instead of three or four extra strings called *cikārī* (or *pārśvatantrī*) put by some players on the larger *sitārs* (Tagore 1879:4,6). The practice of adding one or more extra *cikārī* strings tuned to notes not represented on the other strings was followed, though not widely, into the 20th century. *Sarod* player Karamatullah Khan in his book of 1908 speaks of a *sitār* tuning which can take the place of *tarab*, sympathetic, strings.

The Bengali books call the frets *pardā*, and in the *"Yantra Kshetra Dipika"* two types of *sitārs* are differentiated according to their fretting. A *sacala thāṭ* ("moveable *thāṭ*") *sitār* had seventeen moveable frets, while an *ekrūp* ("single form") *sitār* had frets for all the possible notes and so were not moved (Tagore 1879:4). *Ṭhāṭh* is a Hindi term meaning "framework," "arrangement" or "adjustment" (Platts 1960:361). It was used in Sanskrit texts from the 17th century to refer to the arrangement of frets on a *vīṇā*, earlier expressed by the term *mela*, "assembly." On the *sitār*, *thāṭ* or *ṭhāṭh* became a term for indicating the correct fret setting for each *rāga* (Figures 28-31).

The *acal thāṭ*, though regularly mentioned in late 19th- and 20th-century texts of all regions, was rarely used in practice. The idea imitates the *ekarāgamela* "single-*rāga*-arrangement" and *akhilarāgamela* "all-*rāga*-arrangement" *vīṇās* of Somanātha and later Sanskrit authors. It might have been emphasized as a part of the classicization process of the 19th century. The idea seems to have originated with the Delhi *sitār* players. The author of the *"Sarmāya-i 'ishrat"* says of the Delhi *sitār* players "they put twenty-one frets *(sundarī)* to make it an *acal sitār* and instituted the playing of it in the *bīn* style" (Khan, Sadiq A. 1884:183). Another handbook, *"Tashīl al-sitār"* of 1874 also speaks of the two types of *thāṭs* as an invention of "the Delhi people" (Beg 1884:6).

Other Centers

The popularity of the *sitār* across North India is indicated by the number of handbooks that appear from about 1870. First published largely in Lucknow, Delhi and Patna in Hindi-Urdu using the Persian *dastāliq* script, they appeared in *devanāgari*-script Hindi and Marathi from the 1890s in Baṇaras, Bombay, Pune and other centers. The detailed English account of Indian music by Captain Day also was written in this period. Differences among the *sitārs* described in the handbooks are minor, but significant in what they can indicate about the styles of *sitār* music prevalent in the different centers of North India.

The "*Guldastah-i mūsīqī*" by Ram Bhaju Lal of Patna was published in 1873. Consistent with the history of the *gat*, composition, style called the *Purab* (eastern) *bāj* for which Patna was an important center, the book specializes in fast-speed *gats*. The *sitār* described has sixteen *pardās* and only five strings. Like the smaller *sitārs* of the Bengali descriptions, the Patna *sitār* is tuned Ṃ, Ṣ, Ṣ, P̣ and P̤. The string names are given, respectively, as *bāj*, *joḍī* (two strings), *pañcam* and *mandā*, "low" (Bhaju Lal 1873:20). The lack of *cikārī* strings is noticeable and may reflect the limited technical requirements of the *Purab bāj*.

The "*Qānūn-i sitār*" published, probably in Delhi, in 1871, describes a *sitār* of six strings called *bāj*, *kharaj* (two), *pañcam*, *laraz* and *papīhā*. These became standard terms for the *sitār* strings throughout the Hindi-Urdu language regions of the time and into the early 20th century. The first three strings are tuned Ṃ, Ṣ, Ṣ. The fourth string, made of steel is only described as tuned "less" than the *kharaj* strings. Other systems place the P̣ in that position. The *laraz* (from the Persian, "trembling" or "quivering") is to be tuned "equal to the *kharaj*" (Khan, M. S. H. 1873:26). In later usage *laraz* refers to a thick string, so the implication here is the S̤ of the lowest octave. The *papīhā* (Hindi, a cuckoo or a whistle) is described as a side string tuned to S. *Papīhā* was a name found regularly through the early 20th century as an alternative to *cikārī*. In some cases, however, the two terms are used to refer to the lower *(cikārī)* and the higher *(papīhā)* strings separately. The *sitār* of "*Qānūn-i sitār*" in its having both *laraz* and *papīhā* reflects the complex techniques and the *dhrupad* leanings of the Delhi *bāj*.

The *sitār* existed in the Panjab in a number of forms. One interesting painting of Panjab shows a standing ascetic playing a five-stringed instrument (Figure 33). An 1872 description of three types of *sitārs* is given by B. H. Baden-Powell in his "Hand-Book of the Manufactures and Arts of the Punjab:"

> The instruments are often prettily and elaborately inlaid with ivory or else painted in gold and colors and varnished. The varieties of "Sitár" to be now described are the "Madham Sitár," the "Chárgah Sitár," and the "Tarbdár Sitár." The favourite form of "Sitár" is called "Madham." This is the instrument introduced at Dehli by Amír Khísro in the reign of Kai Kubád ... (Baden-Powell 1872:272)

It has sixteen brass frets "grooved in the middle, so as to retain the catgut belt which holds the fret to the handle" (*ibid*.:272). Larger *sitārs*, he says, have twenty-one frets. Most *sitārs* have five strings, tuned to steel Ṃ, brass Ṣ, P̣ and steel S. When there are six strings a second Ṡ is added, and when seven strings, an additional G. Baden-Powell gives one of the earliest descriptions of the *tarabdār* or sympathetic-stringed *sitār*:

> ... under the frets and under the playing wires a set of very thin steel wires are extended, tuned to the ascending notes of the gamut. The pegs which hold these strings are at the sides of the handle, those holding the playing strings at the head. The *"tarb"* are purely sympathetic strings, vibrating and producing a shrill twang in unison, and by sympathy with the corresponding note struck on the upper strings.[50]

It is representative of the Panjab area from which he writes that Baden-Powell mentions a third *sitār* type, the *chargah,* which has only four strings and no frets. A fretless long lute known as the *dambura* is still found in Pakistan.

The *"Tashīl al-sitār"* by Rahim Beg of Khairabad near Lucknow, was published in 1874. The eight-stringed *sitār* described here has its fourth string tuned to P̣ or Ṃ, according to the *rāga* being played. The fifth string, which is the thickest, is tuned to lowest octave M̤, and three *cikārī* strings are tuned to middle octave S, P and high S (Beg 1874:7-10).

One of the most thorough and informative of the 19th-century books is the *"Sarmāya-i 'ishrat"* by Sadiq Ali Khan, published in Delhi in 1875. It is a good compendium of the oral tradition of its time. In tracing the development of the *sitār*, the author relates the sequence of string additions. According to his account, the original three strings were the *bāj*, one *kharaj* and a steel *pañcam* string. This contrasts Willard's and other early accounts, but is possibly another early tuning. Sadiq Ali goes on to trace the addition of strings in the following order: the second *kharaj*, to form the *joḍī* pair; the thickest string called *laraz* in the fifth position; the *cikārī* strings and *zīl* (a type of cymbals in Arabic and Turkish[51]), a term sometimes used instead of *papīhā* for the highest pitched *cikārī* string and also found as *jhīl* (Azharuddin 1898:7); and finally, in one of the early references to them on the *sitār*, the *tarab* strings (Khan,

Sadiq A. 1884:17, 183). By 1875, then, the *sitār* had acquired five main strings, at least two *cikārīs* and seven, nine or eleven *tarab* strings, practically all the characteristics of its modern form.

Late 19th-century descriptions offer little new information except for variations in terminology and tuning. Captain C. R. Day in "The Music and Musical Instruments of Southern India and the Deccan" of 1891 comments that the *sitār* is also called the *sundarī*, a term which has already been noted as used for the frets of *sitār*. Reflecting the dominant position of the *sitār* in the last decades of the century he says it "is perhaps the commonest of all the stringed instruments of India, being much admired" (Day 1974:117). He describes tunings for *sitārs* having from three to seven strings: M Ṣ P P; M Ṣ P̣ S; M Ṣ P̣ S high *(tār)* S; M Ṣ Ṣ P̣ S high S; M Ṣ Ṣ Ṗ P Ṡ high Ṡ. The tuning here omits the steel string commonly found in the third or fourth positions in 19th-century tunings. Day describes the fixed right hand playing position nicely:

> The instrument is played by means of a plectrum of wire placed upon the forefinger, the thumb being usually pressed firmly upon the edge of the belly, so that the position of the right hand shall change as little as possible (Day 1974:118).

He indicates that "*Taraffedar*" *sitārs* (with sympathetic strings) are less common than simple *sitārs*, saying that they are "sometimes found" (*ibid.*:118). His comments on the tone quality of the *sitār* are amusing:

> The sitar is fairly easy to learn, and much can be made of it by experienced performers; but there is a peculiarity in its tone when played at all loud which greatly mars the effect, the tender charm and colouring of that of the vina being completely absent. To be heard with advantage a sitar should be at a little distance from the listener, the unpleasant jangle of its strings will not then be so apparent, and the melody will be more clear (*ibid*:118).

A *sitār* donated by Day to the Victoria and Albert Museum in London is pictured in Figure 32.

Varieties of tuning continued to be used into the 20th century and up to the present day. In 1908 *sarod* player Karamatullah Khan described methods of tuning six-stringed, seven-stringed and eight-stringed *sitārs*. The five main strings of the six-string *sitār* were to be tuned to M, Ṣ, Ṣ, Ṃ (or G̣) and P̤. The one *cikārī* was to be tuned to middle S. Only the tuning of the fourth string here differs from earlier accounts. His tuning of the seven-stringed *sitār*, however, is quite different. It is M and Ṣ, low P̤, G̣ and lowest S̤. The *cikāris* in this case are to be tuned to Ṅ and middle S. The advantage of this tuning, he explains, is that with the strings tuned to so many different notes there remains no need for *tarab* strings. Karamatullah Khan did not approve of the addition of *tarab* strings to the *sitār* because it changed the character of the original instrument. After so many string additions, he complains, the *sitār* has become a *sau-tār*, "hundred-stringed," instead of *seh-tār*. The eight-stringed *sitār* in his account is tuned like the seven-stringed, except that the fourth is tuned to R, and an eighth string to high S "as in the tuning of the *bīn*" (Khan, K. 1908:173, 177-83). A summary of strings and their tunings according to a number of different sources is given below (Table 1).

Tarab *Strings and Additional* tumbās

Tarab is a Persian word meaning "excitement" or "joy," which has been used in a musical sense from medieval times.[52] At what point and on what instrument the word came into use as the name of sympathetic strings is not known at this time. Such strings existed on instruments in India from at least the early 17th century, noted in an early pictorial occurrence on a *sārangī* by Joep Bor in Bor 1986/87. Bor speculates that the *sārangī* was the earliest instrument in India, and perhaps anywhere, to have sympathetic strings (Bor 1986/87:56; Plate 47). So far no evidence contradicts this speculation. A relationship between *tarab* strings on *sārangī* and *sitār* may be hinted at in the description of an instrument called the *gītār* or *gaitār* by Karam Imam Khan. It is like the *sitār* except for its being played by a bow like the *sārangī*. Unlike the *sitār*, Karam Imam says, it has *tarab* strings. Its pegs are attached in a separate wooden piece alongside the neck (Khan, M. K. I. 1925:58). Judging by a drawing in Rahim Beg's "*Naghmah-i sitār*" that shows a *tarabdār sitār* belonging to Ghulam Muhammad Khan (Beg 1894:53) (cf. Figure 30), *tarab* strings had appeared on the larger *sitārs* by about 1830, the time of that musician's work. The pegs of the *tarab* strings pictured on his *sitār* are also held in a separate wooden piece attached to the right hand side of the *sitār* neck.

The addition of a second gourd *(tumbā)* at the back upper end of the neck of the *sitār* was a final step in the process of modeling the *sitār* on the *bīn*. It was probably instituted by *sitār* players in Delhi and Jaipur who were the most concerned with cultivating a *dhrupad*-based style. Because of the lack of drawings depicting professional *sitār* players, it is not known exactly when the upper *tumbā* first appeared. It is depicted by the 1870s in the handbooks such as "*Naghmah-i sitār*," and probably appeared on professionals' *sitārs* significantly earlier.

N. Augustus Willard (Banda 1834) 3 strings:					"*kharaj*" Ṣ brass	"*kharaj*" Ṣ brass	Ṃ steel
Fanny Parks (Lucknow 1832) 4 strings:				(P̣) steel	Ṣ brass	Ṣ brass	Ṃ steel
F. -J. Fétis (Banaras 1855) 7 strings:	"side" (?) steel	"side" (?) steel	"low-pitched" P̤ brass	P̣ steel	Ṣ brass	Ṣ brass	Ṃ steel
M. K. I. Khan (Lucknow 1856) 6 strings:		"*cikārī*" M˙ steel	"*gandhah*" G̣ brass	"*pañcam*" P̣ steel	"*kharaj*" Ṣ brass	"*kharaj*" Ṣ brass	"*bāj*" Ṃ steel
K. Bandyopadhyaya (Calcutta 1866)	"*cikārī*"	"*cikārī*"	"*ṣaḍaj*"	"*pañcam*"		"*kharaj*"	"*nāyakī*"
7 str./large *sit.*	S	P̣	S̤	P̣	P̤	Ṣ	Ṃ
5 str./small *sit.*	-	-	P̤	P̣	Ṣ	Ṣ	Ṃ
	steel	steel	brass	steel	brass	brass	steel
S. M. Tagore (Calcutta 1872) 7 strings: (large *sitārs*)	"*cikārī*" S steel	"*cikārī*" P̣ steel	"*ṣaḍaj*" S̤ brass	"*pañcam*" P̣ steel	"*kharaj*" Ṣ brass	"*kharaj*" Ṣ brass	"*nāyakī*" Ṃ steel
M. S. H. Khan (Delhi 1871) 6 strings:		"*papīhā*" S steel	"*laraz*" S̤ brass	"less" (?) steel	"*kharaj*" Ṣ brass	"*kharaj*" Ṣ brass	"*bāj*" Ṃ steel

Ram Bhaju Lal (Patna 1873) 5 strings:				*"mandā"*	*"pañcam"*	*"jodī"*	*"jodī"*	*"bāj"*
				P̤	P̣	Ṣ	Ṣ	Ṃ
				brass	steel	brass	brass	steel
Rahim Beg (Khairabad 1874) 8 strings:	*"cikārī"*	*"cikārī"*	*"cikārī"*					
	Ṡ	P	S	M̤	P̣ or Ṃ	Ṣ	Ṣ	Ṃ
	steel	steel	steel	brass	steel	brass	brass	steel
S. A. Khan (Delhi 1875) sequential order of string additions:						*"pañcam"*	*"kharaj"*	*"bāj"*
						P̣	Ṣ	Ṃ
						steel	brass	steel
					"pañcam"	*"kharaj"*	*"kharaj"*	*"bāj"*
					P̣	Ṣ	Ṣ	Ṃ
					steel	brass	brass	steel
				"laraz"	*"pañcam"*	*"kharaj"*	*"kharaj"*	*"bāj"*
				(?)	P̣	Ṣ	Ṣ	Ṃ
				brass	steel	brass	brass	steel
			"cikārī"	*"laraz"*	*"pañcam"*	*"kharaj"*	*"kharaj"*	*"bāj"*
			(?)	(?)	P̣	Ṣ	Ṣ	Ṃ
			steel	brass	steel	brass	brass	steel
		"zīl"	*"cikārī"*	*"laraz"*	*"pañcam"*	*"kharaj"*	*"kharaj"*	*"bāj"*
		(?)	(?)	(?)	P̣	Ṣ	Ṣ	Ṃ
		steel	steel	brass	steel	brass	brass	steel
		also 7, 9, or 11 *tarab* strings						
Karamatullah Khan (Allahabad 1908) 6, 7 or 8 strings:			*"cikārī"*	*"pañcam"*		*"jodī* or	*kharaj"*	*"bāj"*
			S	P̤	M or G	Ṣ	Ṣ	Ṃ
			steel	brass	steel	brass	brass	steel
		S	Ṇ	S̤	G	P̤	Ṣ	Ṃ
		steel	steel	brass	steel	brass	brass	steel
	Ṡ	S	Ṇ	S̤	Ṛ	P̤	Ṣ	Ṃ
	steel	steel	steel	brass	brass	brass	brass	steel

Table 1. Strings and Tunings

Amrtsen of mid-19th-century Jaipur, a famous member of the Jaipur *Senia* branch of *dhrupad*-influenced *sitār* players, is known for having played not a two, but a three-*tumbā sitār*. A portrait in the "*Saṅgīt sudarśan*" shows him with it (Figure 70). Amrtsen's *sitār* has a noticeably thick neck, a feature that would have contributed to an increased resonance of sound, a quality appropriate to his style. Mushtaq Ali Khan credited Amrtsen's line with the addition of the third gourd and said that members of the family called such a *sitār* a "*sitār bīn*."[53] Drawings in the "*Naghmah-i sitār*" and the "*Sarmāya-i 'ishrat*" portray a number of *sitārs* with three *tumbās* (Beg 1876:43) (Figures 29 and 31). They were used to some extent into the 20th century.

Varieties of sitār

The *sitār* appeared in almost as many shapes and sizes as there were musicians and types of music to play on it during the surge in its popularity in the mid to late 19th century. Large sized *tarabdār sitārs* were preferred by *sitār* players specializing in *dhrupad*-influenced music, such as Amrtsen. The author of the 1871 "*Qānūn-i sitār*" comments that "softer" (here lower) notes sound better, and more *mīḍ* (pulling) can be played on large *sitārs* (Khan, M. S. H. 1873:27).

Kachuā, "tortoise," *sitārs* were instruments with their main *tumbā* made from a gourd cut across the natural stem making it flatter than the vertically cut *tumbā*. Fétis' 1855 *sitār* (Figure 26) is an early example of a *kachuā* style *sitār*. Tagore calls it the *kacchapī vīṇā*, and treats it as a standard *sitār* (Tagore 1879:5; 1976:18-9). It is probable that the *kachuā sitār* was the model for the new type of *sitār* created by Ghulam Muhammad, which later became the *surbahār*. *Surbahārs* always have *kachuā*-style *tumbās*. *Kachuā sitārs* were very popular in the first decades of the 20th century and are still seen occasionally today.[54]

Very small *sitārs*, called *sitārī* or *sundarī* were used by amateurs for playing songs and easy *gats* and by professionals for the faster and lighter styles of *gat-toḍā*. They were popular in the urbane society of late 19th-century Calcutta, where paintings and woodcuts show them in parlor settings (Figures 34 and 35). A large variety of experimental, curiously-shaped and highly decorated *sitārs* and *sitārīs* were created in this period, especially in Bengal. Sourindro Mohun Tagore's imaginative collection of instruments may be included in this category. In his collection are *sitārs* made entirely of wood with the body portion in imaginative shapes. There is a *sitār* with a second neck attached alongside the first which he calls "*prasarini vina.*" One he calls "*nadesvar vina*" has a violin or viola body and a *sitār* neck (Figure 36).

Other *sitārs* and *sitārīs* in the Indian Museum in Calcutta and the Metropolitan Museum in New York might have been made by other 19th-century patrons. Two tiny *sitārīs* have ostrich eggs (Figure 37), and one a nautilus shell, in place of a *tumbā*. Captain Day describes a *sitārī* made in South India:

> The small sitar ... is of Deccan manufacture. It is ornamented prettily with ivory carving, and the body of the instrument is formed from a cocoa-nut. Sitars of this kind are much used by native ladies, and their tone is singularly sweet and plaintive, though, of course, not so powerful as that of the larger sitars (Day 1974:116).

Regional *sitārs*, which are outside the scope of this study, were sometimes significantly different from the mainstream instruments. Day describes one:

> ... besides the *sitār* just described, there is another form of the instrument to be met with in Southern India. This might be called the Karnâtik sitar, and it differs from the ordinary sitar in that it is confined in its intonation and is generally made with a much thinner and shorter neck. Its capability is, of course, much less. It is usually shaped somewhat like a tamburi, the body of the instrument being either of gourd or of wood. The manner of stringing is peculiar. The first and second strings only pass over frets, which are about 1/2-inch wide, and raised from the fingerboard; these strings are tuned in unison, and they are placed very much nearer together than the other strings .... The frets are of wood, with an upper edge of metal, only about 1/4-inch in width, and fixed to the fingerboard; the strings cannot therefore be pulled so as to produce "rekhu" without their coming off the frets (*ibid.*:120-1).

This one appears to be influenced by the Karnatak *vīṇā*. Regional *sitār* types such as Day's Karnatak *sitār*, and the Gujarati and Kashmiri *sitārs* have their own stories of development and are not fully accounted for in the story of the mainstream Hindustani *sitār*.

Instruments Related to the sitār

Surbahār

One of the important instruments to appear in late 19th-century Hindustan was the *surbahār*, Hindi-Urdu "springtime of notes," an enlarged version of the *kachuā*, flat gourd, *sitār*. The deep long-lasting sound of this instrument and its capability for extensive pulling of the main string made it suitable for playing music closely imitative of the *bīn*. An early reference to a large version of the *sitār* is found in the diary of Captain Robert Smith, who described and made a drawing of a concert that he attended in Kanpur sometime between 1828 and 1833. The pictured concert group consists of a *sitār* player, a *ḍholak* player and a player of a large *sitār* (Figure 24). Smith says about the players:

> The principal one and he was considered first rate played on the sitar .... The next performer played the bass on an instrument nearly similar to the first except being much larger and with no wire guard on the finger (Smith, R. c.1833:315-6).

This large *sitār* may be some sort of early *surbahār*. The player in Smith's drawing is clearly fingering the instrument, though his high right hand position seems awkward. An intriguing early ensemble!

It is near Kanpur, in the Lucknow of about 1825, to which the origin of the *surbahār* is traced. In the *"Yantra Kosha"* S. M. Tagore states that the *surbahār* was introduced by Ghulam Muhammad of Lucknow "about fifty years ago" (Tagore 1976:34). *Sitār* player Ghulam Muhammad was a disciple of Umrao Khan, a prominent early 19th-century Lucknow *bīn* player. Karam Imam Khan gives us some valuable comments on Ghulam Muhammad's playing although he does not mention the *surbahār* in connection with him. He evidently had heard Ghulam Muhammad and speaks of his expertise in playing a *bīn* style (represented as *ṭhok*[55]) on the *sitār*:

> Yes, in *sitār* first Ghulam Muhammad, recently of Banda, attained amazing mastery, and his *ṭhok* was so clear and expert that I have not heard it like that from any *bīnkārs* or *rabābias*, except Umrao Khan *sāhab*. His *sitār* was not inferior to *bīn* or *rabāb* ... (Khan, M. K. I. 1925:45. My translation).

Fig. 36. Nine instruments, called: 1. prasarini vina; 2. shantika vina; 3. bharata vina; 4. alabu sarangi; 5. nadesvara vina; 6. *fiddle (Nepal);* 7. bipanchi vina; 8. *fiddle* sarbutle, *Madras;* 9. *guitar and bow. S. M. Tagore collection. Victoria and Albert Museum, 22426.*

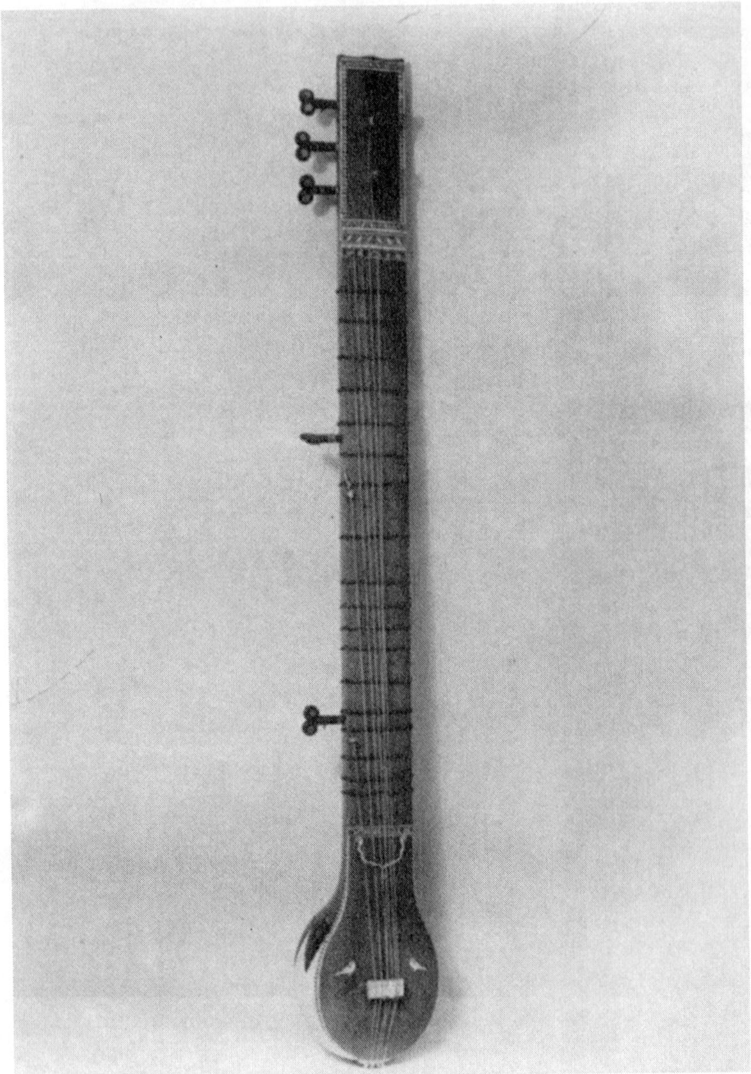

Fig. 37. Sitāri *with an ostrich egg body. The Metropolitan Museum of Art, Gift of Alice E. Getty, 1946. 46.34.6.*

Fig. 38. Bhagawan Chandra Das, sitār *and* surbahār *player. Roychowdhury 1929: 60ff. By permission of the British Library. IOL T 12824.*

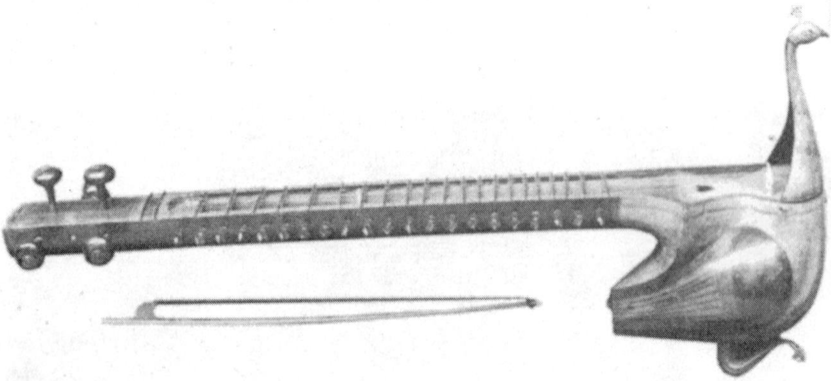

Fig. 39. A tāūs. *Victoria and Albert Museum. I.S. 02119.*

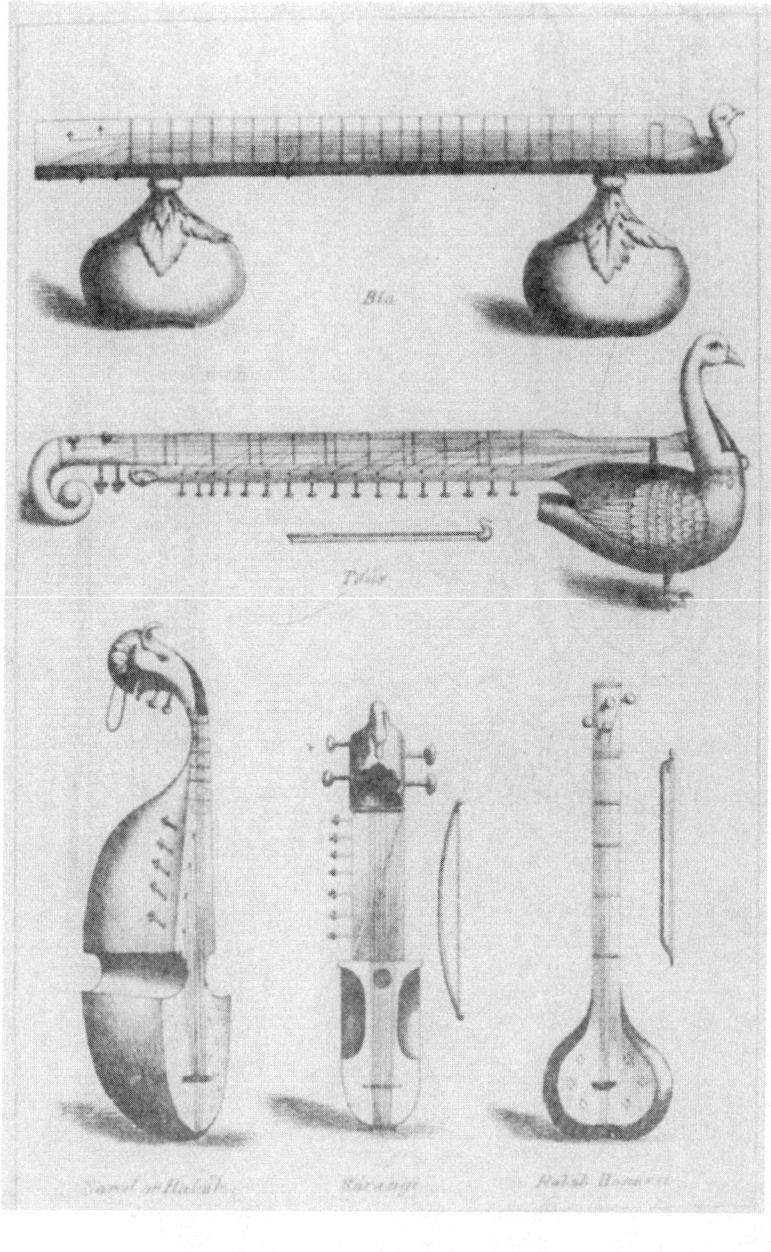

Fig. 40. Tāūs, "sarod or rabāb," and other instruments. Baden-Powell 1872-II:275-6. By permission of the British Library. IOL V 9174.

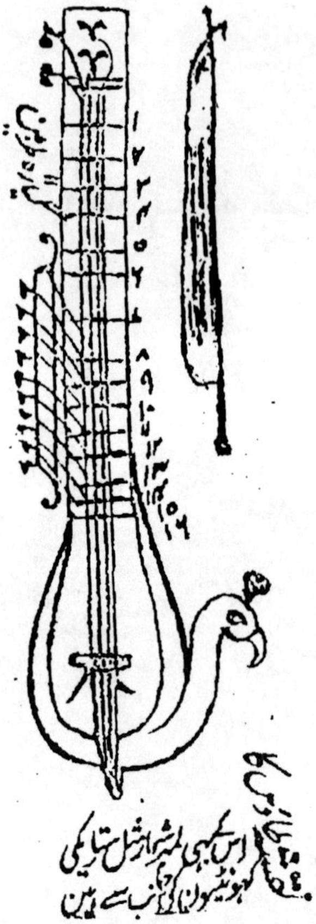

Fig. 41. A tāūs. *Khan, S. A. 1884:278.*

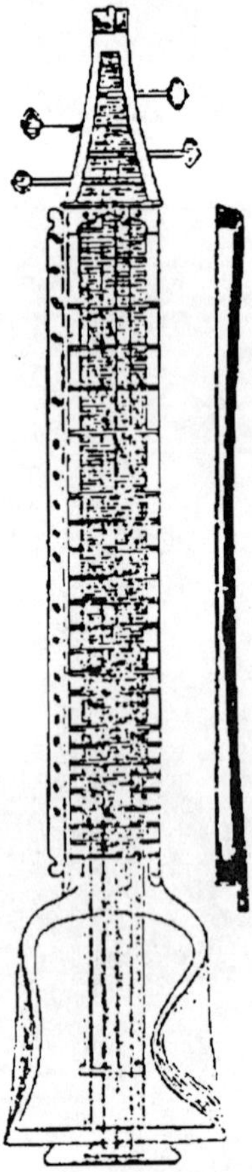

Fig. 42. Tāūs, *or* dilrubā. *19th century. Bahadurji 1887:418.*

Fig. 43. A kamānca *player. Khan, S. A. 1884:277.*

Fig. 44. *Chandrika Prasad Dubey playing* isrāj. *Roychowdhury 1929:38-9. By permission of the British Library. IOL T 12824.*

It is intriguing that Karam Imam mentions the *surbahār*, but not in relation to Ghulam Muhammad or any other player (*ibid*.:229).

There is pictorial evidence that Ghulam Muhammad did in fact create a new type of *sitār*. Rahim Beg in his *"Naghmah-i sitār"* (1876) provides a drawing of a *sitār* which he says was invented by Ghulam Muhammad. The instrument has five strings but no *cikārīs*, a wide neck, an upper *tumbā* and ten *tarab* strings (Figure 30). The text accompanying the drawing tells us:

> These types of *sitārs* are the creation of Ghulam Muhammad, one of the *Purab* people, and that Ustād was accomplished in the playing and making of *sitārs*. The Banaras craftsman Hanuman Dayal made a *sitār* like this in my presence for the Raja Sahab of Rima (Beg 1894:53. My translation).

The strange shape of the main *tumbā* is unexplained. Could it be some sort of stand to hold the instrument? Bengal became the primary center of *surbahār* playing in the late 19th century, where it is closely associated with musician Sajjad Husain or Sajjad Muhammad. Karam Imam tells us that Sajjad Husain is the son of Ghulam Muhammad (Khan, M. K. I. 1925:45).

Tagore discusses the *surbahār*, which he says is no different from a large *kachuā sitār (kacchapī vīṇā)*. It has seven strings, like the *sitār*. It usually has *tarab (taraf* or *pārśvatantrikā)* which are best made of brass. A small bridge *(tantrāsan)* underneath the main one holds these strings. They are to be tuned according to the wishes of the player. The *surbahār* is held and played exactly like the *kacchapī*, Tagore says. Its sound is deep, serious *(gambhīr)*, sweet and longlasting. However, Tagore says, a *kacchapī* made by an expert craftsman will not have a sound at all inferior to the *surbahār* (Tagore 1976:35). Apparently Tagore was not very impressed with the new instrument.

An 1880 catalogue by Victor Charles Mahillon includes descriptions of the instrument collection which Tagore gave to the museum at Brussels. The *surbahār* in Mahillon's description is one metre and a half in length. The two ways of tuning the five main strings and the two *cikārī* duplicate *sitār* tunings found in the Bengali handbooks. They are:

Ṃ (steel), Ṣ (brass), P̤ (brass), P̣ (steel), S̤ (brass), Ṣ, P (steel *cikārīs*)

and

Ṃ (steel), Ṣ (brass), Ṣ (brass), P̣ (steel), S̤ (brass), S, P (steel *cikārīs*).

There are also seven sympatl etic strings according to Mahillon's description of the *surbahār*, to be tuned to a scale from P to M (Mahillon

1893-I:146-7). Ghulam Muhammad's *sitār* in the "*Naghmah-i sitār*" showed ten *tarab* strings. The possibility holds that *tarab* strings were added to the *sitār* under the influence of Ghulam Muhammad and his new *sitār*.

In 1891 Captain Day describes the *surbahār* as "a rather uncommon instrument" which is "merely a large-sized sitar or kachapi-vina, played with a steel plectrum, and specially used for the performance of alapas or ragas." He is astute in recognizing some qualities that kept the *surbahār* a minor instrument: "The tone is rich and mellow like that of the vina, but the large size of the instrument renders its use fatiguing, while the cost is very high" (Day 1974:120).

Late 19th-century *surbahārs*, and those made by the early 20th-century Calcutta *sitār* maker Kanhailal exhibit a few notable structural differences from the *sitār*, including a flatter and wider neck and a decorative hole cut into the face in which the *tarab* strings are fastened (Figure 38). Especially notable on these *surbahārs* are the thin flattened frets, apparently shaped to resemble *bīn* frets.

The music of the *surbahār* is not discussed in detail or notated in the 19th-century handbooks. The instrument's main purpose was to render *ālāp*, the unaccompanied exposition of a *rāga* as played on the *bīn*. *Bīn* music and the techniques of pure *ālāp* were not within the scope of the books, as they were the domain of professional musicians who learned directly from masters. The *surbahār* therefore was a relatively specialized instrument, and never gained a wide amateur popularity. It did, however, attract the attention of both professional *sitār* players and *bīnkārs*.

The *surbahār* was the culmination of the *sitār* family's challenge to the *bīn*. Karam Imam Khan commented as early as 1856 that Ghulam Muhammad was as good as any *bīnkār* or *rabābia*. Karamatullah Khan, by 1908, was of the opinion that *surbahār* players were more knowledgeable and traditional in their techniques than the remaining *bīnkārs* of the day (Khan, K. 1908:168). The *bīn*, fading with the growing popularity of the *sitār*, was virtually eclipsed by the *surbahār*. Although *bīn* technique remained an inspiration for all aspects of *dhrupad*-style *sitār* and *surbahār* playing, and the late 19th-century purists still thought of the *sitār* as "a clumsy imitation" of the *vīṇā* (Tagore 1965:348), the living tradition of *bīn* playing was nearly gone by the beginning of the 20th century.

Tāūs and *kamāñca*

Sometime before the mid-19th century a new type of instrument appeared, one that combined characteristics of the *sitār* with features of the *sārangī*. It had the long neck, and metal strings and frets of the *sitār*, but a skin-covered body, and was played with a bow like the *sārangī*. Karam Imam speaks of two instruments of this type, the *tāūs* and an instrument that he calls the *gītār* or *gaitār*. The *tāūs*, Persian for "peacock," is described by him as being similar to the *sitār* but for its lower *tumbā*, which is in the shape of a peacock, and for the fact that it is played with a bow (Khan, M. K. I. 1925:58). On the *tāūs*, the feet of the peacock's body sometimes extended from the bottom end of the instrument to act as a stand when held upright for playing. The *sitār*-like neck formed the peacock's tail (Figures 39 to 41). Tagore in 1875 stated that the *tāūs* was a very recent instrument, put together in western Hindustan "within the last forty years" (Tagore 1976:57).

Karam Imam mentions the *tāūs* and also the *gītār* or *gaitār*, as an instrument similar to the *sitār* but played with a bow like the *sārangī*. The *gaitār* has *tarab* strings, interestingly a feature not found on the *sitār* in his descriptions. Karam Imam supports Tagore's statement on western Hindustan when he says that both the *tāūs* and the *gaitār* were invented in the district of Panjab (Khan, M. K. I. 1925:59).

The "*Sarmāya-i 'ishrat*" (1875) speaks of the *tāūs*, and of another instrument of the same type called a *kamāñca* which is especially popular in the district of Panjab. *Kamāñca* or *kamānche* is the name of a Persian bowed instrument of the spike fiddle type (also called *ghīchak*) which was present in Mughal India.[56] A "*Sarmāya-i 'ishrat*" drawing of the later *kamāñca* shows it as having the body of a *sārangī* and the neck of a *sitār* (Figure 43). It has *tarab* strings and is quite large. Could it be the same instrument as Karam Imam's *gaitār*? To complicate the matter of terminology regarding these instruments, Pannalal Gosvami in his "*Nād vinod*" of 1895, speaks of the "*kamānca* which is also called *tāūs*" (Gosvami, P. 1895:39). An 1887 article in German originating in Bombay describes an instrument called "*taus*" but pictures it as a *sārangī*-bodied *kamāñca* type (Bahadurji 1887:418-9)(Figure 42).

The name *kamāñca* went out of use, while *tāūs* continued for some time. The peacock-shaped instrument went through a short period of considerable popularity in the second half of the 19th century and continued to be practiced to some extent into the 20th century. Karamatullah Khan mentions it as one of the instruments which his father taught him to play (Khan, K. 1908:162). The *tāūs* eventually disappeared in name, form and practice. From the early 20th century the name *dil-*

rubā, Urdu "heart-ravishing," "bewitching," was applied to the instrument with a flat-bottom *sārangī*-shaped body and a *sitār* neck.

The "*Sarmāya-i 'ishrat*" provides some interesting information on the tuning and playing of the *kamāñca* and the *tāūs*. Both instruments have four main strings and seven, nine or eleven *tarab* strings. The *tarab* strings' pegs are set in a wooden holder attached along the side of the neck. The main strings are a steel *bāj*, two brass *kharaj* strings and a brass *laraz* as on a *sitār* lacking the steel third *pañcam*. The *tarab* strings are to be tuned as on the *sitār*. Sixteen *pardās* are tied to the neck. The following directions are given for tuning and playing these instruments:

> First tune the notes of the *kamāñca* or *tāūs* like those of the *sitār*, then, depending on what *laharā* or *khyāl* or *ṭappa* or the like, of whichever *rāga* or *rāginī* is decided upon, make the *ṭhāṭh* correct and, playing well with the bow, set the fret positions. Tune the *ṭarab* according to what is to be played, or tune each according to what peg it is near; that is, press the fret near each peg and tune the string. Then, when the *sur* and the *ṭhāṭh* are correct, play *laharā* ... (Khan, Sadiq A. 1884: 277-8).

A *laharā*, "wave," is a tune. In regional usage, and perhaps in this context, it is a specific song type for the bowed *surando* or *sarinda* of Sind (Baloch 1966:48). The author of "*Sarmāya-i 'ishrat*" mentions that the *kamāñca*, as well as the *tāūs*, *sārangī*, the *sāzindah* and the *dotāra* (all bowed instruments; the latter two are related to the *sārangī*), is played in accompaniment to singing, and should follow the syllables of the song exactly. He gives the notation for *laharās* in two *rāgas*, and says that when one has gained control over these melodies, one may go on to play easy *ṭhumrīs*, *ghazals* or the like. He provides a tip for vocal accompaniment saying that the singer's notes, including *tān* and *mīḍ*, should be followed as closely as possible, and that the singer's rests should be filled in by the instrumentalist (Khan, Sadiq A. 1884:278), a system followed by accompanists to the present day.

Isrāj

The instrument of the *sitār-sārangī* group to gain the greatest popularity was the *isrāj* or *esrāj*, also called *isrār* or *esrār* in early references. S. M. Tagore speaks of the *esrār* as "a very recent instrument." It has five strings tuned like the *sitār* and also has *tarab* strings. It is used, he says, to accompany women who have soft voices and is also sometimes heard as a solo instrument (Tagore 1976:56-7).

Swami Prajnanananda traces the name *isrāj* to the Urdu words *aish* and *rāj* as meaning "easy" and "greatly," pointing to its function as an easily played alternative to the *sārangī*. The word does not appear in Hindustani dictionaries, although it does in Bengali dictionaries, as *esrāj*. Prajnanananda supplies some details on its origin, information which most likely comes from a Calcutta oral tradition. He reports that the instrument was invented "perhaps by a Bengali artist" during the time Navāb Wajid Ali Shah lived in the suburbs of Calcutta after his ouster from Lucknow in 1856. The instrument was subsequently carried, perhaps, he says, by the *rabāb* player Basat Khan, to the town of Gaya in Bihar (Prajnanananda 1973:468). Basat Khan did go to Bihar from Calcutta in 1858 (Roy Chaudhury 1969:48-9) and Gaya was a center that hosted several well known *isrāj* players. In Gaya, in fact, Kanhailal Dhedhi, a disciple of Basat Khan, is often credited with the invention of the *isrāj*. A disciple of Dhedhi is pictured in Figure 44.

The *isrāj* as it is known in the 20th century has a rounded bottom that contrasts it with the flat-bottomed *kamāñca* or *dilrubā*. One writer compares its rounded shape to the shape of the *tambūrā* (Khan, I. 1912:225) but it more closely resembles other Indian bowed instruments such as the *cikārā* of North India or the *dotāra* of the "*Sarmāya-i 'ishrat*." The associations of Bengal and Bihar with the *isrāj* and Panjab with the *tāūs* and *kamāñca* are notable. It is not clear as to which instrument of this type is the earliest, but the *kamāñca* and the *tāūs* disappeared at an earlier time, and it is tempting to think of them as the predecessors of the *isrāj*.

One motivation behind the creation of an instrument that combined *sitār* and *sārangī* was the desire for an alternative to the *sārangī*. Aside from the difficulty of the *sārangī*'s playing technique, its reputation was socially marred from an early time by its association with dancers and courtesan-singers. Although the *sitār*, especially in its early days, was also used to accompany dance, and shared with *sārangī* a degree of the stigmatization that followed, somehow its subsequent solo use and leaning toward the *bīn* helped it shed most of the stigmatization that remained attached to the *sārangī*.[57] The new bowed instruments were especially taken up by amateur players, although a few professionals specializing in the *isrāj* emerged from Gaya and Calcutta. In 20th-century Bengal it came to be widely used to accompany "*Rabindrasaṅgīt*," the songs of Rabindranath Tagore.

3

Rabāb, *sarod* and Related Instruments

The early history of the *sarod* is more clearly accounted for and far more closely agreed upon than that of the *sitār*. A few differing theories do exist, however, and the main ones are examined here for the sake of record. S. M. Tagore in the "*Yantra Kosha*," attempting to relate all modern instruments to an earlier Sanskrit tradition, calls the *sarod* the *śāradīyā vīṇā* ("the *vīṇā* belonging to the sage Śārada") (Tagore 1976:28). Later scholars make the same statement, taking it either directly from Tagore or indirectly from the Calcutta tradition that he started.[58] *Śāradīyā* is a *vīṇā* name found occasionally in Sanskrit drama and poetry but not in Sanskrit musicological literature. Its characteristics are unknown. Its association with *sarod* is based on an imaginative phonological similarity, and has no historical basis.

The *rudra vīṇā* has also been linked with *sarod*,[59] evidently on the basis of the sound "*rud*," or because of a puzzling idea that the *rudra vīṇā* of the texts was really the *rabāb*, also a thought apparently originating with Tagore (1976:26). The *rudra vīṇā* is clearly described in the 17th- and 18th-century "*Saṅgītapārijāta*," "*Saṅgītanārāyaṇa*" and "*Saṅgīt sār*" as the stick zither that we know as the *bīn*. The idea of any direct relationship between the *rudra vīṇā* and the *rabāb* must be dismissed.

Most theories relate the *sarod* to the *rabāb*, although a lack of clarity concerning the various types of *rabāb* usually characterizes discussions of this instrument. The *rabāb* family in India presents complex problems, but at least three distinct types of *rabāb* can be shown to have existed in mainstream North Indian music in the medieval and the early modern periods. An examination of *rabāb* types and their roles in Indian musical history is a necessary prerequisite to understanding the origin of the *sarod*.

It has been suggested that the *sarod* developed under the influence of the *sursingār*, a modified form of the *dhrupad rabāb* (Mishra 1973:117). 19th-century texts indicate that the *sursingār* and the *sarod* were near contemporary, though of different structural sub-species. Although they are not directly related, evidence allows a possibility that some modifications were made to the *sarod* under the influence of the *sursingār*.

The Persian rabāb *and the Indian* rabāb

The earliest mention of an instrument named *rabāb* was found by Farmer in 10th-century Arabic texts in contexts that indicate it was a bowed instrument (Farmer 1978-I:101-3). Instruments of the same name, transliterated *rubab*, *rebab*, *rabob* and various other ways, proliferated throughout West, Central, South and Southeast Asia. In the Arab world and Southeast Asia, the *rabāb* today appears predominantly as a bowed instrument of the spike fiddle type. A North African type of *rabāb* is a short-necked bowed fiddle, a family of special interest for its possible relationship to the Indian *sārangī* (cf. Dick *et al.* 1984-III:177-83). The complex relationship between the *sārangī* and *rabāb* families has yet to be explored.

The *rabābs* that appeared in India were not bowed, but were plucked fretless lutes. Textual references begin in the earliest of the Persian chronicles, written during the 11th-century Ghaznavid occupation of the Panjab.[60] Amir Khusrau during the 13th-century Delhi Sultanate period mentions the *rabāb* frequently. In one passage he says:

> In order to display the beauty of the bridal-bed of poetry 12 screens [pardah: modes] have been stretched along the fine and thin silken chords fastened to the wooden pegs of the *Rabab* (Askari 1972:110).

A unique and prominent protrusion at the base of the neck of some medieval *rabābs* has caused them to be included in a category called "barbed lutes."[61] The presence in Indian temple art dating to the first centuries A.D. of an early type of barbed lute, often called the "Gandharan lute," is a tempting basis for the claim that this instrument type, and so the *rabāb*, had an early existence in India, predating the Muslim incursions.[62] However, like the 10th-century temple long lutes and their relation to the *sitār*, the Gandharan lute and the later *rabāb* cannot be historically linked in India. The immediate ancestor of the *rabāb* in India is clearly the Persian instrument of the same name.

Indian paintings in the earliest examples show the *rabāb* in the early Mughal courts with frequency and a fair amount of uniformity. These early Mughal *rabābs* have a collar which tapers between body and neck in a characteristic curved or angular shape. The barbed collar is often not as prominent as it would later become. The pegbox is long and bent back at an angle at the end of the neck. The skin-covered body is round or oblong. This type, which is seen in the period of Persian-influenced court life, will be called here the Persian *rabāb* (Figures 45 and 46).

Sometime in the mid-Mughal period a *rabāb* appeared that was to become one of the most prestigious instruments of 18th- and 19th-century Hindustani music. Pictured frequently in late Mughal, provincial and Pahadi miniature painting, it is characterized by its large round skin-covered body and a distinctive and pronounced turned-back collar around the base of the neck. The neck tapers toward the end to a peg-box which is often a distinctively ornamented, rounded or scroll-shaped box positioned behind the upper neck. This unique *rabāb* type, seen only in India, is called here the *dhrupad* or Indian *rabāb*.

In popular tradition, the *dhrupad rabāb* is very often traced to the great Tansen of Akbar's court. Paintings of the 17th century show Tansen or others of his time holding this type of *rabāb* (Figure 47).[63] Since tradition so widely associates the *rabāb* with Tansen, and the appearance of the Indian *rabāb* in painting coincides quite nearly with Tansen's period, it seems possible that Tansen was responsible for innovations relating to *rabāb* performance. Tansen's descendants through his son Vilas Khan are designated the "*rabābia* line" in oral traditions. Later members of this line included both *rabāb* and *sitār* players, among whom was the famous *sitār* player Masit Khan.

The invention of some sort of *rabāb* is sometimes associated with Guru Nanak (1469-1538), the first of the Sikh Gurus. Sikh histories speak of Nanak's disciple Mardana playing the *rabāb* and singing.[64] Paintings show Nanak with Mardana who is playing what is sometimes a small *dhrupad rabāb* (Figure 48). Other paintings show him holding differently shaped instruments. In the "*Sarmāya-i 'ishrat*" a type of *rabāb* having six silk strings which differentiate it from the mainstream gut-stringed one is credited to "Nanak Shah" (Khan, Sadiq A. 1884:283). It is difficult to tell what sort of *rabāb* Mardana would have played, and pre-18th-century sources for the story have not yet been traced.

It is also difficult to know what the process of change was in regard to the *rabāb*. Abu al-Fazl in the "*Ain-i Akbarī*" mentions a "Dekhan rabāb," perhaps providing a clue for the instrument's early use in the courts of Central India (Abu al-Fazl 1894:258). Ibrahim 'Adil Shah, whose court was in the Deccani center Bijapur, refers to it as a four-stringed instrument, but provides no other details. If the Persian *rabāb* followed a course similar to the *tambūr* of the same period, it was gradually modified from its Persian origins to suit aesthetic tastes which were shaped by *dhrupad* music.

The "*Ain-i Akbarī*" mentions twelve and eighteen-stringed *rabābs*.[65] Faqirullah in the 17th-century "*Rāg darpan*" speaks of *rabābs* with six strings but says that some people put on seven or twelve. The twelve-stringed *rabāb*, he says, has some of iron and some of copper which "assist" the six gut strings (Faqirullah 1953:n.p.). These may have been paired with the original six to form double courses.

The 17th-century *"Saṅgītapārijāta"* provides a sketchy description of the *rabāb*. Here it is given the Sanskritized name *ravāvaḥ* with the etymology that it "carries *(vaha)* sound *(rava)*." It is included after the drums under a novel category, *tatānaddha*, "skin-covered string instruments." It is described as being made of wood covered with skin and having seven silk strings, *paṭatantu* or *tantrī*, of which the first string is S and the second M. The rest of the strings are tuned "in order." The stroke is done with a plectrum called a *dāṅśika* or *dāntika*, "made of tooth" (Ahobala 1982:92). This description was adopted by Maharaja Pratap Singh in his *"Saṅgīt sār."* In Singh's description, however, the seven strings are specified as being of gut. They are tuned to a scale from S or M. An interesting playing technique is described here. The right hand is to sound the strings with an ivory plectrum, and the left hand is to play the syllables of the *mṛdang* (the *dhrupad* barrel drum) on the skin face of the instrument (Singh, S. P. 1910-II:74). The playing of *mṛdang bols* (syllables) on the skin of the *dhrupad rabāb* is described in modern oral tradition as well,[66] but the prominence given it in the *"Saṅgīt sār"* makes one wonder if the *rabāb* described here is of a special type.

The *"Saṅgītanārāyaṇa"* gives an 18th-century description of the *rabāb*, called there the *kacchapī* or the *rūpavatī*. The "head," *śira* (probably the body of the instrument), is described as 18 fingers in length. The throat, *galā*, is 5 fingers. The back of it is in the shape of a tortoise. The ivory bridge, *daśika*, is placed in the center of the head and has five holes in it. At the end of the throat is a *karṇikā* ("projection"), measuring ten fingers, in the shape of a half moon at the back of the neck. The neck, *daṇḍa*, is tapered toward the end. The pegbox, *sārīgraha*, has a tail, *puccha*, that is curved in the shape of a fish's tail and ornamented in various ways. The five pegs are called *sārikā* and three are on the right and two on the left of the pegbox. The instrument has five strings, of which three are made of silk and two of silk or gut (Narayanadeva 1966:81-2).

The *"Sarmāya-i 'ishrat"* (Figure 54) describes the *rabāb* as having metal strings, a characteristic that, along with a gourd body and a wooden face, normally distinguishes a related instrument, the *sursingār*, from the *rabāb*. This description may reflect the waning days of the *rabāb* when the *sursiṅgār* was effectively displacing it. The first and fifth string are steel and the second, third, fourth and sixth brass or bronze.

S. M. Tagore in the *"Yantra Kosha"* describes the *"rudra vīṇā* or *rabāb"* as having six gut strings tuned to P R S P G Ṡ. The first finger of the left hand has a thick fish scale tied to it, with which it presses the string.

The right hand gives downward strokes with a stick made of sandalwood or bamboo, or a three cornered plectrum which he says is called *javā* in the Persian language (Tagore 1976:28-9). *Javā* is the normal term used up to the present day, for the *sarod* plectrum. It may be related to the Arabic "*zarb*," the source of the word *mizrāb*.

O. Goswami, similarly to S. M. Tagore, describes the tuning of the six gut strings of the *rabāb* as P R S P̣ Ṃ (or G̣) and Ṣ and reports that their names were *zir*, *miyan*, *sur*, *mandra*, *ghor* and *kharaj* respectively (Gosvami, O. 1957:299), an interesting mix of Arabic, Persian and Hindustani terms. *Zir* was the Arabic name for the highest string on the short lute the *'ud*, and other instruments,[67] *sur*, *mandra* and *kharaj* are Hindustani words. *Ghor* is an Urdu-Persian word meaning "deep."

The *dhrupad rabāb* was a pervasive presence for about two hundred years after Tansen. Along with the *bīn*, it and its players influenced the techniques and music of the *sursingār*, *sarod* and even *sitār*. It will be mentioned in those contexts in later discussions. The *rabāb* had nearly disappeared by the late 19th century, although it continued to be played by a few known artists such as Muhammad Ali Khan of Gaya, son of the famous Basat Khan (Figure 53), and Allauddin Khan, disciple of Rampur's Wazir Khan, into the 20th century. It can perhaps be found in reconstructed form to the present day.[68] Figures 49 to 53 show *dhrupad rabābs* from some 18th- and 19th-century sources.

The Afghani or Kabli rabāb

A *rabāb* of a very different type, probably originating in Afghanistan, appeared in northwestern India and established itself by sometime about the mid-18th century. This *rabāb* does not appear in paintings, and its history in the 18th century is known only through oral tradition. It evidently remained largely in non-urban areas of North India until it entered the mainstream of Hindustani music in the form of the *sarod*. In Afghanistan this *rabāb* exists today as one of the most prominent of that region's instruments. It is also found in Pakistan and Kashmir (cf. Slobin 1976, Sakata 1983). The Afghani *rabāb* is a short lute, and has a deep narrow body with a sharply indented waist. Both body and neck are carved from a single piece of wood and the body tapers into a hollow neck. Because the waist divides the hollow sounding body into two sections, the instrument is sometimes sub-classified as a "double-chested lute." Two to four tied frets of gut are usually present at the upper end of the wooden fingerboard of the Afghani *rabāb*.

The exact origin of this *rabāb* is not clearly known. One scholar notes that Afghanis refer to Ghazni as the place of this *rabāb*'s origin and speculates that it might have been developed at Timur Shah's court in Kabul in the 18th century (Baily 1988:26). The *rabāb* therefore must have travelled rapidly from Afghanistan to have played a role in Indian music from the mid-18th century, which oral tradition and musical evidence says that it did. An even earlier period for the Afghani *rabāb* in India is pointed to in some oral traditions, although this is undocumented. The Afghani *rabāb* type does not appear in any Indian painting, but a curious instrument that might be related to it appears in an early 17th-century Mughal painting of a rural scene by a well-known artist (Figure 55). This short lute, being plucked here like the Afghani *rabāb*, resembles a type of bowed *cikārā*, a North Indian regional instrument, which can still be found (cf. Bor 1986/7)(Figure 39).

Mountstuart Elphinstone arrived in Kabul on a British mission in 1808. In "An Account of the Kingdom of Caubul" he mentions the *rabāb*:

> As soon as a chief of any name dies, songs are made in honour of his memory. Besides these songs, some men recite odes, or other passages from the poets; and others play the flute, the rubaub (a sort of lute or guitar), the camauncheh and sarindeh (two kinds of fiddles), or the soornaum, which is a species of hautboy. The singers usually accompany their voice with the rubaub or the fiddle (Elphinstone 1972-I:309).

The Afghani dancers and musicians, including a *rabāb* player, in an 1880 photograph (Figure 56) are somewhat later representatives of the traditions there. In India a reference to this *rabāb* type is provided by Willard, who in 1834 says:

> This instrument is strung with gut-strings, and in shape and tone resembles a Spanish guitar. It is played with a plectrum of horn held between the fore-finger and thumb of the right hand, while the fingers of the left stop the strings on the fingerboard (Willard 1965:99).

Willard refers to the *rabāb*'s regional concentration saying "The Puthans are remarkably fond of this instrument, which is very common at Rampur," and he reports:

> I have heard some performers on this, who are said to excel, and their performance certainly deserved praise, for the delight with which they inspired their hearers (Willard 1965:99).

The *rabāb* in India is both drawn and described by Fétis in 1869 (Figure 57), who observes that the deep waist is unnecessary on a plucked instrument and would indicate its relationship to bowed instruments. It has six gut strings and seven sympathetic strings, their pegs inserted directly into the body of the instrument (Fétis 1869-II:290-1).

In the 1875 "*Sarmāya-i 'ishrat*" one *rabāb* is called the "*rabāb Sikandari,*" an invention of Alexander, Sikandar, alluding to its northwestern origin. It is described as having four gut strings and seven sympathetic strings. The main strings are tuned to S, S, *(joḍā)*, P, and Ṣ, and the sympathetic strings are tuned to the notes of the octave. Its triangular plectrum is called *javā* (Figure 54)(Khan, Sadiq A. 1884:283).

Modern oral traditions take up the story of the Afghani *rabāb* in the context of its transformation into the *sarod*. These stories create a fairly complete picture of the instrument's history, although any 18th-century visual or written source would be a welcome find. *Sarod* player Karamatullah Khan (Khan, K. 1908), and Calcutta oral traditions, tell us that the Kabli *rabāb* entered India from Afghanistan as a marching instrument played by soldier-musicians who came with the armies of the early Mughals. Karamatullah Khan says that the instrument was used for military purposes because of the fervor and heat that it creates. He puts its entry into India at about 1650 ("two hundred and fifty years ago") (Khan, K. 1908:160). Tagore says that in ancient times the *rabāb* was a travelling instrument. Kings, he says, would send players on elephant or camelback ahead of their processions when they travelled (Tagore 1976:31). References to the 17th-century use of "fiddles" by attacking Rajputs and Afghani thieves is noted by Bor (1986/7:61). Once in India, the *rabābiās* settled in centers near and eastward of Delhi. This region, which came to have a large population of Pathans and Rohillas, groups from eastern Afghanistan, became known as Rohilkhand in the last quarter of the 18th century. Its capital was at Rampur, noted by Willard as a center for *rabāb* playing. The Afghani *rabāb* maintained its identity and its original music in the region of Rohilkhand, according to the oral accounts, until about the mid-18th century, when a line of *rabābias* established contact with Hindustani court musicians. In modern northwest India and in Pakistan, the *rabāb* continues to exist outside of the mainstream Hindustani music tradition (Figures 58 and 59).

The Origin of the sarod

The word *sarod* or *sarūd* was a Persian word for music or singing and may have been a term for a medieval musical instrument as well

(Askari 1972:97). The immediate source of the name in India is not certain. Its mention occurs as early as 1830.[69] It is not clear at what point the name *sarod* came to be applied to the instrument, since the earliest descriptions show none of the modifications that would distinguish *sarod* from the *rabāb*. Two structural differences are normally thought to distinguish the modern *sarod* from the Afghani *rabāb*: the replacement of gut with steel strings, and the covering of the fingerboard with a metal plate. The earliest sources that describe *sarod*, however, report neither of these features. In the *"Ma'dan al-mūsīqī"* it is described as having gut strings. It originated from the *rabāb*, says Karam Imam, but is "one and a half in length" *("qad men ḍevḍhā")* (Khan, M. K. I. 1925:58). As late as 1875 the *"Sarmāya-i 'ishrat"* describes the *sarod* as having four gut strings. There is still no mention of a metal plate. An 1872 drawing in Baden-Powell's "Hand-Book of the Manufactures and Arts of the Punjab" depicting "Sarod or Rabâb" indicates no difference (Figure 40). One scholar has the idea that the name was first applied simply to distinguish it from the *dhrupad rabāb* (Dick 1984a:298).

The *"Ma'dan al-mūsīqī"* and most oral traditions mention a figure, Ghulam Ali Khan, a *rabābia*, who is the earliest musician associated with the instrument called *sarod* (Khan, M. K. I. 1925:47). Descendants give him or his brother Murad Ali Khan credit for creating the instrument (Khan, A. A. 1973:n.p.; Kosar 1956:120). Ghulam Ali Khan was the grandson of a *rabāb* player from Afghanistan, Bandagi Khan. Ghulam Ali lived in Riwa, stayed for some time in Lucknow and finally settled in Gwalior. He learned Hindustani music from musicians in the various courts where he lived. He had died before the *"Ma'dan al-mūsīqī"* was written, so he apparently lived in the first half of the 19th century. Since Ghulam Ali is the earliest figure associated with the instrument called *sarod*, it is likely that he instituted some changes to the *rabāb* and/or called it by the new name. See Part Two for more on Ghulam Ali Khan.

The Changing sarod

An 1864 catalogue of musical instruments by Meadows Taylor describes a curious instrument, *"sarrooda."* Grouped along with the bowed *sārangī* and *cikāra* but larger and "more powerful" than the *sārangī*, it was an instrument that could be either bowed or plucked (Taylor 1965: 257-8). In Karam Imam's Lucknow the *sarod* was a larger version of the Afghani *rabāb*, presumably still with gut strings, wooden fingerboard and sympathetic strings. In 1875 Delhi the *sarod* had four gut strings and seven bronze *tarab* strings (Figure 60) (Khan, Sadiq A. 1884:283).

Changes were beginning to occur, however, around this time. In the same year in Calcutta S. M. Tagore describes the *sarod* (*śarad* or *śāradīyā vīṇā*) as having six strings, and says that players from time to time choose to use steel or other metal strings instead of gut. The strings are tuned to M M S S P P. The two doubled pairs are played as one, an interesting pre-20th-century stringing. The sixth string is used for "accompaniment" (*sur yog*) and seems to be a kind of *cikārī*. There are seven to eleven *tarab* strings. Tagore comments that it is somewhat harsh, not as sweet-sounding an instrument as the *bīn*, *sitār* or *rabāb*. Supporting Karam Imam's note on size, Tagore says the "Arab sarod," probably the Afghani *rabāb*, is somewhat smaller than the Indian *sarod* (Tagore 1976: 28-9). An 1889 *sarod* on exhibit in the Metropolitan Museum, New York, with the Tagore collection and presumably from Calcutta, still has no metal plate. There are six main pegs and places for nine *tarab* strings. It has a somewhat shallower body than the *rabāb* also on exhibit and is highly ornamented, the entire instrument painted elaborately.

Karamatullah Khan tells us that his father, *sarod* player Na'matullah Khan, who lived about 1816-1911, instituted the changes that we think of as defining the modern *sarod*, and identifies a specific time period for the changes. He says that his father instituted three changes in the *sarod* during the time he was living in Navāb Wajid Ali Shah's court-in-exile in Calcutta, from 1858 to 1869. At that time Na'matullah Khan reportedly covered the fingerboard with a brass plate, replaced the gut strings with steel ones and removed two gut frets that had been on the *rabāb*. Karamatullah Khan comments that while almost everyone copied his father's innovations as he made them, some people replaced the two gut frets, which would not hold on a metal fingerboard, with metal frets (Khan, K. 1908:161). From Tagore's comments it seems that, the use of metal instead of gut strings was a trend not attributable to any one person. It is fairly widely agreed upon, however, that Na'matullah Khan introduced the metal plate by which the modern *sarod* is recognized. One Calcutta account says that in the later part of his life even Ghulam Ali played on a metal-plated *sarod* as introduced by Na'matullah Khan (anon. n.d.:3), but Ghulam Ali had died before Na'matullah Khan was supposed to have made the changes, so there is an error in one account or the other.

Drawings by Karamatullah Khan in 1908 illustrate the *sarod* as developed by his father and the *sarod* played by himself (Figures 61 and 62). Na'matullah Khan's *sarod* has six main strings, one *cikārī* string and seventeen *tarabs*. The tuning of the strings is not given, but Karamatullah Khan claimed that his father "changed the tuning *[ṭhāṭ]* of the *sarod* to make it like that of the *sursingār* and the *[dhrupad] rabāb*" (anon.

n.d.:58). The mention of the *sursingār* in this context is notable and might hint at the influence of the *sursingār* on the metal plate and metal strings of the *sarod*. Karamatullah Khan's *sarod* is larger than that of his father. It has a more rounded face, a smaller and rounded waist, a larger deeper body and a fish-shaped peg box bent to the back. It has six main strings, one *cikārī*, and fifteen *tarab* strings whose pegs are in staggered placement in the body, as on modern *sarods*. The older peg placement was in a single line. The addition of the *cikārī* brought the *sarod* to its basic modern form. Later 20th-century developments would alter tunings and shape to some degree and add more *cikārī* and *tarab* strings.

Sursingār

An instrument that emerged prominently in the middle of the 19th century was the *sursingār*, a modified form of the *dhrupad rabāb*. The term is Hindi and Urdu, formed from the colloquial pronunciations of the Sanskrit words *svara* and *sṛṅgāra*, meaning "ornament of notes." It is found in its Hindi-Urdu form, *sursingār*, in the earliest references, such as the "*Ma'dan al-mūsīqī*" (Khan, M. K. I. 1925:59). The Sanskritized version, *sura śṛṅgāra*, or a partially Sanskritized form, *sursṛṅgār*, is seen in Tagore and in later, including modern, references, but the original name is probably *sursingār*. Inayat Khan (later known as Sufi or Hazrat Inayat Khan) calls it *sursanghār* in his 1912 "*Minqār musīqār.*" A smaller but similar instrument in the Metropolitan Museum, New York, has been labelled *sursanga*, probably by Tagore.

Muhammad Karam Imam was a witness to the period of the instrument's rise. He describes it as being similar to the *sarod*, a curious comment that might indicate something about the two instruments' relationship. It has metal strings, an upper *tumbā* "like the *bīn*," and a "long" lower *tumbā*. There is no mention of a metal plate on the fingerboard, a wooden face or a wide bridge, the other characteristics that normally define the *sursingār*. Karam Imam calls it a sweet-sounding instrument and says that it was invented by Pyar Khan (Khan, M. K. I. 1925:59). Pyar Khan was one of the most prominent *dhrupad rabāb* players in early and mid-19th-century Lucknow and is normally credited for the introduction of the *sursingār*. Karam Imam says Pyar Khan died in Lucknow during the time of Sultan Ali, one of Wajid Ali Shah's predecessors.

Metal strings and a wooden body are features of the *sursingār* described in the "*Sarmāya-i ʿishrat*" of 1875 (Figure 63). The six strings are tuned to M S S R G P̣ and two *cikārī* strings called *zīl* are tuned to high octave (*ṭīp)* S. It is a difficult instrument, the author says, and it is used to play *joḍ*, a term for *ālāp*, as on the *bīn*. Interestingly there is no mention of a metal fingerboard here (Khan, Sadiq A. 1884:284). Tagore's *sursingār* has a gourd body with a wooden face. The instrument's neck is covered with a steel cover which he says is called *paṭrī* in Hindi. The strings are tuned to P S P̣ G̣ S and P. It has an upper gourd in imitation of the *bīn*. The right hand uses a metal plectrum. It has a sweet and delicate sound (Tagore 1976:31-3). A description by Captain Day sounds fairly similar:

> The Sur-s'ringara ... is somewhat like the rabôb in shape, but with a wooden belly, and played with an iron plectrum. There are, as a rule, two frets only, the *fingerboard below* the frets being generally of metal, so that the fingers may slide easily over it. The length of the instrument is about four feet, and its tone is rich and mellow, somewhat like that of the pizzicato notes of the violoncello. It ... usually has seven sympathetic strings tuned to the intervals of the raga in which the performer is playing ... (Day 1974:121).

Day gives the string tuning as P R S P̣ Ṣ G and two high S's. The painting given by Day seems to show a metal plate on the fingerboard (Day 1974:116f).

Visual examples of *sursingārs* show that their characteristics differed considerably. In 20th-century examples the *sursingār* has the shape of a *dhrupad rabāb* (Figure 64). The wooden body of *rabāb* is replaced by a gourd, usually cut in the flat *kachuā* style. A wooden face replaces the skin of the *rabāb*. The strings are metal and the bridge is flat-surfaced like that of a *sitār* or *tambūrā*. The fingerboard is covered with a metal plate. The pegbox is straight and unornamented. A second gourd on the upper back of the neck is common. A photograph in Day's book shows a *sursingār* of a considerably different type. The body and gourd resemble a *surbahār* or large *sitār* more than a *rabāb*, while the bulging neck and bent-back pegbox resemble, perhaps, a large *sarod*. In the variety of its shapes, the hybrid quality of the instrument is very apparent. Tagore calls the *sursingār* a combination of the *bīn*, the *kachuā sitār* and the *rabāb* (Tagore 1976:33). In 1912, Inayat Khan comments that the lower portion of the *sursingār* looks like a large *tambūrā* (Khan, I. 1912:225). It is to be remembered that Ghulam Muhammad and his prototype *surbahār* were also in the Lucknow of the 1830s, contemporaneous to Pyar Khan. The two instruments were products of a wave of interest in *dhrupad* that took place at this time. The *sursingār* and the *surbahār* were both modifications of contemporary instruments under the inspiration of the *bīn*.

Karam Imam's mention of the *sarod* in connection with the *sursin-*

Fig. 45. A Mongol chieftain with a rabāb *player. From an album of Emperor Jahangir. Mughal, c1600. Freer Gallery of Art. 52.2 - 1.*

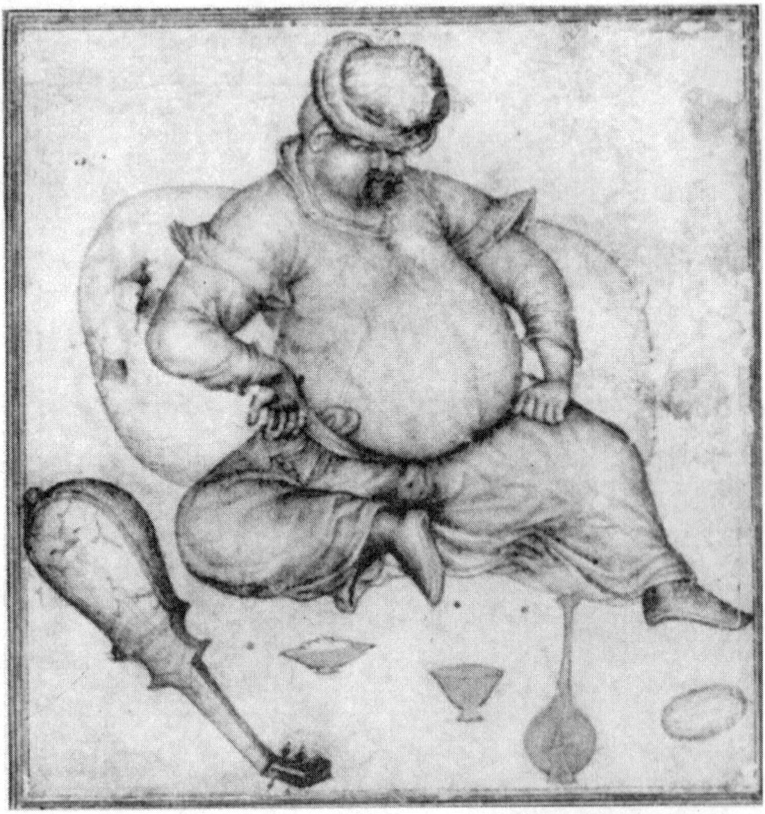

Fig. 46. A seated man and a rabāb*, attributed to Basawan. Mughal, Akbar period, c1580-85. Freer Gallery of Art. 53.60.*

Fig. 47. A rabāb *player with a prince and a* faqīr, *Mughal c1650. National Museum, New Delhi. 50.14 / 11.*

Fig. 48. *Guru Govind, Nanak and Mardana playing* rabāb. *Pahadi, 18th century. Bharat Kala Bhavan. 586 P.*

Fig. 49. A women's concert party with a rabāb *player. Deccan, c1740. Victoria and Albert Museum. CIRC 227-1922.*

Fig. 50. Women playing rabāb *and* daff. *Kangra, 1785-90. National Museum, New Delhi. 87.1251.*

Fig. 51. A rabāb, *decorated with inlay. Victoria and Albert Museum. 36-1890.*

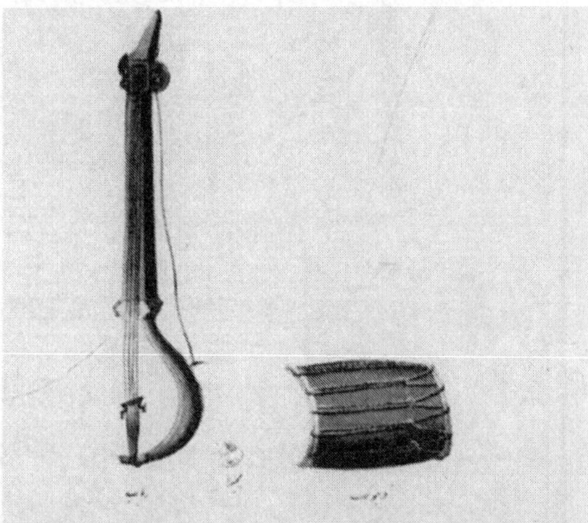

Fig. 52. Rabāb, dholak *and* manjīra. *One of twenty-three drawings of musical instruments, probably Patna, c1820. By permission of the British Library. IOL Add. Or. 2625.*

Fig. 53. Muhammad Ali Khan, rabāb *player. Roychowdhury 1929:52-3. By permission of the British Library. IOL T 12824.*

Fig. 54. Rabāb *and* rabāb sikandarī. *Khan, S. A. 1884:283*

Fig. 55. *Rural scene with a player of an unidentified short lute, by Bichitr. Mughal, early 17th century. Freer Gallery of Art. 48.21 B.*

Fig. 56. Nautch *girls and musicians. Photograph by J. Burke. Afghanistan c1880. By permission of the British Library. IOL Photo 430/3 (60)* Curzon.

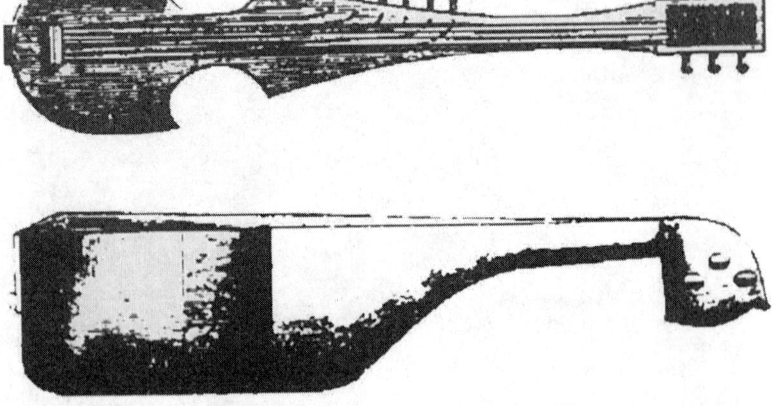

Fig. 57. *A* rabāb. *Fétis 1869-II:290.*

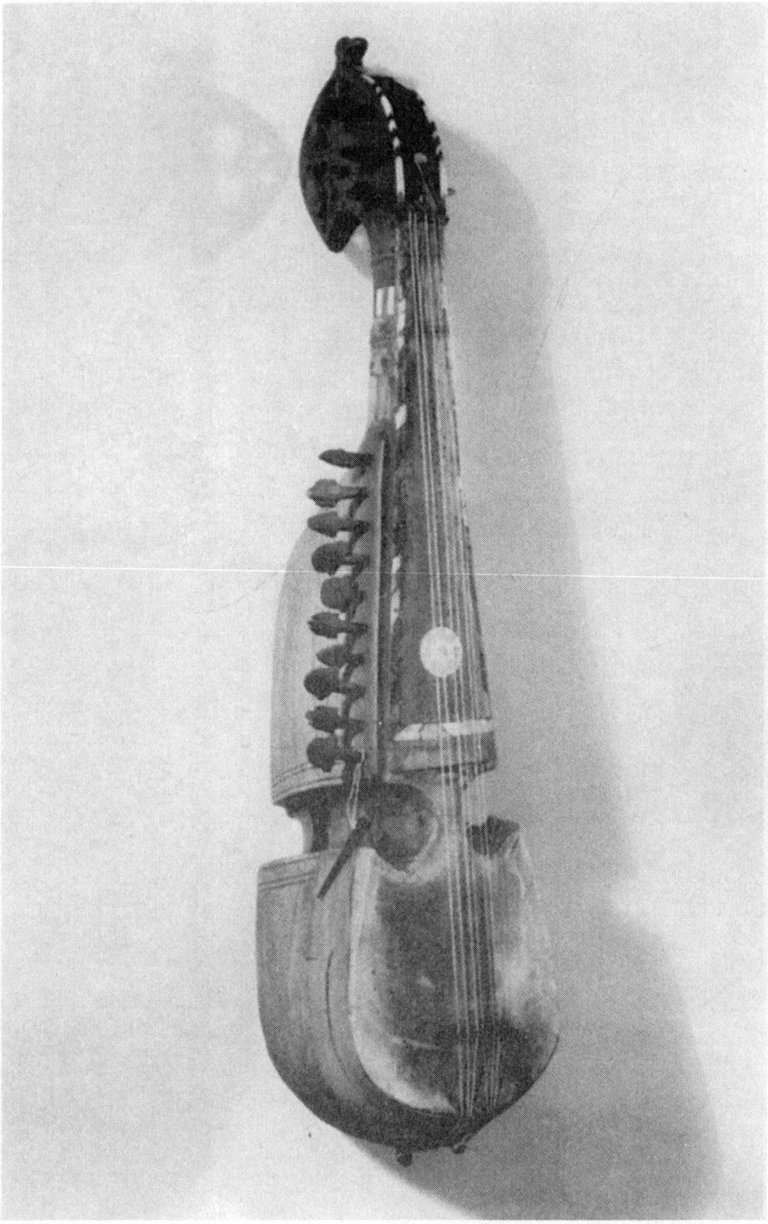

Fig. 58. An Afghani-style rabāb. *The Metropolitan Museum of Art, Gift of Alice E. Getty, 1946. 40.34.24.*

Fig. 59. A rabāb *player, Kashmir. Sangeet Natak Akademi, New Delhi. 1456.*

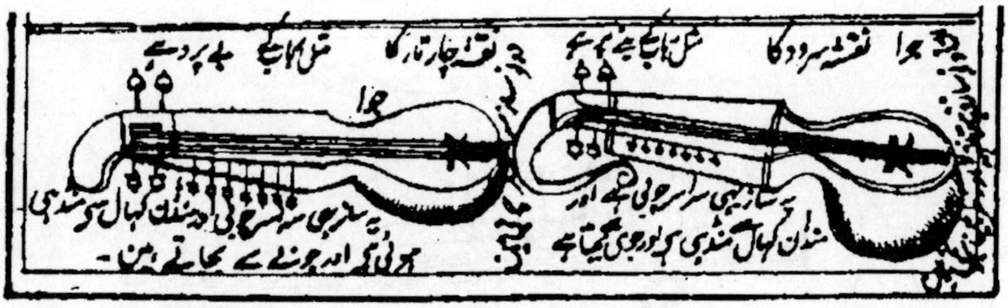

Fig. 60. Cārtār *and* sarod. *Khan, S. A. 1884:283.*

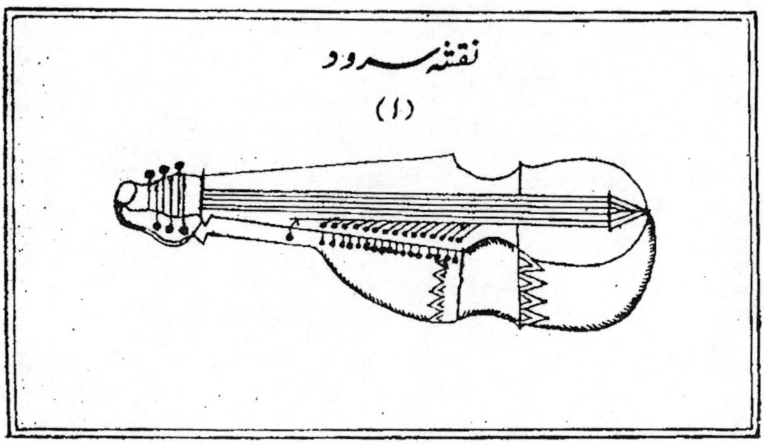

Fig. 61. *Na'matullah Khan's* sarod. *Khan, K. 1908:163.*

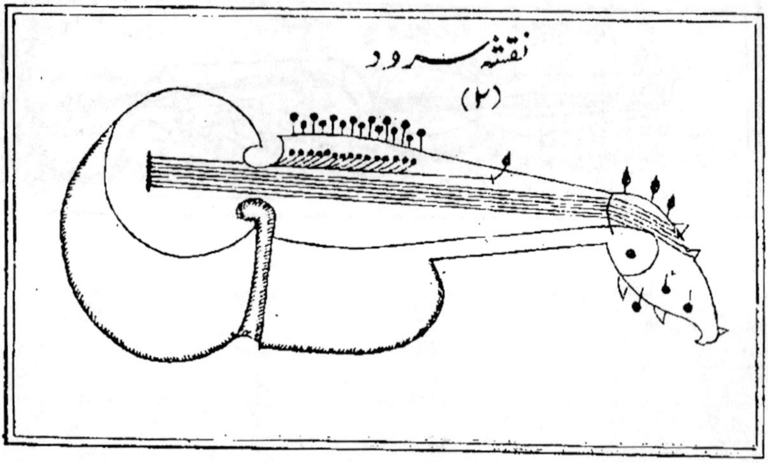

Fig. 62. *Karamatullah Khan's* sarod. *Khan, K. 1908:165*

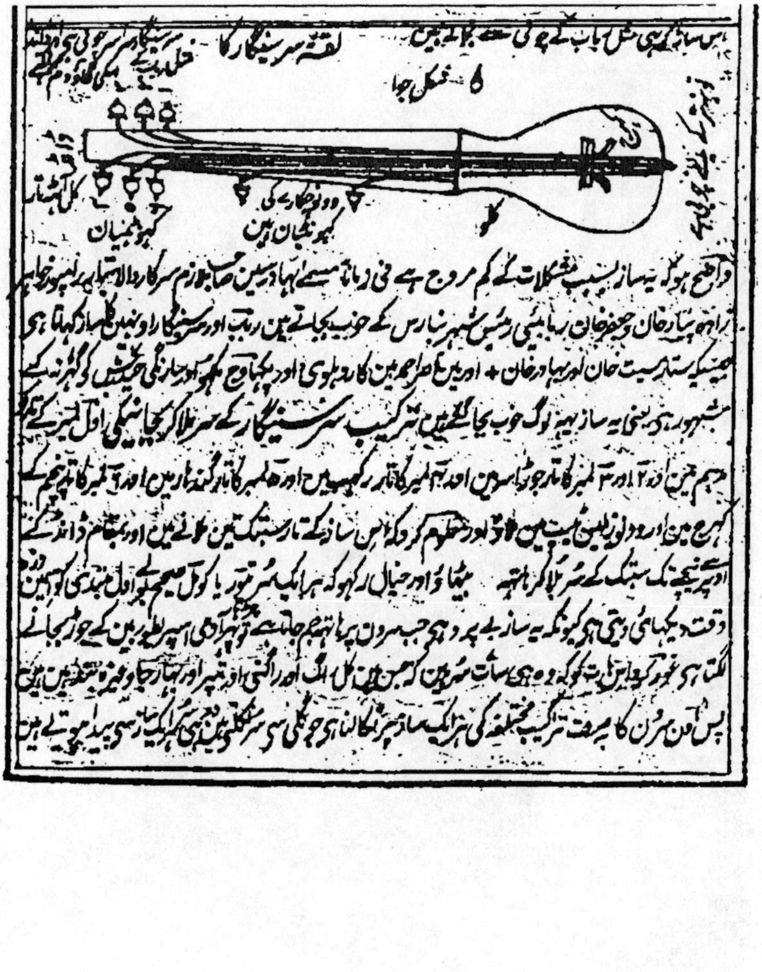

Fig. 63. Sursingār *and its description. Khan, S. A. 1884:284.*

Fig. 64. *Birendra Kishore Roy Choudhury playing* sursingār. *Sangeet Natak Akademi.* 0-1/488.

gār brings up the question of their relationship with respect to metal strings and a metal fingerboard. Ghulam Ali, the earliest player of the *sarod*, is said to have spent time in Lucknow or Farrukhabad and learned from the inventor of the *sursingār*, Pyar Khan, while he was there. His *sarod* fingerboard was probably wooden. Na'matullah Khan was a disciple of Basat Khan, a brother of Pyar Khan, and he probably initiated the changes to his *sarod* in Calcutta after 1858. If the tuning changes that he brought about were inspired by the *sursingār*, as his son writes, then it seems likely that the metal plate and strings as well might have been inspired by the same source. But details of the first appearance of the metal fingerboard plate on *sursingār* are unknown. When did the *sursingār* acquire the plate? Karam Imam does not mention it in 1857. Perhaps it only acquired this feature later in Calcutta.

Created as a more pleasing-toned alternative to the disappearing *dhrupad rabāb*, it was destined for a limited popularity. The *sursingār* reached its peak in late 19th- and early 20th-century Lucknow, Rampur, and Calcutta, but it had already become almost completely obsolete by the mid-20th century. It stands as a symbol for the interest in *dhrupad* and the spirit of experimentation going on at that time.

A few other experimental instruments related to the *sarod* made brief appearances in the late 19th century. One of these was the *surchayan* invented and played by one of the sons of *sarod* player Ghulam Ali. This was some sort of combination of the *sarod* and the *sitār* (anon. n.d.:3-4). In the early and mid-20th century other inventions were the fretless banjo with a metal-plated fingerboard made and played by Karamatullah Khan's brother Kaukabh Khan, and the *candrasārang*, a combination of *sarod* and *sārangī* by Allauddin Khan.

PART TWO:

CENTERS, FORMS AND INNOVATORS

4

The 18th Century: Late Mughal Delhi and Other Centers

The stable courts of the three "Great Mughals," Akbar, Jahangir and Shah Jahan, from the mid-16th to the mid-17th centuries were centers known all over the world for their wealth, art and culture. The reign of Akbar (1556-1605) is famous for its ecumenical policies under which Muslim, Hindu and even Christian elements existed side by side in aspects of imperial policy. In music, large numbers of Indian musicians were called to Delhi to join the Persians and Turks who had until then dominated court music. Figure 65 shows a court scene with musicians from the Akbar period. The fervent creative activity of the musicians produced the *darbārī* (court) music of Tansen and his descendants, the main pre-18th-century source of Hindustani performance practice. This music had some of its roots in the long tradition of court and temple performance described in the Sanskrit music treatises. In part it grew out of the music developed in the earlier Indo-Persian courts. Some time in the Mughal period it came to be known as *dhrupad*, and set the classical standard for North Indian art music. The peak of Mughal *darbārī* music extended through the reigns of Jahangir (1605-1627) and Shah Jahan (1628-1658), when the music became sophisticated and highly stylized under the cultivation of the court elite. An attention by connoisseurs of the time to elaborate detail and design is evident in the exquisite miniature paintings that were produced under Jahangir and Shah Jahan's patronage. A comparable refinement and precision can be imagined to have been present in the music. The elusive substance of musical performance cannot be traced, but oral performance traditions give a substantial idea of the form and aesthetics of early *dhrupad* music, and pictorial and textual-based examinations of this important hundred-year period in Indian musical history have now begun to come out.[70]

The court in Delhi was not the only center for music in the 17th century. Of the provincial centers, the stable and most prosperous courts were naturally those in which music could be supported to a significant extent. Musical history recognizes a number of centers of patronage. In Gwalior, Raja Man Singh was famous for his contribution of many of Akbar's topmost musicians including Tansen himself. In Jaunpur, Sultan Husain Sharqi is credited with the introduction of the *ṭappā* and sometimes the *khyāl* vocal form. Baz Bahadur of Gujarat is named in all the Persian texts on music for his contributions at this time, and in the Deccani court of Bijapur, Ibrahim 'Adil Shah promoted poetry, music and music-inspired painting. Of these centers, only Gwalior was to re-emerge in the modern period. Faqirullah, in the "*Rāg darpan*," speaks of four musicians who formed the four pillar styles *(bānī)* of *dhrupad* music. They are Tansen of Gwalior; Braj Cand of Dangar, near Delhi; Raja Sammokhan Singh of Khandahar, Rajasthan; and Sricand, a Rajput of Nauhar, Rajasthan (Khan, M. K. I. 1925:23-4). In Rajasthan, the rulers of Jaipur (then Amber) and Udaipur (then Mewar) supported leading family lines of *bīn* players, a tradition that continued through the 18th and 19th centuries.

Aurangzeb and the Beginning of the 18th Century

The reign of Aurangzeb (1659 to 1707) is infamous in popular music history, known as a time when musical activity was ruthlessly suppressed by this fundamentalist ruler. During the beginning of his rule Aurangzeb was said to have been a good judge of music, and the records show that he supported it for a number of years. A gradually growing religious fervor, however, led him to disband the court musicians in the eleventh year of his reign, according to contemporary accounts, or in 1688,[71] and he finally banned the practice of music altogether among the citizens of Delhi. He even appointed an officer to head a special department to enforce his orders. Contemporary Italian traveller Niccolao Manucci writes:

> Aurangzeb took steps against the excessive number of musicians. In Hindustan both Moguls and Hindus are fond of listening to songs and instrumental music. He therefore ordered the ... official to stop music. If in any house or elsewhere he heard the sound of singing and instruments, he should forthwith hasten there and arrest as many as he could, breaking the instruments (Manucci 1907-II:5).

Evidently there had been a great deal of music going on in the city, as Manucci says "thus was caused a great destruction of musical instruments" (*ibid.*). The reaction of the musicians to Aurangzeb's harsh orders resulted in an often told story:

> About one thousand of them assembled on a Friday when Aurangzeb was going to the mosque. They came out with over twenty highly-ornamented biers, as is the custom of the country, crying aloud

> with great grief and many signs of feeling, as if they were escorting to the grave some distinguished defunct. From afar Aurangzeb saw this multitude and heard their great weeping and lamentation, and, wondering, sent to know the cause of so much sorrow. The musicians redoubled their outcry and their tears, fancying the king would take compassion upon them. Lamenting, they replied with sobs that the king's orders had killed Music, therefore they were bearing her to the grave. Report was made to the king, who quite calmly remarked that they should pray for the soul of Music, and see that she was thoroughly well buried.[72]

Aurangzeb's puritanical attitude applied also to the watching of dance. He "would as soon tolerate idolatry as a Nautch" (Lane-Poole 1964:263), and he ordered female dancers and "public women" to "either marry or clear out of the realm" (Manucci 1907-II:6).

Although Aurangzeb's policies meant a stoppage of support to music and a suppression of it to some degree, it did not mean a total shutdown of Delhi's musical scene. Manucci says that in spite of the strict regulations, "the nobles did not cease to listen to songs in secret" (*ibid.*). Historians Ikram and Spear say:

> During Aurangzeb's reign music ceased to enjoy royal patronage, but of course the popularity of the art with the Mughal nobility was, by now, too firmly established to allow it to suffer. Perhaps the art even gained by being cultivated by its true votaries and those keenly and sincerely interested in it ... (Ikram & Spear 1955:52).

Manucci reports that Aurangzeb continued to allow music in his *zenāna*:

> In spite of Aurangzeb's having forbidden all music, he nevertheless continued always to entertain in his palaces, for the diversion of the queens and his daughters, several dancing and singing women; and even conferred special names on their mistresses or superintendents (Manucci 1907-II:312-3).

He lists thirty-three superintendents of the dancers and singers, and says "The queens and the other ladies pass their time in their rooms, each with her own set of musicians" (*ibid.*:313). Brhaspati thought that Aurangzeb's repression had no real effect on the musical atmosphere of the court at all (Brhaspati 1974:78; 1976:335-6). There was evidently a high level of intellectual music-related activity that continued during this time, as both the *"Rāg darpan"* and the *"Tuḥfāt al-Hind,"* two of the major Persian works on music, were written during Aurangzeb's reign.

A large number of musicians stayed in Delhi under Aurangzeb, but there is mention of musicians leaving the Delhi court at this time for centers such as Alwar in Rajasthan (Sharma, B. R. 1980:106), and there is little question that Aurangzeb's attitude had some effect on music in late 17th-century Delhi. The emperor had been a leading force whose taste (and funds) had directed trends in performance style. When the emperor's monetary patronage ended, musicians must have turned to the nobility residing outside the court. There their music would have been exposed to more diverse audiences. Ikram and Spear recognize a growth in patronage outside the court and suggest that it was a reaction to Aurangzeb's puritanism, with the result that "... even the nobles and princes began to have as much interest in music as they formerly took in war and other vigorous outdoor exercises" (Ikram & Spear 1955:52). Shifts in patronage almost always promote stylistic and formal changes in musical performance. The musical history of the late Mughal period following Aurangzeb is a story of large-scale fundamental changes.

After Aurangzeb's death in 1707, the Mughal empire began a steady decline. The late Mughal period, which extended for the great length of one hundred and fifty years, was a scene of political degeneration. Historian K. K. Datta calls it a "dark and tragic period in the history of India" and states dramatically that

> virtual collapse of governmental authority and consequent disappearance of administrative order and peace throughout the dark and dismal years of the 18th century ... caused a grievous social anarchy gnawing at the very vitals of Indian civilization and culture (Datta 1972:7).

Records of treasonous plots inside the court, and the gradual falling away of territories outside Delhi, speak of the weakness of the emperors following Aurangzeb and the decadence surrounding the throne at Delhi. But a closer look at the period reveals other aspects of the history of the time. Major developments in music and language were among the gifts of the 18th century to modern India. Historian Percival Spear says:

> The "Time of Troubles" is dubbed a degenerate age. But it is a mistake to suppose that the public stage was filled by weak-kneed or effeminate triflers. These are the by-products of prosperity and power. With few exceptions, the actors were vigorous and hardy, brave and warlike ... . Thus it comes about that individual degeneracy though the prelude, is not the accompaniment of social collapse, and the ages of social and political decay are commonly periods of exceptional energy and activity (Spear 1951:10).

A look at developments in the 18th century will reveal that a powerful surge of creative activity rose out of the political decay and gave new direction to musical history.

The Successors of Aurangzeb: the Court Favorites

Aurangzeb had brutally repressed his sons out of the fear that they would usurp the throne, and he had not appointed a successor before he died in 1707. His will stated that the empire should be divided among his three sons. The eldest, Muazzam, titled Shah Alam I or Bahadur Shah I, took the throne after a power struggle in which the two competing brothers were killed. Reports are that he was courageous and intelligent, but that his father's repression had harmed his abilities.

> All accounts agree in representing Bahadur Shah as a man of mild and equable temper, learned, dignified and generous to a fault .... Although not a great sovereign, Bahadur Shah may be called, at least in comparison with his successors, a fairly successful one (Irvine 1971-I:137).

Support to music was apparently renewed during his brief rule of five years, as *dhrupad* compositions containing his name can be found (Brhaspati 1974:78), and it was in his court that Na'mat Khan, the most famous of the 18th-century musicians, began his training. The *"Risāla-i ẕikr-i mughannián-i Hindustān"* and the *"Mir'āt-i āftāb numā"* speak of Na'mat Khan's learning from musicians of Bahadur Shah I's court, among whom were Tatari Qavvāl, Lala Bangali Naṭvā and Devdat Kabīshar.[73]

In 1712 when Muazzam Shah died, his son Jahandar Shah took the throne after a struggle in which his three brothers were killed. Described by historians as "a worthless profligate," "utterly incapable and incurably vicious,"[74] Jahandar Shah was the first of a line of increasingly ineffectual late Mughal rulers. Music, however, thrived under his brief reign, and it is at this time that the *"Mir'āt-i āftāb numā"* reports Na'mat Khan attained his first wave of fame (Rehman 1803-4:folio 466).

Fascinating references show a new and surprising side to musicians' activities under Jahandar Shah's patronage. The name of Lal Kunwar appears prominently in the chronicles of Jahandar Shah's career. She was a singer, dancer and a favorite concubine of Jahandar Shah since before he took the throne. It is apparent that Lal Kunwar held more than a little power in influencing his decisions and activities. Contemporary sources say that she was the daughter of one Khasusiat Khan, a descendant of Tansen,[75] and tell us that the famous Na'mat Khan was one of her brothers. Historians give us a startling picture of their activities during Jahandar Shah's short rule:

> During these months the fiddlers and drummers, who were Lal Kunwar's brothers and relations swaggered through the streets, commiting every sort of outrage. Lal Kunwar was dignified with the title of *Mumtiaz Mahal*, Chosen of the Palace, and immense treasures, the spoils from Azim-ush-shan's and Jahan Shah's camps, were made over to her. Her whole family was ennobled, father, brothers, and brothers-in-law. Her middle brother was the most oppressive of all to the people. All the brothers were granted the *naubat*, or the right to play music at stated intervals, and the use of kettle-drums when on the march. Their titles were Niamat Khan, Namdar Khan and Khanazad Khan. Some of the finest confiscated mansions in the city were given to them, and as Kanwar Khan says, "the owl dwelt in the eagle's nest, and the crow took the place of the nightingale" ... (Irvine 1971-I:193).

One incident indicates how thoroughly Na'mat Khan was involved in political affairs. The Emperor at one point had apparently decided to grant the entire governorship of Multan to Na'mat Khan, and ordered his chief minister to draw up the appropriate papers. The disapproving *vazīr*, however, delayed the proceedings, and Na'mat Khan approached him to find out the reason for the delay. The *vazīr* told Na'mat Khan that it was customary for him to receive payment for work of this sort, and when asked for the amount, replied "one thousand tamburs:"

> The stupid fellow, not seeing the ironical nature of the reply, worked his hardest and in a week sent as many as two hundred tamburs to Zulfiqar Khan. The Wazir insisted on the full number. Niamat Khan complained to His Majesty of the excessive bribe demanded from him. Jahandar Shah, when next he saw the Wazir, asked him the reason of collecting so many tamburs. The answer was that when musicians were sent to govern provinces, nobles must discard their weapons and learn to play on the tambur. This remonstrance induced Jahandar Shah to cancel the appointment (Irvine 1971-I:193-4).

Another account of the incident mentions the involved musician as Khushhal Khan (Elliot 1877-VII:432-3), which may be Na'mat Khan's original name (cf. section below on Na'mat Khan). This reputation hardly seems in accord with his later achievements and with the expectations set by his alleged descent from the great Tansen. Na'mat Khan's expertise as a *bīn* player and his originality as a composer, however, eventually outshone all his other exploits, and later history knows him as a major contributer to 18th-century music. Details of his early career are now little known. Corruption and political power in the courts involving musicians will figure again in the history of the later *navābs* of Avadh, especially Wajid Ali Shah, where the musician most involved was again one of the most prominent of his time, the *sitār* player Ghulam Raza Khan.

Jahandar Shah lost the throne to his nephew Farrukh-Siyar in 1713. Described as another weak and ineffectual ruler, he was dominated by two powerful nobleman brothers, known as the Saiyyids, who brought him to power.

> For seven years the State was in a condition of unstable equilibrium … . Feeble, false, cowardly, contemptible, it is impossible either to admire him or regret him (Irvine 1971-I:396).

In 1719 Farrukh-Siyar was blinded, imprisoned, and finally murdered by the order of the Saiyyids. In the one year following his death four puppet emperors were put on the throne by the Saiyyid brothers and kept under their control. Each died within a short time. No musical references are found relating to this period. It can be imagined that the cultural activities of the court might have slowed between 1713 and 1719 in the midst of such chaos. On this backdrop Prince Roshan Akhtar, given the title Muhammad Shah, was placed on the throne in 1719, where, despite the unpromising circumstances, he was to complete a reign of twenty-nine years.

Politics, the Social Scene and Music under Muhammad Shah

> Muhammad Shah had received from his ancestors dominions of large extent, which they had, by dint of prowess and successful exertion wrested from other illustrious kings and annexed to the territories already under the rule. But instead of attending to the affairs of his kingdom, and turning his ernest attention as becoming an Emperor towards the management of the country, Muhammad Shah, from the commencement of his reign displayed the greatest carelessness in his government, spending all his time in sport and play … .[76]

Powers inside the court controlled Muhammad Shah and the throne: "The capital was the scene of incessant intrigues and treasons unworthy of record or remembrance" (Smith, V. A. 1958:434). As the governors of important provinces declared independence from the empire and dropped away from Mughal control one by one, powerful Maratha forces from the Southwest threatened Delhi. They were turned away only by two remaining allies, Asaf Jah, Muhammad Shah's *vazīr*, and Sa'dat Khan, who later themselves left to rule the territories of Hyderabad and Avadh respectively.

Then, in 1739, in the midst of the internal and external troubles, the infamous raider Nadir Shah arrived at Delhi from Persia, having conquered Mughal territories to the North. His sacking of Delhi stands out as one of the most disastrous events in Delhi history. In a six-hour massacre ordered by him, the number of lives lost has been estimated at twenty thousand. At least one hundred fifty million rupees were lost (Irvine 1971-II:368-71). Along with money and jewelry from the treasury went the great Peacock Throne, the prized possession and the symbol of the line of Mughal rulers. Nadir Shah is also said to have carried away a "celebrated illustrated Persian manuscript on Hindu music written under the command of the Emperor Muhammad Shah" (Majumdar, Raychaudhury & Datta 1967:526).

Dargah Quli Khan, a nobleman and ancestor of later rulers of Hyderabad, came to Delhi in 1738[77] and wrote the account known as the "*Muraqqa'-i Dehlī*" shortly after Nadir Shah left. He notes Muhammad Shah's mood at the time:

> these days on account of Nadir Shah's attacks the Badshah remains downcast, and has lost his interest in music. He feels completely uninclined to ease his heart by listening to song or instruments, and the Badshah's company of musicians has been disbanded by written order (Khan, D. Q. B. 1933:90).

If the Emperor made any attempts to restore the government after Nadir Shah left, they were ineffectual:

> The condition of the country after the departure of Nadir Shah was worse than before. The "amirs" took what they liked. The Emperor spent what remained to him in sports and pastime.[78]

Aside from the one comment in the "*Muraqqa'-i Dehlī*," few hints of the tragedy appear in the rest of this exuberant work, which describes famous places of pilgrimage, bazaars, poets and performers in Delhi. Evidently a great number of citizens of Delhi were busy in a thriving social and cultural scene. Translator Hasan Nizami comments:

> It is surprising that even after such a big historical event as the massacre of three lakh Delhi people, the revelries and entertainments

> continued as ever, but this is entirely in the character of Delhi. (Khan, D. Q. B. 1933:5-6 footnote).

Figure 66 is a contemporary painting of Muhammad Shah with some of his female musicians.

The description of more than fifty musicians, dancers, and performers of various sorts in the "*Muraqqa'-i Dehlī*" confirms popular history that speaks of Muhammad Shah's Delhi as a teeming center for music. It is a colorful scene populated by large eager audiences and diverse and innovative performers. There are *qavvālī* singers, *khyāl* singers, and singers of a form called *kabit*, players of *bīn*, *tambūr*, *rabāb*, *sārangī*, *pakhāvaj* and *ḍholak*, someone who plays on a grass blade, and one who plays *pakhāvaj* and *ḍholak bols* on his stomach. There are male and female dancers, eunuchs, and mimics. A picture emerges of musical gatherings held throughout the city, attended by large numbers of Delhi citizens. Musicians are noted here in terms of popularity and the large audiences that crowd their performances. In regards to mainstream music, a look at the "*Muraqqa'-i Dehlī*" gives a good idea of the environment of the time.

Qavvālī, *dhrupad* and *khyāl*

Notable in the "*Muraqqa'-i Dehlī*" is the strong presence of *qavvālī*, and the number and popularity of its singers. The foremost is Taj Khan, father of Ghulam and Jani Rasul, two figures later famous in the history of *khyāl*. *Qavvālī* is mentioned as performed both at special sittings such as that at the home of Taj Khan on the seventh of every month. and at religious functions such as at the tomb of the Sufi saint Nizamuddin Auliya. This event continues to be held today. *Qavvālī* appears to have been the single most widespread form of the time, and one held in high musical regard.

It is difficult to speculate on the musical characteristics of 18th-century *qavvālī*. The 14th-century Amir Khusrau in speaking of *qaul*, a medieval Persian sung form, refers in his writings to the use of various ornaments such as *tahrīr* and *zamzama* and singing vigorously in a high speed in the upper ranges. One of his phrases is "the voice rode high and came down in broken particles ..." (Sarmadee 1975b:40, 49, 50). We get the idea of a fast-moving, energetic and ornamented music, not unlike the *qavvālī* known today. *Qavvālī*'s degree of influence on the new *khyāl* type that emerged from Delhi has been a matter of disagreement. From this text there can remain little doubt *qavvālī* was a potent force in

Delhi, and it is known that a number of *qavvālī* singers later became well-known *khyāl* singers.

Dhrupad is mentioned only once by name in the "*Muraqqa'-i Dehlī*," in connection with singers Rahim and Tan Sen. They belonged to the lineage of Tansen. Their control and the volume of their voices, the powerful effects of their music and the respect with which they were held by other musicians are noted by the author. It would seem, however, that the two could not support themselves as *dhrupad* singers, since they were both employed as singers of *kabit*, some sort of song style involving poetry (Khan, D. Q. B. 1982:177; 1833:69-7). From its meager treatment in the "*Muraqqa'-i Dehlī*," it appears that *dhrupad* music existed in a relatively minor role.

The early history of *khyāl* is problematic. Disagreements parallel those on the origins of the *sitār*. While some writers believe that *khyāl* was a modification of *dhrupad*, which had its roots in the music described in the Sanskrit texts, others point to *qavvālī*, which is associated with Amir Khusrau and the Sufism of Nizamuddin Auliya, and say that *khyāl* originated there.[79] The *qavvāl bacche* ("children of *qavvāls*") *khyāl* singers in the 19th and early 20th centuries indeed traced their tradition to Amir Khusrau (cf. Bhatkhande 1970-5-IV:48). The "*Muraqqa'-i Dehlī*" gives us evidence that *khyāl* was in existence before Na'mat Khan introduced a new *khyāl* type. There are several references to *khyāl* singers without mention of Na'mat Khan. Some of these had close contact with *qavvālī* singers. Rahim Khan Jahani is associated with the *qavvāl* Burhani Amir Khan. Allabande is the son of a *qavvāl* (Khan, D. Q. B. 1933:72, 81). In contrast to these singers, Kamal Bai stands alone. She is described as singing the *khyāls* of Na'mat Khan which are associated with the royal court, and singing in the style, or with the feeling *(andāz)* of a *kalāvant* (Khan, D. Q. B. 1933:91; 1982:201). The title *kalāvant* carries the association of a musical lineage of high standing. Panna Bai[80] was also a disciple of Na'mat Khan who sang *ghazals* with a feeling for his style. Both singers are noted for their voice quality and range, and are said to be highly regarded by other musicians.[81] The hints are that Na'mat Khan's *khyāl* was of a more rigorous and classical style than the earlier variety of *khyāl*. The idea, well established in popular history, that Na'mat Khan instituted a slow speed *khyāl*, later called *baḍā khyāl*, infused with *dhrupad* elements, gains support here.

It is vital, then, to distinguish between two types of *khyāl* when speaking of the 18th century. The earlier was possibly a song form not strictly based on *rāgas*. It might have had long-standing connections to *qavvālī*. The fast speed *khyāl* known today as *choṭā khyāl* may have its roots in this early form. The other was a *khyāl* form classicized through an addition of *dhrupad* elements by Na'mat Khan. The fact that the name was retained is evidence that in the original mixture of the earlier *khyāl* and the *dhrupad* genres, the balance tilted toward the former. One recent writer proposes that the new form allowed courtesans to sing the *rāgas* that were previously restricted to *dhrupad* singers (Meer 1980:57-8). This might have applied to Kamal Bai when she sang the *khyāls* of Na'mat Khan. Who was this great figure, Na'mat Khan, then, who made such an important contribution to the music of the time?

Na'mat Khan

> In Hindustan, the presence of Na'mat Khan is itself a blessing *[na'mat]*. In the art of music and in creating new compositions, he is incomparable. Famous courtesans boast of their association with him, and he is expert at presenting many delicate musical *khyāls*. He is a competent man. He has written in various languages on several different topics. But at this time, without a doubt, he is the leader among all the musicians of Delhi, and he is so proud that, except for the Badshah, he will not concede to anyone's requests ... .
>
> He himself organizes a party on the twelfth of each month which all the noblemen *[amīr]* and the men of rank *[raīs]* and all the respectable citizens of the city attend. They begin arriving in the morning of that day, and by evening the *mahfil* is so completely filled that there remains no room even to put a seed. On the twelfth the party goes on all night, and it is during this time that Na'mat Khan demonstrates the merits of his mastery. His singing in various *rāgas* and *rāginīs* has no less effect than magic, and the perfection *[kamāl]* that Na'mat Khan has obtained in his *bīn* playing ... ! It can be claimed that never in the world was there born such a magician of a *bīn* player, nor is there any hope of one's ever being born. When he begins to play the *bīn*, when the notes of the *bīn* throw a spell on the world, the party enters a strange state: people begin to flutter like fish out of water ... . As long as the *bīn* keeps sounding, or he is involved in letting the *tāns* fly, people remain out of their normal state, and no one has any sense of others or oneself. But when the music grows lighter, then from every direction come great exclamations of "Wah! Wah! Well done!" and various acclamations and praise, and there is such a clamor that the whole place rises in echo. Na'mat Khan is acquainted with all aspects of music. Na'mat Khan is considered unequalled and is the pride of the people of Delhi (Khan, D. Q. B. 1933:66-7).

Some contemporary accounts seem to indicate that Na'mat Khan's original name was Khushhal Khan, and that he was a brother of Lal Kunwar, the favorite courtesan of Emperor Jahandar Shah.[82] But Lal Kunwar's father was named Khasusiat Khan, while we know from contemporary texts that Na'mat Khan's father was Nirmol Khan.[83] Na'mat Khan might have been a cousin or been otherwise related to Lal Kunwar. Contemporary sources say that Lal Kunwar's father was a descendant of Tansen. In popular history, Na'mat Khan is thought to be descended from Tansen through his daughter's line. But Brhaspati, on the basis of unspecified sources, claims that Na'mat Khan was not a descendant of Tansen, and that this was a story spread in the 19th century (Brhaspati 1976:346). The "*Muraqqa'-i Dehlī*" makes no reference to Na'mat Khan's family background, while it says specifically of two other singers that they are descendants of Tansen.[84] The "*Risāla-i ẕikr-i mughanniān-i Hindustān*" and the "*Mir'āt-i āftāb numā*" only mention that his father's name was Nirmol Khan. Accounts of his first music teachers, who were obviously not of Tansen lineage, indeed counterindicate a Tansen-associated background. Anyway, Na'mat Khan was not popularly associated with a Tansen lineage during his own time. It might be suggested in general in this regard that the stress placed on the relationship of musicians to Tansen, beginning in the 19th century and continuing to the present, should be considered more symbolic than actual. An association with Tansen is often simply a statement of a performer's high standing in the classical tradition.

Na'mat Khan is popularly thought of as a *dhrupad* performer. The "*Risāla-i ẕikr-i mughanniān-i Hindustān*" calls him a composer of *dhrupads*, although the "*Muraqqa'-i Dehlī*" does not mention *dhrupad* by name in its long description of him. In contemporary texts his earliest musical training is credited to three musicians in the court of Jahandar Shah: Tatari Qavval, Lala Bangali Natva and Devdat Kabishar. By their titles, the three are a *qavvālī* singer, an actor and a poet, all fascinating sources behind this musician's distinguished career. The source of his training in regards to *bīn* and *dhrupad* is left unmentioned, although it might be assumed that he learned from his father, Nirmol Khan. As well as being noted as a great *bīn* player and a composer of *dhrupad*, Na'mat Khan is noted as a composer of *khyāl*, and also of *tarānā* (Khan, Inayet 1961:30). In the "*Muraqqa'-i Dehlī*," we have seen that he is praised for creating a variety of colorful new *khyāls*, and for composing lyrics in several languages. The musical environment of the time, his background and his enormous popularity as described in the "*Muraqqa'-i Dehlī*" indicate that Na'mat Khan's music would have been an eclectic and innovative mixture of the musical elements of the day.

An early association with courtesan singers and their associates is thought to have kept pre-19th-century *khyāl* irreconcilably apart from the *dhrupad* tradition. Thus, popular tradition says that Na'mat Khan composed *khyāls* but did not perform them himself in deference to his standing in the prestigious Tansen lineage. The "*Muraqqa'-i Dehlī*" seems to support the popular belief that Na'mat Khan did not perform his *khyāls* himself. It says "how many colorful khyāls he has created! - there are examples of his compositions in several languages." (Khan, D. Q. B. 1982:173) In contrast, descriptions of Rahim Khan Jahani (*ibid.*:179-80), and the four brothers Rahim Khan, Daulat Khan, Gyan Khan and Haddu (*ibid.*:188-9) as well as others, explicitly mention these musicians as good singers of *khyāl*.

An anecdote from later oral tradition illustrates popular belief about Na'mat Khan's *bīn* playing, the origin of his new *khyāl* and the pen-name Sadarang. Vocalists among Muhammad Shah's musicians once took to taunting the instrumentalists, calling them *nirjīv* ("lifeless") instead of *sajīv* ("full of life") like them. It then occurred to Muhammad Shah to order Na'mat Khan and his nephew to accompany the vocalists. When they began to be called *sāzinda* (Urdu, "instrumentalist," taken as a derogatory reference to dance accompanists) Na'mat Khan objected. He tried to influence the Emperor to change his orders through court intermediaries, but the Emperor refused, and Na'mat Khan left Delhi along with his nephew, Firoz Khan. Away from the city they began to compose *khyāls* in a slow tempo, which they called *muṇḍhī dhrupad*, "hidden *dhrupad*." To cover their identities, the two took the pen-names Sadarang and Adarang. When their compositions in praise of the Emperor reached Delhi, the Emperor was so pleased that he invited them back (Josi 1935:141-3). In another version of the story Na'mat Khan taught his new *khyāl* to two young beggars outside of Delhi, who eventually performed before the Emperor (Sastri 1916:Introduction, 18-9).

A curious point in the "*Muraqqa'-i Dehlī*" relating to this is the separate mention of Sadarang, a signature name found in numerous *khyāl* compositions still in use today, and long assumed to belong to Na'mat Khan. Here, however, it is found in only one instance, in association with a eunuch, Raji Amard, who is adept at singing the "*khyāls* of Sadarang, which are popular in today's Delhi" (Khan, D. Q. B. 1982:190). Any connection to Na'mat Khan remains unstated. Either the identity of Sadarang was hidden at the time, or the longstanding identification of Na'mat Khan with that name needs re-evaluation.

Instrumental Music

The *bīn* (Figure 67) in the hands of Na'mat Khan was the foremost instrument in Muhammad Shah's Delhi, in prestige and also in popularity. Na'mat Khan's brother, probably named Khusrau Khan, his nephew, Firoz Khan, and perhaps his disciple, Qasim Ali, mentioned in "*Muraqqa'-i Dehlī*," can be assumed to have played the *bīn* as well. A later oral tradition mentions another *bīnkār* disciple of Na'mat Khan's named Hasan Khan who was assigned the job of teaching in the court *zenāna*, the women's quarters (Josi 1935:143). 18th-century paintings show *bīnkārs* both alone and in groups that include singers and other instrumentalists. Na'mat Khan evidently performed only as a soloist. The musical roles of the other *bīnkārs* in Delhi is not indicated in contemporary literature. The weak position of *dhrupad* music in 18th-century Delhi, however, the prominence of *khyāl* and *qavvālī*, and the musically experimental environment of the time make it likely that the music of the *bīn* was a mixture of elements.

Na'mat Khan's brother probably had a role in the introduction of the *sitār* in Delhi. A translation of his description in the "*Muraqqa'-i Dehlī*" was given above in Chapter 1. He is also noted as a good singer. Na'mat Khan's nephew, Firoz Khan, is noted for playing the *sitār*, and for being able to play anything on it that any other instrument could play. He will be an important figure in the post-Muhammad Shah period in instrumental music both in and outside of Delhi. He is more famous in the popular history of *khyāl*, however, where he is known as the composer who signed his compositions with the name Adarang. The "*Mir'āt-i āftāb numā*" indeed cites him for his excellence as a composer of *dhrupad*, *tarānā* and *khyāl*.[85] His background in *tarānā* is especially intriguing in relation to his later contributions to instrumental music.

Among other instrumentalists mentioned in the "*Muraqqa'-i Dehlī*" are Baqar, a *tambūr* player, Hasan Khan, a *rabāb* player, and Ghulam Muhammad, a *sārangī* player. It is clear that Baqar the *tambūrcī* was very popular:

> When Baqar's fingers move on the strings of the tambūr and sweet notes are born from it, all the listeners' hearts go out of control, and the melody of the *tambūr*, like the cool morning breeze, creates a singing and excitement in the soul. He himself becomes intoxicated while playing and also intoxicates the people. The Badshah respects Baqar very much, to say nothing of the common people and the rich who are Baqar's passionate admirers (Khan, D. Q. B. 1933:68-9).

Did Baqar play *rāgas* on his *tambūr*? The drawing of the *tambūr* in the "*Tuḥfāt al-Hind*" manuscript with *śruti* positions marked on its neck, and the *nibaddh tambūr* pictured in the Persian "*Pārijātak*" manuscript with the note positions for the *rāga rāmkalī* indicate that he would have. Further than this, though, we cannot know what sort of music was played on the *tambūr*. One might imagine that lively melodies were suited to the instrument, which had limited sustain, and that it used rhythmic patterns suited to a free-hand strumming action.

Physical similarity makes it logical to suppose that the music of the *tambūr* played a significant role in influencing the earliest stage of *sitār* music. Similarly in the case of *khyāl*, the shared name makes it likely that the early *khyāl* influenced Na'mat Khan's later creation. In fact, the relationship of *tambūr* to *sitār* seems to reflect and parallel the relationship of the early *khyāl* to the *khyāl* of Na'mat Khan. Both early *khyāl* and the *tambūr* were Indian transformations of Persian forms. The new *khyāl* and the *sitār* were in turn modifications of these, effected through the addition of *dhrupad*, and *bīn*, elements. Musically, Na'mat Khan's *khyāl* gave a new, more classically acceptable character to the earlier form, and the same must have been true for the *sitār*. The relationship of *sitār* to *khyāl* is more than coincidental. The same family, the same musical environment and the same Delhi public were directing the course of musical innovation in both cases.

Dargah Quli Khan tells us little of Hasan Khan *rabābī*'s music but gives us a sympathetic picture of the man:

> On this difficult instrument, Hasan Khan has full mastery. And he has passed most of his life in playing the *rabāb*. It is now the last part of his life, and his entire body continually shakes like the strings of the *rabāb*. He is constantly troubled by impoverishment. Nevertheless he still has the spark of life in him, and the blessings of God are on him. In playing *rabāb* he is proof of that blessing, and no one can compete with him. He is one of the famous figures of Delhi (Khan, D. Q. B. 1933:69).

We assume that the *rabāb* spoken of here is the Indian *rabāb*. There are no indications that the Afghani type *rabāb* was in Delhi at this time.

Delhi's leading *sārangī* player was Ghulam Muhammad. It is notable that Dargah Quli Khan's work appears unstained by the prejudice against the *sārangī* that was to become prominent in the 19th century:

> In playing the *sārangī*, Ghulam Muhammad's reputation is known far and wide. The exquisite way Ghulam Muhammad plays the sad and serious *rāgas* on the *sārangī* can be matched by no one in Hindustan. It pierces just like an arrow. His fingernails move gently and ef-

> fortlessly on the *sārangī* and he casts magic on every musical sitting he attends. All of Delhi agrees that in this art there is no one to equal him. He is respected by everyone. He is modest and unpretentious and enjoys making acquaintances (Khan, D. Q. B. 1933:69).

The large assembly of musicians gathered under Muhammad Shah was not matched again in later Delhi, but Delhi would always remain a center of some prestige. As musicians moved to other cities and courts, the inspired work of Na'mat Khan and his colleagues formed the basis for further innovations.

The Later 18th Century

Delhi: Firoz Khan and Masit Khan

After the death of Muhammad Shah, the court, immersed in political and economic troubles, was unable to continue with its high level of patronage. Musicians carrying new ideas and instruments began to move to areas that they saw emerging as more prosperous centers. The provinces of Rajputana, Rohilkhand and Avadh would soon stand out as important centers in the next phase of music history. For *sitār* music, however, Delhi remained the focus of formative activity until at least the end of the 18th century. Here the *gat-toḍā* form emerged as the first codified instrumental music independent of vocal forms, and techniques from the *bīn* and *dhrupad* music gradually and systematically began to be applied to the *sitār*.

Historians recount the dismal plight of the Mughal empire at the end of Muhammad Shah's reign. The court was corrupt with murderous intrigues, and little authority remained to the throne. The situation in the court was so lawless that when Muhammad Shah died in 1748 while his son was away, his courtiers kept his death a secret, fearing the throne would be usurped. They wrapped the body in a cloth from the kitchen and kept it in "the wooden box of a European clock" until the son returned (Elliot 1877-VIII:111). The son, Ahmad Shah, perhaps like his father "gave himself up entirely to pastime and sports, and bestowed no thought on the weighty affairs of the kingdom" (*ibid.*:112). Outside of Delhi, most of the former Mughal territories were now out of Mughal control:

> By 1751, the Moghul Empire had crumbled to pieces and was limited to the upper Doab and Gujarat. The Marathas had become a leading

> power in the Deccan, and Ahmad Shah Abdalee ruled over Kashmir, the Punjab and Sind. Mysore was under a Hindu raja while Oudh, Bengal, Bihar, Rohilcund, Hyderabad and the Carnatic were under Muslim Sultans (Srinivas & Rao 1960:38).

After six years Ahmad Shah was deposed and imprisoned, and the youngest son of former emperor Jahandar Shah was enthroned under the title Alamgir II. He allowed himself to be controlled by the *vazīr*, and, trying to emulate his hero Aurangzeb (Alamgir I) "shunned the usual diversions of royalty, such as dance and song" (Sarkar 1966-II:1). In 1757 Delhi was invaded by the Afghan conqueror Ahmad Shah Abdali, and again Delhi residents were subjected to a month-long bout of looting. The same year, Alamgir II was murdered through a plot of the *vazīr*.

This period saw a major exodus of musicians from Delhi. While the lack of royal encouragement and the looting of Delhi would have been enough cause for musicians to seek out other sources of patronage, the wealthy and rising court of Shuja ud-Daula, the third *navāb* of Avadh, provided an attractive destination. References to an influx of musicians in the Avadh court are made by Karam Imam (Khan, M. K. I. 1925:30). Smaller courts in Rohilkhand and Rajputana also began to attract musicians, among whom was Firoz Khan.

Firoz Khan is known to have remained in Delhi during the period of Alamgir II, since *dhrupad* compositions of his in praise of that emperor are to be found (Brhaspati 1976:338). We know that he formulated an instrumental style, which we find as a *gat* type or *bāj* (style) in 19th-century written sources and in some living performance traditions. 20th-century *sarod* player Radhika Mohan Maitra described Firozkhani *gats* as having a number of specific characteristics. They are suited specifically to a medium speed, they have stroke (*bol*) patterns set in varied and interesting rhythms, their melody lines cover the entire gamut of the *rāga* and their melodic movement is characterized by large intervallic jumps.[86] It is not possible to make definitive statements on the music of Firoz Khan himself, but there are enough examples of the Firozkhani style, and enough other evidence of his work in music, to grant his contributions and this style or *gat* type historical validity (despite some instrumentalists' doubts as to its authenticity[87]), and an increased recognition as the earliest *gat* type. The core elements associated with the Firoz Khani style are not unsuited to what the earliest *sitārs* would have been like, with their limited capabilities for pulling techniques and sound production. When Firoz Khan left Delhi for Rohilkhand sometime before 1760, according to records there, his movement was an important event in the history of instrumental music. It was there that his music established itself among a wider group of instrumentalists, the *rabābias*. Evidence will indicate that these people helped initiate later important developments in music in Lucknow.

For fourteen years after the demise of Alamgir II, no emperor ruled in Delhi, which was subject to various court powers. During this time the British East India Company, centered in Bengal, became a leading power in India. The *navābs* of Avadh, submissive to the British, rose in political and cultural importance. The fierce Marathas vied for power, alternately befriending and opposing the Delhi throne. In 1771 Shah Alam, the legitimate heir to the throne, was able to gather enough support to return to Delhi. Although hardly able to restore any authority, he is known to have been a kind and generous person, and was highly regarded as a writer who knew several languages (Francklin 1798:138). The "*Nādirāt-i shāhī*" is a collection of his poems, which contain a number of musical references. It is unfortunate that he was unable to take action against the treachery that was rampant during his reign. A tragic culmination of events came in 1788 when a half deranged Afghan general named Ghulam Qadir usurped the throne. He blinded the Emperor, subjected him and the residents of the royal household to horrible torture and looted what remained of the wealth of the palace. Shah Alam was afterwards restored to the throne by Maratha forces who captured and executed Ghulam Qadir. The Marathas had to support Shah Alam since there were no funds in the treasury, but he was supported so poorly that it is said he had to remove some of the inlay and ornaments of the palace just "to buy bread for himself and his children" (Heber 1829-II:311). The British authorities, eventually discovering his poverty, granted an allowance to him and his son. He lived until 1806.

It must have been in the Delhi of around this time that the most famous of the early *sitār* players, Masit Khan, lived. Uncertainty surrounds the background of this important musician. No contemporary literature has been found that mentions him, and later accounts differ on his family background, although he is always described as a descendant of Tansen. In an account that seems close to his line, he is said to be the son of Firoz Khan.[88] We know from references in Rohilkhand that Firoz Khan left Delhi sometime shortly before 1760. Masit Khan's son, Bahadur Khan, died around 1841, according to a contemporary source (Khan, Saiyyid A. 1964:688). Given the time periods of his father and his son, a likely span for Masit Khan's life is from about 1750 into the first quarter of the 19th century. In Delhi, the disastrous condition of the court makes it likely that Masit Khan lived largely independent of royal patronage.

Masit Khan turned the course of *sitār* music. He is famous for introducing the genre called *gat-toḍā*, a term that came to stand for all solo *sitār* music in the early period. A *gat* is a composition for the *sitār* or *sarod* that is set into *tāla*, a fixed rhythmic cycle. It has both fixed strokes and a fixed melody. The word is probably related to *gati*, "movement" in Sanskrit, and is found in the "*Nāṭyaśāstra*" to describe manners of walking in dance and drama. *Gat* became a term used in both dance and in drumming. We see its use in respect to a *ḍholak* player in the "*Muraqqa'-i Dehlī*:" "When he plays *gat*, even the earth and the sky seem to be dancing."[89] Either drumming or dance was probably the source of its use in *sitār*. When the term first came into use is unknown, but it is likely to have predated Masit Khan, since his *dhrupad* leanings make it seem unlikely that he would choose terminology from dance. *Toḍās* are the melody lines played in *sitār* music which expand on, and are interspersed with, the *gat*. One meaning of *toḍā* is a chain-type ornament worn at the ankle, and this may be the sense in which it was borrowed from dance terminology.[90] *Sitār* player Inayat Khan used to say that *toḍās* punctuated the rhythm of the *gat* just as ankle bells did in dance.[91] Mushtaq Ali Khan describes the meaning of *toḍā* as "a bouquet of flowers, with each in its proper and beautiful place." *Sitār toḍās* are similarly beautiful arrangements of strokes and melody.[92] It is possible that both terms are relics of the *sitār*'s early use in dance accompaniment.

Masit Khan created a *gat* form in which *rāga* melody was placed in a fixed framework of strokes. The possible sources of his inspiration are discussed in Chapter 8. In these compositions, the same stroke framework, with minor variations, was common to all Masitkhani *gats*. The melody was created for each *gat* according to *rāga* rules as dictated in the *dhrupad* tradition. Masit Khan is credited for adopting actual *dhrupad* compositions for melodies to use in his *gats* (Bandyopadhyaya, S. 1937:n.p.). For this work he was highly respected as a classicist by later *sitār* players, and his descendents in *sitār* playing trace themselves through him to the Tansen tradition. Masitkhani *gats*, imitative of *dhrupad*, were to be played at a slow speed, but early Masitkhani styles show that this was considerably faster than the speed practiced today.

All the melodic, ornamental and rhythmic content of the Masitkhani style outside the *gat* was contained in the *toḍās*, the extensions of the *gat*. The earliest examples of written *toḍās* indicate that their ordering followed in general the pattern of *dhrupad* exposition, expanding successively into wider ranges of tonal space and rhythm. The "*Sarmāya-i 'ishrat*" claims that Masit Khan filled his *gats* and *toḍās* with all the techniques of the *bīn* such as "*mīḍ-māḍ, ṭhonk and jhārā*" (Khan, Sadiq A. 1884:203).

The origin of the *sitār*'s drum accompaniment may have had connections to *qavvālī*. The "*Sitār śikṣā*" of Krisnadhan Bandyopadhyaya gives the notation for what we know as *tīntāl*, the sixteen-beat cycle used most often with *sitār* music, but calls it "*qavvālī tāl*."[93] In the "*Muraqqa'-i Dehlī*" there is no mention of the *tablā*, which is the drum later associated with *sitār* music and with dance. The *ḍholak* and the *pakhāvaj* were drums used for dance accompaniment. The *ḍholak* is seen in 19th-century paintings and drawings accompanying the *sitār* (Figures 24, 74, 88, 89), and it seems likely that it was the drum most commonly used for accompaniment.

It should be noted that the emphasis placed by later *sitār* players on Masit Khan's *dhrupad* influence must be balanced with an idea of the physical capabilities of his instrument. Paintings show that the *sitār* was a small, thin-necked instrument. It must have had relatively little capability for sustained tone and elaborate pulling techniques. Moreover, the *sitār* was not a mere imitation of the *bīn*: one of the qualities for which it was admired was its ability to adapt the best aspects of all the genres of the day. Still, Masit Khan and his followers raised the status of the *sitār* through the use of *dhrupad* elements.

Rohilkhand: Firoz Khan and the *rabābias*

In the early and mid-18th century a territory east of Delhi on the Nepal border came under the control of Rohillas, a people from Afghanistan. Some had come in search of employment and some as adventurers, and many finally settled in India (Gazetteer 1911:80). Their first leader, Ali Muhammad, was a contemporary of Muhammad Shah, and was given the title of Navāb by him early in his rule. Ali Muhammad had captured the area which became Rohilkhand by about 1741. It was later divided among his three sons, of whom Faizullah Khan received the portion that was to become Rampur.

It is said that Ali Muhammad once accompanied Muhammad Shah to Delhi, where he was so impressed with the musical and literary environment of the court that he "came to acquire all the attributes of art appreciation fitting to a navāb of the times."[94] As a result of the Navāb's contact with Delhi, some of that city's musicians came to Rohilkhand. Among them was Firoz Khan, who settled under the patronage of one of Muhammad Ali's sons, Sadullah Khan (Brhaspati 1976:356). Sadullah Khan had his court about thirty miles south of what would be Rampur city. When he died in 1761, Firoz Khan evidently moved to the court of Ali Muhammad, where a Rampur source mentions him in that

Fig. 65. A Mughal court scene, by Basawan. Akbar period, 1596-97. Bharat Kala Bhavan. 9069/3 M.

Fig. 66. *Emperor Muhammad Shah with some of his musicians. Mughal, 18th century. Courtesy Kasturbhai Lalbhai Collection, Ahmedabad.*

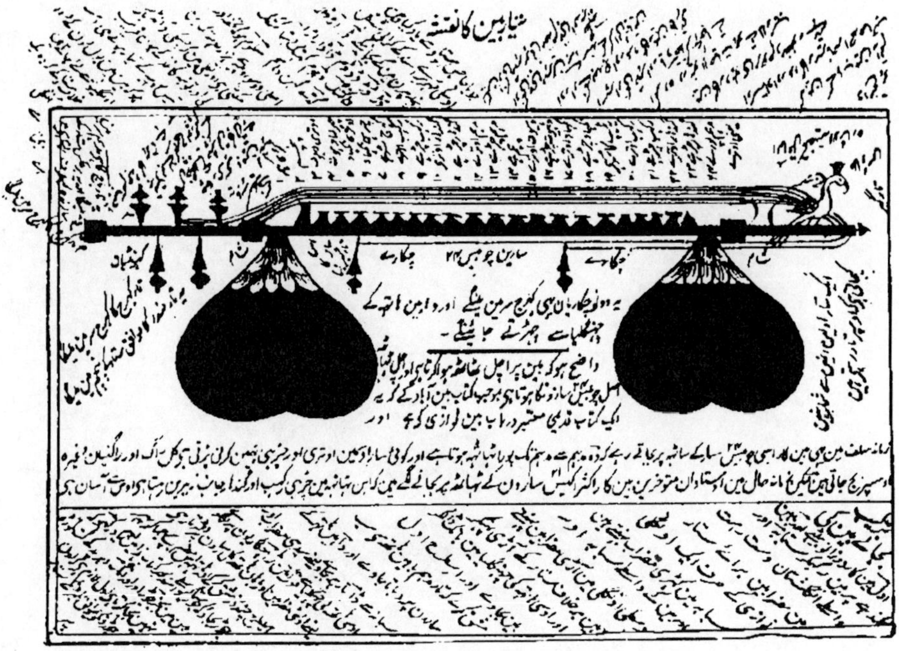

Fig. 67. A bīn. *Khan*, S. A. 1884:181.

Fig. 68. "Tumboora." Solvyns 1808/10-II:Plate IV. By permission of the British Library. BL 460.h.1.

context (Khan, Sa'dat Ali 1921:4). In 1775 Rampur city was founded by Faizullah Khan. It became a cultural center immediately: "A large number of learned men came and settled in Rampur just about this time, and their tombs and descendants still exist in the city" (Gazetteer 1911:58).

Many of the instrumentalists who lived in the Rohilkhand region were players of the Afghani *rabāb*, as later noted by Willard and others. Present day descendants and disciples of these *rabābias* tell us that their ancestors were largely non-professionals who played the melodies of their native Afghanistan.[95] The arrival of Firoz Khan and other Delhi musicians brought these non-professionals their first extended contact with North Indian mainstream court music. Some of the musical remnants of the *rabābias* are represented in the *sarod* playing of their descendents. It is no surprise, then, to find the Firozkhani *bāj* alive in some of these traditions. Radhika Mohan Maitra, representing a line descended from the Rampur *rabāb* and *sarod* player Ghulam Ali, told me that Firozkhani was the main *gat* form used in his Ustad, Amir Khan's, style.[96] A familiarity with the middle speed Firozkhani style continues in this line of *sarod* players to the present day. Firozkhani *gats* have an association with the *sitār* as well, as they are mentioned in several of the 19th-century *sitār* handbooks, where they must be considered the earliest of all recorded *gat* forms.[97]

The music of Firoz Khan and the *rabābias* also moved southeast, where it had a formative influence on the important Purab, eastern, *bāj* of *sitār* playing. There is evidence of contact between Rohilkhand and the court of Avadh beginning in the last quarter of the 18th century. Sadullah Khan is said to have had a close relationship with Shuja ud-Daula (Brhaspati 1976:356), and in 1774 the territory of the Rohillas, including Rampur, was brought under the political control of the *navāb* of Avadh.[98] Ghulam Ali of Rampur, the first *sarod* player, was well-known in Lucknow, and two of the leading early 19th-century *sitār* players, Ghulam Raza, the famous inventor of the Razakhani *bāj*, and Qutub ud-Daula, a contemporary, were Rampur natives. The Purab *bāj* is a style that was formed in the first quarter of the 19th century, and will be discussed in that context. It contrasted with Delhi instrumental style with its faster speed, constant variety and focus on non-*dhrupad* styles and *rāgas*.

Jaipur, Lucknow, Banaras, Gwalior, Bengal

Rajasthan was especially noted from the period of the Mughal emperor Akbar for its famous *bīn* players, beginning with Tansen's son-in-law Sammokhan Singh, the first of the Tansen line of *bīn* players. A tradition of *bīn* associated with Rajasthan extended into the 20th century. Rajasthani miniature paintings show the *bīn* with great frequency.

The city of Jaipur was founded in 1727 by Sawai Jai Singh, who is known for the observatory he built there and for his interest in architecture and culture in general. Jaipur was one of the few politically stable courts throughout the turbulent years of late Mughal rule. Under Jai Singh a treatise on music entitled "*Hastkār ratnāvalī*" was supposed to have been written.[99] A strong interest in music was shown by Maharaja Sawai Pratap Singh, who compiled the "*Saṅgīt sār.*" Another text, "*Svar sāgar,*" was also allegedly written by one of his court musicians, Chand Khan.[100] The "*Saṅgīt sār,*" as we know, describes the *sitār* in considerable detail. It had probably recently arrived in Jaipur from Delhi. The only hint as to the music of *sitār* is that it is used to "play *rāga*" (Singh, S. P. 1910-II:7). This indicates at least a *dhrupad* orientation, and probably a solo music. It is impossible to say whether Masit Khan's *gat-toḍā* had reached Jaipur by the end of the century, but the degree of contact that existed between the cities makes it likely that it had, in some form. We do not, however, find any names of prominent *sitār* players at this early time in Jaipur. Rajasthani and the related Pahadi style miniature paintings of the late 18th century show a number of *tambūrs* as well as *bīns*, but no *sitārs.* The large number of *rāgamālā* paintings that appeared at the time indicates a peaceful environment and a surge of aesthetic interest among the leisured rulers. Jaipur and other cities of Rajasthan would be the center of the activities of Masit Khan's followers in the 19th century, who would form the important Jaipur Senia line of *sitār* players.

The first two *navābs* of Avadh, Sa'dat Khan (1732-1739) and Safdar Jang (1739-1753), were strong and wealthy rulers who played a prominent political role in North India during Muhammad Shah's reign. Under the third *navāb*, Shuja ud-Daula, the court at Faizabad was built into a major center of trade and culture:

> Fyzabad had risen to a height of unparalleled prosperity under Shuja ud-Daula and almost rivalled Delhi in magnificence; it was full of merchants from Persia, China and Europe, and money flowed like water ... (Neville 1928:223).

Coinciding with the disastrous court scene after the death of Muhammad Shah, this period saw the beginning of an influx of Delhi musicians and the rise of Avadh as a musical center. Shuja ud-Daula's successor, Asaf ud-Daula, moved the capital from Faizabad to Lucknow and built it up, according to a contemporary writer, until "the wealth and magnificence of the court began to surpass even that of the emperor in Delhi"

(Hay 1939:14). He was compared to "the most splendid sovereign in Europe" (*ibid.*:17). Cooperation with the British East India Company increased under Asaf ud-Daula. In 1775 the territories of Jaunpur and Ghazipur, including Banaras, a noted music center, were ceded by him to the Company. The Navab, despite a tendency toward extravagance, was well liked by the population (*ibid.*:18), and musicians continued to migrate from Delhi. Lucknow reached its first musical peak. Asaf ud-Daula died in 1798.

Muhammad Karam Imam gives an account of the musicians who were supported by the Navābs Shuja ud-Daula and Asaf ud-Daula. Notable and prominent among the vocalists are Ghulam Rasul and Jani, known as the first of the Lucknow *khyāl* singers. It is to be recalled that the "*Muraqqa'-i Dehlī*" had mentioned these two as prominent *qavvālī* singers in Delhi. Their *qavvālī* background is not recognized in most modern music histories, where they are sometimes even said to have had a *dhrupad* background (Josi 1935:52). Evidently they took to *khyāl* as it gained in acceptability and prestige.

Dhrupad music had a strong revival in Lucknow beginning at this time and extending through most of the 19th century. Its exponents were musicians who traced themselves to Tansen. Foremost among the instrumentalists mentioned by Karam Imam were the brothers Chajju Khan and Jivan Khan, *dhrupad rabāb* players. Genealogical charts compiled by Vimalakant Roy Chaudhury from unknown sources show their father to be Gulab Khan, a sixth generation descendent of Tansen's son Vilas Khan, and a musician in Muhammad Shah's Delhi court (Roy Chaudhury 1975:168). Karam Imam says about Jivan Khan that he was "an accomplished exponent of both Marg and Desi *rāgas*," hinting, perhaps, at the influence that he would later have on the non-*dhrupad* music of Lucknow.[101] Karam Imam states that they both died during Asaf ud-Daula's rule. Their sons and disciples would shape instrumental music in Lucknow. Perhaps not quite so prominent at that time as these *rabābias* were the *bīn* players. Karam Imam states that a number of descendants of *bīnkār* Sammokhan Singh, Tansen's son-in-law, came from Delhi to Lucknow during the time of Shuja ud-Daula (Khan, M. K. I. 1925:34). Among them, Umrao Khan would be one of the most prominent of the 19th-century *bīnkārs*.

Despite the influx of musicians from Delhi, it is interesting to note that no *sitār* player is mentioned for this period in Lucknow, either by Karam Imam or in oral histories. Apparently Delhi continued to dominate as a center for the new *sitār* music.

Banaras was a part of Avadh until 1775 when Asaf ud-Daula surrendered Raja Cait Singh's land to the East India Company. Despite the

British control, a Hindu ruler was maintained there, and the Banaras court was the scene of a high level of musical patronage through the late 18th and the entire 19th century. Two important *bīn* players lived in Banaras in the last quarter of the 18th century. Jivan Shah and his brother Pyar Khan were the foremost *bīnkārs* of their time. They are not to be confused with the Lucknow *rabābia* Jivan Khan who had a nephew Pyar Khan. Francis Fowke was the British Resident for the East India Company in Banaras for seven years between 1771 and 1786 (anon. 1919:27, footnote). Apparently an accomplished musician himself (cf. Bor 1988: 56), he wrote a detailed description of the *bīn* for the Asiatic Society of Bengal, "On the Vina or Indian Lyre." In it he includes a drawing of Jivan Shah, and mentions that his brother, "*Pear Cawn* is a performer very little, if at all, inferior to *Jeewan Shah*" (Fowke 1965:195). Fowke was only partly impressed with the music of the *bīn*.

> The style of music on this instrument is in general that of great execution. I could hardly ever discover any regular air or subject. The music seems to consist of a number of detached passages, some very regular in their assent [sic] and descent; and those that are played softly, are most of them both uncommon and pleasing ... . The open wires are struck, from time to time, in a manner that, I think, prepares the ear for a change of modulation ... but the ear is, I think, always disappointed ... . Were there any other circumstances, respecting the *Indian* music, which lead to suppose that it has, at some period, been much superior to the present practice, the style, scale and antiquity of the instrument, would, I think, greatly confirm the supposition (Fowke 1965:197).

Jivan Shah and Pyar Khan of Banaras are highly regarded in performance tradition. Pyar Khan is sometimes known as "Anguli Kaṭ" ("Cut Finger"),[102] and is given credit for influencing the Pūrab *bāj* of *sitār* playing. The Purab area included both Lucknow and Banaras. One of the most well-known of all *sitār gats* in the *rāga kāfī* is attributed to Pyar Khan by Radhika Mohan Maitra, and denoted as a Firozkhani style *gat*.

Gwalior was an outstanding center for music during the earlier Mughal period. It contributed a large number of musicians, among them Tansen, to the court of Emperor Akbar. After the 17th century, continuous military efforts undertaken by the Gwalior rulers undermined continued patronage. Their Maratha armies were powerful forces throughout the late Mughal period. But at the end of the 18th century under Daulat Rao Sindia (1794-1827) Gwalior began to re-emerge as a center of musical patronage. The first of the musicians who is said to have moved to Daulat Rao's Gwalior was vocalist Kadir Baksh, who came with his sons Haddu and Hassu Khan from Lucknow.[103] These *khyālias* would make Gwalior a dominating force in the development of *khyāl* in the 19th century. Gwalior never became a leading center for *sitār* music, as it was for *khyāl*, but it hosted a number of known instrumentalists at different periods. Dulha Khan, a nephew of the *sitār* player Masit Khan, is reported to have lived about this time in the Gwalior court (Sastri 1916: Introduction, 26).

Bengal was the center of British power in India. Although the region had its own musical history, it is not noted for any well-known mainstream musicians in the 18th century. Toward the end of the century, however, a notable event took place relating to the British presence there. In 1784 Sir William Jones, a judge in the Supreme Court of Calcutta and a pioneering figure in the field of Indological studies, founded the Asiatic Society of Bengal in Calcutta for research in the history, sciences, arts and languages of India and Asia. Jones provided one of the inspirations for the surge of European and Indian interest in Hindu learning centered in 19th-century Europe and Bengal. Jones' treatise "On the Musical Modes of the Hindoos" was a serious inquiry into the variety of *rāgas* and the Sanskrit literature on music. English-educated Bengalis would subsequently direct their interest toward the building of cultural and national pride, in a movement known as the Hindu or Bengal renaissance.

Contrasting William Jones' scholarly and serious inquiry is the writing of Belgian artist F. Baltazard Solvyns, who represents perhaps a more typical late 18th-century European view of Indian music. His insulting opinion of vocal music and Indian musicians emerges by way of a discussion of the "*Tumboora*" (Figure 68):

> A great deal has been said upon the music of the Hindoos. The transactions of the Society of Calcutta among others, contain many treatises upon the subject, which is notwithstanding but very imperfectly known in Europe, for this simple reason, that the instruments which they use have never been described with sufficient precision, which ought to have been the principal object, for they are much more remarkable than the music itself. Their instruments have been carried successively to a surprising degree of perfection; but those improvements have not reached their music, which still remains in its infancy. It is impossible not to make this remark in seeing a Hindoo play upon the *Tumboora*; in his hands it is a magnificent instrument, covered with paintings and gilding, ornamented to an excess of luxury, and we are naturally led to imagine that he is to draw from it the most enchanting sounds; but on the contrary he remains for hours together in the same attitude, singing a monotonous air, and touching from time to time one of the four chords which compose this instrument. This is the only use he makes of it, the only

> pleasure which he seeks from it. And for him even this is a great deal: seated on a carpet or a piece of white cloth, he gives himself up to the pleasing sensations which the vibrations of the single chord produce, and probably he would give up even this enjoyment, if it required the smallest exertion. Everything about him must be proportioned to his natural taste for laziness and indolence (Solvyns 1808/10-I:26, n.p.).

Fortunately, European attitudes such as this had virtually no impact on the history of Indian music performance.

5

The 19th Century to 1857

The beginning of the 19th century saw the British East India Company in control of North India from the Upper Doab, surrounding Delhi, eastward through Bihar and Bengal. Only Rampur and Avadh controlled their own territories among the upper provinces. The Rajput and Maratha territories remained independent. The British presence did not encourage court or indigenous culture, as

> all over India the British attitudes to things Indian were changing. The old interest in and respect for Indian civilization was changing to criticism and distaste (Spear 1951:50-1).

Dance and music were prominent features of many court cultures, and were now especially associated by many of the British with irresponsibility and degeneracy. And it had recently been discovered in the pioneering European studies on Sanskrit literature that a glorious early period of Hindu culture contrasted the current scene. Even Captain Willard, who is very sympathetic toward music, expresses a strong negative opinion on the current state of the art:

> In Hindoostan, music arrived at its greatest height during the flourishing period of the native princes, just a little before the Mahomedan conquest, and its subsequent depravity and decline since then, closed the scene with the usual catastrophe ... . At present most native performers of this noble science are the most immoral set of men on earth, and the term is another word for all that is abominable, synonymous with that of the most abandoned and profligate exercises under the sun (Willard 1965:28-9).

To what degenerate music of the time was Willard referring? Perhaps it was the music of the *"nautch,"* performed with great frequency in the 18th and 19th centuries for the entertainment of royalty and visitors:

> The wealthy Mahometans, Hindoos, and Parsees, frequently entertain their friends at their garden houses: but in these mixed companies no women are present, except the dancing girls, or tolerated

> courtesans, who are accompanied by musicians, playing on instruments resembling the guitar and violin. These singing men and singing women, are hired at festivals and grand solemnities, among all sects and professions in India (Forbes 1813-I:80-1).

A contemporary of Willard's sees occasional glimpses of what he thinks of as a more glorious age:

> Still in these degenerate days there are exceptions, and the sacred Vin may still be heard pouring forth a strain of rhapsody that carries the imagination back to the fabulous age of Rishis and Gandharbas (anon. 1965:236).

However, in the oral traditions of music history carried by performers, we do not hear of degeneracy, but of outstanding centers of culture in the early 19th century where illustrious musicians were expanding and solidifying the innovative forms introduced by the preceding generations.

Delhi: the Generation after Masit Khan

The last of the Mughal emperors in Delhi were Muhammad Akbar II, called Akbar Shah (1806-1837), and Bahadur Shah Zafar (1837-1857). Both were virtually powerless under the controlling force of the East India Company, and both are given harsh treatment by later historians. Bahadur Shah was a patron of literature, and was a poet and philosopher himself. Under him Delhi saw one of its greatest periods for Urdu literature. Mirza Ghalib, one of India's most outstanding literary figures, was a poet in his court. A description of the Red Fort, the seat of Mughal power, appears in Bishop Reginald Heber's "Narrative of a Journey Through the Upper Provinces of India From Calcutta to Bombay 1824-1825." The Fort was outwardly beautiful but inside dilapidated and dirty. Flower inlays were missing, plucked from the walls by Shah Alam in his days of poverty. The fountains were dry, and old furniture and tools were lying around in piles. The great *darbār* hall was filled with lumber and old boxes, and the throne was soiled with pigeon dung. The old part of Delhi appeared like a slum extending "as far as the eye could reach," although other parts of the city were clean and had prosperous *bāzārs* (Heber 1829-II:290, 302-5). Despite its poor condition, Delhi retained a great prestige throughout this period, and continued to set the standards for language, dress and manners, and functioned as a center for "all arts and crafts" (Spear 1951:83). An example of the quality of artistic activity going on in mid-19th-century Delhi remains in the brilliant work of Mirza Ghalib, who infused new levels of poetic meaning and exquisite nuances of expression into the Urdu *ghazal* form.

A number of musicians remained in Delhi despite the lure of richer centers. Pannalal Gosvami in his "*Nād vinod*" of 1895 tells us that his musician ancestors came from Multan to Delhi with the Emperor Humayun, Akbar's father, and remained attached to the court until the ouster of Bahadur Shah in 1857. His father was supported by funds from a treasury at Meerut even after Shah Alam was looted of his wealth by the raider Ghulam Qadir. It was only in 1857 when the British took official control in Delhi, that his father finally sent him and his brothers away in search of patrons outside of Delhi (Gosvami, P. 1895:5-8).

The *sitār* had two prominent exponents in early 19th-century Delhi, Bahadur Khan and Dulha Khan. According to Sastri in the "*Saṅgīt sudarśan*," Bahadur Khan was Masit Khan's son, and Dulha Khan was Masit Khan's sister's son.[104] Sastri notes that Bahadur Khan was especially famous for his *gat* and *toḍā* compositions, and indeed, *gats* attributed to him are found in some of the 19th-century handbooks.[105] Bahadur Khan had a female disciple, Biba Jan Sahiba. A student of hers wrote the "*Qānūn-i sitār*" in 1870. According to him, Bahadur Khan was originally a *bīnkār*, and he took to *sitār* after a hand injury prevented him from playing the *bīn*. He adapted certain *bīn* techniques to the *sitār*, and created new types of *toḍās* based on them. The *toḍās* were so difficult, the author says, that he had seen no one able to execute them properly except Biba Jan (Khan, M. S. H. 1873:17). Several important techniques are mentioned in the "*Qānūn-i sitār*," but it is not possible to say which of them was introduced or used by Bahadur Khan. The *gats* attributed to Bahadur Khan, however, regularly contain two techniques, *mīḍ* and *zamzama*.[106] It is likely that these were among the earliest of named *sitār* techniques. According to a contemporary source, Bahadur Khan died in 1841 or 1842 (Khan, Saiyyid A. 1964:688).

While Bahadur Khan was noted as a composer, Dulha Khan seems to have been an outstanding performer. Sastri calls him an expert in both *dhrupad* and *bīn*, and a major *sitār* player of his time (Sastri 1916: Introduction, 26). Josi notes him for the great amount of hard practice that he did, which helped win the *sitār* an increased popularity (Josi 1935: 250). The *sitār* was still a very new instrument in India's musical scene. Sastri says Dulha Khan stayed for some time in Gwalior, but he must have been a visitor there, as Gwalior *sitār* traditions do not mention him.

The development of a new solo music based on ideas from *dhrupad* was the work of the four generations between Khusrau Khan and Dulha Khan. *Dhrupad* elements must have enhanced the repertoire and the reputation of the *sitār*. To contrast this *sitār* style with another that soon emerged in Lucknow, the *gat-toḍā* of Masit Khan and his followers came to be called the Delhi *bāj*. Despite the emphasis on *dhrupad* that later writers give in describing the Delhi style, written *gats* and performance tradition show that it was very much a genre of its own, one having the qualities of experimentation and eclecticism that characterized *sitār* music throughout its history.

There were other noted musicians who remained in Delhi during this time. Mir Nasir Ahmad was the leading *bīnkār*,[107] and a *sitār gat* attributed to him appears in the *"Naghmah-i sitār"* (Beg 1876). Even *bīn* players apparently had to concede to the growing popularity of the *sitār* in their teaching and composing. Karam Imam tells us

> Mir Nasir Ahmad Saheb is a Sayyed but he married a girl from the Kalawant class in Delhi in order to fulfill his desire to learn *Been*. He is proficient in it."[108]

Rahim Khan, son of the *bīnkār* Umrao Khan is mentioned by Karam Imam in relation to Delhi as well as Lucknow (Khan, M. K. I. 1925:34). He was one of the teachers of the writer Rahim Beg, and *gats* attributed to him are found in Beg's book (Beg 1884:3).

Leading vocalists in Delhi were Tanras Khan, who "sings *ghazals* and to some extent *khyāl* quite well,"[109] and is thought of as the founder of the Delhi school of *khyāl*, and Yusuf and Wazir Khan, nephews of the foremost singer of the time (Baḍe) Muhammad Khan, then in Lucknow. Karam Imam describes the latter two as "shining in Delhi like the Sun and the Moon" (Vidyarthi 1959:19). Karam Imam, however, shows his allegiance to Lucknow when he says "Apart from these there are in Delhi hardly three or four musicians of the type you find in Lucknow."[110] Figure 73 may represent the dignified atmosphere of the best performances of this time.

The Early Senias: Rahimsen and Amrtsen

When, after the time of Bahadur and Dulha Khan, the descendants of Masit Khan moved from Delhi, a new phase in *sitār* music began with the *sitār* player Rahimsen (Figure 69). Around this time, the title *"sen,"* and the designation *"senia,"* came to be considered a mark of the family line descended from Tansen, and Masit Khan and his son Bahadur Khan began to be called Masitsen and Bahadursen by some followers. The so-called Senia *sitār* line was subsequently traced to them. It is more expressive of the developmental phases of *sitār* music, however, to separate Masit Khan, Bahadur Khan and Dulha Khan and their Delhi followers from the *sitār* players in Rajasthan beginning with Rahimsen. The latter are widely known as the Senia *sitār* players, and this designation is followed here. Sudarsanacarya Sastri, author of the "*Saṅgīt sudarśan*," was a disciple of Rahimsen's line, and he provides a great deal of colorful detail on the history of the Senia *sitār* players. Sastri's account will form the basis for the following look at the early *sitār* music of this line.

Rahimsen is said to have been a descendant of Tansen through his son's line, and was the first among them to play the *sitār*. His father was Sukhsen, a *dhrupad* singer.[111] Sastri tells us how Rahimsen got his start on the *sitār*. Rahimsen was married to Dulha Khan's daughter. He was learning *dhrupad* from his father but had not completed his training when Sukhsen died. Unwilling to learn *dhrupad* from anyone else, he took up the *sitār* under his father-in-law, Dulha Khan.

> At that time the *sitār* was a simple instrument. Someone therefore taunted Rahimsen saying "now just go ahead and play *diṛ dā diṛ dā ṛā*." Rahimsen, swallowing his anger replied, "friend, doubtless *sitār* isn't worth two cents compared to *dhrupad*. *Dhrupad* is a jewel and *sitār* is just a pebble, but I will change this pebble to such a degree that it will equal a jewel." Thereafter he applied so much thought and effort that he filled the *sitār* with *vīṇā*, *dhrupad* and *khyāl*, after which time great musicians began to bow their heads before his *sitār* (Sastri 1916:Introduction, 62).

Rahimsen was employed in the court of the small state of Jhajjar, located about forty miles west of Delhi. He was appointed to the prestigious position of the Navāb's teacher. He had a large number of disciples, among whom was his younger brother Husain Khan, who settled in Indore and became well-known as a musician there. Rahimsen's first and most famous son, *sitār* player Amrtsen (Figure 70), was born in 1814. His two younger sons, Na'matsen and Lalsen, also became *sitār* players, but neither reached the fame of their eldest brother. Sastri does not give the year of Rahimsen's death. He was still alive in 1847 when the "*Āsāru al-sannādīd*" was written (Khan, Saiyyid A. 1964:688), but since the "*Saṅgīt sudarśan*" does not mention him after the discussion of the uprising of 1857, it seems he had died before that.

Rahimsen was evidently very conscious of the *dhrupad* and the *bīn* music that surrounded him in Jhajjar and formed his family tradition.

But the new *khyāl* was also a potent force in the early 19th century, especially under the influence of the great Baḍe Muhammad Khan in Gwalior. Rahim Khan's efforts in infusing the still lowly *sitār* with elements of both *dhrupad* and *khyāl* appear to have been a necessity for acquiring the balance of respectibility and popularity that he sought. He was highly successful in his endeavor. Rahimsen played *joḍ* ("joining," an early term for instrumental *ālāp*) evidently in a relatively full and successful imitation of that played on the *bīn*. He followed it with *tāla*-bound *gats* and *toḍās*, as developed by his Delhi predecessors. He followed that with *fikre*, (Persian/Urdu, "sentence or refined speech"), passages played in imitation of a section called *fikrebandī* in a *khyāl* performance. Sastri says that he did not leave out any aspects of *bīn* music, and that in fact his music even outshone the *bīn* because of the addition of *tāla*-bound work. Sastri says that *bīnkārs* began to fear Rahimsen's *sitār* (Sastri 1916: Introduction, 26-7). We get a picture of a highly competitive musical atmosphere in the courts of the early 19th century.

Rahimsen, who had been struggling financially, was appointed to the prestigious position of the Navāb's teacher just before Amrtsen was born in 1814. Sastri says that Amrtsen was so lucky during his life that people used to say he was "born and died on a throne." Amrtsen is one of the greatest figures in the 19th-century history of the *sitār*. His reputation even overshadowed that of his father. He began to perform in public with his father at the age of ten and independently at the age of thirteen. When he was fourteen he was granted his own salary by the Navāb of Jhajjar. Travel had become common among musicians at this time, and Amrtsen travelled and performed with his father in all the prominent courts of the day. His salary at Jhajjar, and later at Alwar and Jaipur, included a grant of villages *(jāgīr)*, servants and numerous luxuries, and it is said that he lived like a nobleman (Sastri 1916:Introduction, 41-3). After the uprising of 1857, Jhajjar was taken over by the British, and he moved to Alwar and then to Jaipur, the city with which his family came to be most closely associated. His activities there will be followed later. Amrtsen died in 1893, his career having spanned most of the 19th century.

The *sitār* music of Rahimsen and Amrtsen can be spoken of in terms of the constituents that Sastri mentions as making it up: *bīn* and *dhrupad*, *khyāl*, and elements unique to the *sitār*. Although later exponents of this line often stress the *dhrupad* element in this *sitār* style, oral and written tradition show that *dhrupad* is only an equal partner in the whole. Here the constituents are discussed in a historical context; a more technical discussion and examples are given in Part Three.

Rahimsen and Amrtsen's *sitār* music was first of all characterized

Fig. 69. Rahimsen. Sastri 1916:n:p.

Fig. 70. Amrtsen. Sastri 1916:n:p.

जयपुरनरेशके जागीरदार श्रीअमृतसेनजीके पुत्र उत्कृष्टसितार-
वादनके द्वितीयखलीफा मीयां निहालसेनजी

Fig. 71. Nihalsen. Sastri 1916:n:p.

Fig. 72. Amir Khan. Sastri 1916:n.p.

by their minute attention to the correctness of the *rāgas* they played. The contemporary *"Āsāru al-sannādīd"* says about Rahimsen that "the six *rāgas* and thirty-six *rāginīs* are slaves and slave girls to the strings of his instrument" (Khan, Saiyyid A. 1964:688). Mushtaq Ali Khan, a modern representative of the style, said that the greatest contribution of the Senias was their establishing a musical definition for each *rāga*. They refined the individuality of each *rāga* to such an extent that a *rāga* was actually manifest in each one of its notes alone. It is indicative of their high status in the field as a whole that the rules they set in regards to the musical specifications of each *rāga* established standards accepted by the performers and the theoreticians of the day.[112] Sastri says "Rahimsen and Amrtsen's *gats* are just like definitions of the *rāga*," and "whoever knows *gats* of theirs in any *rāga* knows the *rāga* so completely that he can improvise in it at will." He calls Amrtsen the "Badshah of *rāga*" (Sastri 1916:Introduction, 51-2). Mushtaq Ali Khan and others who claimed a connection to the Senia line retained such minute training in each *rāga* that they saw each note and phrase as an entity that could be expressed uniquely for each particular *rāga*. The *gats* notated in the *"Saṅgīt sudarśan"* represent a very large number of *rāgas*, some very rarely seen. The emphasis on *rāga* and *rāga* purity is one of the characteristics of their music obtained from the *dhrupad* tradition.

Ālāp, the *dhrupad*-based solo exposition of a *rāga*, usually preceding the performance of the *gat*, was not a part of the Delhi *bāj* of Masit Khan and his followers, even into the 20th century. Their entire repertoire of techniques was incorporated into their elaborate *gats* and *toḍās*. From the *"Saṅgīt sudarśan,"* we learn that Rahimsen and Amrtsen played an *ālāp* in imitation of the *bīn*, which they called *joḍ*. They played it, in at least all the major *rāgas*, before the *gat* and *toḍā*, as is normal in modern practice. In one sense, *joḍ* must have been considered a phrase or set of phrases, probably covering a scale-section of the *rāga*. Thus, Sastri speaks of Amrtsen's playing "eight or ten *joḍs*" to show another *sitār* player the *rāga* (Sastri 1916:Introduction, 26-7). In the most common modern usage, *joḍ* is the term for the middle-speed section in a full exposition of *ālāp*. There is an instrumental style of short *ālāp* called *joḍ*, however, still to be found at present among senior musicians. It is a somewhat simplified and faster-moving *rāga* development than the extremely slow modern *ālāp*, and might have been the prevalent *ālāp* style in pre-20th-century instrumental music. See Part Three for more on *joḍ*.

Mushtaq Ali Khan stated that although the Senias knew *ālāp* from their *dhrupad* training they did not perform it in public.[113] His statement is contradicted by Sastri, but it points to the practice of the Delhi *bāj* players, and to some disciples of the Senia line as well, who did not play *ālāp* in public performances. Barkatullah Khan, a Senia-trained *sitār* player of the early 20th century, specialized in the Masitkhani *gat-toḍā* and did not normally play *ālāp*. He was the source of Mushtaq Ali Khan's relationship to the Senia line.

The *khyāl* influence in the *sitār* music of the Senias has been overlooked in popular music history. Sudarsanacarya Sastri and Mushtaq Ali Khan both spoke of it clearly. The most influential *khyāl* singers of the 19th century, Baḍe Muhammad Khan and Haddu and Hassu Khan, in the Gwalior court, were contemporaries of Rahimsen and Amrtsen. They specialized in high-speed *tāns* and probably brought them into *khyāl* music. Under the phenomenal influence of their innovations, new concepts of *khyāl* were taking hold in centers all across North India. Sastri mentions an occasion when Amrtsen and Haddu-Hassu Khan performed at the same gathering. The brothers said "Today we have heard the *sitār* for the first time." Amrtsen returned a similar compliment (Sastri 1916: Introduction, 20). There is little doubt that Haddu-Hassu Khan's most well-known innovations, varieties of fast speed *tāns*, had an impact on Senia *sitār* music, despite the prevalent modern view that fast *tān* playing was instituted in the early 20th century. Sastri relates a story of Amrtsen's playing with the famous *pakhāvaj* player of the time, Kudau Singh. In order to show his accomplishment in *tāla*, Amrtsen first played at such a slow speed that Kudau Singh had trouble and asked him to speed up. Amrtsen then began to play so fast that Kudau Singh could not keep up with him. Amrtsen said "Singhji! Both your hands are working, and only my one finger is doing all the work, look!" Kudau Singh replied, "Except for you, Mīyañjī, today there is no one who can surpass my speed" (Sastri 1916:Introduction, 45-6). Sastri states that the *fikre* of Rahimsen and Amrtsen's *sitār* music was an imitation of the *fikrebandi* of *khyāl*. *Fikra* became an important term in *sitār* music, which had a range of meaning. In some of the 19th-century handbooks it is a particular type of *toḍā*. Mushtaq Ali Khan used it as short rhythmic interjections into the *gat*. Mushtaq Ali Khan said that the Senias distinguished two types *(aṅg)* of *gats*, *dhrupad* and *khyāl*. The playing differed more in the style than in the notes, and incorporated differences in technique and ornamentation. The *khyāl* influence in *sitār* music is normally thought to have begun seriously with the great early 20th-century *sitār* players Imdad Khan and Inayat Khan. History shows that *khyāl* influence had an early phase in the music of the Rahimsen and Amrtsen. *Sitār* music has always responded quickly to the musical trends of its times.

As much as for its adoption of *dhrupad* and *khyāl* influences, Rahimsen and Amrtsen's *sitār* music was noted for its originality. Their *gats* are said to have had a special quality about them. Sastri calls them "priceless jewels." They were "difficult in *laya* [rhythm] and filled with *mīḍ*" (Sastri 1916:Introduction, 52). To play them properly was no easy matter. And if the *gats* were difficult, says Sastri, their "*toḍa fikre,*" are impossible to imagine (*ibid.*). Amrtsen's *layakārī*, rhythmic work, astounded all the musicians with its difficulty. He would not depend on the *pakhāvaj* player, but keep rhythm with his foot through the entire *gat-toḍā-fikra* performance. Sastri says the two were protective of their special *gats*, and taught them to no one outside the family (*ibid.*).

Lucknow

In the most extravagant court of Hindustan a whole new trend in *sitār* playing was taking form. The *navābī* culture of Lucknow, now displacing Delhi with its wealth and its exquisite refinement in dress, language and social graces, had attracted some of the outstanding musicians of the time. We will see that the new trends in instrumental music were being set on the one hand by descendants of Tansen, who were now teaching non-*dhrupad* instruments, and on the other hand by the colorful and corrupt "head of the singers," Ghulam Raza, to please the less tradition-minded of the Lucknow aristocracy.

By the end of the reign of Asaf ud-Daula in 1798, the Lucknow court had become the richest in Hindustan and the *navābs* known for their luxurious life style. Karam Imam lists a large number of musicians who were supported by these early *navābs*. State affairs were reportedly well-handled until Asaf ud-Daula's adopted son, Wazir Ali, mishandled the state's wealth and initiated a negative trend. He was deposed after only four months, and Sa'dat Ali Khan became the next Navāb. In 1801, Sa'dat Ali was coerced into ceding large tracts of land to the British East India Company, placing Avadh in the midst of British-controlled territory. Afterwards repentent, he is said to have vowed to abstain from vice. Karam Imam informs us that he did not take an interest in the arts, and that during this time a number of musicians left Lucknow for other courts (Khan, M. K. I. 1925:30).

In 1814 Sa'dat Ali Khan was poisoned, and his son Ghaziuddin Haidar inherited the throne. Bishop Reginald Heber travelled through Avadh during Ghaziuddin Haidar's rule. Heber was favorably impressed with the industry of the people of Avadh and their desire for continued sovereignty (Heber 1829-II:88-90). He writes:

> I was pleased ... and surprised after all which I had heard of Oude, to find the country so completely under the plough, since were the oppression so great as is sometimes stated, I cannot think that we should witness so considerable a population, or so much industry (Heber 1829-II:49).

Heber notes the use of Urdu, as opposed to Persian, as the court language and says:

> I suppose this has arisen from the king's desertion of his old allegiance to the house of Timur since when it has been a natural policy to frame the etiquette of this court on a different model from that of Delhi (*ibid.*:69).

The ending of Avadh's support for the Mughal emperor was marked by the British gift of the title "king" to Ghaziuddin Haidar of Avadh. In general, Ghaziuddin Haidar supported literature and the arts, and the continuity of family lines spoken of by Karam Imam indicates that a number of leading musician families remained in Lucknow during the relatively dull period of the early 19th century. Dance was a mainstay of court entertainment, and Heber witnessed at least two *nautch* performances during his tour. The *sitār* functioned as an accompaniment to dance in Lucknow at this time.

In 1827 Ghaziuddin Haidar's son Nasiruddin Haidar took the throne:

> Since Delhi has been shorn of its splendour, and become a dilapidated burlesque of what it once was, there is no native court in India to vie with that of Oude in wealth and magnificence (Knighton 1856:8).

So writes the anonymous author of "The Private Life of an Eastern King." However, in this sensationalist account of the scandal and degeneracy in the court, we hear outrageous stories of Nasiruddin Haidar's period on the throne. The author of this book was a European who lived in favor in Haidar's court. Haidar's five European "friends" were a tutor, a librarian, a German painter-musician, a captain of the bodyguard and a barber. The barber, a Mr. Derusett, was held in special regard, and held inordinate influence with the king. He eventually fled, allegedly taking with him more than twenty-four lakh rupees from the treasury (*ibid.*:278), which had already been depleted by the king's expenditures on such favorites. The "Calcutta Review" said about this period:

> All decency and propriety were banished from the court. Such was more than once the king's conduct ... that Colonel Lowe, the resident, refused to see him, or to transact business with his minions.[114]

The author of "The Private Life" makes the most of the frivolity, capriciousness and cruelty of the king in this work which became popular in contemporary England. In regards to music, the author says "At the present time, the court of Hyder is the most brilliant in India; and his company of performers is without contradiction the first" (Knighton 1856:24). However, from the descriptions of the court, the musical environment did not do justice to the caliber of Nasiruddin Haidar's performers. Every evening with dessert after his meal, the king would watch such entertainers as tumblers, jesters, magicians and snake charmers, or watch puppet shows or cock fighting on the table. While these entertainments were going on there would usually be a group of female dancers and their musicians performing elsewhere in the room:

> There is, for the most part, a comedy every night, that commences about eight in the evening, and lasts till eleven. It is intermixed with dances and songs .... Attendant musicians played upon a species of lute and tambourine behind them, advancing and retreating with them, and accompanying the instruments with their voices. The instrumental seemed the principal part of the musical performance; the voice accompanied it rather than it the voice (Knighton 1856:23).

Karam Imam hints at the capriciousness of the king when he says that the king cut a portion of the salary of one singer for refusing to attend the court (Khan, M. K. I. 1925:37). In "The Private Life" a much more sinister side of his character is pointed to in an account of a beautiful Kashmiri dancer and singer who was in great favor in the court until the king tired of her and she vanished (Knighton 1856:91-6).

After the departures of the "friends" and the barber in 1837, new servants were brought into the court and within four months Nasiruddin Haidar was poisoned. The British intervened to prevent one of the queens from enthroning her son, and instated Muhammad Ali Shah, one of Haidar's uncles. He is said to have begun to refill the depleted treasury (Hay 1939:45). Karam Imam mentions that he restored the salary and position of the punished musician (Khan, M. K. I. 1925: 37). When Muhammad Ali died in 1842, he was succeeded by his son Amjad Ali, who is said to have then taken up a life of excess and vice, caring little for government and spending most of his time in the *zenāna*. At one point he was warned by the British Resident to improve the situation (Hay 1939:49-51). No separate mention of music for his time are found. His son and successor was Wajid Ali Shah, whose nine year rule saw an extraordinary flood of musical activity.

Wajid Ali Shah: Ghulam Raza and the "Singers and Fiddlers"

Wajid Ali was not the heir-apparent to the throne at Lucknow and therefore had not been provided training in government affairs. He had spent his time as a prince

> learning music and writing verses ... . He was preoccupied with 'mushā'irās' and 'maḥfils' [poetry readings and musical sittings], and soon became a poet and musician of considerable repute (Bhatnagar 1968:4).

From a young age he was surrounded by young courtesans called *parī* (fairies), who lived in the *parī khāna* and "learned music and dancing from reputed musicians of the time" (*ibid.*:6). Apparently already from this time a group of the musicians had begun vying for his favor in order to gain positions of status and power. Headmost among this group was one of the teachers of the *parīs*, Ghulam Raza Khan, famous in modern music as the originator of the Razakhani *gat*. An early exploit of Ghulam Raza's sets the tone for his later adventures in the Avadh court:

> One day Ghulām Raḍā and Chajjū Khān [a thumri singer mentioned by Karam Imam] were in attendance upon the prince when all of a sudden an unknown person made a prearranged mock attack upon him with a sword. Both Chajjū Khān and Raḍā Khān at once pounced upon him and ultimately overpowered him. They were handsomely awarded for their fidelity and appointed as bodyguards (Bhatnagar 1968: 7, n. 42).

Ghulam Raza was a musician of the *ḍhārī* class, a group associated with dancers and accompanists who figured low in the musico-social hierarchy.[115] His father was Natthu Khan, also known as Ghulam Ali Khan, a musician who had held a post under Navab Ahmad Ali Khan (1822-1840) in Rampur. Ghulam Raza was given the title Razi ud-Daula and his father the title Najib ud-Daula by Wajid Ali Shah in Lucknow (Bhatnagar 1968:232). Karam Imam says "Raziuddaula who was a Dhari was honoured with the title of 'Abai'."[116] William Crooke, speaking of the musicians' classes *ḍom*, *mirāsī* and *ḍhārī* says: "The most famous of them in recent times was Raji-ud-daula, who ruled the court of Oudh" (Crooke 1896-III:497). The surprising latter part of the statement will soon gain substantiation.

Ghulam Raza had one brother named Hassu Khan (not the famous Gwalior figure) who stayed in Rampur and was known as a *ṭhumrī* singer. Two other brothers were given the titles Wahid ud-Daula and Bashasat ud-Daula by Wajid Ali Shah (Jan 1950:112). Ghulam Raza's sister was also in Lucknow. Her husband was a musician named "Dumman Khan" (Sleeman 1858-I:105). Another relative was Anis ud-Daula, a *sārangī* player or a *tabla* player.[117] Ghulam Raza had a son, Ali Raza, who appears in the post-1857 period in Patna.

When Wajid Ali Shah took the throne, Ghulam Raza and his relatives and a number of other musicians established themselves as his special favorites in the court, and began to figure significantly, and mischievously, in the political history of his reign. Records of his exploits are gathered here from the reports of Colonel W. H. Sleeman, the British Resident in Lucknow, and from other sources of Lucknow history. The story adds a new dimension to the history of Lucknow *sitār* music and to our understanding of the environment of the time.

For his overly close association with musicians and entertainers, Wajid Ali Shah began to incur the displeasure of the British representatives in Lucknow right at the beginning of his reign. Colonel Sleeman wrote:

> The present king has, from the time he ascended the throne, manifested a determination to take no share whatever in the conduct of affairs; to spend the whole of his time among singers and eunuchs, and the women whom they provide for his amusement ... (Sleeman 1858-I:lxviii).

Only four months after he was enthroned, the then Resident sent a letter to the Navāb protesting appointments of musicians to government offices:

> Has not (another) Corps been lately ordered to be raised by Gulam Ruzza Russee ood Dowlah a singer, and is it not notorious that the sepoys presenting themselves for enlistment are required to pay rupees sixteen each? ... Will your majesty be pleased to consider how the appointment of Kootub Ulee [*sitār* player Qutub ud-Daula] (whose birth and profession must be well-known to Your Majesty, and who, though able to read and write is yet entirely inexperienced in matters of Government) to the Court ... can possibly conduce to the welfare of your country? (Bhatnagar 1968:34).

Wajid Ali Shah replied to the Resident's letter defending his appointments. Razi ud-Daula, Ghulam Raza, he says, is neither

> an inexperienced child nor a woman behind the curtain. His father held an honourable post in Rampur during the time of Nawab Ahmad Ali Khan (*ibid.*).

Even Karam Imam who was proud of Lucknow's musical environment, noted with gentle criticism the Navāb's special promotion of musicians: "the patronage extended to artists by the Nawab was so great that even Dharis were raised to the position of nobles" (Vidyarthi 1959:25-6). Appointments of musicians to unsuitable positions of administrative power continued. Ghulam Raza and Qutub ud-Daula were given commands in the army, and an extreme was reached when Ghulam Raza was appointed Deputy Prime Minister. Upon the Resident's persistent objections, Wajid Ali Shah consented to remove Ghulam Raza from some of his positions, and after considerable continuing efforts, the Resident had managed by the end of his term to draw up a draft of an agreement that would prevent "eunuchs and singers from holding office and practising nepotism" (Bhatnagar 1968:50). Under the agreement the Resident was granted power by the king to banish any eunuch, singer or other improper person who broke the agreement.

Colonel Sleeman took over as the British Resident in Lucknow in 1849, a year after the agreement banning singers from office. His work, "A Journey through the Kingdom of Oude in 1849-1850" (Sleeman 1858), provides a detailed account of the workings of Avadh under its last Navāb. The story as Sleeman presents it is one of power in the hands of corrupt underlings, and wide mismanagement of state matters. Evidently the agreement on the singers brought about by Sleeman's predecessor did little to correct the musicians' monopoly of the Navāb's attention. In an official correspondence of 1849 Sleeman complains of Wajid Ali Shah's behavior, and notes signs of mental depression as well:

> The King continues to show the same aversion to hear anything about public affairs, or to converse with any but the singers, eunuchs and females .... He does not suffer bodily pain, but is said to have long fits of moping and melancholy, and he is manifestly hypochondriac. He squanders the state jewels among the singers and eunuchs, who send them out of the country as fast as they can (Sleeman 1858-I:lxxi-ii).

As the psychological state of the Navāb was degenerating, Ghulam Raza's audacity was increasing:

> The king is in constant dread of poison, and would do anything to get relieved from that dread, and all further importunity on the state of the country. His chief wife would poison him to bring on throne her son, and restore to her her paramour, who is now at Cawnpoor, waiting for such a change. He is afraid to admonish his other wife for her infidelities with the chief favourite and singer lest she should

> poison him to go off with her paramour to Rampoor, whither he has sent the immense wealth that the king has lavished upon him. (Sleeman 1858-I:lxxiii-iv).

The musicians' and entertainers' influence on Wajid Ali Shah began to be intolerable for Sleeman. He reports with disgust:

> He eats, drinks, sleeps and converses with the singers and eunuchs and females alone, and the only female who has any influence over him is the sister of the chief singer Rusee-od Dowlah, whom he calls his own sister. No member of the royal family or aristocracy of Oude is ever admitted to speak or to see his Majesty, and these contemptible singers are admitted to more equality and familiarity than his own brothers or sons ever were; they go out, too, with greater pomp than they or any of the royal family can; and are ordered to be received with more honours as they pass through the different palaces. The profligacy that exists within the palace passes all belief; and these things excite more disgust among the aristocracy of the capital than all the misrule and malversion that arise from the King's apathy and incapacity (Sleeman 1858-I:lxxv-vi).

Sleeman includes the Navāb's Prime Minister, Ali Naqi Khan, also a *sitār* player and singer, in his stark summary of the situation:

> we have a fool of a king, a knave of a minister, and both are under the influence of one of the cleverest, most intriguing, and most unscrupulous villains in India (*ibid.*:xxii).

Was he referring to our Ghulam Raza? It seems so.

A series of complicated events would end in the banishment of Ghulam Raza and Qutub ud-Daula and their families from Avadh altogether. In 1849 the musicians were caught perpetrating a massive fraud on the Navāb. It seems they had brought in a *faqīr* to cure him of disease, and had convinced the Navāb to give large payments to the *faqīr* over the course of several months. One of the king's wives disclosed to him that it was a fraud, and the *faqīr* soon confessed that he was in conspiracy with the singers. The king had allegedly paid two lakh rupees to the fake, which he had then shared with the musicians. The king became angry at Ghulam Raza, and Captain Bird, Assistant to Sleeman who was then away on tour, took the opportunity to bring up the subject of Ghulam Raza's illicit relations with the second queen. He extracted a promise from the king to banish Ghulam Raza and Qutub ud-Daula "across the Ganges" into British territory. The king confronted Ghulam Raza saying "'All the evil that I have so often heard of you, men of Rampoor, I have now with my own eyes seen realized'" (Sleeman 1858-I:45):

> The king, in the latter end of November 1849, divorced Surfaraz Mahal, and sent her across the Ganges, to go on a pilgrimage to Mecca. She had long been cohabitating with the chief singer, Golam Ruza, and was known to be a very profligate woman (*ibid.*:47).

The king's anger, however, did not last:

> The minister reports to the Resident on the ninth, that the king had relented, and wished to retain the singer, Ruzee-od Dowlah, and his sister, and Kotub Allee at Lucknow, with orders never to approach the presence (*ibid.*:49).

The king, apparently under pressure from his favorites, subsequently denied to the Assistant Resident that he had ever found Ghulam Raza guilty. He placed his hand on the head of his prime minister and said:

> "I swear, as if this was my son's head, and by God, that I believe Gholam Ruza to be entirely innocent; and that I never promised to turn him out, or to send him across the Ganges." Captain Bird then heard a movement of feet in the next room behind closed doors. He was horrified ... (*ibid.*:104).

The Assistant used strong language and threats in attempting to have the king honor his promise, but Wajid Ali Shah was adamant:

> "This case has reference only to my house—it has no connection with the Government; but if you wish to use force, take me also by the beard, and pull me from my throne!" (*ibid.*:104).

The next day in a show of defiance, Ghulam Raza and "his relative the fiddler, Anees-od Dowlah" were seen riding behind the king in his carriage where they

> paraded through the city, as in full possession of his favour. After the King had alighted from the carriage at the palace, the coachman drove the two singers to their apartments in the Mukbara, seated as before in the Khuwas, or hind seat (*ibid.*:105).

On May 25, 1850, Ghulam Raza and his relatives and Qutub ud-Daula and his family with other musicians, fourteen in all, were put into prison. On June 2, all except Ghulam Raza and his sister's husband were taken across the Ganges and left in British territory. Sleeman says that on July 23 those two were taken likewise:

> The immediate cause of the King's anger was the discovery that his divorced and banished wife, Surfaraz Mahal, had actually come back, and remained concealed for seven days and seven nights in the palace, in the apartments of the chief singer, Gholam Ruza. They were all made to disgorge the Company's notes and jewels found upon them, but the king visited Gholam Ruza the day before his departure, and treated him with great kindness, and seemed very sorry to part with him (*ibid.*:106).

According to the *"Tārīkh-i Avadh,"* Ghulam Raza was banished along with the other musicians on June 2. He travelled in a cart with Wahaj ud-Daula (mentioned as a *sāzinda* player by Karam Imam [Khan, M. K. I. 1925:47]), while Qutub ud-Daula rode in another cart with Najib ud-Daula, Ghulam Raza's father. Qutub ud-Daula's cart is said to have turned over and injured its passengers, but no one was permitted to touch or assist the exiles, and they were not even provided water despite the heat of the summer. Across the river, they took a house on rent. In July, Ghulam Raza and Wahaj ud-Daula went off in the direction of Kanpur (Khan, M. N. 1919-IV:169).

So ends the career of Ghulam Raza and some of his colleagues in Lucknow. To Sleeman's disgust, however, some musicians who remained in Lucknow continued with similar activities. He reports that "all the singers are despicable domes; but the two, who govern the King, are much worse characters than any of those who were banished" (Sleeman 1858-II:129).

However strong Sleeman's distaste for the Navāb's way of running his government, the British intention to take over Avadh did not have his approval, and he counseled against it. But after Sleeman retired in 1854 the next Resident urged that "extreme measures" be taken aginst the ill-governed state, and in 1856 the British under Dalhousie annexed Avadh to their territory. Wajid Ali Shah refused to sign the treaty, but relinquished the throne with an emotional speech. He left for Calcutta with about one hundred followers on March 13, 1856, amid strong demonstrations of sorrow by the Lucknow citizenry, and arrived in Calcutta two months later (Bhatnagar 1968:70-88, 111, 147-55).

Life in *navābī* Lucknow

Sleeman's descriptions of the corrupt adventures of Ghulam Raza and the court scene under Wajid Ali Shah are one side of the picture, and somewhat misrepresent the overall quality of the cultural and social life in *navābī* Lucknow. Lucknow sources and the city's cultural legacy show that its contributions to some musical, literary and social aspects of 19th- and early 20th-century North Indian urban life were unparalleled.

The aristocratic families of early 19th-century Lucknow led a life of refined extravagance that even surpassed that of Muhammad Shah's Delhi. Language, dress and etiquette were given special attention. It was a high period for Urdu literature, especially poetry, inspired and influenced by Delhi's Urdu period under Bahadur Shah. Ghalib's influence was strongly felt. Composing poetry at all levels and on all topics was a major pastime. In dress, finely embroidered coats, headwear and shoes, and fine, semi-transparent cotton were the specialties of Lucknow. The cultivation of etiquette, *adab*, was a Lucknow social priority. Kite flying, cock fighting, and playing board games were fashionable pastimes. Among musical activities, dance took a foremost position:

> The nautch girls of Lucknow are celebrated for their sociability and education, the generality of them possessing a colloquial knowledge of Persian. They pre-eminently excel the nautch girls of Delhi by their exquisite singing as well as their beauty.[118]

The *kathak* style of dance, which after this time became North India's major classical dance form, is known to have been cultivated under the guidance of Wajid Ali Shah. Karam Imam mentions a number of Hindus of the *kathak* caste from Banaras involved in the musical scene of the time. In vocal music, the Lucknow of this period is known for producing the *ṭhumrī*, a semi-classical form originally associated with dance. *Ṭhumrī* later became a major form in Hindustani music. Karam Imam speaks of *ṭhumrī* only rarely and there in a negative context, such as in connection with Ghulam Raza's *sitār* style (Khan, M. K. I. 1925:44). It was evidently a recent and non-classical style of vocal music. *Dhrupad*, *khyāl*, *ṭappā* and *tarānā* are frequently mentioned by Karam Imam and were obviously established and frequently performed genres of the time. *Khyāl* was sung by male and female singers, and seems to have become accepted even by musical families steeped in *dhrupad* tradition. Karam Imam's sections on the contemporary Lucknow musicians is a mine of information on the musical personalities and the dynamics of the genres of time. An exuberant Company style painting conveys something of the lively musical atmosphere of the time (Figure 74).

Instrumental music must be discussed under two different categories. One consists of the instrumentalists with a family background of *dhrupad* music. Many of these either taught or played non-*dhrupad* instruments during this time. In the other category are the non-*dhrupad* instrumentalists. The dynamic contributions of both types of Lucknow instrumentalists profoundly changed the repertoire and style range available for *sitār* and *sarod* players of the following generations.

Dhrupad Instrumentalists and the Purab *bāj*

Three *dhrupad* instrumentalists stand out in early and mid-19th-century Lucknow. They are Basat Khan, Pyar Khan and Ja'far Khan, sons of Chajju Khan, a descendent of Tansen who had come to Lucknow during the time of Navāb Shuja ud-Daula. Karam Imam comments that "the playing of the *rabāb* ends with these brothers" (Khan, M. K. I. 1925: 33). Although the *rabāb* survived for one or two generations after them, these three stand out as the last of the great players. Ironically, their later fame comes less from the *rabāb* than from their roles in founding and teaching the Purab *bāj* of *sitār* and *sarod* music, some of which was influenced by the *ṭhumrī* music of the time. They composed *gats* that are preserved in performance tradition and in written records, and produced numerous disciples who were important figures in the history of this style.

Basat Khan was born in 1787, according to the tradition of his disciples.[119] He left Lucknow to go to Calcutta with Wajid Ali Shah in 1856, and later moved to Gaya, where he is said to have lived to the age of one hundred. His main disciples were his son, Muhammad Ali Khan, a *rabāb* player, and *sarod* player Na'matullah Khan, both of whom emerged in the last quarter of the century. Basat Khan is said to have written a book, which exists in handwritten form.[120] Among the three *rabāb*-playing brothers, Pyar Khan was the most prodigious teacher. He was Navāb Wajid Ali Shah's *ustād*, and he had a number of disciples who became topmost instrumentalists of their time. He is credited authoritatively by Karam Imam, for the invention of the *sursingār*, the metal-stringed hybrid instrument of the 19th-century *dhrupad* revival (Khan, M. K. I. 1925:33). The *sursingār*'s leading player would be a nephew of Pyar Khan's, Bahadur Husain or Bahadur Sen, in Rampur. The instrument also went to Calcutta with Basat Khan, and was taken up by some of Basat Khan's students there. Pyar Khan died sometime around 1857, before Karam Imam wrote his *"Ma'dan al-mūsīqī."* Ja'far Khan was a good singer as well as a *rabāb* player, according to Karam Imam. He must have lived for some time in Banaras, as in some references he is called Ja'far Khan "Banarsi" (Khan, Sa'dat A. 1921:5). The three brothers are found mentioned in connection with Rampur in the years 1854-1864 (Khan, S. M. R. A. 1956:49). They probably increased their contacts there after the annexation of Avadh by the British.

In *bīn*, Karam Imam tells us that Umrao Khan was the leading player of the day. His brother, Muhammad Ali, was a *bīnkār* in the service of the Mahārāja of Banaras. Umrao Khan's sons Rahim Khan and his elder brother Amir Khan were also noted *bīn* players. Ali Naqi Khan, Wajid Ali Shah's prime minister, also learned the *bīn* under Umrao Khan's direction, and played it as well as the *sitār* (Khan, M. K. I. 1925:43-4).

The Lucknow in which Basat, Pyar and Ja'far Khan lived was far different from the Mughal environment of their ancestors. In 19th-century Lucknow they, as the descendents of Tansen, were the conservators of the *dhrupad* and the *rabāb* tradition, but all around them *khyāl*, *ṭappā*, *tarānā* and the *sitār* were dominating musical performance. Although *dhrupad* and the *rabāb* were appreciated by such aristocratic connoisseurs as Karam Imam Khan, the demand for the newer forms must have been great. Increasingly also, amateurs or students from non-musical family backgrounds were interested in learning instrumental performance. The Tansen line is noted for its policy of keeping its traditional knowledge within the family line. Karam Imam says: "Those people do not teach the rules of the *bīn* even to any family members except their sons" (Khan, M. K. I. 1925:44). The Lucknow *rabābias*, therefore, taught their new disciples the *sitār*, the most popular instrument of the time.

Ghulam Muhammad is noted by Karam Imam as one of the great musicians of the time. He was a disciple of Umrao Khan, and evidently learned a great deal of the techniques and style of the *bīn* on the *sitār*, since he played *ṭhok* as well as any *bīnkār* or *rabābia*, except Umrao Khan himself. Ghulam Muhammad is an important figure for his development of a new *sitār* which later came to be called *surbahār*. We recall here the work of the *sitār* players Rahimsen and Amrtsen in Jhajjhar, Rajasthan, who were filling their *sitār* music with all the elements of the *bīn*. Karam Imam mentions Rahimsen as the leading *sitār* player of the Masitkhani *bāj*. Influences must have been exchanged.

Another *sitār* player was Babu Isvari Prasad, "Babu Jan," who Karam Imam notes was young and highly respected for his playing in "middle speed" and "*chālā*" (*jhālā*?). Karam Imam says that his grasp of *rāga* is also good, and that he holds the hope that his reputation will match that of Ghulam Muhammad in the future (Khan, M. K. I. 1925: 45). Another well-known *sitār* player was Sanvalia Khan of Farukhabad, one of the non-family disciples of Pyar Khan.

Performance tradition and the 19th-century handbooks describe the *sitār* style of these Lucknow *sitār* players as the Purab *bāj*. The Purab *bāj* is known for its varied and interesting *gats* in the middle and fast speeds. Ghulam Raza, who we know invented a new style of fast speed *gat*, was a contemporary of these *sitār* players. In common present day usage, Razakhani is an alternate term for Purab *bāj gats*. However, evidence indicates that there was a clear distinction between the original Purab *gats* and the *gats* of Raza Khan. The *dhrupad* instrumentalists would not have either adopted or taught a style that was recently created by Ghulam Raza. Karam Imam's comments on Ghulam Raza's style show us that it was unique to its inventor. Specialists in the Purab *bāj gats* also tell us that the Razakhani style *gat* had a specific definition, which will be discussed presently. The "*Saṅgīt kalādhar*" of Dahyalal Shivram labels *gats* separately as belonging to the Purab *bāj* or the Ghulam Raza *bāj*. Firozkhani *gats* also maintained a separate tradition in this and other performance lines, while they do not appear at all in some, and are considered a subset of the Purab or Razakhani *bāj* in others.

The Purab *bāj sitār* player Ghulam Muhammad and the disciples of the *dhrupad rababias*, then, played *bīn*-inspired *ālāp* and *jhālā*, and also middle or fast speed *gats*. From the 19th-century handbooks and the performance practice of modern traditionalists, we can see that the *gats* were characterized by variety in *mizrāb* patterns, syncopated and complex rhythmic movements and quick melodic movement over the range of the *rāga*. Karam Imam noted Babu Jan's grasp of *rāga*, a point that distinguishes that style from Ghulam Raza's, which he says pays very little attention to *rāga*.

We know the source of the *bīn*-inspired side of the Purab *bāj*. What, then, was the inspiration for the middle speed *gats*? It is very likely that the idea came from the musicians who had come from Rampur, bringing with them the music of Firoz Khan and the Afghani *rabāb*. The connections between Lucknow and Rampur may go to an even earlier time. The "*Falsaf-i mūsīqī*" of Rampur reports that the grandfather of Basat, Pyar and Ja'far Khan had been in the court of Ali Muhammad, the first ruler of Rohilkhand, along with Firoz Khan (Khan, Sa'dat A. 1921:4). The early Rampur music for the *sitār* and *rabāb* was very likely the basis for *gats* that the *dhrupad rabābias* and *bīnkārs* created and taught to their non-family disciples. Since *rabābs* were especially suited to rhythmic work, the strong presence of both the *dhrupad* and Afghani *rabāb* can help explain the emphasis on fast and varied *mizrāb* work in this style.

Three figures stand out in later performance tradition as important composers and performers of the Purab *bāj* in the generation following Basat, Pyar and Ja'far Khan. They are Qutub Ali, Barkat Ali Khan and Hashmat Jang, all disciples of Pyar Khan. Qutub Ali, given the title Qutub ud-Daula, is perhaps the most well-known. He was mentioned in connection with Ghulam Raza and his cohorts. Qutub Ali was a native of Bareilly, near Rampur, according to Karam Imam. Colonel Sleeman says that he sent the wealth he collected from Wajid Ali Shah to Rampur, and references to him there indicate that he settled there after his exile in 1850.[121] He had a brother, Sahab Ali, who was exiled along with him. Karam Imam says of Qutub Ali that he "has a power" in his *sitār* playing (Khan, M. K. I. 1925:46). Another Lucknow source says that he practiced hard, and became the best of his class among *sitār* players (Halim 1971:153). *Gats* of his in both the Purab and the Masitkhani styles are found in written and oral tradition. It is interesting to note here the appearance of the first generation of *sitār* players who performed or composed both the Purab and Delhi, or Senia, styles. Perhaps this was the influence of Rahimsen and Amrtsen finally showing itself in Lucknow.

Barkat Ali Khan, called Sanvalia Khan, and Navab Hashmat Jang, a nobleman, were the other prominent *sitār*-playing disciples of Pyar Khan. Despite their teacher's *dhrupad* background, both are remembered in performance tradition for the fast *gats* they composed on the basis of *ṭhumrī* music. Hashmat Jang's *gats* are characterized as difficult and original. Sanvalia Khan is said to have composed *gats* on the basis of *khyāl* and *tarānā* as well as *ṭhumrī*.[122] Were these *sitār* players responsible for introducing the *ṭhumrī* influence into *sitār* playing, or was Ghulam Raza the first to do it, as Karam Imam seems to indicate? Sanvalia Khan and Hashmat Jang were contemporary to Ghulam Raza, if not earlier. It may not be possible to determine the precise order and authors of the innovations that came about at this eventful time.

Ghulam Raza and the Non-*dhrupad* Instrumentalists

Ghulam Raza's *sitār* style was somewhat like his life style both in its success and in its disregard for traditional propriety. Karam Imam's disapproving comments indicate that it ignored the classical priorities regarding *rāga* and technique:

> And concerning the style of Ghulam Raza, I have not found anyone good at it except Ghulam Raza himself. First of all this *bāj* is only suited for *atāīs*[123] and is unsystematic. Its *gats* in *titāla* are without *rāginī* and *dhun*, and are composed on the basis of *ṭhumrī*. I have found them neither complete nor well-formed. Yes, Ghulam Raza had such an original style that I found it enjoyable. But the people of that *bāj* are really mad over it. It has no *ṭhok* or *jhālā* or scope for *rāga* except for one or two. *Ustāds* disapprove of this *bāj* and intelligent listeners are ashamed of it. Ghulam Raza invented this *bāj* only for the sake of the nobles of Lucknow.[124]

Fig. 73. *Portrait of a vocalist with his disciples and accompanists. 19th century (?). Indian Museum, Calcutta. 13436 / S.287.*

Fig. 74. A musical performance. Company painting, c1850. National Museum, New Delhi. 58.13/74.

Fig. 75. Standing sitār *player. One of 35* mica *paintings by a Banaras artist, c1830-40. By permission of the British Library. IOL Add. Or. 370.*

Fig. 76. A standing **sitār** *player. One of a series of 12 mica paintings, Patna, 19th century. By permission of the British Library. IOL Add. Or. 421.*

Karam Imam makes his points clearly. Ghulam Raza was not concerned with the systematic approach of the *dhrupad*-influenced styles. Another Lucknow source is even more blunt about Ghulam Raza's merits, saying that he was not an exceptionally good musician but that he gained his fame primarily through royal favor (Halim 1971:153).

There are no *gats* available in written or oral traditions attributed directly to Ghulam Raza, although some are specified as belonging to his style. Ilyas Khan spoke of the original Razakhani *gats* as having sixty-four *mātrās*. His examples show intricate, fast and rhythmically challenging *gats*, but they are difficult to distinguish from other Purab *bāj gats*. The earliest available *gats* specifically of this style are attributed to Ghulam Raza's son, Ali Raza, and are found in written and oral traditions. Some examples are given in Part Three.

The fact that he was heartily disapproved of by both the political and the musical establishment was apparently of no concern to Ghulam Raza. He seems to have pursued his activities with energy, abandon, and a great deal of resulting popular acclaim. His *ṭhumrī*-based music must have had a phenomenal appeal to the non-specialists of Lucknow, and it certainly made a lasting impact on later instrumental music. Today the Purab *bāj* is virtually identified by modern musicians with Ghulam Raza through the term Razakhani. Karam Imam's clear separation between Ghulam Raza and the other Lucknow *sitār* players shows that this modern identification is not entirely correct, but it is probable that aspects of Ghulam Raza's experimental style permeated the Purab *bāj*. His music can be followed in a later period to Patna where he apparently went after his banishment, and where his son continued on after him.

Rampur: Ghulam Ali and the sarod

In the late 18th century, Rampur had been a center for the Afghani *rabāb* and the Firozkhani instrumental style under Navāb Ali Muhammad. For the period of the two following Navābs there is no record of outstanding musical activity, although musicians can be assumed to have remained at the court. Karam Imam mentions the fourth Navāb, Ahmad Ali Khan (1822-1840), as being a good patron of music (Khan, M. K. I. 1925:47). Bishop Heber makes an unflattering comment about him, saying "like almost all the nobility of India, the Nawab of Rampoor is a mere drunkard and voluptuary" (Heber 1829-II:259). Musical patronage and political weakness are again linked. It was in Ahmad Ali's court that Natthu Khan, Ghulam Raza's father, was a musician, and Ghulam Raza probably had his musical background here. The instrumental music of Firoz Khan and the *rabābias* must have been an important force. It is at this time that Captain Willard notes the *rabāb*'s strong presence in Rampur.

One of the outstanding figures associated with early 19th-century Rampur was Ghulam Ali *rabābia*, the first player of the *sarod*. Karam Imam refers to him as a native of Rampur and says that he was of the *ḍom* musicians' class. Family accounts of the 20th-century *sarod* player Hafiz Ali Khan, who was a descendent of Ghulam Ali, give us a few details on his life. His father was Ghulam Bandagi Khan Bangash, a soldier-equestrian from Afghanistan who played the *rabāb* as a hobby. He settled in Riwa where the ruler supported a number of Hindustani musicians. Ghulam Ali, according to these accounts, began learning Hindustani music from the Riwa Maharaja. He subsequently travelled and performed all over India. In Lucknow he is said to have learned a bit from Pyar and Ja'far Khan, and he finally settled in Gwalior (Khan, Amjad A. 1973:n.p.). Evidently Ghulam Ali's association with Rampur is loose, perhaps only as a *paṭhān* whose family had settled in that area. Ghulam Ali had died before Karam Imam wrote the *"Ma'dan al-mūsīqī."* Josi gives the year of his death as 1850 (Josi 1935:164).

Family tradition describes Ghulam Ali's music as *"dhrupad ang,"* a mixture of Afghani *rabāb* music and *dhrupad* forms (Khan, Amjad A. 1973:n.p.). Information given by Radhika Mohan Maitra indicates that the Firozkhani style was prominent among the early *sarodias* of this line, although representatives of some *sarod* families do not believe in the authenticity of the Firozkhani *bāj*. If Ghulam Ali played in the Firozkhani style, its middle-speed, *rāga*-based *gats* were a mixture of *dhrupad* elements and Afghani *rabāb* style. A link between Ghulam Ali and the Firozkhani style is found in at least one written source. Bakhtavar Singh, author of *"Svar tāl samūh,"* was a disciple of Ghulam Ali. Firozkhani is the only *gat* type, aside from the universal Masitkhani, that he gives. His Firozkhani *gats* may represent the sort of music that Ghulam Ali played. In the *sarod* playing of the 20th century, fast percussive rhythms and strokes may represent the style of the *rabāb* and early *sarod* players like Ghulam Ali.

In the decade or so preceding 1857, Rampur lost a number of its musicians to Lucknow, which dominated the area's music scene. Ghulam Raza and his family and friends were among those who went to Lucknow at this time. Rampur would again emerge as an important center for music after Lucknow's fall to the British.

Banaras and Banda: Umrao Khan and Ghulam Muhammad

Figure 75 is one of a series of Banaras figures painted colorfully on thin pieces of mica. The face of the *sitār* player, on a separate piece, was to be held behind the painted figure from where it would show through the transparent mica. If not able to vie with Lucknow in the early to mid-19th century, Banaras was still an active cultural center, and was the home of the one of the foremost *bīn*-playing lines of the time. The Banaras Maharaja Udit Narayan is mentioned by Karam Imam as one of the outstanding patrons of the day. Several of his court musicians are also mentioned. Topmost among the musicians of Banaras, and first among all contemporary musicians named by Karam Imam is Umrao Khan *bīnkār*. Willard mentions Umrao Khan as an excellent *bīn* player and the grandson of Jivan Shah, the former leading *bīnkār* of Banaras (Willard 1965:91, 122). Neither writer refers to the generation between Jivan Shah and Umrao Khan. Traditions represented in Josi and Roy Chaudhury say that Jivan Shah's son was Nirmal Shah and that Nirmal Shah's brother was Choṭe Naubat Khan, who was Umrao Khan's father (Josi 1935:144; Roy Chaudhury 1975:171). References to Nirmal Shah are heard in oral tradition, but Choṭe Naubat Khan is a more obscure figure. Umrao Khan's sons were Amir Khan and Rahim Khan *bīnkārs*, who became prominent in Rampur after 1857.

Umrao Khan was a contemporary of Pyar and Basat Khan, and like them played a role in non-*dhrupad* music by teaching the *sitār* to disciples outside his family. Two *sitār* players already mentioned as Purab *bāj* disciples of Pyar Khan, Qutub ud-Daula and Hashmat Jang, are said to have been disciples of Umrao Khan as well (Roy Chaudhury 1975: 172). But Umrao Khan's most outstanding disciple was Ghulam Muhammad Khan who was a very important trend setter in *sitār* music.

Ghulam Muhammad was living in Banda when Karam Imam spoke of him. He was a *sitār* player of the Purab style, probably playing fast speed and *ṭhumrī*-based *gats*, but he also adopted *dhrupad* forms to the *sitār*, and Karam Imam's comments hint that he might have been responsible for instituting full-scale *bīn ālāp* as a part of *sitār* playing. In the translation by Vidyarthi:

> In sitār playing Ghulam Muhammad Khan now residing in Banda has achieved mastery. His thok is so clear and precise that I have not found an equal to him either among Beenkars or Rababias with the possible exception of Umrao Khan Beenkar. His sitar was in no way inferior to Been or Rabab, and according to the Ustads of the day there was no sitar player in India who could attain his standard (Vidyarthi 1959:23).

Ṭhok or *ṭhonk* is a section and a technique of *bīn ālāp*. Another source speaks of Ghulam Muhammad's influence in the spread of the *dhrupad*-based repertoire of the Purab *bāj*. Jani Sahab of Rampur says: "with the help of other *rabābias* and *bīnkārs* he gave perceptible impetus to the spread of the Lucknow *bāj*." Jani Sahab speaks of the Lucknow *bāj* as that "used by *rabābias* and *bīnkārs*" (Khan, M. A. A. c.1925:62-3). It is an important comment on the Purab *bāj*, reminding us that its normal association with fast-speed *gats* should be balanced with the knowledge that it was formed primarily by *dhrupad rabābias* and *bīnkārs* and their disciples, who played *dhrupad*-based music more prominently than the *ṭhumrī*-based *gats*. Such was certainly the case with Ghulam Muhammad. His successors played *bīn ālāp*, often on the *surbahār*, and fast speed Purab *gats* on the *sitār*. Ghulam Muhammad developed a new type of *sitār* for his playing. It is pictured in the *"Naghmah-i sitār,"* of Rahim Beg, and is by all evidence the precursor of the *surbahār*.

Mushtaq Ali Khan makes an intriguing statement, that Ghulam Muhammad learned the *surbahār* from *khyāl* singer Baḍe Muhammad Khan, who also played the *bīn*.[125] Lack of any other references to Baḍe Muhammad Khan as an instrumentalist makes this statement impossible to back up. It emphasizes, however, the possibility of exchange between these two contemporaries. Ghulam Muhammad's son, according to at least one tradition, was named Muhammad Khan.[126] Ghulam Muhammad's most famous follower was his son (or grandson according to some), Sajjad Muhammad. Sajjad Muhammad became a very influential *sitār* and *surbahar* player in late 19th-century Bengal, and will be discussed in that context.

It is appropriate to compare at this point the work of *sitār* players in the various centers of North India. In Delhi, *sitār* players concentrated on the *gat-toḍā* genre of Masit Khan. They incorporated all of their techniques, including *bīn* techniques and *jhāla* into their *gats* and *toḍās*. Rahimsen in Jhajjhar, Rajasthan, was intensely working on the infusion of *bīn* techniques into the *gat-toḍā* inherited from Delhi. His style focused on the intricacies of *rāga*, and included for the first time some sort of *bīn*-style *ālāp*. He and his son Amrtsen further expanded their style by an addition of techniques of *khyāl*, probably in part inspired by the new fast *tān* techniques of the great Baḍe Muhammad Khan in Gwalior. Karam Imam, despite his loyalty to Lucknow, comments that he had heard Rahimsen, and that in truth he was one of the great *sitār* players of the day. Ghulam Muhammad played a *dhrupad ālāp* that compared favorably with that performed by others on the *bīn*. It was probably the first time full-scale *ālāp* attempted on the *sitār*, and it required a large *sitār*, later *surbahār*, for its proper execution. He played fast speed

Purab-style *gats*. Ghulam Raza played only fast, attractive and non-conventional *ṭhumrī*-based compositions.

Other Centers

Daulat Rao Sindia's rule in Gwalior from 1794 to 1827 marked the re-entry of Gwalior into the Hindustani music scene. Tod comments in his "Annals and Antiquities of Rajasthan," written in 1829, that "Sindia, some years since, carried away the most celebrated vocalists of Oodipur ..." (Tod 1950-I:514) indicating that Daulat Rao was intentionally building up the musical atmosphere of his court. Baḍe Muhammad Khan was among those he brought to his court. Under him and his famous followers Haddu and Hassu Khan, Gwalior was established as the leading center for innovative *khyāl* music, in which position it remained throughout the 19th century. In the period following Daulat Rao's death, although there was no special stimulus given to music, Baḍe Muhammad Khan was active, and according to a well-known story, Haddu and Hassu Khan were secretly copying his style. Sometime in the later part of Alijah Jankoji Rao Sindia's rule, Baḍe Muhammad Khan left Gwalior for Riwa, and Haddu and Hassu Khan were given positions in the court (Josi 1935:61).

A thriving period for music in the Gwalior court was the rule of Jayaji Rao Sindia from 1843 to 1866. Although Alwar and Jaipur were contemporary courts which had even more musicians than Gwalior, Haddu and Hassu Khan were the most outstanding *khyāl* singers of the time, and they kept Gwalior high in prestige.

One famous *bīn* player appears in association with this period in Gwalior, although he lived elsewhere for most of his career. Bande Ali Khan was born in 1826, and in the period following 1857 until his death in 1890, he was one of the foremost *bīn* players of India. He was married to Haddu Khan's daughter. Because the greater part of his career came after 1857, he will be discussed in that context. Among other instrumentalists, Masit Khan's nephew Dulha Khan spent some time in Gwalior, but non-*dhrupad* instrumental music does not appear to have been a noteworthy facet of the Gwalior scene at this time.

In Rajasthan the early 19th-century rulers kept up an unbroken tradition of musical patronage. Tod talks of the Rana of Mewar "who is a great patron of the art" and comments that

> Indeed, we may enumerate this among the principal amusements of the Rajpoots; and although it would be deemed indecorous to be a performer, the science forms a part of education (Tod 1950-I:514).

As to the prevalent musical forms, he speaks of instrumental bands, and in vocal music says "The tuppa is the favourite measure. Its chief character is plaintive simplicity; and it is analogous to the Scotch, or perhaps still more to the Norman." He traces its origin to Panjab (*ibid.*).

In Alwar and Jaipur, in the courts of Shivdan Singh and Ram Singh, musical patronage was generous. Tod speaks of Shivdan Singh's serious interest and knowledge even before he came to the throne:

> He was proficient in musical science, and could discourse most fluently on the whole theory of Sangíta, which comprehends vocal and instrumental harmony. He could explain each of the *ragas*, or musical modes, which issued from the five mouths of Siva and his consort Mera, together with the most endless variations of the *ragas*, to which each are allotted six consorts or *raginis*. He had attached to his suite the first vocalists of Méwar, and occasionally favoured me by letting them sing at my house ... (Tod 1950-I:513).

He speaks of the Raja's musical sittings and mentions an instrumentalist, perhaps a *sitār* player or a *rabāb* player:

> The chieftains of Saloombra, the chief of the Suktawuts, and others, frequently joined these parties, as well as the Maharaja; for all are partial to the dance and the song, during which conversation flows unrestrained. Sadoola, whose execution of the guitar would have secured applause even at the Philharmonic, commanded mute attention when he played a *tan* or symphony, or when, taking any of the simple *tuppas* of Oein as a theme, he wandered through a succession of voluntaries (*ibid.*).

After 1857 the courts of Alwar and Jaipur would again be famous for the important *bīnkār* line of Rajab Ali Khan, and the later Senia *sitār* players.

6

Changes after 1857

The Western Centers

Delhi, Alwar and Jaipur

The Indian army revolt of 1857-1858 ended in a series of severe reprisals by the British, and basic changes in British administration in India. The period following saw consequential changes in Indian culture as well as government. One of the most obvious centers of change was Delhi, the seat of the last Mughal Emperor, Bahadur Shah Zafar. Upon recapturing the city, the British removed the Emperor, whom the rebelling soldiers had declared their leader, and sent him in exile into Burma. Under the new administration the famous culture of Delhi began to change. Percival Spear says

> the end of the Court involved a break in cultural as well as political tradition, and ushered the garish period of utility into Indian life when education came to mean knowledge of English, and culture foreign imitations (Spear 1951:83).

Life in Delhi now revolved around the British who made it their "center and haven." They did not support "native culture," but in deference to old Delhi culture they did continue to attend *nautch* parties given by the Muslim nobility, even "after the practice was stopped in other parts of the country" (*ibid*.:137-40, 150). Hasan Nizami, early 20th-century author and translator of the "*Muraqqa'-i Dehlī*" assures us that the traditions of Delhi did not stop completely, saying that even through the bullets of 1857 the esthetes of Delhi did not give up their pleasures (Khan, D. Q. B. 1933:6 n.). But there is no question that Delhi suffered a transformation. Many nobles and music patrons left the city, and some became supporters of the new order, adopting the accoutrements of British culture. Pannalal Gosvami in his "*Nād vinod*" tells of his and his brothers' positions after 1858. When "the Timur dynasty died, and all its wealth was being disbursed through treaties," he and his brothers decided to leave

Delhi. Recalling some of the great past patrons of Delhi, their father told them:

> Now you will not find such men, so go out and find your livelihood according to your own abilities. ...
>
> You see to what state the Bādshāhs have been reduced ... evil times are falling on the great kings and emperors ... . Now you will find in Delhi no one who will satisfy your spirit. So go and seek out *mahārājās*, wise men and saints (Gosvami, P. 1895:5-8).

Some Delhi musicians moved to the thriving courts of Alwar and Jaipur, some to Rampur and Lucknow, and others to smaller centers to the north, south and east.

Still remaining in Delhi, however, were lesser known *sitār* players who still represented the Delhi *bāj* of *gat-toḍā* music. The publication of handbooks after 1870 for learning the *sitār*, such as "*Sarmāya-i 'ishrat,*" "*Nād vinod,*" "*Qānūn-i sitār*" and "*Talīm us-sitār*" (Figure 82) show that disciples of the earlier stars remained, and that interest among amateurs was thriving in Delhi. From the notations in these books, and from performance tradition, we know that the Delhi instrumentalists played almost exclusively the Masitkhani *gat-toḍā* style until the end of the century. Into this system they incorporated the entire range of their techniques. Safdar Husain Khan, the Delhi author of "*Qānūn-i sitār,*" criticizes the new, difficult and limited Purab *bāj* fast *gats*, and says of his own style:

> As to the Masitkhani *bāj*, God is good; what can be said of it! All types of *bāj* are played in it, and the scope for elaboration is such that one *gat* can be played for as long as one likes (Khan, M. S. H. 1873:17).

Other musicians remaining in Delhi were two noted *bīn* players, Rahim Khan and Mir Nasir Ahmad, and the *khyāl* singer Tanras Khan, who founded what became known as the Delhi school of *khyāl*.

Following the events of 1857-58, the stable and already musical court of Raja Sivdan Singh in Alwar, then called Mewar, grew and thrived. Sudarsanacarya says that it had the best gathering of musicians of any contemporary state (Sastri 1916:Introduction, 46). Its period of musical eminence would end in the 1860s, however, due to a run-in with the British. Rajab Ali Khan and his nephew Musharraf Khan in Alwar were among the most prominent *bīnkārs* of their time. However, they are more frequently associated with Jaipur, where they later moved along with many of the Alwar musicians. They will be discussed in that context. A prominent figure of the Alwar court was the *dhrupad* singer Bahram or Bairam Khan, one of the predecessors of the outstanding *bīnkār* Bande Ali Khan of Indore. This *dhrupad* and *bīn* playing tradition is represented today by the Dagar family of musicians.

Foremost among the *sitār* players in the court of Alwar was Amrtsen (Figure 70). *"Saṅgīt sudarśan"* gives a detailed account of Amrtsen's arrival in Alwar and his stay there, providing a good picture of the time. The following is a summary of that account. The Navāb of Jhajjar, where Amrtsen lived with his father, was convicted of conspiracy in the events of 1857-58 and hanged by the British. Saddened at his patron's fate, Amrtsen left Jhajjar for Delhi. Alwar's Sivdan Singh invited him from there to his own court, and instated him with the same generous salary and allowances he had been receiving in Jhajjar. Amrtsen was appointed as the Mahārāja's *ustād*, and enjoyed a position of great prestige and luxury for six years until his patron fell into difficulty with the British authorities. The British blamed Sivdan Singh for neglecting state affairs and spending his time and attention on various diversions. A court case was filed against him, and an ultimatum presented that he dismiss his "hundreds" of state musicians. He would be allowed to keep only four or five, for whom the government would provide. But Sivdan Singh rejected the offer, insisting that he would keep all his musicians or none. In the midst of this trouble, Amrtsen decided to leave Alwar. He returned to Delhi in about 1864. Hearing the news that the famous Amrtsen had left Alwar, the rulers of Gwalior and Jaipur, Jayaji Rao Sindia and Ram Singh, both sent messengers to invite Amrtsen to their courts. Ram Singh's messenger arrived first and Amrtsen went with him to Jaipur. Amrtsen had settled in Jaipur by 1866 where he would remain for twenty-seven years until his death at the age of eighty (Sastri 1916:Introduction, 45-8).

One *sarod* player deserves mention in the context of the Alwar court of Sivdan Singh. Karam Khan was the son of Hasan Ali Khan, a player of the Afghan *rabāb* based in Bulandshahar. He was one of the predecessors of the important *sarodia* Na'matullah Khan, who will be discussed in the context of Bengal. Karam Khan later moved to Jaipur along with many of the Alwar musicians.

After Alwar's brief but illustrious period of musical patronage, Jaipur emerges as the leading musical center in Rajasthan. Mahārāja Ram Singh's court is famous in modern oral tradition for having maintained, it is said, at least one hundred and fifty musicians who were the leading *ustāds* of their fields (Khan, V. H. 1957:28). It is said about the Jaipur court of this time that there were musicians who specialized in very specific aspects of music, and were given such titles as "Captain of *tān*," "Marvelous in Intonation," "*ustād* of *boltān*," "Singer of *sthāī* and *antara*," "Emperor of *ālāp*" etc. (*ibid*.:28).

The famous 20th-century vocalist, Vilayat Husain Khan, gives us an anecdote about a meeting between the rulers of Jaipur and Gwalior around this time. The Gwalior Maharaja, Jayaji Rao, had come to Jaipur where Ram Singh had a musical program arranged. He brought with him the pride of his court, *khyāl* singers Haddu and Hassu Khan, announcing "I have chosen these two roses from my garden." Ram Singh responded that he had not just roses, but numerous flowers in his garden, which "I have watered ... with my heart's blood." The Gwalior ruler had to concede that "truly in all the states of Hindustan there is no garden such as this" (*ibid*.:28). But it was generally agreed upon that Haddu and Hassu Khan were the leaders in *khyāl* singing (Josi 1935:61).

The most prominent *bīnkār* of Ram Singh's Jaipur was Rajab Ali Khan. He was the Maharāja's *ustād* and the official head of the court musicians, and was so highly placed as to have been granted a village land holding. Rajab Ali Khan was the founder of an important *bīn* tradition. His main disciple was Musharraf Khan, who is said to have practiced all night every night for twenty-two years, seated on a rock in an isolated spot, until the marks of his knees were left imprinted on the stone.[127] Musharraf Khan became one of the leading *bīn* players of the late 19th century. His line was carried on by his son Sadiq Ali Khan and is represented today by his grandson Asad Ali Khan.

Amrtsen was the leading *sitār* player in Jaipur. There he lived with the same high salary and luxurious facilities that he had enjoyed in both Jhajjar and Alwar. A landgrant provided him with extra income, and the Maharaja regularly gave him monetary gifts as well. He lived extravagantly, using silver utensils and wearing expensive shawls. When he travelled or performed outside the court he received five hundred to a thousand rupees for each performance. He became famous all over India, and was a prized court personality in Jaipur. (Sastri 1916: Introduction, 42) When Jayaji Rao of Gwalior asked Ram Singh to let Amrtsen come to his court, Ram Singh replied "If you take Amrtsen, then take me also" (*ibid*.: Introduction, 44).

Besides Amrtsen, there were other members of the Senia family who established themselves as *sitār* players in the late 19th century. Amrtsen's two younger brothers, Na'matsen and Lalsen, were noted in Jaipur. Na'matsen learned from Amrtsen while Lalsen learned from their father Rahimsen. Amrtsen also taught his cousin's son, Hafiz Khan, who served as a court musician in Tonk and Rampur. Hafiz Khan died about 1906. Other disciples were Amrtsen's sister's sons, Nihalsen and Amir Khan (Figures 71 and 72). Of all these family members, Sudarsanacarya says that Amir Khan became the best and most famous, but that he still "did not reach one quarter of the standard of Amrtsen" (*ibid.*:Introduction, 11). Amir Khan gained much of his fame after he moved to Gwalior, where he was the leading *sitār* player. He died in about 1916 (*ibid.*: Introduction, 53). See the section on Gwalior below.

Characteristics of the Senia *sitār* style were overviewed in the context of the earlier Jhajjar period and the formative work of Rahimsen. In regards to Amrtsen's later style, it can be seen from the material in "*Saṅgīt sudarśan*" that the technical complexity, the range of speed and variety of genre borrowings in his playing were much wider than generally came to be remembered of the Senias in the 20th century. The Senias later acquired a reputation for strictly limited and severely *dhrupad*-oriented playing. Thus D. T. Joshi says they "allowed for no compromise with vocal or lighter forms."[128] Ravi Shankar says that the style was almost devoid of *ālāp* and *mīḍ*.[129] Mushtaq Ali Khan, representing the line, said that the Senias rarely played *ālāp*, and only for very special audiences, preserving the Masitkhani as a form complete in itself. But we know from Sudarsanacarya's accounts that Amrtsen played *ālāp*, was fully alive to developments in *khyāl* and its new fast-speed *tāns*, and that he used difficult and complex techniques. It seems that after Amrtsen, later Senia representatives began to direct the style in a way that placed increasing emphasis on a conservative purity, shunning any but the most austere of musical elements.

In the field of *sarod* playing, we hear that Karam Khan had moved to Jaipur from the Alwar court. The *sarod* is apparently present in all the major courts of the period, though in far fewer numbers than *sitār*. Four or five family lines altogether constituted mainstream *sarod* playing, which maintained its concentration in the Rampur area.

Gwalior and Indore

Despite up-and-down relations with the British through mid-century, Gwalior under Jayaji Rao Sindia was a stable political and cultural center. Haddu and Hassu Khan were the leading musical figures, and their followers in *khyāl* kept Gwalior the leading center for *khyāl* into the 20th century. Hassu Khan died about mid-century as a result, so the story goes, of singing his famous "*kaḍak bijlī ka tān*" ("lightening bolt *tān*") in *rāga miyāṅ malhār* (Josi 1935:58, 64). Haddu Khan is said to have sung less well after his brother's death, but he was an important court figure in Gwalior until his death in 1875. When Haddu Khan died, the Gwalior ruler is said to have fasted and taken a vow of silence for seven days (Tripathi 1977:318).

In *dhrupad* instrumental music, the famous Bande Ali Khan had an early association with Gwalior, but he moved to Indore and is normally associated with that court. Two late 19th-century *bīnkārs* are less well-known outside Gwalior. Eknath Pandit was the brother of the Gwalior *khyāl* singer Shankar Pandit, father of the modern Gwalior singer Krishnarao Shankar Pandit. He and Balvant Rao Bhaiya learned *bīn* from Bande Ali Khan, and Eknath Pandit is said to have learned from Musharraf Khan as well. Eknath Pandit took to *sitār*, which he learned under one Bapu or Babu Khan of Gwalior (who is not to be confused with the more widely known Babu Khan of Indore). Bapu Khan is said to have been a good Purab *bāj sitār* player (Pandit 1933:4). Eknath Pandit spent several years in Pune as a professor with the Poona Gayan Samaj (see section on Pune), and he assisted A. H. Fox-Strangways, author of "The Music of Hindostan."[130] One of his disciples was Bhaiya Sahab Mavlankar, father of my own Dada Guru, Shivram Ramchandra Mavlankar (c.1915-1986).

Amir Khan (Figure 72) was the most famous *sitār* player in Gwalior. He was the *ustād* of the ruler Jayaji Rao, and of his successor Madhav Rao Sindia after 1886. Amir Khan evidently developed a style of his own, as the Amirkhani *bāj* is sometimes spoken of in Gwalior references. One writer refers to Amirkhani as an alternate term for the Delhi *bāj* (Avtar 1958:10), emphasizing the relationship of the Senias with Delhi. Magical stories are told about Amir Khan's musical abilities. Once Amir Khan was to play the *sitār* at the tomb, *dargāh,* of Faqīr Chingashah in Gwalior. He took with him only a defective *sitārī* which had a cracked *tumbā*, only eight or ten *pardās* and only three strings: a *bāj*, a *joḍā* and a *laraj*. When he played for the *faqīr*, it sounded like a fine instrument. He began with *joḍ* and then *gat* in *rāga khamāj*, but after a while was stopped by the *faqīr* and requested to play his well-known "*Alaiya Madhyam*," a morning *rāga*. Amir Khan said "In God's evening you want me to play Alaiya?" The *faqīr* insisted. After ten or fifteen minutes of playing, birds in the trees all around awoke and began chirping. Amir Khan wished to stop, but at the *faqīr*'s command played for twenty minutes more amidst the chirping of birds. Then he began a wonderful *gat* in *tilak kāmod* (an evening *rāga*), and within five minutes the birds were silent (Bajpeyi 1936:n.p.). Another story about Amir Khan reflects a practical attitude that he held regarding the playing of *bīn*. Once asked why he did not play *bīn*, Amir Khan replied:

> In order to play the *bīn*, one must learn it; if I take up the *bīn*, I will not be able to play it properly and my *sitār* will suffer besides. I have no desire to pass myself off as a bogus *bīnkār*, as some people do (Josi 1935:157).

Amir Khan's son, *sitār* player Fida Ḥusain, also became well-known in Gwalior. He later went back to Jaipur.

The Gwalior *sitār* players, according to later written sources and performers, played both Delhi, by this time sometimes called the *Paścim* (western) style, and Purab style *gats*. They also played light pieces. One of Amir Khan's pieces, which he is said to have played at the end of performances, is a fast "*gat lahara*," in *rāga sarparda*, which he used as the basis for a *rāga* series in the style of pieces presently called *rāgamālā*. Part Three contains some examples of *gat* styles in Gwalior.

Among *sarod* players, Ghulam Ali had finally settled in Gwalior, but had probably died by 1857. Two other *sarod* players were noted in Gwalior after 1857, Sa'dat Khan and Nanhe Khan. Descendants of Nanhe Khan state that he was Ghulam Ali's son, but Nanhe Khan lived during the rule of Madhav Rao Sindia, who succeeded Jayaji Rao in 1886, and seems to be a significantly later figure than Ghulam Ali. Gwalior sources say that Nanhe Khan's father was Sa'dat Khan. Nanhe Khan's brother was Murad Ali Khan who settled in Darbhanga, Bihar. Another brother was Husain Ali, a lesser known musician. Nanhe and Murad Ali Khan are also mentioned in connection with Rampur, and must have lived there for some time.

Descendants' accounts provide some information on the *sarod* music of Nanhe Khan. He had inherited a style that blended Afghani *rabāb* and *dhrupad* music, and was perhaps influenced by the Purab *bāj* of Pyar Khan. To this he is said to have added the fast *tāns* of the newly evolving *khyāl*. Nanhe Khan's son was the great 20th-century *sarod* player Hafiz Ali Khan, who states:

> Perhaps because of the great influence in Gwalior of the great Khyalias, Ustads Haddu Khan and Hassu Khan, my father incorporated this technique in his playing (Khanna 1973:n.p.).

The influence of Haddu and Hassu Khan on all the music of the time and following generations cannot be overstated.

The Maratha court of Indore appeared as a center for music after the end of its political struggles in the late 19th century. The most outstanding instrumentalist was the famous Bande Ali Khan who has been called the "greatest veena player of modern times" (Chaubey 1958:n.p.). It is true that Bande Ali is the most widely known *bīnkār* of the time in oral tradition, but Umrao Khan, Rajab Ali and Musharraf Khan were all top 19th-century *bīnkārs*. Bande Ali Khan was born in 1826 in Kirana. He lived first in Gwalior then in Indore, and died in Pune in 1890. His father, a *bīnkār* named Sadiq Ali Khan, is an obscure figure. His maternal uncle was Bairam Khan, a prominent *dhrupad* singer of Alwar and Jaipur. There is some controversy over Bande Ali Khan's source of training. Some accounts say that he was a disciple of Nirmal Shah of Banaras, son of Jivan Shah (Roy Chaudhury 1975:182), but Nirmal Shah's period would seem too early for this relationship. Other accounts say he learned from Umrao Khan, but there is no record of Bande Ali's having lived in Banaras. One scholar claims to have found records indicating that he was trained by his uncle Bairam Khan in Jaipur before the 1857 period.[131]

Bande Ali Khan is an intriguing figure. He was a practicing Sufi, and stories tell of unusual powers that he possessed. Although primarily known as a *bīnkār*, he is associated with *khyāl* as well, and is considered the founder of the Kirana *khyāl gharāna*. Through his associations with the Kirana *gharāna*, he has also been associated with *sārangī* playing.[132] He married the daughter of Haddu Khan. Shamsuddin Faridi, a present day *bīn* player whose family traces its tradition to Bande Ali Khan, stated that Bande Ali added elements of *khyāl* to his *bīn* playing, but that he did so without compromising the *bīn* idiom.[133] Bande Ali Khan was a powerful force in his time and seems to have been an innovative musician. Josi comments that although many *bīn* players claimed to be disciples of Bande Ali Khan, he did not really teach anyone (Josi 1935:147). A number of other *bīnkārs* did appear in Indore, however, who were said to be his disciples or followers. Wahid Khan was a disciple whose line is represented today by Shamsuddin Faridi. Latif Khan and Majid or Masjid Khan were two other disciples. They later married into the family of Imdad Khan, the famous late 19th-century *sitār* player.

Notable for the history of *sitār* in Indore is Murad Khan, one of the disciples or followers of Bande Ali Khan. He later moved to Rajasthan and died in 1927. He is known mainly because his disciple, Babu Khan of Indore, became a prominent *sitār* player in Western Hindustan in the early 20th century. Babu Khan's noted disciple is the present day *sitār* player Abdul Halim Jafar Khan.

Imdad Khan, one of the most important figures in the 20th-century history of the *sitār*, also had associations with Indore, and some say with Bande Ali Khan (Roy Chaudhury 1975:183). For the main part of his career, however, he was in Calcutta and will be discussed in that context.

Rampur

In the period after 1857, Rampur maintained a prosperous court as an independent state under British supervision. Once again it became a center for music, after the arrival of musicians fleeing other cities, especially Lucknow. Late 19th-century Rampur is especially noted .for its *dhrupad* instrumentalists, although some important non-*dhrupad* players were also present. Muhammad Yusuf Ali Khan became the sixth Navāb of Rampur (1855-1864) after the death of his father. Perhaps because his father had been brought to the throne by the British, Muhammad Yusuf Ali remained their friend during the period of the rebellion. Consequently Rampur escaped the purges and reprisals that followed. Rampur was an attractive destination for musicians effected by the events of 1857-58. The Navab was a good patron of the arts and was himself a poet of considerable merit (Brhaspati 1976:357). Yusuf Ali Khan's period was followed by one even more conducive to musical activity. The rule of Kalbe Ali Khan from 1864 to 1887 has been called Rampur's "golden age" for art and learning (*ibid*.:357). The last part of the century under Navāb Hamid Ali Khan saw the rise of some of the musicians who would shape 20th-century music.

First among the Rampur musicians in the period following 1857, and foremost among *dhrupad* instrumentalists, was Bahadur Husain, or Bahadur Sen, a *rabāb* and *sursingār* player from Lucknow. He was the nephew and disciple of Pyar Khan. Karam Imam says that *sursingār* playing stopped with him (Khan, M. K. I. 1925:33). He also comments that he and his family were "extremely proud" and "notorious for stinginess and jealousy" (Vidyarthi 1959:18, 23). Bahadur Husain was the teacher of the Navab's nephew, Navab Haidar Ali Khan of Bilsi, who was a prominent figure in Rampur's musical history. This enthusiastic patron learned from several of the Tansen-descended musicians of late 19th-century Rampur. His son, Muhammad Ashafaq Ali Khan, called Jani Sahab, wrote a book "*Naghmāt al-Hind*" (Khan, M. A. A. c.1925). In it he tells us an amusing story concerning Bahadur Husain. He says that Bahadur Husain knew a larger set of traditional *sargams* for *bīn*, *sitār* and *rabāb* than anyone else in India. In order to learn these *sargams*, Jani Sahab's father, Haidar Ali Khan, paid Bahadur Husain one lakh rupees. Jani Sahab gives us these *sargams* in his book as syllabic, *pakhāvaj*-style *bol* patterns (Khan, M. A. A. c.1925:65-73). Josi has another story involving Navāb Haidar Ali Khan and Bahadur Husain. According to him, Haidar Ali Khan presented Bahadur Husain with three lakh rupees so that he would teach him and no one else (Josi 1935:165). But several disciples of his are mentioned in musical history nevertheless. His prominent Rampur disciple was Jani Sahab's elder brother, Navāb Sa'dat Ali Khan, called Chamman Sahab. Chamman Sahab was supposed to have been the best *sursingār* player in India after Bahadur Husain's death. He lived in Bilsi, near Rampur, moved back to Rampur in 1915, and died at the age of forty-four in 1922. He wrote a book, *"Falsaf-i mūsīqī"*(Khan, Sa'dat A. 1921).

Other *dhrupad rabābias* in Rampur were the sons of Ja'far Khan, named Kazim Ali, Sadiq Ali and Nisar Ali. The first two are also associated with Banaras, as is their father. They must have lived there for some time. Kazim Ali became known in Rampur, according to Chamman Sahab, as a *khyāl* singer. Perhaps the presence of Bahadur Husain lessened his prestige in Rampur as a *sursingār* player. Karam Imam does say "Bahadur Sen plays better than Sadiq Ali, Kazim Ali and Nisar Ali" (Khan, M. K. I. 1925:44). Kazim Ali's daughter married the Rampur *bīnkār* Amir Khan, discussed below. Kazim Ali's son never came to Rampur but stayed in Lucknow and went to Calcutta with Wajid Ali Shah. Sadiq Ali Khan, was another of Navāb Haidar Ali Khan's *ustāds* (Khan, Sa'dat A. 1921:5). Sudarsanacarya gives us a story about an encounter Sadiq Ali and Kazim Ali had with Amrtsen. According to him, the two were inordinately proud, and used to "ruin the prestige of smaller musicians and grab the instruments from their hands" (Sastri 1916: Introduction, 33). Once they came to Alwar, where Amrtsen greeted them with the respect due their status, and as "younger brothers." They played the *sursingār* so well at Amrtsen's house that cries of appreciation came from the hundreds of musicians gathered. When Amrtsen was asked to perform, he politely declined in deference to his guest performers. But upon their request he conceded, and Sudarsanacarya says that he first played everything that they had played, and then developed on it in his own style. The two were humbled, as they had considered themselves the best instrumentalists of the time (Sastri 1916: Introduction, 33-4).

Amir Khan, son of Umrao Khan of Banaras, was Rampur's leading *bīnkār* at this period. He was another of Navāb Haidar Ali Khan's *ustāds*. Amir Khan's brother, Rahim Khan, also in Rampur, is also mentioned by Karam Imam and the Rampur writers. He was one of the teachers of Rahim Beg, author of *"Tashīl al-sitār"* and *"Naghmah-i sitār"* (Beg 1884:3; 1876:3). Amir Khan's son was the legendary Wazir Khan, a figure well-known in modern performance traditions, especially for being the teacher of the two most famous mid-20th-century *sarod* players, Allauddin Khan and Hafiz Ali Khan. Wazir Khan played *rabāb* as well as *bīn*, which he is said to have learned from Bahadur Husain (Roy Chaudhury 1975:170). Wazir Khan was a contemporary of Chamman Sahab. One writer says that the two had long musical sittings in which Wazir Khan and Chamman Sahab faced each other competitively (Kosar 1956:121).

Among non-*dhrupad* instrumentalists in the Rampur court of Yusuf Ali Khan was Qutub ud-Daula, the *sitār* player who had been banished from Lucknow along with Ghulam Raza. Sleeman had mentioned that he was a Rampur native like Ghulam Raza. Another *sitār* player there was Hafiz Khan, Amrtsen's disciple and his cousin's son. He had come to Rampur from Tonk in Rajasthan, and died there about 1906.

In the period of Navāb Hamid Ali after 1889, we hear of a *sitār* player and *bīnkār* Nabi Bakhsh Khan (Khan, S. M. R. A. 1956:51). Karam Imam mentions him as a brother of a courtesan-singer from Panjab, and says that he was a disciple of Ghulam Muhammad (Khan, M. K. I. 1925: 46). Rahim Beg's "*Naghmah-i sitār*" contains Masitkhani *gats* composed by him. Beg gives us the amusing note that the Rampur Navāb wished to put one of Nabi Bakhsh's *gats* into notation, but was not permitted to do so by Bakhsh because he was not satisfied with the salary he was being given (Beg 1876:51).

In *sarod*, Munduru Khan was a Rampur native who had been in the service of the Banaras court for many years. He returned to Rampur after 1858 and died there around 1884 at the age of seventy or seventy-five (Jan 1950:115). A present day descendant of this line, Salamat Ali Khan, spoke of a *sarodia* named Ghulam Murtaza Khan, who seems to be the same person. He was a disciple of Pyar Khan.[134] Ghulam Murtaza's (or Munduru Khan's) son was Haji Abid Ali Khan and his son was Ahmad Ali Khan. Both were noted Rampur *sarod* players. Ahmad Ali is also mentioned in connection with Bengal, and probably lived there for some time. He was one of the early teachers of the great 20th-century *sarod* player Allauddin Khan. Fida Husain Khan was a second Rampur *sarod* player, representing a separate line. His father and grandfather, Hasan Ali Khan and Khaler Khan, were Afghani *rabābias* of Shahjahanpur who are said to have had no contact with the *dhrupad*-playing descendants of Tansen. In Rampur, Fida Husain became a disciple of Amir Khan *bīnkār*, creating the first *dhrupad* link in his family.[135] He was another of the early teachers of Allauddin Khan. He is said to have been a confident performer, and he was counted among the best *sarod* players of the day. Fida Husain died in 1927 (Josi 1935:165). Two other instrumentalists, Nanne Khan and Murad Ali Khan, are found in contemporary sources in connection with the Rampur court of Kalbe Ali Khan (1864-1887). They are probably the well-known *sarod* players who were father and uncle of the 20th-century *sarod* player Hafiz Ali Khan. They are more often associated with Gwalior. Murad Ali Khan settled in Darbhanga, Bihar.

Rampur, true to its historical connection to Afghani *rabāb* and early *sarod*, appears as the center for several lines of *sarod* players in the late 19th century. Descendants say their music consisted of the *ālāp* style called *joḍ*, begun after contact with *dhrupad* musicians, and fast *gats* of the Purab *bāj*. Examples and discussion of *gats* from these *sarod* traditions are given in Part Three. It is appropriate at this point to summarize the available information on the family lines of *sarod* players centered in western Hindustan.

Shahjahanpur *sarod* Families

Umar Khan spoke of three lines which he called the Shahjahanpur *sarod* families. The details and dates given below were provided by his records.[136] The first members of all the lines were Afghan *rabāb* players who had settled in various areas of Rohilkhand and what is now Uttar Pradesh. Their original centers outside of Rohilkhand were Farukhabad, Shahjahanpur, Bulandshahar and Jalalabad near Delhi in northwestern Uttar Pradesh. Ghulam Ali, the first player of the *sarod*, headed the first of the Shahjahanpur family lines. According to family accounts his three sons were Nanhe or Nanne Khan, Murad Ali and Husain Ali. But further genealogical information is required for Ghulam Ali since other accounts do not relate Nanhe Khan to him. Nanhe Khan and Husain Ali are spoken of in connection to Gwalior. Murad Ali moved to Darbhanga, Bihar. Nanhe Khan's line continued with his son Hafiz Ali Khan and his grandsons, the present days *sarod* players Mubarak Ali and Amjad Ali Khan.

A second Shahjahanpur line was that of Afghan *rabābia* Najaf Ali Khan (1705-1760), Khaler Khan (1730-1782), Hasan Ali Khan (1752-1809) who lived at the Rajasthan courts of Kota and Bundi, in Rajasthan, and Hasan Ali's son Fida Husain, who settled in Rampur. Fida Husain was the first in the family to establish a *dhrupad* connection when he became a disciple of Amir Khan *bīnkār*. The line came to be represented in the 20th century in part by Allauddin Khan, who had some contact with Fida Husain in Rampur.

A third Shahjahanpur *sarod* family began with an Afghani *rabābia* named Hingan Khan. His son Inayat Ali Khan was a court musician in the state of Bhaval where he learned from a Tansen-descended musician Kasim Ali Khan, a grandson of Lucknow's Ja'far Khan. He lived from the first quarter of the century until about 1890. His son was Shafayat Ali Khan who lived from 1848 to 1920. Shafayat Khan's son Sakhawat Husain Khan (1875-1954), was one of the leading *sarod* players of the first half of the 20th century. His sons were the modern *sarod* and *sitār* players Umar Khan (1916-1982) and Ilyas Khan (1920-1989).

An independent *sarod* line based in Bulandshahar was one that produced the two famous *sarod* players Na'matullah Khan and Karamatullah Khan in the late 19th and early 20th century. The originators of this line were again Afghanis who had come to India as soldiers and musicians in early Mughal times. One of them, Gul Khan (1728-1779), was a trader who supplied horses to the army. He was presented a property grant in Bulandshahar. His *rabāb* and *sarod*-playing descendants were Gul Muhammad Khan, Hasan Ali Khan, Haqdad Khan and his son Na'matullah Khan. Na'matullah Khan was the first in the family to establish a link with *dhrupad* musicians when he learned from Basat Khan in Calcutta after Wajid Ali Shah's exile from Lucknow. He became one of the most prominent *sarodias* of this time, and will be discussed at some length in relation to Calcutta. His two sons were Karamatullah Khan and Asadullah, called Kaukabh or Kaukab Khan, also well-known *sarodias*. A son of Hasan Ali Khan's was Karam Khan, who was a *sarodia* at the time of *dhrupad* singer Bairam Khan in mid 19th-century Alwar. His son, Kifait Khan, was in service in Alwar and Bhopal. One of Kifait Khan's sons in 20th-century Bulandshahar was *sitār* player Shafiqullah Khan, who played the *sitār* with two *mizrāb's*, of which a recording exists. Descendants of this line are said to remain in Bulandshahar.

Intermarriage among the last three *sarod* families brought together the lines of Sakhawat Husain, Na'matullah Khan and Fida Husain. Shafiqullah Khan married Na'matullah Khan's sister; Shafayat Ali married Na'matullah Khan's daughter and his sister married Fida Husain. Sakhawat Husain married Kaukab Khan's daughter.

The Eastern Centers

Lucknow, Banaras, Bihar

Safdar Husain Khan of Delhi, the author of "*Qānūn-i sitār*," says of the playing of *sitār* players in the east:

> This recent *bāj* is somewhat difficult because its *bols* are *āḍ* [complex] and the movement of the *gats* is fast, which is why *addhā tāla* is played. And the elaboration of these *gats* is also troublesome. When this writer was in the east and the south, often friends there would play Purbī style *sitār*. Although I was with them for months, I never

> heard anything from them but *gat* and *toḍā*, and if they got separated from the *tāla*, then only God was their keeper (Khan, M. S. H. 1873: 17).

At mid-century, Lucknow, Patna and Banaras remained the centers of the lively Purab *bāj* style of *sitār* music, while the slower and more elaborate Delhi or Masitkhani style retained prominence in the environs of Delhi and Jaipur. Calcutta would soon emerge as the melting pot of 19th-century instrumental music. By the end of the century the movement of musicians all over North India would bring both styles into the repertoire of all professional *sitār* players. Compositions in both styles attributed to artists of the last half of the 19th century still make up much of the prized repertoire of traditional instrumentalists.

With the British takeover of Avadh, the departure of Wajid Ali Shah for Calcutta with a large number of musicians, and one year later the fighting and aftermath of the rebellion, Lucknow's musical activites were more or less suspended. Karam Imam says that a musician who returned after the British takeover saw that "the connoisseurs of Lucknow had ceased to hold musical concerts because of fear of the new regime" (Vidyarthi 1959:26). In popular history, little is heard of Lucknow in this period. Lucknow books on music such as the "*Ghunchah-i rāg*" (Khan, N. M. A. 1879), and the "*Ma'dan al-mūsīqī*" (Khan, M. K. I. 1925), however, indicate that musical interest remained strong in the post-1858 period there. One instrumentalist is associated with Lucknow right after the rebellion. Azam Khan of Kalpi (between Lucknow and Jhansi) was a *bīn* player, *dhrupad* singer and *sitār* player. He had learned from his father, Husain Khan, a *bīnkār* who lived in Jahanabad, near Jhansi. He played in a *dhrupad* style on the *sitār*, and is said to have helped introduce *dhrupad* elements into Lucknow *sitār* playing (Srivastav 1976:n.p.).

The last decade of the 19th century saw a revival of musical activity in the Lucknow area. S. K. Chaubey calls it a "second awakening," and says that it saw "the ultimate flowering of genius in Lucknow music" (Chaubey 1958:n.p.). *Kathak* dance, *tablā* playing and *ṭhumrī* music were the specialties of late 19th-century Lucknow, and modern performers trace their traditions to near legendary artists of that day. In instrumental music, Azam Khan's son Abdul Ghani, was a prominent *sitār* player in the small state of Khajurgaon, Rai Bareli, near Lucknow. Abdul Ghani was addicted to opium, and it is said that every day the Rājā of Khajurgaon would send a horse to Lucknow to bring sugar cane, opium and sweets for Abdul Ghani. He lived until 1938. His main disciple was a well-known 20th-century Lucknow *sitār* player, Yusuf Ali Khan (1870-1962).[137] Modern Lucknow's Ilyas Khan was a disciple of

Yusuf Ali Khan. Besides Abdul Ghani and Yusuf Ali Khan, a *sitār* player named Hamid Husain appears in this period. He traced his learning tradition to the original Purab *bāj* through Barkat Ali, called Sanvalia Khan of Farukhabad, a disciple of Pyar Khan. Hamid Husain was the son of Tulan Khan who was a Lucknow *sārangī* player known along with his brother Turab Khan. Their father was a musician named Izzat Khan (Srivastav 1976:n.p.). No *sarod* players for this period are mentioned, but in the 20th century *sarod* would return to Lucknow with Sakhawat Husain at the Marris, later Bhatkhande, Music College.

Karam Imam speaks of the Banaras ruler, Udit Narain Singh, as one of the best patrons of the mid-19th century. A few instrumentalists stand out in the post-1858 period. Two sons of Ja'far Khan, namely Kazim Ali and Sadiq Ali Khan, mentioned in connection to Rampur, are associated with Banaras, and must have spent some time there. A *bīnkār* in the late 19th-century Banaras court was Waras Ali Khan, adopted son of Makhu Khan of Tilianaga near Rajghat in Banaras. Waras Ali is said to have learned *bīn* from Baḍe Muhammad Khan, "Jagat (World) Guru."[138] It seems likely that Waras Ali Khan's teacher was not the *khyāl* singer, but Muhammad Khan, the son of Ghulam Muhammad, *sitār*/*surbahār* player and disciple of *bīnkār* Umrao Khan. References to Muhammad Khan *bīnkār* and *surbahār* player are found in connection with Bengal. Waras Ali's son, Abbas Ali, became a *bīnkār* at the court of Hyderabad. An important disciple of his was his nephew Ashiq Ali Khan, to whom he taught *surbahār* in a *bīn* style using three *mizrābs*.[139] Ashiq Ali was the father of the important modern *sitār* player Mushtaq Ali Khan.

Tagore says that *sitār* players Pannalal Bajpai and an amateur named Babu Mahesh Chandra Sarkar, a Bengali, "were two of the best Setar players of Benaras of the modern day" (Tagore 1963:60). Bajpai was a Banaras Brahmin. Karam Imam says about him

> He plays *sitār* very well with two *mizrābs* and earns his living in this way. But he is an *atāī* [untrained musician]. His hand is sweet, but his grasp of *rāga* is doubtful (Khan, M. K. I. 1925:45).

Recordings of two early 20th-century *sitār* players, Waliullah Khan and Shafiqullah Khan, also of Purab background and players who used two *mizrābs*, show that they used them rapidly in succession for an occasional emphasis of the inward "*dā*" stroke. Purab *gats* attributed to Bajpai are found in the repertoires of some traditional *sitār* players. They are fast, melodically interesting and rhythmically complex.[140] Bajpai appears to have been someone from a non-musical lineage who learned from scattered sources. As such he represents a group who would contribute significantly to the development of 20th-century *sitār* playing. Bajpai also stands out as one of the few Hindus who were prominent in the 19th century. His success as a *sitār* player is indicated by the presence of his *gats* in later performance tradition.

In Bihar, Patna, Darbhanga and Gaya stand out for contributions in the history of instrumental music. Patna was a city of strong British presence and *navābī* nobility, and it saw a certain amount of musical activity in the 19th century. We find that the ambitious and clever Ghulam Raza had settled there with his son, Ali Raza, after their banishment from Avadh. Ghulam Raza established himself as a nobleman; he probably had brought with him a great deal of wealth from Lucknow. For the post-rebellion period, more is heard of Ali Raza than of Ghulam Raza, and Ali Raza is sometimes given credit for founding the Razakhani *bāj*. *Gats* attributed to him are to be found in modern performance tradition. He evidently was effective in legitimizing his father's style. It is satisfying to note the conclusion of the colorful and successful career of Ghulam Raza. Books published in Patna, such as the "*Guldastah-i mūsīqī*" (Bhaju Lal 1873) and "Sangit or the Rudiment of Hindustani Music" (Bhatt 1880) contain exclusively Purab style *gats*. No other outstanding musicians are spoken of in relation to later 19th-century Patna. Figure 76 is a company-style painting of an unnamed Patna *sitār* player.

Darbhanga was a prosperous though small music center from the late 18th century, and continues to be the home of a prominent line of *dhrupad* musicians to the present day. The musical history of Darbhanga begins with Bhupat Khan, said to be a son of Na'mat Khan himself. Bhupat Khan was the teacher of the first in the line of Mallik family musicians, a family that came to dominate Darbhanga *dhrupad* music. Vocal music was predominant in the Mallik family, although instrumentalists are spoken of as well. Naval Mallik was a *bīn* player of the early 19th century, and Ganu Mallik, somewhat later, a *sitār* player (Mallik n.d.:1). S. M. Tagore tells us in 1896 that the Maharaja of Darbhanga, Sir Laksmisvar Singh, himself "plays on the *Setár* ... excellently well" (Tagore 1963:76). By far the most famous *sitār* player of Darbhanga, and one of the leading *sitār* players of his time, was the early 20th-century Ramesvar Pathak. He is said to have learned from Basat Khan who had moved to Bihar after living for some time with Wajid Ali Shah in Calcutta, or from Basat Khan's son Muhammad Ali Khan. Ramesvar Pathak played in both the Purab and Delhi styles, and his style and technique had a significant impact on 20th-century *sitār* music. His grandson was the modern *sitār* player Balram Pathak.

The Darbhanga court also supported a prominent *sarod* line. Murad Ali Khan, brother of Nanhe Khan of Gwalior, came to Darbhanga, and is recognized as one of the leading *sarod* players of his time. In at least one source he is given credit for being the first to put metal strings and a metal fingerboard plate on the *sarod* (Kosar 1956:120). His son, who also stayed in Darbhanga, was Abdullah Khan. S. M. Tagore writes that the Darbhanga Maharaja "has in his service a performer on the Sarod, who is considered one of the best players on the instrument of the present day" (Tagore 1963:76), referring to either Murad Ali or Abdullah Khan. Abdullah Khan's son was *sarodia* Amir Khan, who moved to Calcutta and was the teacher of the important modern *sarod* player Radhika Mohan Maitra.

The city and district of Gaya is notable in the history of instrumental music after mid-century. Basat Khan settled in the area when he went from Calcutta to Tikri state in 1859 (Roy Chaudhury 1969:48-9). After that time, Gaya felt the influences of other Bihar centers such as Darbhanga and Bettia, a center also known for its *dhrupad gharānā*, and Calcutta. Maula Bakhsh of Gujarat is among the prominent musicians who had contact with Gaya (Dayal n.d.:n.p.). Although Gaya never became famous for its *sitār* or *sarod* players, it did become notable for its cultivation of two more unusual instruments, the *isrāj*, and later the harmonium. Swami Prajnanananda writes of the *isrāj*,

> When Md. Basat Khan, a renowned Mohammedian [sic] artist settled from Calcutta at Gaya, perhaps he took it and introduced it at Gaya. Then the renowned artists like Kanailal Dhedji and others of Gaya took this (easily accessed) instrument Esraj with care, and began to culture, [sic] and this instrument was much appreciated at Gaya, and gradually was appreciated in Bengal too (Prajnanananda 1973:468).

Oral tradition names several of the *isrāj*'s most prominent players as residents of Gaya. The harmonium was probably introduced to Indian musicians in Calcutta, where it had been brought from England. The time of the harmonium's introduction into India is difficult to pinpoint, but it must have been used in British households before it was taken up by Indian musicians. One of its earliest references is in the Bengali "*Gīta sūtra sār*" (Bandyopadhyaya, K. 1885:140). Books devoted entirely to harmonium appear not long after.[141] In Gaya it gained some prestige as a solo instrument in the 20th century.

Bengal

It was only after 1858 that Calcutta and wider Bengal began to emerge as centers of mainstream activity, but Bengal quickly became a preeminent music center in late 19th-century India. Musicians in urban Bengal became so numerous that it is helpful to think of them in at least three categories: professional musicians from outside Bengal, Bengali scholars and professionals, and amateurs. The interchange among the categories created the Bengal music scene. Wajid Ali Shah's dethronement and arrival in Calcutta with a large number of musicians was the main source of the first category. A historically significant set of social and educational factors in Bengal was behind the phenomenal rise of the second and third groups.

The first quarter of the 19th century saw a movement for English education that was to shape the history of modern India. In Calcutta it began in 1817 with the founding of the Hindu College, the work of the great reformer Ram Mohun Roy. It soon was followed up by British policy, so that in 1835 a resolution was passed "that the great object of the British government ought to be the promotion of European literature and science." Funds should "be henceforth employed in imparting to the Native population knowledge of English literature and science through the medium of the English language" (Spear 1978:127). Consequently, institutions for English education were set up, and through English, new sets of values and ways of thinking were introduced on a large scale to the upper and middle classes of urban Bengal. Around 1870, an "educational explosion" saw the Bengali public taking over the initiative in setting up more schools and pressing for more universities (*ibid.*:167). The result of English education was the emergence of individuals who would be the leaders in new cultural and religious movements. In the cultural sphere, the interest in Indian history, especially of classical Hindu India, that had been initiated by scholars such as Sir William Jones in the late 18th century, was now taken up by Indians. Beginning as a rediscovery of lost cultural traditions, it was to gradually take on a nationalist lean.

A prominent Calcutta music scholar was Ksetra Mohan Gosvami, author of "*Ṣaṅgīt sār*" (1870) and other books in Bengali, and a teacher of Sourindro Mohun Tagore. He was the first to create a system of musical notation that became widely accepted. Krisnadhan Bandyopadhyaya was another important writer on music. His "*Sitār śikṣā*" of 1866 is among the earliest handbooks for learning the *sitār*. Its large number of *gats* and songs are carefully formulated in Western notation. Technical information is admirably detailed. His "*Gīta sūtra sār*" of 1885 is an early modern study of Indian music theory.

Sir Sourindro Mohun Tagore was a member of one of the prominent aristocratic families of 19th-century Calcutta. Educated at Hindu College, he made music his chosen field, and studied with a number of teachers, including European musicians. His work in music education and his numerous books on theory, history and practice make him one of the most visible figures in the 19th-century Bengali music field (cf. Rosse 1980:525-6). In his books and schools Tagore interpreted musical tradition for urban Bengalis and defended it from attacks by British critics. In 1871 he founded the Bengal Music School, the first institution for music learning in India. It was a place

> where vocal music and some of the drawing room instruments began to be taught with the aid of books and according to a system of notation (Tagore 1963:87-8).

In 1881 he founded the Bengal Academy of Music, a larger version of the earlier school with a wider scope of activity:

> The object of this institution is mainly to encourage the study and practice of Hindu music by the establishment of schools and by the awarding of complimentary titles and insignias thereof to distinguished musicians (*ibid.*:88).

The schools were built on Western models, but their aim carried out the ideas of the Bengal renaissance, renewed awareness of and pride in Indian history and culture. On the model of Tagore's pioneering work, institutions for learning music began to appear in other parts of India. The first in western India was the Gayan Samaj in Pune, established in 1879. It carried out a program of concerts and lectures, teaching and publishing, and its records are valuable sources for the music of the period. Such music institutions nourished the growing amateur enthusiasm, encouraging the participation of larger and larger numbers of people.

Tagore wrote books in Bengali for the middle classes of Calcutta. His important "*Yantra Kshetra Dipika*," published in 1872, is a detailed account of the *sitār* and contains a large and sophisticated collection of *gats*. One of his English publications is a valuable collection of early writings by Englishmen on Indian music. It was first published in 1875 and again with a second part under the title "Hindu Music" in 1882. By this time there was an English-reading Bengali public interested in the history and theory of its music. In the article "Hindu Music" Tagore defends their interests, responding to a British criticism of Indian music:

> We are sorry to perceive that Mr. Clarke still persists in his original misconception of the real character of Hindu music. ... We believe he is a searcher after truth, and if he will, in a kindly spirit, accept the light which we, in all humility, offer to him, he may yet find out that priceless treasure (Tagore 1965:339).

Scholarly advocates of Indian music like Tagore could now eloquently reply in English to criticisms by prejudiced foreigners. His campaign built elaborate arguments for the scientific and historical equality of Indian with European music:

> There is nothing to make us regret that the principles of Acoustics, as they exhibit themselves in our music differ in form from the European system. We shall have occasion to shew as we proceed that the science of Acoustics, as it exists among the Hindus, is quite sufficient for all purposes as regards the application of its principles to music (*ibid*.:340).

After a detailed and technical retort of Mr. Clarke's criticisms he says:

> If this paper satisfies Mr. Clarke that in advocating the national system we are simply following reason, truth, and history, we will consider ourselves amply repaid (Tagore 1965: 387).

His "*Yantra Kosha*" (1875) includes discussions of Greek instruments, and attempts to establish the antiquity of Indian instrumental forms. Later among Tagore's works was the "Universal History of Music," a pioneer attempt at a discussion of the musics of different parts of the world.

Amateur Music in Calcutta: *sitār*

In the late 19th century across North India, a degree of amateur musical performance ability became an admired social grace, a phenomenon evidently inspired by British social life. While amateur participation thrived across India at this time, in Calcutta musical involvement extended to an especially wide cross-section of the public. The medium for acquiring a rudimentary practical skill was usually "the simplest and most popular musical instrument in use amongst the natives of this country" (Tagore 1965:346), the *sitār*. In Calcutta it was played by amateurs who varied widely in their musical sophistication. Calcutta woodcuts and Kalighat paintings depict gentlemen and ladies seated on chairs in parlor settings (Figures 34 and 35). Some amateurs made serious efforts at learning the classical forms. Those who wanted a working knowledge of *gat-toḍā*, *tāla*, and techniques could attend Tagore's school, or use *"Sitār śikṣā"* (Bandyopadhyaya K. 1866) and *"Yantra Kshetra Dipika"* (Tagore 1879) which offered *gats* in a large number of *rāgas*. Most fortunate among amateur players were a number of wealthy landowners and aristocrats who could afford to promote and study under prominent professionals of the day. Tagore mentions the names of several "aristocratic families of Bengal and especially of Calcutta who were generous patrons" (Tagore 1963:86). He says of Calcutta patron Babu Ashutosh Deb, "popularly known as Shatu Babu" that "He was a skilful player of the *Sétar*, and the composer of many songs" (*ibid.*). The Tagore family itself was among the most famous of Calcutta patrons and supported some of the leading musicians of the day. On the background of the booming amateur musical environment of late 19th-century Calcutta, we now turn to the professional activity in instrumental music there.

Professionals from Lucknow: Basat Khan and Family

In 1856 Wajid Ali Shah brought with him to Calcutta a large number of musicians who eventually spread and settled in various centers of the east. In his court in Matia Burj in the suburbs of Calcutta, Wajid Ali Shah supported musicians until his death in 1887, but the scene around him was not comparable to what it had been in Lucknow. Musicians found other enthusiastic and generous patrons, and many left the service of Wajid Ali Shah after a short time. Most important among *dhrupad* instrumentalists who came from Lucknow was Basat Khan. He, his two sons and his brother Ja'far Khan's grandson, Kasim Ali, lived with Wajid Ali Shah for two years (Roy Chaudhury 1969:48-9). In Calcutta, he taught one of the outstanding figures in *sarod* playing, Na'matullah Khan. Basat Khan soon left Calcutta, and settled in Tikri state in the Gaya district of Bihar, where he died in 1887.

After Basat Khan's death, his eldest son, Ali Muhammad, went to Banaras where he lived until his death in 1898. The second son, Muhammad Ali, became well-known in Bengal as the last *rabāb* player in his line (Figure 53). It is said of Muhammad Ali that he was originally a vocalist, and took up *rabāb* only after his father's death. Calcutta oral tradition tells us that Muhammad Ali, when young, used to ask his father for money for extravagant or trivial purposes, such as buying pigeons. Once, his annoyed father gave him the money that he had asked for, but made him declare that in exchange he would give back all the *tālīm*, training, that he had received. Muhammad Ali made the declaration, and after that time was never the same. He would sometimes forget what he was singing and sing the *sthāī* (first line) of one *rāga* and the *antarā* (second line) of another.[142] Muhammad Ali moved to the court of Gidhaur, and also stayed for some time in Banaras after his brother's death there. In the early 20th century he lived for a time in Rampur where he taught Chamman Sahab, in Lucknow where Thakur Navab Ali took his help in writing his "*Maarifun naghmāt*" (Khan, M. N. A. 1927), and finally in the Mymen Singh district of Bengal at the estates of the famous Roy Chaudhury family, where some family members became his disciples. Among his disciples were the musician-scholars Birendra Kishore Roy Choudhury of Gauripur, and Jyotish Chandra Chaudhury of Bhavanipur, the latter one of my own teachers in Banaras.

Basat Khan's grand-nephew, Kasim Ali, had left Calcutta with him but went to Nepal, which was a center for some well-known musicians of the time. Kasim Ali is remembered in relation to both Calcutta and Nepal, and had disciples in both places. The movements of Basat Khan and his family are representative of the lives of many professional musicians in the 19th and early 20th centuries. The family's musical career began in Delhi. When the court failed they moved to Lucknow and Banaras, and after mid-century spread in different directions to Rampur and Calcutta. From Calcutta they moved to whatever center they could find patrons.

Despite the presence of Basat Khan and his family, Calcutta never became a strong center for *dhrupad* music. A center in Bengal that did become known for its *dhrupad* music was Vishnupur, located about seventy miles northwest of Calcutta. The Vishnupur line of Bengali musicians is traced to an unnamed disciple of Basat Khan's cousin, Bahadur Khan. One of the prominent members of the line, Jadu Bhatt, is also said to have learned from Kasim Ali (Roy Chaudhury 1975:185). The relationship of the Vishnupur line to Basat Khan's family seems strong. Later exponents of the Vishnupur line played *bīn*, *sitār* and *isrāj*, and also sang *khyāl*, *ṭappā* and *ṭhumrī*. Vishnupur musicians stand out for their multi-faceted interest and for their attention to the details and unique characteristics of each separate form. Vishnupur will appear again in the discussion below.

Sitār and *surbahār* in Bengal

The single most outstanding and influential instrumentalist of later 19th-century Calcutta was Sajjad Muhammad Khan, son of Muhammad Khan and grandson of Ghulam Muhammad of Lucknow. There is some question over the identity of Muhammad Khan. Many sources do not mention him, saying that Sajjad Muhammad was Ghulam Muhammad's son. But the time gap between the two would point to a generation between them, and Bengal sources mention Muhammad Khan as a *bīn* and *surbahār* player. Satya Kinkar Banerji, representing the Vishnupur oral tradition, spoke of Muhammad Khan as Sajjad Muhammad's father, and said that he was a musician in the state of Govardanga, about thirty-five miles northeast of Calcutta.[143] A letter by the Gujarati musician-scholar Maula Bakhsh written sometime before 1874 in support of Ksetra Mohan Gosvami's notational system has the signature of Muhammad Khan *bīnkār*.[144] It is an appropriate time for Sajjad Muhammad's father to have lived. References also occur in oral histories of this line to a musician named Ghulam Abbas. His identity and relationship to the line are not clear. He may be the same person as Muhammad Khan since one source names Ghulam Muhammad's son as Abbas Muhammad Khan (Khan, K. 1908:168). More genealogical information on this line needs to be collected and sorted out.

Sajjad Muhammad lived under the patronage of S. M. Tagore's brother Jatindra Mohan Tagore and had a wide impact in Bengal in both *sitār* and *surbahār* playing. He is known for playing *dhrupad ālāp* on the *surbahār* and Purab *bāj gats* on the *sitār*. Satya Kinkar Banerji had in his *sitār* repertoire *gats* composed by Sajjad Muhammad. According to him and demonstrated in the *gats*, Sajjad Muhammad specialized in the use of *kṛntan*, a left hand technique, and used it a great deal in his playing (see Part Three). Sajjad Muhammad's influence is indicated by the strong presence of the *surbahār* in late 19th-century Bengal. Fox-Strangways in 1914 speaks of the *surbahār* as "a large satar common in Bengal" (Fox-Strangways 1970:172). Ghulam and Sajjad Muhammad were so important for the *surbahār* that practically all musicians who carry a tradition of *surbahār* playing trace some connection to them.

One of the most outstanding *sitār* players of late 19th-century Bengal and the figure of the time most known by modern musicians was Imdad Khan. Imdad Khan lived at various centers during his life but gained most of his fame in Calcutta where he was a musician at Jatindra Mohan Tagore's estate along with Sajjad Muhammad. Imdad Khan was born at Etawah, about eighty-five miles northwest of Kanpur. His father, Sahabdad Khan, was a *sārangī* player who is said to have learned from the famous Gwalior *khyālias* and also from the *bīnkār* Nirmal Shah (Roy Chaudhury 1975:203). Sahabdad Khan is also said to have played *sitār* and *surbahār*, and credit for inventing the *surbahār* is given to him by family members and disciples. Some also claim that he was the first to put *tarab* strings on the *sitār* and *surbahār*. The evidence that Ghulam Muhammad was responsible for both of these innovations is overwhelming, but Sahabdad Khan's presence in the same time and area allows for a possibility that he played some role. Sahabdad Khan rigorously trained his son from an early age and then directed him to become a disciple of a Tansen-descended musician.[145] In Indore, Imdad Khan is said to have learned from the great *bīnkār* Bande Ali Khan. Two of his granddaughters married Majid and Latif Khan, disciples of Bande Ali (Roy Chaudhury 1975:202). Leaving Indore, Imdad Khan stayed for some time in Banaras, which was at the forefront of developments in *ṭhumrī* music and *tablā* playing. From there he was invited to Calcutta by Jatindra Mohan Tagore. After Tagore's death in the early 20th century, he lived at the estate of another Calcutta landowner, Tara Prasad Ghosh. Sajjad Muhammad had an important influence on his playing during this time.[146] Imdad Khan became famous for a unique and innovative style, which later made him known as one of the fathers of 20th-century *sitār* playing. He later returned to Indore, where he died around 1920.

A number of musical influences figure in Imdad Khan's background, and they all played a part in the creation of his *sitār* style. A familiarity with *sārangī* and *khyāl* came from his father. In Indore, Bande Ali Khan was a source for *bīn* techniques and innovative style. From Banaras came the influences of *ṭhumrī* and *tablā* and from Calcutta the *dhrupad* and Purab styles of Sajjad Muhammad Khan. Imdad Khan played *surbahār* in a *dhrupad* style, but he is most well-known for his innovative *sitār* playing. He is credited with the addition to *sitār* of a number of vocal ornamentations and *tāns*, generous use of *mīḍ*, and certain specific types of *jhālā* patterns. Representatives of his line say that his special gift was the addition of vocal *khyāl* techniques at a time when other instrumentalists, especially the late Jaipur Senias, were taking a strict stand against mixing vocal forms in their music. In the light of our knowledge about Rahimsen and Amrtsen's use of *khyāl* techniques, however, it would be more appropriate to propose that Imdad Khan contributed a daring new range of ideas and techniques to *sitār* which were perhaps directly imitative of vocal *khyāl*.

Imdad Khan played both slow and fast *gats*. His style in rendering them was so unique that it came to be called the Imdadkhani *bāj* in some circles. Imdadkhani *gats* have been described differently by different members of the line. D. T. Joshi says that the slow Imdadkhani *gat* used only a three-*mātrā* (three-beat) *mukhḍā* (lead-in phrase) instead of the normal five-*mātrā* one. Imdad Khan's grandson, Imrat Khan, described the fast Imdadkhani *gat* as one having the *bol* pattern "*dā dir dā rā -- dā -r dā dā -- dā rā dā rā dā rā.*" Mainly, however, the Imdadkhani *bāj* was not a *gat* type but an overall playing style. Imdad Khan's son, Inayat Khan, carried his father's work further and became one of the most innovative and popular artists of his time. They both contributed a number of now universally employed elements to *sitār* playing. Inayat Khan's style and period extends beyond the scope of this study and deserves detailed research in its own right, as do the contributions of his elder son, Vilayat Khan, one of the greatest *sitār* players of our time, and his younger son, Imrat Khan.

In Vishnupur, *sitār* playing sprang out of the center's own musical resources, an outcome of the phenomenal popularity of the instrument in the 19th century. Members of this line mention no outsiders' names for the origin of its *sitār* style, saying it is "traditional." However, contact with Calcutta and other centers was evident in the repertoire of Satya Kinkar Banerji. Among his *gats* were compositions by Ali Raza of Patna, Bajpai of Banaras and Sajjad Muhammad of Calcutta. In *ālāp*, he played in a style that could have come directly from the Vishnupur *dhrupad* tradition. Another 20th-century *sitār* player in Vishnupur was Gokul Nag, who settled in Calcutta, and was the father of the modern-day *sitār* player Manilal Nag.

In the late 19th and early 20th centuries, other *sitār* players lived in various cities of Bengal. Bhagvan Das Sitaria (1852-1931) was a native of Bihar who settled in Dacca and became a well-known *sitār* player of the region (Figure 38).[147] Waliullah Khan, grandson of *sarodia* Na'matullah Khan, was an early 20th-century *sitār* player in Bengal. He played *sitār* with two *mizrābs* and recordings of him provide a good source for the style of that line.

Sarod in Bengal

Later 19th-century Bengal is noted for a few outstanding *sarod* players. The earliest in the area was Na'matullah Khan, who learned from Basat Khan in Matia Burj under Wajid Ali Shah's patronage. He is said to have added metal strings and a metal fingerboard to his instrument at this time, and it is likely that he was the author of these changes. Na'matullah Khan remained for eleven years with Wajid Ali Shah, and then moved to Nepal, where he remained in service in the court for thirty years. In 1903 he left Nepal and returned to Delhi, where he died not long after (Khan, K. 1908:161). Descendants provide additional details about Na'matullah Khan and his family. They say that he initiated a tradition of "music with education." The generations following him took pride in obtaining a high degree of education, and made it a point to associate with members of the upper classes.[148] Members of Na'matullah Khan's line claim that he was the first *sarod* player to play in the Masitkhani style on the *sarod*. Other lines make the same claim for their ancestors. While middle and fast-speed *gats* were predominant on early *sarod*, it is reasonable to accept that both *ālāp* and the slow *gat* style began to be played on that instrument from around mid-century.

Na'matullah's two sons were prominent instrumentalists. The elder was Karamatullah Khan. Born in the family home of Bulandshahar about 1848, Karamatullah Khan lived in Nepal, then moved around to various places until settling in Allahabad where he opened a private school and taught a large number of students. He travelled frequently to other centers, including Calcutta, where he had more students. He is said to have collected lakhs of rupees in wealth (Munib 1925:10). Although Karamatullah Khan played both slow Masitkhani and fast Purab style *gats*, almost all of his *gats* found in performance tradition are in the Purab style. Na'matullah Khan's second son was Asadullah, called Kaukabh or Kaukab Khan, who was born in Nepal about 1858. He was highly educated and had even studied the Sanskrit language. He married the daughter of vocalist Taj Khan, another of Wajid Ali Shah's former musicians. A member of the Tagore family brought Kaukab Khan from Nepal to Calcutta where he gained much of his fame. In 1908 Kaukab Khan and his brother were taken by Motilal Nehru, father of Jawaharlal Nehru, to Paris and England for demonstrations at an international exhibition at Wembley. The story goes that Kaukab Khan's *sarod* was broken on the trip, and when he got to Paris he was given a Western banjo. He removed the frets, put a metal plate over the fingerboard, and played it like the *sarod*. His success on the new instrument was such that he continued to play it even upon his return to India. He became more famous on the banjo than on the *sarod*. Some recordings of his banjo playing and other recordings cf family members show extremely high-speed work. Kaukab Khan died in Calcutta in 1917.[149]

In the *sarod* line of Ghulam Ali *rabābia*, his grandson (according to his descendents), Asghar Ali, was well-known in Calcutta. He is said to have had a very sweet touch, and could make the *sarod* "sound like the flute" (Roy Choudhury 1973:n.p.). He died in the early 20th century. Ghulam Ali's great grandson was Amir Khan, son of Abdullah Khan of Darbhanga. Amir Khan lived at estates in the Bengal districts of Rajshahi and Gauripur and taught some of his patrons. His most prominent modern disciple was Radhika Mohan Maitra (cf. Maitra n.d.:n.p.).

In a second line, Ahmad Ali Khan, a *sarod* player mentioned in connection with Rampur, is also associated with Dinajpur, Bengal. He

Fig. 77. Maula Baksh. *Photograph of a portrait from the collection of Manmath Roy. Sangeet Natak Akademi. 278/o.*

Fig. 78. Sitār *player Anna Gharpure. Day 1974:116.*

Fig. 79. *Musicians from Aurangabad, Maharashtra, c1870. By permission of the British Library. IOL Photo: 2/10 (16a).*

Fig. 80. *Musicians from Dhar, Maharashtra, 1902. By permission of the British Library. IOL Photo 430/23 (18d) Curzon.*

Fig. 81. *A dancer and accompanists. Russell & Hira Lal 1916-II:374-5. By permission of the British Library. IOL T 36651.*

was another of the early teachers of Allauddin Khan. It is said of his playing that he "played tarana like a singer" (Maitra n.d.:n.p.), an indication of a trend to imitate vocal genres directly.

Allauddin Khan, one of the fathers of 20th-century instrumental music, was born about 1881 in Comilla, Tripura district, now in Bangla Desh, the son of Sadu Khan. He went to Dacca and then Calcutta, where he joined the school opened by S. M. Tagore and studied a number of different instruments. His subsequent move to Rampur and his concentration on the *sarod* under Ahmad Ali, Fida Husain and especially Wazir Khan is legend to modern musicians. His story and that of his daughter Annapurna Devi, his son Ali Akbar Khan and his disciple Ravi Shankar, are the subjects of a number of recent and ongoing studies.[150] His profound contributions to 20th-century instrumental music require separate treatment, and can only be alluded to here.

Other Centers: Gujarat and Maharashtra

Although Gujarat is not popularly recognized as a main center for instrumental music in the 19th century, certain cities and princely states there were active and worthy of mention. Baroda was a state known in the late 19th century for its courtly culture. An outstanding musician and scholar associated with Baroda is Maula Bakhsh (Figure 77). He was an acclaimed writer and demonstrated a knowledge in a wide range of forms and instruments, including the music of South India. He travelled extensively. In Calcutta he received a gold medal at the Bengal Music School in 1874 (Tagore 1963:66). He wrote a petition in support of Ksetra Mohan Gosvami's notational system which Tagore appended to his article "Hindu Music." He must have spent some time in Gaya, as he is mentioned in that connection. He returned and settled in Gujarat where he opened an institute for music in Baroda in 1881. It later became the Music Department of Baroda University.[151] One of the efforts for which he was famous was a system of musical notation in Gujarati script, which followed upon that of Ksetra Mohan Gosvami. Maula Bakhsh had professional ties to Bombay, with which he is often associated. He died in 1896. His grandson was Inayat Khan, an accomplished *bīnkār* and *sitār* player, better known as Sufi Inayat Khan. He gained a tremendous following in Europe and America after he spent many years there in the 1920s. Sufi Inayat Khan wrote a number of books on Sufism and at least two on music. His Urdu "*Minqār mūsīqār*" published in Allahabad is a detailed and scholarly work providing valuable information and a number of *sitār gats* (Khan, I. 1912). In Baroda, another *bīnkār*, Jamaluddin Khan, is mentioned by Josi (Josi 1935:148), but no other information is provided.

Bhavnagar was another princely court in Gujarat known for its cultivation of music. It became especially known for its *dhrupad* musicians. A tradition of *sitār* playing in Bhavnagar is represented in the "*Saṅgīt kalādhar*" of 1900 (Shivram 1938), of which a large part is devoted to *sitār*. It is a carefully written and precise work presenting a good record of *tālas* in notation, and a large number of high standard *sitār gats*. *Gats* of four types are separately labelled. There are Masitkhani *gats*, Purbī *bāj gats*, Ghulam Raza *bāj gats* and Firozkhani *bāj gats*. Our survey of the 18th and 19th centuries has indicated that all of these categories are historically distinct. In the scholarly center of Bhavnagar, they evidently retained their distinction. Thus, the "*Saṅgīt kalādhar*" provides valuable resource in efforts to musically differentiate *gat* types.

Jamnagar was another scene of musical activity in late 19th-century Gujarat. The ruler, Aditramji, is said to have "systematized the whole of music art and science with fresh modal compositions" (Vyas 1916:2).

Pune and Bombay, centers of English society and education from a relatively early time, emerge as the scene of a prosperous British-influenced culture in post-1858 Hindustan. The English education movement was strong in these cities, which had a good deal in common with contemporary Calcutta. The Gayan Samaj exemplified this movement, founded in 1874 following on Tagore's Bengal Music School. The Gayan Samaj in Pune was organized by a group of professionals, lawyers and government employees who saw their mission as one "to revive a taste for our musical science amongst our brethren of the upper classes, and to raise it up in their estimation," and also

> to introduce and promote the cultivation of music as a domestic amusement amongst the Hindus who were now passing their B.A.'s in the educational movement of the 19th century (Sahasrabuddhe 1887:33).

We hear as further motivation for the Samaj a familiar view on the degenerate state of the art:

> The art became eventually obscured, and the science sank into oblivion until, at the present time, instances of men advanced in the art to any degree of accurate proficiency are few and far between (*ibid*.:3-4).

The Gayan Samaj was supported by the royalty of various surrounding states, and events were even attended by British royalty, officers and dignitaries. A nationalist stance, however, which outdid Tagore's with its strong political overtones, is expressed in reports and papers. The Secretary says:

> It was one of the outgrowths of an ambition to revive the ancient Arts and Sciences of India, and to restore to the land, under the great seal of time, the glory and the prestige which have been usurped by the nations of Europe.

The Samaj was to be

> instrumental in preserving our nationality in the sense of our possessing an indigenous art of singing, which, unlike English music has challenged all attempts at its being reduced to writing.[152]

The Gayan Samaj sponsored publications, lectures, demonstrations and concerts for members, guests and the public. Some references to instrumental music give us a picture of the environment:

> Perhaps the most popular of the contributers to the concert was Professor Balkoba Natekar, an accomplished singer, with a voice capable of sweetest modulations. His Satar accompaniments were remarkable for their dexterity of fingering ... (Sahasrabuddhe 1887:77)

The *sursingār* is also mentioned in a report of one demonstration:

> The first to exhibit his skill was Professor Moorar Bawa, whose many stringed instrument, the Sura Shringara, was most skilfully manipulated in the rendering of an air or two to the raga Bhimpalasha (*ibid.*).

The violin is given an early mention, described as being played by a Mr. Naidu and held in a "painfully cramped position" (*ibid.*).

The music sponsored by the Gayan Samaj as described here appears hardly representative of the professional music which was being performed in court settings across North India. However, some professionals became involved in the institution, and some good Maharastrian instrumentalists emerged out of the movement. Eknath Pandit, *bīnkār* and *sitār* player from Gwalior, worked with the Gayan Samaj for six years, presumably as a teacher, and he became a well-known figure in the Pune area.[153] A Pune patron, Dr. Vinayak Rao Limaye, invited *sitār* player Bicchu Khan, who was famous in the court of the Maharaj of Satara (in Madhya Pradesh) to Pune. Limaye became an accomplished performer and promoter of the *"Gulamrazā bāj"* (Limaye 1970:121). His disciple was Anna Gharpure (Figure 78) a government employee from a family of Sanskrit scholars, who became quite a famous *sitār* player in the early 20th century. Anna Gharpure worked with the Gayan Samaj, started a monthly periodical on music and wrote several books on *sitār* (Josi 1935:155). Josi makes the comment that Gharpure played the *sitār* like the *bīn*. There may be representatives of this *sitār* line in Pune today.

Bombay was a great urban center where, as in Calcutta, educated upper and middle classes were taking a growing interest in music in the later 19th century. Two amateur *bīnkārs* are mentioned in connection with Bombay. They both were in government service. Damodar Pant Malpekar worked in the railways, and Mangesrao Telang worked in the High Court (*ibid*.:149). In *sitār*, one professional musician is mentioned as prominent: Jivanji Maharaj played "both *vilampad* and *gat*" (Josi 1935: 156) and taught several students. One of his disciples was Visvanath Bua Kale, a lawyer who began a monthly periodical on music and wrote books on *sitār* and *tablā* (*ibid*.). Ethel Rosenthal, in "The Story of Indian Music and its Instruments" of 1928 remarks that the *sitār* was a prominent instrument in Bombay, more visible than the South Indian *vīṇā*, and that it was used by Parsi ladies to accompany their own singing (Rosenthal 1928:36-7). Bombay stands out as a center for amateur interest in the 19th century.

A number of *sitār* players were renowned in other cities of Western India. Astewale of Ujjain is said to have played both "*vilampat*" and *gat*, and was very popular. His son was named Bhaiya Sahab. In the city of Kolhapur, Rahmat Khan was a well known *sitār* player who lived into the 20th century and made a number of early recordings.[154] Figures 79 to 81 are late 19th- and early 20th-century photographs of musicians' groups from Maharashtra.

PART THREE:

TECHNIQUES AND COMPOSITIONS

7

Techniques and *ālāp*

Techniques from the bīn: gamak, mīḍ, sūt

Elements of continuity in Indian music are clear and traceable from the ancient period in textual sources, but over-emphasis on continuity is misleading if it obscures the changing musical times. A large number of instrumental techniques are described in Indian musicological texts, beginning with the *dhātu*, hand movements for harp-type instruments, in the *"Nāṭyaśāstra"* of Bharata. The 13th-century *"Saṅgīta-ratnākara"* represents a growing tradition, and in it techniques called *hasta* or *hasta vyāpāra* ("hand," or "hand movements"), for instruments using a small stick in the left hand to stop the string, number twenty-four. Twenty-four *gamakas*, ornamental techniques, are also listed in terms of vocal music. Techniques for the fretted *vīṇā* are found in texts dating from the 17th century. The *vādanabheda,* "types of instrumental playing," in the *"Rāgavibodha"* are so well described that they can be interpreted and demonstrated with little trouble (cf. Ayyangar 1980). The *"Saṅgītapārijāta"* and the *"Rāgatattvavibodha"* also contain descriptions of a number of *gamakas* with their methods of production on the *vīṇā.* Although modern performance techniques have strong ancestral connections to those recorded in the Sanskrit texts, many of the techniques handed down in the professional performance traditions have their immediate sources in the colloquial terminology of the Mughal or late Mughal period. A brief survey of some of the most important pre-20th-century *dhrupad* instrumental techniques follows, with reference to their Sanskrit sources only where the terminology is directly related.

Figure 67 is a drawing of a *bīn* with its description from the *"Sarmāya-i 'ishrat."* Oral histories speak of the *rudra vīṇā*, or the *bīn*, from the time of Tansen and his son-in-law Naubat Khan. It had been used for both accompaniment and solo music in a variety of musical settings. Later, partly under the pressure of competition from the *sitār*, it became concentrated in specialized circles, and *bīn* techniques became the prized and guarded possession of a few family lines. The antiquity, the high musical standard expected of its players, and the increasing secrecy of professionals regarding techniques gave the instrument a special mystique, especially as it was disappearing in the late 19th century. On the basis of the information that was carried by traditional instrumentalists into the 20th century, and from the 19th-century sources, it is possible to isolate many of the techniques of the *bīn* that were retained in *sitār* playing.

Dhrupad tradition tells us that exchange between vocal music and the *bīn* was an ongoing process, with influences moving in both directions. While the *bīn* tried to adopt vocal patterns, the voice also took ideas from instrumental techniques. *Gamaka* was a general term for ornamental techniques in medieval and late Sanskrit texts. Both vocalists and instrumentalists speak of a variety of *dhrupad*-related *gamak* techniques surviving in their traditions. Vimalakant Roy Chaudhury in his "*Bharatiya Sangeet Kosh*" lists twenty-two belonging to the tradition of the Tansen descendents.[155] Roy Chaudhury was a disciple of Dabir Khan, grandson of Rampur's *bīnkār* Wazir Khan, and is probably recording the tradition as learned from him. Some of the *gamaks* he lists are closely related in name to those in the Sanskrit texts. While some of these names were probably living in performance tradition, it is likely that others were artificially reintroduced from Sanskrit sources. 19th-century sources use the term *gamak* in its modern sense of a specific ornamental technique. In modern performance practice, it is a quick sliding movement which touches a higher note and returns to the original, and is usually repeated in a quick series. In fretted instruments it is performed by deflections of the string, and in non-fretted instruments by left hand slides. Some 19th-century descriptions of *gamaka* specify deflection *(mīḍ)* and others specify sliding.

Mīḍ or *mīnḍ*, a continuously sounded slide, is one of the most basic technical terms in Hindustani music. It has primarily been associated with stringed instruments that use a deflection of the string to produce a continuous sound over an interval of two or more notes from one fret position. The term does not resemble any of the named *gamakas* in the Sanskrit texts and first appears in the 18th century. Its origin was probably the Hindi *mīḍnā*, "to crush thoroughly" or "to rub with the hands." It is mentioned in the "*Saṅgīt sār*," where Pratap Singh says that it is used by *kalāvants* (trained musicians) as an equivalent to *gharṣaṇa*, (Sanskrit "rubbing") (Singh, S. P. 1910-12, Part 4:11). Karam Imam says *mīḍ* is played on the *bīn* by pressing the left thumb, pulling the main string and playing the stroke *dāūn* (Khan, M. K. I. 1925:227). The use of the term in vocal music and with non-fretted instruments may postdate its use with the *bīn*. It is one of the most fundamental techniques of *sitār* playing and is notated in the earliest written sources.

Another term associated with *dhrupad* stringed instruments is *sūt*. It denotes a sliding along the string of an instrument from one note to another, usually over an interval of several notes. The intervening notes are sounded lightly as the finger passes over their frets or positions on the neck. The term may derive from the Sanskrit *syūta*, "sewn together." *Syunt* is one of the Tansen descendents' *gamaks* listed by Roy Chaudhury. At the present day, *sūt* is normally thought of as a technique applicable to non-fretted instruments, and *ghasīṭ* (Hindi "drag" or "pull") the same technique on fretted instruments. The use of the word in the 19th-century *sitār* handbooks, however, shows that *sūt* was a term frequently used for the *sitār*, and it was probably used for the *bīn* before it. *Ghasīṭ* is found less frequently in 19th-century books.

Ālāp, joḍ, jhālā, ṭhonk, sargam *and Related Techniques*

A large number of *dhrupad* instrumental techniques formed the bases for sections or subsections of *ālāp*. In this section, a number of written and oral sources of *dhrupad* instrumental performance are scanned for the terms and technique-derived parts of *ālāp* they describe. *Joḍ* is an important term in this context. Written and oral traditions often use *joḍ* as a term for instrumental *ālāp*, applying equally to *bīn*, *sitār*, *surbahār*, *rabāb*, *sarod* and *sursingār*, distinguishing it from the longer and slower *ālāp* of vocal *dhrupad* music. Examples of instrumental *joḍ* as a faster-paced *ālāp* still exist in the performance repertoire of traditional musicians.[156] The word later came to be used as the term for the middle speed sections of *ālāp* after a slower-paced, full-scale *ālāp* began to be played on *sitār* and *surbahār*.

Four terms are fundamental to a discussion of *dhrupad*-based *ālāp* or *joḍ*. *Sthāī*, *antarā*, *sañcārī* and *ābhog* are the four sections that describe the internal range of melodic development in both *ālāp* and fixed *dhrupad* compositions. *Sthāī* (Sanskrit "standing," "constant") covers the middle range of the *rāga* from middle S to M or P. The *antarā* (Sanskrit "between") covers the higher range to high S. The definitions of *sañcārī* and *ābhog* differ in different traditions. *Sañcārī* (Sanskrit "wandering") is defined by some *dhrupad* performers as the section in which the melody line extends into the lower register, moving between Ṃ and M or P and Ṗ.[157] Others describe it as the section in which the melody jumps among the registers, mixing the phrases of the earlier sections.[158] *Ābhog* is usually defined as the melody line that moves into the upper register, above the *antarā* range. Some say it involves a working back from the upper range to middle S.[159] In *dhrupad* compositions, *ābhog* often begins with a leap from middle S to a note in the upper range, and gradually resolves back to middle S. In some traditions the *ābhog* section preceeds *sañcārī*.

Two written sources and two oral sources are used here to outline the sections and subsections that make up a full *ālāp* in some traditions. This is followed by an examination of the specific terms mentioned.

Karamatullah Khan represents the teaching of *rabābia* Basat Khan in his *"Israr-i karāmat."* He does not use the terms *sthāī*, *antarā*, *sañcārī* and *ābhog*, but follows a related pattern. In his account (Khan, K. 1908: 86-8), *ālāp* has three large sections, *bilampat*, *madh* and *drut* (Sanskrit *vilambita*, "slow," *madhya* "medium" and *druta*, "fast"). Bilampat has four subsections called *sancār*. The first *sancār* begins at the *bādī* (Sanskrit, *vādī*, the most important note of the *rāga*), and reaches as far as the S. It evidently begins from lower M or P. The second *sancār* begins at S and reaches to the *sambādī* (Sanskrit *samvādī*, the second most important note, usually a fourth or fifth from the *vādī*). Khan may mean the middle M or P. The third *sancār* begins from the S, moves to the *bādī*, *sambādī*, *bibādī* and *anubādī* (the probable reference is to the notes in decreasing hierarchy; in Sanskrit where these terms originate, the meanings are a disallowed note and a helping note), and returns to the S. The fourth *sancār* progresses to the notes higher than the high S, returns to R or G, touches the middle S three times, wanders over all the notes once more, and finally returns to middle S. In the entire *bilampat* section the strokes were in "single" rhythm *(ṭhā lay)*, but the four subsections of *bilampat* increased slightly in speed. Khan expresses this as

> one part stroke to two parts *tān* [here *tān* is simply note movement], one part stroke and three parts *tān*, one part stroke and four parts *tān* and two parts stroke and two parts *tān* (Khan, K. 1908:87).

If the strokes increase too much in speed, he says, it will become the *madh* section, called *joḍ*. Here the term *joḍ* is used in its modern sense. In *joḍ*, the strokes increase in frequency "but not too much" (*ibid.*:87). *Joḍ* has twelve subsections. In the first, the three elements melody *(sur)*, rhythm *(lay)* and stroke *(bol)* are all equal. He calls this *laḍī* (*ibid.*:88). In the second, the notes are "shaken," and this is called *gamak*. In the third, some notes are passed over to arrive at others. This is called *chūṭ*. In the fourth part, all three techniques, *laḍī*, *gamak* and *chūṭ*, are present, and this is called *dahak*. In the fifth section of *joḍ*, several notes are played in one stroke, and it is called *lahak*. Both *laḍī* and *chūṭ* are found in the sixth part, which is called *laḍguttāv*. *Gamak* and *laḍī* are found in the seventh part, which is called *muran*. *Gamak* and *chūṭ* together make up the eighth part, again called *dahak*. *Laḍī* and *dahak* are found in the ninth part. *Dahak* and *chūṭ* are found in the tenth part, and its rhythm is *āḍī* (complex). The eleventh part consists of *gamak*, *laḍak* and *dahak*. The twelfth has *dahak* and *lahak*. The twelve-part *joḍ* is followed by the *drut* section of *ālāp*, which Khan says is also called *ṭhonk*. Its strokes and rhythm are in double speed, although its melody is not. Its rhythms are complex, and *jhārā* is played here. This ends *ālāp*, but Khan goes on to list twenty-two *gamaks* out of the "*Rāgavibodha*" (Khan, K. 1908:88), and then lists and describes twenty-two, of unknown origin, based on Sanskrit terms.[160]

Vimalakant Roy Chaudhury in his "*Bharatiya Sangeet Kosh*" lists thirteen parts, *aṅga*, of *ālāp* (Roy Chaudhury 1975:11-14). This corresponds closely to the *ālap* described to me by Jyotish Chandra Chaudhury, who was also one of the disciples of Dabir Khan. The thirteen parts of Roy Chaudhury's *ālāp* are: (1) *vilambit*, (2) *madhya*, (3) *drut*, (4) *jhālā*, (5) *ṭhok*, (6) *laḍī*, (7) *laḍgutthī*, (8) *laḍlapeṭ*, (9) *paraṇ*, (10) *sāth*, (11) *dhūyā*, (12) *māṭhā*, and (13) *parmāṭhā*. The *vilambit* section consists of the *sthāī*, *antarā*, *sañcārī* and *ābhog*. Similarly to Karamatullah Khan's description, *vilambit* is played in three parts, each of which slightly increase in speed. They are called *vilambit-vilambit*, *vilambit-madhya* and *vilambit-drut*. The *madhya* or *madh*, middle-speed, section of *ālāp* is likewise divided into three parts of slightly increasing speed. The *madhya-vilambit* increases its use of *cikārī*, *mīḍ* and *syunt*. Ornaments, *alaṅkāras*, such as those listed in the "*Saṅgītaratnākara*" are also used here, says Roy Chaudhury (*ibid*.:12). The *madhya-madhya* part is called *madhya joḍ*, or *barābar kī joḍ*. A technique called *gamak joḍ* begins here. In this section, says Chaudhury, instrumentalists play largely on the frets, and do not use pulling techniques (*ibid*.:13). The *madhya-drut* part gets the term *laḍī joḍ* and hardly any *cikārī* is used in playing it. The fast section of *ālāp* again consists of three parts. *Drut-vilambit* employs *cikārī* only occasionally. *Drut-madhya* and *drut-drut* increase in speed. The important *jhālā* section of *ālāp* now begins. In *jhālā* the melodic movement is slow, but *cikārī* is heavily used. *Pakhāvaj* accompaniment may begin at this point. After *jhālā* the *ṭhonk* section begins, in which *jhālā* techniques are also used. *Jhālā*, *ṭhonk* and the next four mentioned *ālāp* sections, *laḍī*, *laḍgutthī*, *laḍlapeṭ* and *paraṇ* are discussed separately below. The techniques called *dhūyā*, *māṭhā* and *parmāṭhā* which make up the last three sections in Roy Chaudhury's *ālāp*, are not mentioned in other traditions. They are described by him as the playing of *laḍī*, *laḍgutthī* and *paraṇ* on various combinations of the main string and the *cikārī* strings (Roy Chaudhury 1975:11-5).

Mushtaq Ali Khan, representing the tradition of the Jaipur Senias and Muhammad Khan *bīnkār*, described four main parts of *ālāp* called *vilampat*, *madhya*, *drut* and *jhālā*. Each section has a number of subsections and specific techniques. *Vilampat* consists of *sthāī*, *antarā*, *sañcārī* and *ābhog*. In the *madhya* section, rhythmic movement, *gati*, is added, which becomes faster in the drut section, where techniques such as *gamak*, *palṭā*, *tān*, *āmad kī tān*, *kalam lagāna*, *kulfī lagānā* and *bāl pench* are used. The last six terms are taken from *khyāl* music and are fast techniques metaphorically describing different types of *mizrāb bols* and shapes of melodic movement. *Gamak*, *palṭā* and *tān* are terms commonly used in later *sitār* tradition, while the others are less used and are not commonly known, at least in name. Mushtaq Ali Khan said that in the last section called *jhālā*, the techniques *laḍī*, *laḍgutthāv* and *ṭhonk* are to be employed. These are discussed below.

Asad Ali Khan, representing the Alwar *bīn* tradition, states that *ālāp* was called *joḍ* in instrumental traditions, and that it moved somewhat faster than vocal *ālāp*. This seems to conform to the use of the term *joḍ* in several 19th-century sources. In Asad Ali Khan's tradition, the slow section consists of *sthāī*, *antarā*, *ābhog* and *sañcārī*. The second section, called *gamak joḍ*, uses techniques such as *huḍak*, *sur lagão*, *lagão*, *lāg ḍānṭ and tīkh chokh*. *Huḍak* is a *gamak*-related technique used by *dhrupad* vocalists. The others are specific *dhrupad* techniques now known by name within only a few specialized traditions. The third section, *jhālā*, consists of *joḍ jhālā*, *ṭhonk jhālā*, *laḍī* and *laḍgutthāv*.

In all the accounts surveyed here the slow speed portion of *ālāp* is described in similar terms. In regards to the second section of *ālāp*, however, D. T. Joshi, expressing what our descriptions here show, said that the middle speed portion in traditional instrumental *ālāp* had no set system, but differed from school to school.[161] Several techniques, however, are shared among most of the accounts. They are *laḍī*, *laḍgutthāv*, *laḍlapeṭ*, *jhālā*, *ṭhonk* and *tār paran*. These are also the techniques found the most frequently in later *sitār* and *sarod* performance traditions.

Laḍī, "chain" in Hindi (Mushtaq Ali Khan explained the word as meaning a "string of flowers"), musically refers to series of stroke combinations that form running, linked patterns. It is associated by some performers with the middle-speed portion of *ālāp* and by others with the fast *jhālā* section. The specific stroke patterns used for *laḍī* differ from school to school. Umar Khan defined *laḍī* for *sitār* and *sarod* as the *tāns* executed only with "*dā*" strokes in the section of *joḍ* preceding *jhālā*. He placed the related techniques *laḍgutthāv* and *laḍlapeṭ*, however, in the *jhālā* section. D. T. Joshi described *laḍī* as occurring in the second phase of *joḍ*, following on the beginnings of *gamak* called *lahak*. He said that *laḍī* uses stroke combinations such as:

dā rā dā rā dā rā dā rā dā rā rā rā;
dā dā dā rā, dā dā dā rā;
dā dā rā rā, dā dā rā rā;
dā rā dā dā rā dā, dā rā dā dā rā dā;
dā -- dā rā, dir dā rā dā dir dā rā dā
dā rā dā dā dir dā -- rā, dā rā dā dā dir dā -- rā
dā rā dā dir dā dā rā dā.

Ali Akbar Khan identifies *laḍī* with the continuous *bol "dārādārā"* used to form an important segment of middle-speed *joḍ*. Asad Ali Khan and Mushtaq Ali Khan spoke of *laḍī* in the context of the *jhālā* section of *ālāp*. Vimalakant Roy Chaudhury refers to it as a section played after *jhālā* and *ṭhonk*. He describes it as the imitation and expansion of a small section of a *pakhāvaj* pattern. An example he gives consists of the *pakhāvaj* strokes *"dhumakiṭa tak tak."* He writes that it might be expanded on as *"dhumakiṭa tak tak tak dhuma kiṭatak dhumakiṭatakadhumakiṭataka dhumakiṭa* etc." (Roy Chaudhury 1975:14).

Laḍgutthāv or *laḍgutthī* is the forming of *laḍī* patterns into knots (Hindi *guthnā*, "to knot"), by internal changes in strokes or melody. Mushtaq Ali Khan described it as the shaping of a straight garland into another beautiful form. D. T. Joshi said it involves adding more *"dir"* and rhythmic changes to *laḍī*. *Laḍlapeṭ* is another variation of *laḍī*, where *laḍī* is "wrapped" or "wound" through melodic or *mīḍ* movement (Hindi *lapeṭnā*, "to wrap"). As is the case with so many instrumental techniques, practical definitions differ widely from school to school.

Jhālā is a term familiar to all modern instrumentalists. In modern performance, it makes up the climax of both *dhrupad ālāp* and fast *gat* performance. It uses the *cikārī* strings in combination with strokes on the melody strings to form fast right hand patterns. The term is sometimes found as *"jhārā"* in 19th-century texts. This word is mentioned by Somanātha in the *"Rāgavibodha"* as a colloquial for *jīvā*, the thread placed between the flat bridge and the string to produce a desired buzzing effect. Whether *jhārā* as a playing technique was in use at Somanatha's time is not possible to say. Pannalal Gosvami, in his *"Nād vinod,"* traces the word *jhālā* to the Hindi *jhulānā*, "to swing," saying that it means "to swing the *rāga*" (Gosvami, P. 1895:40). More often, the word is linked to the Hindi *jharnā*, *jhār*, or *jhārā* meaning a stream of water, waterfall or drizzling rain, to which the sound of the instrumental technique is compared.[162]

Notation and descriptions indicate that early and mid-19th-century conceptions of *jhālā* differed somewhat from modern practice. Karam Imam mentions it as the third of three sections of *bīn* playing: *ālāp*, *ṭhonk* and *jhālā*. He defines it as the interplay *(laḍant)* of two *mizrābs*, and says it is known for its speed. On the *bīn*, he says, its *bols* are "*ghā*" and "*nā*," and the notes are up to the player, according to the chosen *rāga*. The inward *mizrāb* stroke, he says, produces the sound "*ghā*" or "*jhā*," and the reverse stroke produces "*nā*." *Jhālā*, he says, should be played so that the play *(laḍant)* of one *mizrāb* sounds like that of two, a technique dependent on the speed of the hands (Khan, M. K. I. 1925:228). Karam Imam also gives a description and examples of a distinct but related set of patterns which he calls *sargam*.

Jani Sahab in his "*Naghmāt al-Hind*," gives a long list of *sargams* which his father had purchased from *rabābia* Bahadur Husain, and *jhārā* is a subset of patterns among them. The *jhārā bols* as Jani Sahab gives them are "*gha nā nā nā nā*" with a series of simple variations (Khan, M. A. A. [c.1925]:65-73). *Sargam* is discussed more below.

Pannalal Gosvami in his "*Nād vinod*" gives examples of "*ṭhok* and *jhālā*" which use a variety of *pakhāvaj*-style sounds (Gosvami, P. 1895:Introduction, 40-1):

> *ḍāge ḍagaḍa ghinānā, ḍagaḍa ghinānā ḍāge;*
>
> *kiḍadhākiṭa kiḍadhān, ghighitiṭa kiḍadhān, kiḍadhākiṭakatain, ghighitiṭakatain, kiḍadhākiṭa* (3 times) *kiḍadhān, ghighitiṭa* (3 times) *kiḍadhān*;
>
> *ḍaga ḍaga ḍiga ḍiga ḍhūṅki ḍhāṅki diga thaung diga thaung ḍigi ḍagi ḍagi.*

Gosvami says the last example belongs to the tradition of Svami Haridas, Tansen's guru (*ibid.*: Introduction, 41). It is not possible to say exactly how these *jhālā* patterns would have been recreated on the strings of the instrument. Gosvami says some *jhālā* patterns are made with strokes on the *madhyam* string and the *cikārī* while others use the *madhyam* string, the *kharaj* strings and the *cikārī* in sequence. He says that intelligent players need only a hint to understand the technique (*ibid.*:Introduction, 41).

It is apparent from 19th-century notations and descriptions that *jhālā* was originally one of the ways to create *pakhāvaj*-inspired rhythms. *Pakhāvaj bols* were translated into *bīn* strokes using a system that was lost when "*dā*" and "*rā*" replaced these *pakhāvaj* sounds for stringed instruments. Oral traditions speak of large numbers of *jhālā* variations, one hundred twenty-two,[163] or three hundred sixty in the case of Wazir Khan of Rampur.[164] In modern performance, large numbers of *jhālā* variations and other *bīn* techniques are still in use, and some are named, but performers have dropped much of the inclination toward naming and analysis of earlier times.

Both Karam Imam and Jani Sahab also speak of three hundred sixty *bol* patterns, but in connection with *sargam* instead of *jhālā*, indicating that for them *sargam* was a more encompassing term. Today the term *sargam* is used to designate a special vocal or instrumental composition that demonstrates *rāga* movement without words or fixed strokes. It also is used to refer to vocal passages in *khyāl* or *ṭhumrī* sung with the *svara* names *Sa*, *Re*, *Ga*, *Ma* etc. instead of words, hence the name. For both Karam Imam and Jani Sahab, however, *sargam* appears to have been a general term for *bol* patterns to be played on the *bīn*. Chosen patterns were to be put into use for *ṭhonk* and *jhālā*. Karam Imam gives us eleven *sargams*:

(1) *ghan nan ghan nan*
(2) *ghan ghan jhanān*
(3) *ghan nāna ghan nāna*
(4) *ghan ghan ghanān ghan ghan ghanān*
(5) *ghan gha nan ghān ghan gha nan ghān*
(6) *ghan gan gha nan ghan gan gha nan*
(7) *ghan ghan ghana nan ghan ghan ghana nan*
(8) *ghanā nā nā nā nā nā nā ghanā nā nā nā nā nā nā*
(9) *ghan ghanān ghan ghan ghanān nanā ghan ghanān ghan ghan ghanān nanā*
(10) *ghan ghana nan ghanān ghan ghana nan ghanān*
(11) *ghan ghānan ghana nan ghān ghān ghana nan ghān ghān*
(Khan, M. K. I. 1925:228)

Sitār has no *sargams*, says Karam Imam, but he says that those for *bīn* may be played on the *sitār* if the hand is sufficiently prepared (*ibid*.:227). Below are a few of the three hundred sixty *sargams* which Jani Sahab's father purchased from Bahadur Husain for one lakh rupees:

ghana ghana nana;
ghana ghana gha nā nā;
ghana ḍā ghana dhā ghane dhā gha nā nā nā;
ḍagara ḍagara ghanana ghanana;
ḍagaraḍagara ḍagara gḍā;
taka takata;
taka taka taka dhalāng;
dhara ghe da dhāt;
taka dham kaṭa taka taka taka
(Khan, M. A. A. c.1925:65-73).

The first three examples are also labelled *capkā*. We can assume that the exact method of production for all these different sounds was a part of the *bīn* and *rabāb* learned tradition, something that was lost as *pakhāvaj*-based *bols* were replaced by the syllables denoting the specific stroke directions on the *sitār*.

Ṭhonk or *ṭhok* was a technique related to *jhālā*. The word in Hindi means "strike" or "hammer," and the technique uses forceful strokes to emphasize certain beats of a fast running pattern. Again, the specific technique differs from school to school. Pannalal Gosvami gives a definition of *ṭhok* as striking the *bol* "*ṇā*" "to illuminate certain places of the *ālāp*" (Gosvami, P. 1895:40). Asad Ali Khan defines *ṭhonk* as the pattern "*ḍa ga ra ra,*" consisting of strokes on the main string by the second and first finger *mizrābs* respectively followed by two strokes on the *cikārī*.[165] Zia Moinuddin Dagar defined *ṭhonk jhālā* as one stroke on the *cikārī* and three strokes on the melody string. Simple *ṭhonk*, in contrast, he defined as a combination of first and second finger alternating strokes on the melody string without the use of *cikārī*.[166] Roy Chaudhury gives the strokes of *ṭhok* as "*ḍre ḍār ḍār ḍā ḍārā ḍārārārā,*" to be played in conjunction with the *cikārī* work of *jhālā*. *Ṭhonk*, he writes, is a section that concentrates on rhythm more than on melody. In some instruments it also involves an incidental striking of the plectrum on the wood (or skin) of the instrument's face (Roy Chaudhury 1975:13). We remember Karam Imam's praise of Ghulam Muhammad's *ṭhok* on the *sitār*, which may refer to this fast speed work.

Paraṇ, *paran*, *tār paran* or, as Karam Imam calls it, *gat paran* was a section of solo *dhrupad*-style playing usually accompanied by *pakhāvaj*. It was the translation of complete *pakhāvaj* compositions onto the strings of the instrument. Karam Imam speaks of it in connection with *ṭhok* (Khan, M. K. I. 1925:228). The *mizrāb*, or the *javā* in *rabāb* playing, where *paran* was especially important, imitated the strokes of *pakhāvaj* compositions as closely as possible, adding to them the element of melody. Roy Chaudhury describes the process of playing *tār paran*, saying that the instrumentalist began by stroking the rhythm of an appropriate *tāla* on the *cikārī* strings. After the *pakhāvaj* player joined in, the instrumentalist played a *pakhāvaj* composition on the *bāj* string. He then returned to the basic *tāla* on the *cikārī* strings while the *pakhāvaj* player replied with a composition of his own. *Tār paran* sometimes functioned as an alternative to a *dhrupad* composition following an *ālāp* in a solo performance (Roy Chaudhury 1975:14).

Some *dhrupad* instrumental terms are not univerally known, but are used by more than one school. One is *lahak* (Hindi "wave"). D. T. Joshi described *lahak* as a small *gamak*-like attack on each note, and said that it is used at the beginning of middle speed *ālāp*. Umar Khan agreed, saying they are small *gamak*-like *tāns*. Umar Khan spoke of *lapak*, "jump" as a similar technique where one jumps an octave with *gamak*-like effect: P P PPPP. Karamatullah Khan describes *lahak* as a technique where several notes are played in one stroke. Numerous other techniques are named by instrumentalists of different schools, and need categorizing in a detailed study of 20th-century style.

*Early Non-*dhrupad *Techniques*

Since pulling techniques came only with the reshaping of the *sitār* neck and frets under the influence of the *bīn*, the narrow-necked, flat-fretted earliest *sitārs* can be assumed to have had a set of techniques somewhat resembling their predecessors, the Persian *setār* and the *tambūr*. *Zamzama* is a technique basic to *sitār* playing that may date to this early time. In modern usage, it is normally thought of as a trill, where the fret of the adjacent note is touched by the second playing finger rapidly two or three times in succession. It is described in the same way in most 19th-century books, but it has also been defined as a pulling on one fret instead of a trill (Varma 1899:48). The term is Persian, and its presence in the writings of Amir Khusrau hints that it might have been a term first used in India in connection with *qavvālī* music (Sarmadee 1975b:40). It was also used in connection with *khyāl* from an early time. Karam Imam praises Baḍe Muhammad Khan for his "*tān*, *palṭa*, *tahrīr* and *zamzama*" (Khan, M. K. I. 1925:35). Baḍe Muhammad Khan is known to have had an association with *qavvālī*. *Zamzama* is found in association with *bīn* playing as well as *sitār*, but it is not likely to be a *dhrupad*-based term. *Zamzama* and *mīḍ* are the two ornamental techniques notated in the earliest attributed *gats* of the *sitār* handbooks, those of Masit Khan's son Bahadur Khan.[167]

In regard to the earliest right hand techniques for the *sitār*, the instrument's known relation to Persian *setār* and *tambūr* playing directs our attention to the possible influence of their free-hand stroking style. West Asian instrumental playing is often characterized by a fast tremolo-like action of the right hand. In *sitār* playing, the *mizrāb* was adopted from the *bīn*, but unlike on the *bīn*, here it was used for both inward and outward strokes. A versatile back-and-forth movement helped form the *sitār*'s most fundamental style, and may be a gift of its West Asian predecessors.

Bengali Terms and Later sitār *Techniques*

In some of the late 19th-century books, and especially in the Bengali language books, some peculiar names and some new techniques appear. Many of them can be attributed to Bengali translations of earlier terms, or to Sanskritization, a part of S. M. Tagore's mission to reform the music of the day. Others reflect a growing repertoire of named techniques for the *sitār*.

Āś (Hindi: *ās*, "resonance") in the Bengali books is the term for a slide of any length along the frets from one note to another. The first note is described as predominant and the following ones lightly heard (Bandyopadhyaya, K. 1866:23). It appears to be the exact equivalent of *sūt* or *ghasīṭ*. Alternatively, says Tagore, it is known as *gharṣaṇ*, from the Sanskrit *gharṣaṇa*, "dragging" (Tagore 1879:98). *Vikśep* and *prakśep*, (Sanskrit "throw to and fore") are slides in ascent and descent respectively, differing from *āś* in that the intervening notes should not be audible (*ibid.*:86). *Mūrchanā* is a Bengali term for *mīḍ*, spoken of as a movement from one note to another without a break in sound. It is also described as a note "played loudly or with stress" (Bandyopadhyaya, K. 1866:23). The original and unrelated musicological usage of the Sanskrit *mūrcchanā*, "increasing," "augmenting," was a modal shifting of scale tones.

Kṛntan (Sanskrit, *kṛntana*, "cutting") is a technique well-known in modern practice and notated copiously in the Bengali books. Interestingly, it is not found by this name in non-Bengali books dating before 1900. It is seen in Sudarsanacarya's "*Saṅgīt sudarśan*" as *kāṭ katar*, and in Bajpeyi "*Sitār kī tīsrī pustak*" as *kaṭṭhāṃ*. Satya Kinkar Banerji said that it was a technique in which Sajjad Muhammad Khan specialized, and demonstrated a *gat* of Sajjad Muhammad's in the Purab style that used it prominently. The "*Sitār śikṣā*" describes *kṛntan* as a descending *āś* in which the second finger "strikes lightly" (*ibid.*). This agrees with modern practice where it is normally three notes or more in descending order, sounded by left hand plucking and hammering actions on the frets after a single *mizrāb* stroke. Tagore describes it simply as a pressing and pulling off of the second finger on an adjacent fret so that the note on which the first finger rests sounds clearly (Tagore 1879:58).

In the "*Yantra Kshetra Dipika*," a technique described as a single hammering by the left second finger to sound a note one interval above that on which the first finger rests is called *sparś*. *Sparś kṛntan* is a hammering-on and pulling-off movement (*ibid.*:46, 72). In modern terminology, *kaṇ* is a term sometimes used to refer to a single touch on the lower or higher adjacent note by left hand plucking-off or hammering.

The term for *jhālā* in the Bengali instructional books is *cheḍ*, (Bengali and Hindi, "stroke,") and is described as two or more strokes on the *cikārī* strings or the brass strings or both, in repeating patterns interspersed with the melody. Satya Kinkar Banerji used a type of *jhālā* in which the brass strings instead of the *cikārīs* were struck. The *"Sitār śikṣā"* gives a number of practice exercises where *cheḍ* is mixed with other techniques, such as *"āś cheḍ," "kṛntan cheḍ," "gamak cheḍ"* and *"mīḍ cheḍ"* (Bandyopadhyaya, K. 1866, Part II:4).

Gitkārī is a technique described in the *"Sitār śikṣā"* as a series of short, fast *āś* slides, or as "*āś* having *bhūṣikā*" (*ibid.*, Part I:24). *Bhūṣikā*, Sanskrit "ornament," is described as a short sliding attack on any note from above or below. The related term *giṭkiri* is found in modern use in connection with *khyāl*, and has definitions that differ from school to school. Another related technique in the Bengali books is *kartit bhūśikā*, which is described as a short, sliding attack in which the first note is "cut" with a *kṛntan* (*ibid.*). *Kañcan* is a term unique to the Bengal school of terminology and is described as a series of fast strokes, each ornamented with a *kampan* (*ibid.*, Part II:4). *Kampan*, Sanskrit "trembling" or "shake," is a term found in Sanskrit texts and recognized in modern music but little if ever used. It is used in the Bengali books of this period, and may have been revived from the Sanskrit texts by Tagore under the inspiration of the Western use of vibrato. *Svar saṃyog* (Bengali and Sanskrit, "note combination") is a technique not described in any but the Bengali tradition. It refers to two notes sounded simultaneously. Tagore specifies that the notes used should be in accordance with the *vādī* and *saṃvādī* of the *rāga* being played. This chord effect is very likely a direct product of Western influence.

Outside the Bengali tradition, two other terms out of the *khyāl* vocal tradition came into use late in the 19th century. *Murkī* is a technique well-known to modern performers, where it is a turn around a note using a quick pulling action. The *"Rāg prakāśikā"* of 1899 refers to a technique by this name, but does not describe it (Varma 1899:48). *Khaṭkā* is a similar turn, also used in *khyāl*, which came to be conceptually paired with *murkī* in the 20th century.

A novelty technique probably originating in the later 19th century is *capkā* or *chapkā*. This is a striking or slapping of the left hand fingers onto the brass strings or all of the strings of the *sitār* or *sarod*. It produces a percussive tone without a right hand stroke. On *sitārs* with double *joḍī* strings, notes of the lower register, Ṛ, G̣, Ṃ and P̣ could be clearly sounded by a *capkā*. It appears occasionally as a special effect in the *joḍ* or *gat-toḍā* of traditional players. Roy Chaudhury gives a second definition of the technique, in which the right or left hand suddenly damps the sound of the strings after a light stroke on all of the strings. Umar Khan said the term originally meant "bird trap," but its definition "splash" seems to be just as likely a source of its usage here. Numerous other terms from the *dhrupad* and *khyāl* repertoire of *gamaks* and ornaments came to be used by some *sitār* players without becoming universal to *sitār* playing.

Some Examples of 19th-Century sitār ālāp

We know that although a number of *bīn* and therefore *ālāp* techniques were incorporated in the *gat-toḍā*, *ālāp* was not a part of the performance repertoire of the early followers of Masit Khan and the Delhi *bāj*. The playing of *ālāp* on *sitār* and *sarod*, called *joḍ*, probably began with the Purab instrumentalists who were trained under the Lucknow *dhrupad* instrumentalists. It is fairly certain that Ghulam Muhammad and the other professionals of his time played it, and that he created the prototype of the *surbahār* to suit this style of playing. However, by soon after mid-century, it must have been a part of the repertoire of most professional *sitār* players, since we hear that even Rahimsen and Amrtsen, leaders in the Masitkhani *bāj*, knew and played *joḍ* in the important *rāgas*.

Safdar Husain Khan in his "*Qānūn-i sitār*" says that "*joḍ*, that is *ālāp*" is difficult to play, but that he is including a few samples in his book (Khan, M. S. H. 1873:18). He also uses the term *muhara*, "face" (in music often a leading or repeating line) as synonymous with *joḍ* (*ibid.*). A notation for a *joḍ* in *rāga eman kalyān*, below, reveals a complete melodic development structured in lines of increasing melodic range. This *joḍ* is produced by a flowing iteration of *mizrāb* strokes. In the notation below, the melodic range of each line is noted in parentheses next to the line number. At the end of line number 1 is what is known to modern performers as "showing *sam*," a characteristic cadence around S ending each line of *ālāp*. Elements of Safdar Husain Khan's notation are retained here. He uses parentheses around some *bols*, apparently for phrasing, and a horizontal line below the notes to indicate what he calls "*sam mīḍ*," apparently a short *mīḍ* with a return to the original note. Repetitions of line 1 are noted. *Tīvra*, raised, M is notated here as 'M. A careful reading will uncover a simple, yet complete 19th-century *joḍ*:

line 1 (Ṇ-G-S)

G R S-R R G R Ṇ-R S S _ Ṇ-R Ṇ S
(dā r dā) dā rā (dā rā dā dā rā dā) (dā rā rā) (dā dā) dā

line 2 (P̣-R-S)

Ṇ P̣ Ḍ R Ṇ-R S
(dā rā) dā dā rā dā r dā (play line 1)

line 3 (G-Ġ-S)

G P D Ṙ- Ṡ-N N Ṡ Ġ Ṙ ṠṘ Ṙ
(dā r dā) dā r dā (dā r dā) dā rā) dā rā (dā (dā r dā) (dā r dā) dā rā

Ġ Ṙ N-ṘṠ Ṡ N-Ṙ Ṡ D Ṙ N Ṙ Ṡ N D Ṙ 'M _
dā dā rā dā (dā rā rā) (dā dā(dā(dā r dā) (dā dā rā dā rā dā rā (dā rā dā)

G _ _ R _ _ S-R R G R Ṇ S S Ṇ-R S
dā rā dā) (dā rā dā (dā rā dā dā rā dā (dā rā rā) dā dā (dā

line 4 (G-D-S)

G P D 'M D P 'M G R
(dā r dā) dā r dā (dā r dā) dā rā dā rā dā rā (play line 1)

line 5 ('M-S-Ṙ-S)

'M G 'M G D P 'M G R S N D N D Ṙ Ṡ
dā r dā dā r dā dā rā dā rā (dā rā dā) dā r dā dār dā dā rā

N D P 'M 'M G R G 'M P D P 'M G R
dā rā dā (rā dā) (dā r dā) dā dā rā dā rā dā rā dā rā dā (play line 1)

line 6 (Ṃ-D-S)

Ṇ Ḍ Ṇ Ḍ R S Ṇ Ḍ P̣ 'Ṃ P̣ Ḍ Ṇ S R Ṇ S
dā r dā dā r dā r dā rā də rā (dā rā dā) dā rā dārā dā rā dā rā

R G 'M P D D P 'M G R
dā rā dā rā dā dā rā dā rā dā (play line 1)

line 7 (Ṇ-Ġ-S)

N S R G 'M P D P 'M G R S Ṡ N D P
dā rā dā rā dā rā dā rā dā rā dā (rā dā) dā rā dā rā

'M G R S   Ṇ S R G 'M P D N Ṡ Ṙ Ġ Ṙ
dā rā dā (rā dā) dā rā dā rā dā rā dā rā dā rā dā rā

Ṡ N D P   'M
dā rā dā (rā dā) dā r dā (play line 1)

line 8 ('Ṃ-Ṡ-S)

'Ṃ P̣ Ḍ Ṇ S R G 'M P D P 'M G R S Ṡ N D P 'M G
dā rā dā rā dā rā dā rā dā rā dā rā dā rā dā dā rā dā rā dā rā

R S Ṇ S R G 'M P D P 'M G R
dā (rā dā) dā rā dā rā dā rā dā rā dā rā dā (play line 1)

Ex. 1. Muhara rāga eman kalyān *(Khan, M. S. H. 1873:42-4)*

Figure 84 is a notation of a "*muhara* or *joḍ*" from Sadiq Ali Khan's "*Sarmāya-i 'ishrat*" (1875). In his discussion of "*joḍ* and *muhara* which is called *ālāp*," Sadiq Ali Khan says:

> If at this time Ustāds Bahadur Khan, Hasan Khan, Rahimsen and Mir Nasir Ahmad were present, their *muharas* also, of rare authority, would be written just like this (Khan, Sadiq A. 1884:254).

The *joḍ* below, from the "*Sarmāya-i 'ishrat*," shows stroke patterns not dissimilar to Safdar Husain's, and a use of simple but effective *mīḍ*. Appropriately for the *rāga darbārī kānharā* as we still know it, he specifies that one should "swing" *(jhulānā)* the *mīḍ*, notated here as (m), on each G. The short horizontal lines below G̲, D̲ and N̲ here denote not *mīḍ* but the flattened versions of those notes. The commas are taken from the author's notations. The final S, R, S of each phrase is marked as *sam*. The terminology for the four main lines follows *dhrupad* style, but the *antarā* comes in the third position:

āsthāī

(m) (m) (m) (sam)
S R G̲ -- R R -- S S Ṇ̲ Ṇ̲ S,R,S
dā r dā dā r dā dā -- dā r dā -- dā dā rā dā rā dā dā dā

(m) (sam)
P M M,P G̲ R S Ṇ̲ S,R,S
dā rā dā dā dā r dā dā dā rā dā rā dā dā dā

(m)
S R G M P D N D P M,P G R
dā rā dā rā dā dā rā dā dā rā dā dā -- dā r dā

(m) (sam)
S N N S,R,S
dā dā rā dā rā dā dā dā

sañcārī

(m) (m) (m) (m) (m) (m) (sam)
N S N S G R G R S N N S,R,S
r dā r dā dā r dā dā rā dā rā dā rā r dā dā r dā dā dā rā dā rā dā dā dā

joḍ on the *kharaj* strings (play on both *kharaj* strings simultaneously)

(m) (m)
S R G R S
dā rā dā dā dā dā r dā dā

second *joḍ* on the *kharaj* strings

(m) (m)
S R M P -- D N D P M,P G R S S
dā rā dā dā rā dā -- dā rā dā dā rā dā dā dā dā

antarā

(m) (m) (m) (m)
Ṡ N Ṡ D N D P M G R
dā r dā dā rā dā rā dā ra dā ra dā ra dā rā dā rā dā dā r dā

(m) (sam)
S N N S,R S
dā dā rā dā rā dā dā dā

bhog

(m) (m) (m) (m) (m)
Ṡ N Ṡ Ṙ Ġ Ṙ D N D N D
dā r da dā rā dā rā dā dā dā rā dā rā dā dā r dā dā rā dā rā dā rā

(m) (m)
P M,P G R S N N S,R,S
dā rā dā dā dā r dā dā dā dā dā

Ex. 2. Muhara *and* joḍ dārbari kānharā (*Khan*, *Sadiq* A. 1884:255-6)

A *joḍ* in *rāga bhairavī* from the 1899 "*Rāga prakāśikā*" of Rāja Fatah Sinha Varma shows similarities to both earlier examples in both stroking style and melodic development. It is a bit more sophisticated in its use of several notes to one stroke (m = *mīḍ* to given note). It is an attractive piece:

M (M G R S) R S R S D M D N S R G (G R S)
dā r dā dā rā dā dā rā dā dā rā dā dā rā dā dā

(sam)
S N (S R G M) (M G R S)
dā rā dā rā dā dā rā

second type

(m) (m) (m) (m)
S S--M S--G R S S--M S--G R S S
dā dā r dā dā rā dā rā dā dā r dā dā rā dā dā rā dā dā rā

N G R S N (S R G M) (M G R S)
dā dā r dā dā dā rā

sañcārī

(m) (m)
S G R P (P D N) N P-D
dā rā dā rā dā dā rā dā dā rā dā rā dā dā r dā dā rā dā rā

(m)
P (P M G) M P (P D N D P M) M P (P D N D P) G
dā dā r dā dā rā dā rā dā dā dā rā dā dā rā dā rā

(G R S) S S R G M (M G R) S R G R S N S
dā r dā dā rā dā dā rā dā dā r dā dā rā dā dā rā dā rā

S (S N D) D M D N S G (S R G) R S S N (S R G M) (M G R S)
dā dā r dā rā dā dā rā dā dā r dā dā rā dā rā dā dā rā

antarā

(m) (m)
(P D) P M P D N Ṡ (Ṡ Ṙ Ġ Ṁ) Ṡ Ġ
dā r dā dā rā dā dā r dā dā r dā dā rā dā dā rā

(m) (m) (m)
Ṡ Ṙ Ṡ (Ṡ N D) D (P D N Ṡ)(Ṡ N D P) D (Ṡ Ṙ Ġ Ṁ) Ṡ (Ṡ Ṙ Ġ Ṁ)
dā dā rā dā dā r dā dā rā dā dā rā dā r dā

Fig. 82. Cover from Hasan Rizvi 1876. By permission of the British Library. IOL VT 1190.

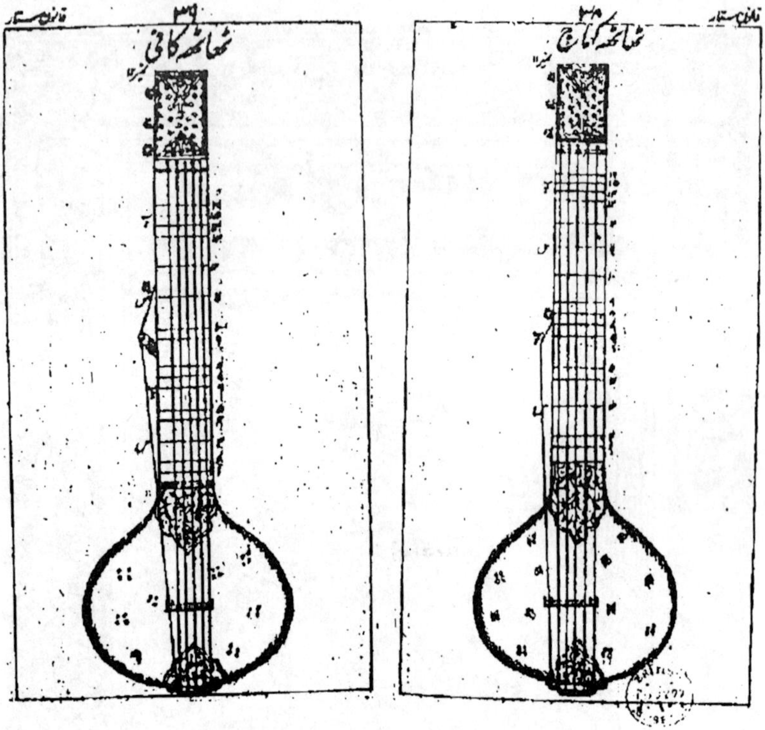

Fig. 83. The ṭhāts *of* rāgas khamāj *and* kāfī. *Khan, M. S. H. 1873:38-9.*

بیان ستار کا است ادہیایا ۲۵۶ مہرے اور جوڑ

مہرہ اور جوڑ بھیم پلاسی کا

جوڑ استائی کا

Fig. 84. *A notation for* muhara a*nd* joḍ, bhīmpalāsī, *and* joḍ, *Kedārā." Khan. S. A. 1884:256.*

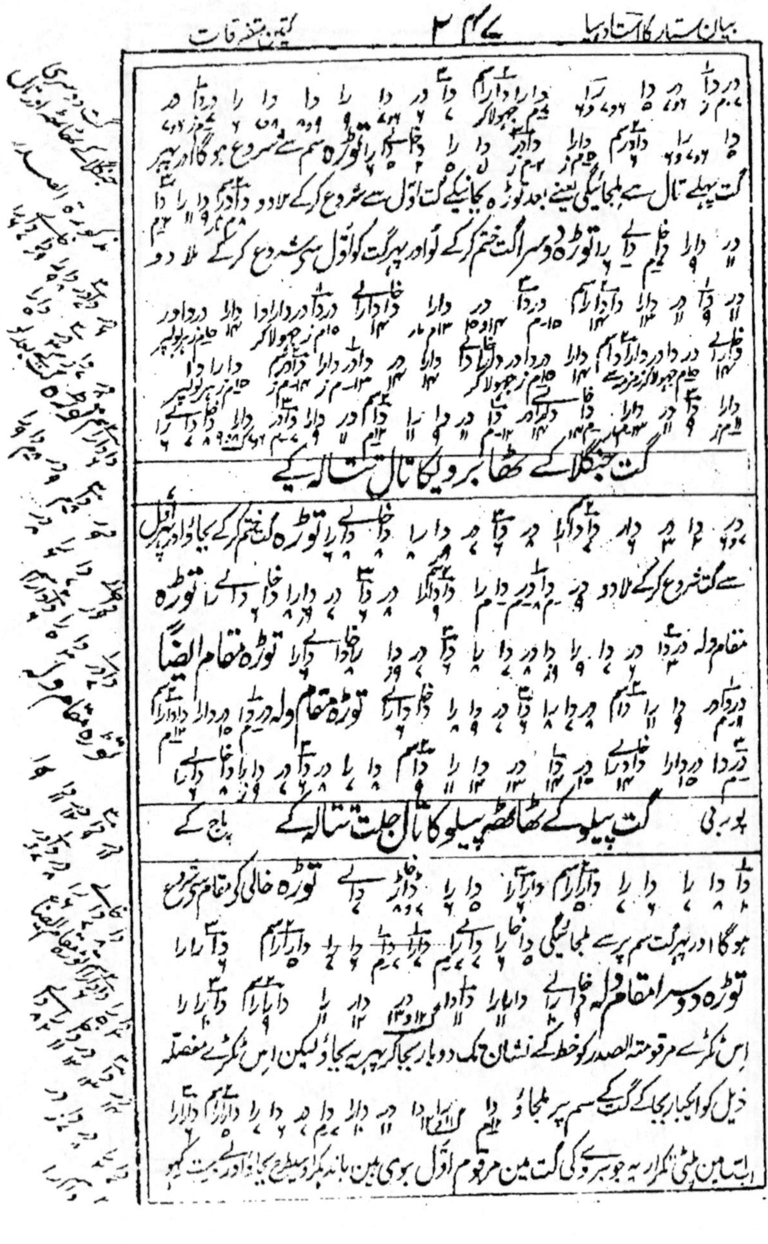

Fig. 85. Notations for gats barvā, janglā *and* pīlū. *Khan, S. A. 1884:247.*

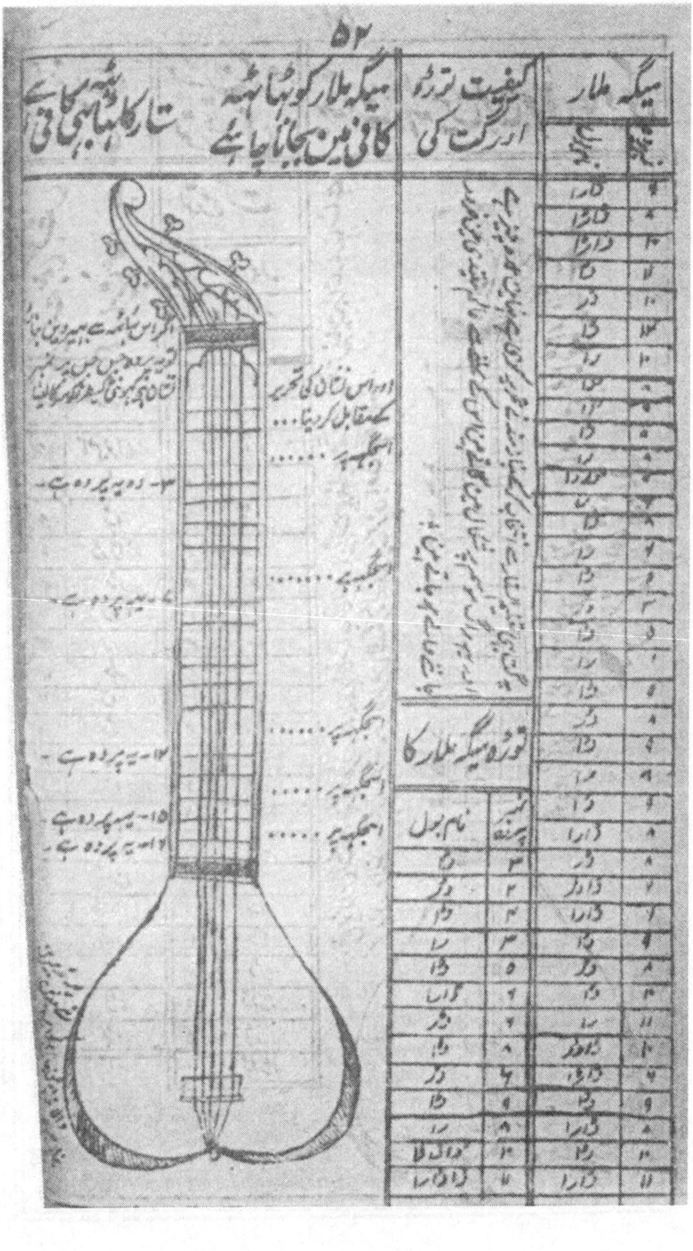

Fig. 86. Notation for gat megh mallār. *Beg 1876:52.*

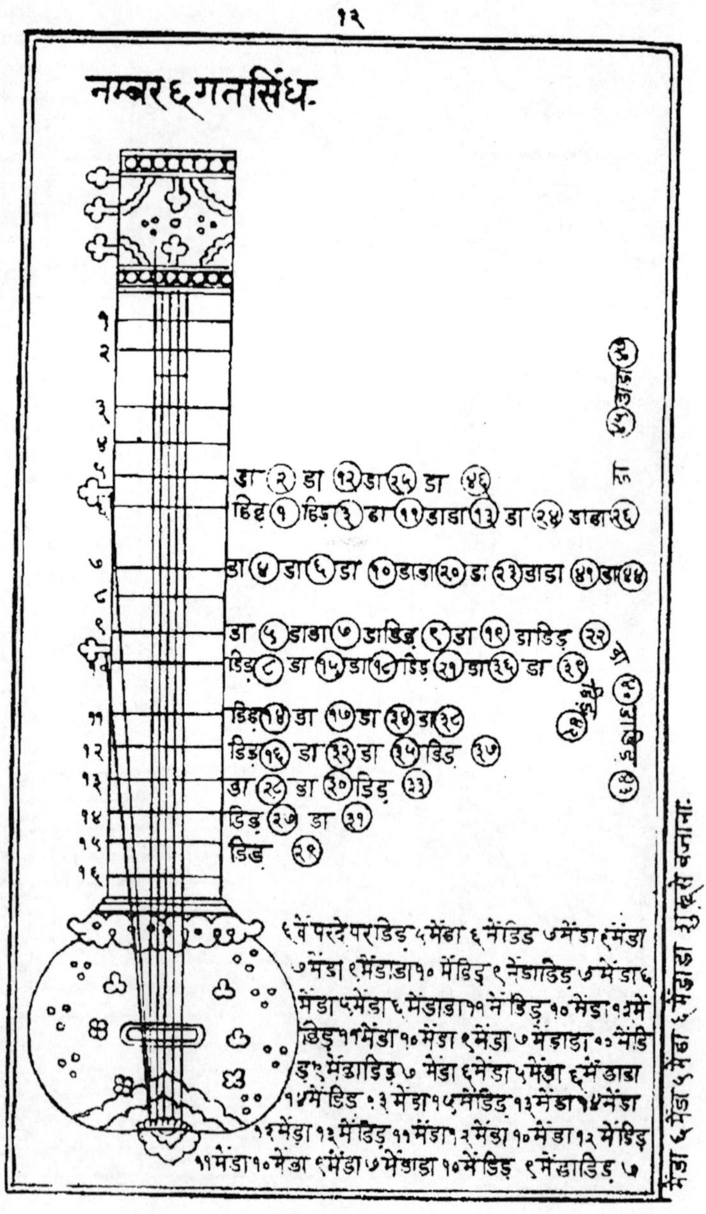

Fig. 87. Notation for gat sindh. *Vastad 1893:12.*

Fig. 88. Sitār *and* ḍholak *players. Khan, S. A. 1884:197.*

Fig. 89. Sitār, jaltarang *and* ḍholak *players. Khan, S. A. 1884:275.*

(m) (m) (m) (m) (m) (m) (m) (m)
ṠĠ̲ ṠṘ̲ Ṡ (ṠṘ̲Ġ̲Ṁ) ṠĠ̲ ṠṘ̲ Ṡ (ṠṘ̲Ġ̲Ṁ) ṠĠ̲ ṠṘ̲ Ṡ Ṡ
dā rā dā dā rā dā dā r dā dā rā dā dā rā dā dā r

(ṠN̲D̲) N̲ (ṠṘ̲Ġ̲Ṁ̲) Ṡ
dā dā rā dā dā r dā dā rā dā rā dā dā dā rā dā

(ṠN̲D̲) P M G̲ M P (PD̲N̲D̲) (D̲PM) G̲ (SR̲G̲R̲S)
dā r dā dā rā dā dā rā dā dā r dā dā dā dā rā

R̲ G̲ M (MG̲R̲) (R̲SN̲) S (N̲D̲P)M N̲ N̲ G̲ R̲ S M
dā dā rā dā dā r dā dā r dā dā r dā dā dā r dā dā

S N̲ (SR̲G̲M̲) (MG̲R̲S)
rā dā rā dā dā rā

Ex. 3. Joḍ bhairavī (Varma 1899:89-91)

The author instructs the player to follow this *joḍ* with phrases "set into *mizrāb bols* and *jhālā*, at faster tempos" (Varma 1899:91).

Sarod players, according to oral histories, also began playing *joḍ* sometime after mid-century. Techniques for playing *joḍ* on *sarod* were in part inspired by the style of the *dhrupad rabāb* and the *sursingār*. These instruments followed the same patterns as the *bīn*, but specialized in the middle and fast speed movements, and are especially remembered for their practice of *tār paran*. An intriguing practice sometimes employed was the playing of *pakhāvaj bols* with the hands on the skin of the *rabāb* or *sarod* (Roy Chaudhury 1975:136).

8

The Delhi or Masitkhani *bāj*

The gats *of Masit Khan and Bahadur Khan*

The representation of instrumental strokes, which had existed from an early time in India, was simplified on the *sitār* into two syllables to represent the two possible strokes, the inward, "*ḍā*" or "*dā*" and outward, "*ṛā*" or "*rā*." These two sounds could be shortened and joined to create any desired rhythmic combination. Jani Sahab gives us the five basic *sitār bols* as "*ḍā, ṛā, ḍiṛ, ḍāṛ* and *ḍṛā*" (Khan, M. A. A. [c.1925]:64). "*Diṛ*" is twice the speed of "*ḍā ṛā.*" If "*ḍā*" is considered one beat, "*ḍāṛ*" is one and a half and "*ḍṛā*" a half and one. These syllabic stroke representations formed the core of the *gat-toḍā* style created by Masit Khan in late 18th-century Delhi. To a fixed pattern of *mizrāb* strokes set within the *tīntāla* cycle of sixteen beats, he set a melody line composed in *rāgas* as they were known from the *dhrupad* repertoire. Some of the early notated *gats* contain four lines that resemble in their ranges the *sthāī*, *antarā*, *sañcārī* and *ābhog* of *dhrupad* compositions.

The Masitkhani *gat* seems to have a strong original relationship with *tīntāla*, the sixteen-*mātrā* rhythmic cycle that predominates in instrumental music to the present day. Masitkhani *gats* are occasionally found in other *tālas* in the 19th-century books, but their stroke pattern is an obvious modification of the *tīntāla* version. The origin and history of *tīntāla* is a subject about which very little is known. Krsnadhan Bandyopadhyaya's "*Sitār śikṣā*" seems to point to an early relationship of *tīntāla* to *qavvālī*. There the *tāla* having the strokes we know as *tīntāla* is called *qavvālī tāla* in the middle speed, and *dhīmā qavvālī* ("slow *qavvālī*") or *dhīmā titāla* in the slower speed. This is the *tāla* most frequently indicated for use with the Masitkhani and other *gats* in the book (Bandyopadhyaya, K. 1866, Part II:1).

The primary Masitkhani *bol* pattern as found in 19th-century accounts is identical to that known (but now not always followed precisely) in modern performance tradition. It fits into the cycle of *tīntāla* as shown below. "*x*" indicates *sam*, the first *mātrā* of the *tīntāla* cycle, and "*o*" indicates *khālī*, the ninth *mātrā*. The vertical lines are division markers, and carry no rhythmic value.

		x		o	
dir	| dā dir dā rā	| dā dā rā dir	| dā dir dā rā	| dā dā rā	

Pattern 1a

The pattern consists of two identical halves. The first five *mātrās* lead to the *sam* of the *tīntāla* cycle. 19th-century books give no name to this group of five but simply call it the beginning of the *gat*. Modern performers know it as the *mukhḍā*, "face." The second line found most frequently in conjunction with pattern 1a is as follows:

		x		o	
dir	| dā dir dā rā	| dā dir dā rā	| dā dir dā rā	| dā dā rā	

Pattern 1b

The origin of these patterns is unknown. Popular tradition sometimes says that they are based on the rhythm of a *bhajan* or a *kirtan* of the time, Hindu devotional song genres, which Masit Khan had heard. The large number of poetic metres in the Sanskrit literary tradition includes two that correspond closely to Patterns 1a and 1b. A ten-syllable metre called *uddhāta* is:

S S S I I S I I S S ("I" is half the measure of "S").

The rhythm corresponds to the Masitkhani pattern 1a as played from *sam*. Part of the rhythmic pattern of line 1b is found in the ten-syllable metre called *campakamālā*:

S I I S S S I I S S (Velankar 1949:124).

Any direct relationship between the Masitkhani pattern and Sanskrit poetry is unlikely, but it is possible that a popular devotional song of the same pattern in the colloquial may have been the model for the Masitkhani pattern.

A second pattern found commonly in the 19th-century books is Pattern 1a shifted so that it begins at *sam*. It is identical to the *uddhāta* metre:

x		o	
dā dā rā dir	dā dirdā rā	dā dā rā dir	dā dirdā rā

Pattern 2

The third most frequently seen pattern is identical to Pattern 1b and the *campakamālā* metre, but it begins at *sam*. Differing starting places change the character of the Masitkhani pattern and determine melody. They cannot be considered identical:

x		o	
dā dirdā rā	dā dirdā rā	dā dā rā dir	dā dirdā rā

Pattern 3

A survey of the notated *gats* in several 19th-century books shows that only Patterns 1a and b appear in the *gats* attributed to Bahadur Khan, Masit Khan's son, while Pattern 3 appears in several of the *gats* attributed to Rahimsen. Pattern 3 may be a later, and perhaps a Senia type.

A number of other pattern types found in written and oral collections differ slightly from the first three. One begins from the seventh *mātrā* of the *tīntāla* cycle and covers two cycles:

	o		x	
dā dir	dā dā rā dir	dā dirdā rā	dā dā rā dā	dā rā
	o		x	
dā dir	dā dā rā dā	dā rā dā rā	dā dā rā dā	dā rā

Another is very close to Pattern 2:

x		o	
dā dā rā dā	dā rā dā dir	dā dā rā dir	dā dirdā rā

Another is identical to Pattern 3, but the *sam* and *khālī* are reversed. It begins at *khālī*:

o		x	
dā dirdā rā	dā dirdā rā	dā dā rā dir	dā dirdā rā

One of the Jaipur Senia patterns is another variation on Pattern 3:

x		o	
dā rā dā rā	dā rā dā dir	dā dā rā dir	dā dirdā rā

Other variations also appear in written notations, but the overwhelming frequency of Patterns 1a-b in written and oral sources allows us to assume that they make up the definitive and probably the original Masitkhani *gat* pattern.

A collection of examples of Masitkhani *gats* found in 19th-century books follows. The skeletal nature of the notation in these books does not permit a high degree of practical interpretation as to the playing style of Masit Khan and his immediate followers. Examples of the diverse styles of notations for Masitkhani *gats*, Figures 85 to 87, make this fact clear. Oral tradition also cannot be said to contain pure examples of the earliest styles. It is unavoidable, therefore, that speculation and imagination play some part in reconstructing details of actual performance and technique in the early period.

The *mīḍ* of early *gats* as notated in 19th-century collections is specified in various ways which may indicate degrees. Simple "*mīḍ*," may refer to a short pull and immediate return to the original note; "a little *mīḍ*" may mean a slightly longer glimpse of the adjacent note, and "*mīḍ*-" with a specification of the fret number or the note clearly denotes the note to which the string is to be pulled, one or two notes away from the original. In the following *gat* and *toḍā*, *mīḍ* and *zamzama*, *(m)* and *(z)*, are used not only for ornamentation, but for bringing out the correct phrasings of the *rāga*. We know from a familiarity with the *mallhār* family, that these *rāgas* often require the combinations G̱ M R and frequent use of M R M R. The following *gat* is in *rāga khās mallār* and is attributed to Bahadur Khan:

		--(z)--		x - (m to M) -		(m to G̱)		o (m to M)
R	I	R S Ṇ S	I	R R R R	I	R G̱ M P	I	G̱ G̱ R
dir	I	dā dir dā rā	I	dā dā rā dir	I	dā dir dā rā	I	dā dā rā

toḍā (1b)

(m to G̱)				x - (m to Ṡ) -		(m to Ṉ)(little m)		o (m to M)
R	I	R G̱ M P	I	Ṉ̣ Ṉ Ṉ Ṉ	I	Ṉ Ṉ P M	I	G̱ G̱ R
dir	I	dā dir dā rā	I	dā dir dā rā	I	dā dir dā rā	I	dā dā rā

Ex. 4. Gat-toḍā khās mallār *(Patterns 1a, b) (Beg 1876:132)*

A *dhrupad* quality is felt in the generous use of *mīḍ* and the sweep from Ṉ̣ to Ṉ. In this *gat*, as in most notations in the 19th-century books, the word *toḍā* denotes the second line, corresponding to the line known as the *antarā* by modern *sitār* players, extending to the upper range of the scale, at least to upper S.

Another *gat* attributed to Bahadur Khan in *rāga darbārī kānhaḍā* uses both *mīḍ* and *zamzama* on Ḏ and G̱, which we know need such ornaments for the correct melodic contour of the *rāga*:

				x				o (m)(m)(m)
R	I	Ṉ̣ S Ḏ̣ P̣	I	P̣ S S S	I	SṈ̱S R R	I	G̱ G̱ G̱
dir	I	dā dir dā rā	I	dā dā rā dir	I	dā dir dā rā	I	dā dā rā
		---(z)---		x (m) (m)		(m)		o (m)
G̱	I	G̱ M P P	I	G̱ R S G̱	I	R S Ṉ̣ G̱	I	R S Ṉ̣
dir	I	dā dir dā rā	I	dā dir dā rā	I	dā dir dā rā	I	dā dā rā

toḍā

				x ---(m)---		(z)		o (m) (z)
M	I	M M P P	I	P Ṡ Ṡ Ṡ	I	Ḏ Ḏ P P	I	G̱ G̱ M
dir	I	dā rā dā rā	I	dā dā rā dir	I	dā dir dā rā	I	dā dir dā
		(m)(z)		x (m) (m)		(m)		o
P	I	Ḏ Ḏ P P	I	G̱ R S G̱	I	R S Ṉ̣ G̱	I	R S Ṉ̣
rā	I	dā dir dā rā	I	dā dir dā rā	I	dā dir dā rā	I	dā dā rā

Ex. 5. Gat-toḍā darbārī kānhaḍā *(Patterns 1a,b) (Khan, Sadiq A. 1884:222)*

The *gat* and the *toḍā* are each two *tīntāla* cycles long. The *toḍā* represents the high range *antarā*. The use of low notes in the *gat* is appropriate to the character of *rāga darbārī* which emphasizes the lower octave and lower half of the scale. The melodic jumps from P to S in both octaves are typical to *dhrupad* movements in this *rāga*.

Toḍās in *sitār* music explore different areas of the gamut of a *rāga*, and systematically introduce rhythmic variations. The three or four *toḍās* that immediately follow a *gat* sometimes represent the ordered lines of a *dhrupad* composition. Ilyas Khan demonstrated a *gat* in *rāga chāyānaṭ* that clearly had a *sthāī*, *antarā*, *sañcārī* and *ābhog*. A *gat* from the "*Naghmah-i sitār*" with its *toḍās* seems to be constructed in the same manner. The *gat* covers the range of Ṇ to P conforming to the definition of *sthāī*. The first *toḍā* begins at high R and descends almost directly back to S. The second *toḍā* explores the lower and middle ranges. The third *toḍā* reaches to high S, then works its way back to middle P and finally middle S. The last *toḍā* restates the *sthāī* range. The *gat* is in *rāga deś* and is also attributed to Bahadur Khan:

(z)	(z)	x (z)	--(z)--	o
S	Ṇ S R G	M P M G	R R S Ṇ	S S S
dir	dā dir dā rā	dā dir rā dir	dā dir dā rā	dā dā rā

toḍā 1 (1a)

		x		o
Ṙ	Ṡ N D P	M G R M	G G S Ṇ	S S S
dir	dā dir dā rā	dā dā rā dir	dā dir dā rā	dā dā rā

toḍā 2 (1a)

		x		o
Ṗ	Ṃ Ṗ Ṇ S	R R R R	R R G S	R R R
dir	dā dir dā rā	dā dā rā dir	dā dir dā rā	dā dā rā

		x		o
R	R R M P	D D P M	G R S Ṇ	S S S
dir	dā dir dā rā	dā dir dā rā	dā dā dā rā	rā dā dā

toḍā 3 (1b)

	--------(z)------	x	(m) (z)	o
N	N N N D	N Ṡ Ṡ Ṡ	N D P M	P P P
dir	dā dir dā rā	dā dir dā rā	dā dir dā rā	dā dā rā

```
          (z)      x            (z)        o
R    | R R M P  | D D P M  | G R S Ṇ  | S S S
dir  | dā dirdā rā | dā dirdā rā | dā dirdā rā | dā dā rā
```

toḍā 4

```
                   x                       o
M    | G M R G  | M P M G  | R G S Ṇ  | S S S
dir  | dā dirdā rā | dā dā rā rā | dā dirdā rā | dā dā rā
```

Ex. 6. Gat-toḍā deś *(Beg 1876:134)*

A third *gat* attributed to Bahadur Khan is in *ektāla* of twelve *mātrās*, and shows an early use of other *tālas*. The *gat* is in *rāga bhupālī*. N and 'M do not occur in this *rāga* in modern practice:

```
3        4         x         o          2         o
                   (m) (m)   (m) (z)
NS  Ḍ   | S R     | G G     | G R      | G D     | P P
dā  dir | dā rā   | dā dā   | rā dir   | dā dir  | dā rā

3        4         x (m)(m) o (m)(z)   2          o
G   Ṇ   | Ṇ S     | G G     | G P      | G 'M    | G R
dā  dir | dā rā   | dā dā   | rā dir   | dā dir  | dā rā
```

Ex. 7. Gat bhūpālī-ektāla *(Khan, Sadiq A. 1884: 226)*

Early toḍās *and their Techniques:* ṭhā, dūn, āḍ, tān

In the earliest notations, all the material following the *gat* is presented as numbered *toḍās*. The first one, two or several *toḍās* closely adhere to the Masitkhani *bol* pattern while exploring the range of the *rāga*, sometimes reflecting the ideas of *antarā*, *sañcārī* and *ābhog*. The sets of *toḍās* that follow these in the early notations bring in rhythmic patterns that break away from the original *bols* of the *gat*. Safdar Husain Khan in the "*Qānūn-i sitār*" gives us *toḍā* types named "*toḍā āḍ*," "*toḍā mizrāb*," "*toḍā tān*," "*toḍā gamak*," "*toḍā sūt*" and "*toḍā jhārā*." He says that of all the *toḍā* types, almost any can be fitted into any *gat*, so that "more than fifty" can be played with each *gat* (Khan, M. S. H. 1873:18). He reminds us, however, that the ones chosen should have a likeness to the pattern of the *gat* (*ibid.*). Sadiq Ali Khan, in the "*Sarmāya-i 'ishrat*," tells us that such rhythms (*laykārī*) as *dūn*, *āḍ*, *kuāḍ* and *baḍāḍ* are used for *toḍās* in the Masitkhani style (Khan, Sadiq A. 1884:203). *Ṭhā* is also a term used in this connection. *Ṭhā* refers to single speed, a speed equalling that of the basic *mātrās* of the composition. Thus, *toḍās* in *ṭhā* are the first extensions of the *gat*, such as those shown above, where melodic variations are imposed on the *bol* pattern of the *gat*. *Dūn* refers to a rhythm double that of *ṭhā*, and *dūn toḍās* are usually the first to follow *ṭhā*. A *gat* type called *ṭhā-dūnī*, containing both single and double rhythms, will be mentioned in a later section. The term *āḍ* today usually refers to rhythmic divisions placing a rhythm of three over two *mātrās*, or one-and-a-half over one *mātrā*. In the 19th-century *sitār* books, the term is used for simple syncopated rhythms. The terms *kuāḍ* and *baḍāḍ* have definitions that vary from school to school. They are either variations of *āḍ* or, as in Roy Chaudhury's tradition, the division of the sixteen-*mātrā* cycle into rhythms of seven or nine (Roy Chaudhury 1975:21, 78). All of these rhythmic terms were used in drumming, and to an extent in *dhrupad* music, which specializes in systematic *mātrā* division for its rhythmic variations. Either could have been the source of the terms' use in *sitār* music. Besides their function for describing *toḍā* types in the 19th-century books, the terms are used for clarifying rhythmic changes occurring within *toḍās* or *gats*.

One of the most wide ranging terms in Hindustani music is *tān*. A few words on the background of this important term is appropriate here. It comes from the Sanskrit verb root "*tan*" and its derivative *tāna* which means "spreading" or "expansion." It was used technically in ancient and medieval music texts for scales in which certain notes of the octave were omitted in accordance with prescribed rules (Śārṅgadeva 1989:179-228). A more general usage was one meaning simply music or musical phrases. In performance-related tradition traceable to *dhrupad* and *dhrupad*-influenced music, the term is used in speaking of a phrase, such as particular short phrases that characterize a *rāga*, or each of the small phrases that make up a larger *ālāp*. Thus traditional artists such as Ilyas Khan would speak of the correctness and ordering of each particular *tān* in *ālāp*. This definition of the term, however, has been overshadowed by another, by which it refers to the melodic runs that are found in so much variety and abundance in *khyāl* vocal and also instrumental music. High speed *tāns* became famous from the time of Baḍe Muhammad Khan and his followers Haddu and Hassu Khan in Gwalior. Roy Chaudhury lists seventy-two *tāns* with their descriptions. He treats the term as a general one for any sort of medium to fast-speed melodic movement. A great number of named *tāns* are still known to traditional vocalists and instrumentalists, although the trend of naming techniques in general has lost its strength in the later 20th century. It is often claimed that the use of fast-speed *tāns* in *sitār* music came about under a period of *khyāl* influence that occurred in the early 20th century. We have been told in the writings of Sudarsanacarya and others that *khyāl* elements were introduced by Rahimsen and Amrtsen. Notations in "*Qānūn-i sitār*" and "*Sarmāya-i 'ishrat*" also indicate that a *khyāl* influence, and with it *tāns*, were a part of 19th-century Masitkhani *sitār* music. It is generally agreed, however, that much of the *tān* work actually known to and used by current performers was introduced by the great *sitār* player Imdad Khan and his successors.

"*Mizrāb*" refers to *toḍās* that use various rhythmic combinations of strokes. Characteristic of *mizrāb toḍās* in the "*Qānūn-i sitār*" are patterns such as:

dir dir dā -- dir dir dā --
dā -- dir dir dā -- dir dir
dir dā dir dā
dir dir dir dir.

Toḍās called *gamak*, *sūt* and *jhārā* contain the techniques having those names, which were discussed earlier.

Some Masitkhani style *toḍās* from the "*Qānūn-i sitār*" are good examples of an early system of *gat* elaboration. A *gat* in *rāga jhinjhoṭī* has a series of twenty-three *toḍās*, classed into five types. The first six are *ṭhā*, single-time, and follow the *bol* structure of the *gat*. The *gat* and the first three *toḍās* are as shown in Example 8a. A melodic development related to the *dhrupad* four-line system is visibie here. The *gat* itself covers a range between P and Ṗ. The lower range is normally emphasized in *rāga jhinjhoṭī*. The first *toḍā* ascends to high S as a brief *antarā*. The second explores the middle range from S to P, and the third reaches the highest notes, conforming to some definitions of *ābhog*. Whether the notes notated above the main melody line are to be played by *mīḍ* or *sūt* is not specified:

	(RGM)	x (GM)	(RGM)	o (z)
P̣	I Ḍ S S G	I R G G P	I M G S G	I S R S
dir	I dā dir dā rā	I dā dā rā dir	I dā dir dā rā	I dā dā rā

toḍā 1 (1b)

R		x	(RGM)	o (z)
G	I G P D Ṡ	I P D D D	I G S S G	I S R S
dir	I dā dir dā rā	I dā dir dā rā	I dā dir dā rā	I dā dā rā

toḍā 2 (1b)

		x	(z)	o (z)
P	I M P M P	I G M R G	I S R P G	I S R S
dir	I dā dir dā rā	I dā dir dā rā	I dā dir dā rā	I dā dā rā

toḍā 3 (1b)

		x	(z)	o (z)
Ġ	I Ṙ Ṡ N D	I P M G R	I S R P G	I S R S
dir	I dā dir dā rā	I dā dir dā rā	I dā dir dā rā	I dā dā rā

Ex. 8a. Gat-toḍā jhinjhoṭī *(1a-b) (Khan, M. S. H. 1873:101-2)*

Toḍā 7 is the first of those that vary from the pattern of the *gat*. The rhythm in *toḍā* 7 is still *ṭhā*, but now each note is ornamented with a *zamzama*. The method of executing the *zamzama* is described by the author: the written note is to be fretted with the second finger, and the *zamzama* is to be played by raising it to sound the next lower note fretted by the first finger. Thus, *zamzama* on M would be a short trill between M and G:

toḍā 7

(z)	(z) (z) (z) (z)	x (z) (z) (z) (z)	(z) (z) (z) (z)	o (z) (z) (z)
M	I M G G P	I P G M M	I M G G S	I S R S
dir	I dā dā rā dir	I dā dā rā dir	I dā dā rā dir	I dā dā rā

Ex. 8b. Toḍā jhinjhoṭī *(Khan, M. S. H. 1873:103)*

The next few *toḍās* are in *dūn*, double-time, and they start from *sam*. The *bols* are now independent of those of the *gat*. "*d*" is half the length of *dā*. One of them is as follows:

toḍā 8

x   o
S P M P P GM | GM M R G RG | G S SRS S
dādir dārā dā dādir | dārā dā dādir dārā | dādd dddā rā

Ex. 8c. Toḍā jhinjhoṭī (*Khan, M. S. H. 1873:103*)

After the *toḍās* in *dūn* are some in *āḍ*, using the *bol dār* or *d dā*:

toḍā 11

                                x   o
P | 'M D P G | M P M R | G M D Ṇ | S R S
dir | dār d dirdir | dār d dirdir | dār d dirdir | dār d dir

toḍā 20

x   o
ĠṘ ĠṠ ṘN ṠD | NP DM PG MR | GS RN S
d dā d dā d dā ddā | d dā d dā ddā d dā | d dā d dā d

Ex. 8d. Toḍā jhinjhoṭī (*Khan, M. S. H. 1873:104, 107*)

Toḍā tān follow on *toḍā āḍ*. For the most part they consist of the *bols* "*dā rā*" and have one note to each stroke, conforming to the basic modern idea of a *tān*:

toḍā tān 12

x
G R | G P DṠ DṠ ṘĠ | ṠṘ ṘṘ ṠN D P
dā rā | dārādārādārādārā | dd dd dārā dārā

Ex. 8e. Toḍā jhinjhoṭī *(Khan, M. S. H. 1873:104)*

Some *tāns* combine *āḍ* and *tān*. Next in the series come *mizrāb tāns* such as the following:

toḍā mizrāb tān

x
Ṡ Ṙ | Ṡ N
dir dir dā -- dir dir dā -- | dir dir dā -- dir dir dā --

o
D P | M G
dir dir dā -- dir dir dā -- | dir dir dā -- dir dir dā --

x o
Ġ Ṙ Ṡ N | D P M G | R S Ṇ
dā dir dā rā | dā dir dā rā | dā rā dā

Ex. 8f. Toḍā jhinjhoṭī *(Khan, M. S. H. 1873:108)*

This *gat* in *jhinjhoṭī* ends with a long *toḍā mizrāb*.

A second *gat* in *rāga jaijaivantī* is an attractive composition, and contains another *toḍā* type called *toḍā gamak*:

x o (z)
R R R R | R G G S | R R R P | M G RG S
dā dā rā dir | dā dir dā rā | dā dā rā dir | dā dir dā rā

toḍā 1

x(m) (m) (m)(m) o (m)(m)
Ṉ̣ S Ṉ̣ S | R R S S | Ḍ Ḍ Ṉ̣ R | S Ṉ̣ Ḍ P̣
dā dir dā rā | dā dir dā rā | dā dā rā dir | dā dir dā rā

toḍā gamak 5

```
x(m)      (m)            (m)               o                        (z)
DD P--   DD P--    |  DD P--   DG M--  |  DP M--  GG S      |  M G R S
dārā dā-- dārā dā--  |  dārā dā-- dārā dā-- |  dārā dā-- rādā dir  |  dā dir dā rā
```

Ex. 9. Gat-toḍā jaijaivantī *(2) (Khan, M. S. H. 1873:94-5)*

The *gamak* here (m) is executed by a short pulling described as *sam mīḍ*.

A *gat* in *rāga bhairavīn* also has a *toḍā* called *toḍā gamak*. The *toḍā* contains *sūt* as well:

```
x    (z)            (z)   o             ---(z)---
P P N̲ D̲ | D̲ D̲ D̲ P | M G̲ R̲ M  | M R̲ S S
dā dir dā rā | dā dir dā rā | dā dā rā dir | dā dir dā rā
```

toḍā 1

```
x             (m)(m)(m)(m)  o
Ḍ̲ Ṇ̲ S S | G̲ G̲ G̲ G̲ | S R̲ R̲ M  | M R̲ S S
dā dir dā rā | dā dir dā rā | dā dā rā dir | dā dir dā rā
```

toḍā gamak 9

```
x                                            o --(sūt)---  ---(z)---
Ṇ̲SR̲ SR̲G̲ R̲G̲M G̲MP | MPD̲ PD̲N̲ D̲N̲Ṡ N̲ṠṘ̲ | Ġ̲    R̲ M  | M R̲ S S
dā   dā   dā   dā  | dā   dā   dā   dā  | dā dā rā dir | dā dir dā rā
```

Ex. 10a. Gat-toḍā bhairavīn *(3) (Khan, M. S. H. 1873:61-4)*

The technique to play this *tān* is explained as follows. For the *gamaks* in the first half, in one "*dā*" stroke the first finger frets the first note then slides "like *sūt*" to the second note. The second finger is then brought down onto the third fret for the third note. The second half of the *toḍā* contains a long descending *sūt*. The author specifies that on the two "*dā*" strokes three notes each should be covered in descent. On the "*rā*" stroke the first finger returns to S and the second comes down on R̲ (*ibid.*:64). The next two *toḍās* use long mostly descending *sūt*:

toḍā sūt 10

```
x (sūt)          (sūt)          o  (sūt)
Ġ̲ ----- G̲       | Ṙ̲ ----- R̲     | Ṡ ----- S  M    | M R̲ S S
dā dir dā rā    | dā dir dā rā  | dā dā rā  dir   | dā dir dā rā
```

toḍā sūt 11

```
x (sūt)          (sūt)          o  (sūt)
Ġ̲ ----- N̲       | S --- Ġ̲ Ṙ̲ Ṡ    | Ġ̲ ----- S  M    | M R̲ S S
dā dir dā rā    | dā dir dārā   | dā dā rā  dir   | dā dir dā rā
```

Ex. 10b. Toḍā bhairavīn *(Khan, M. S. H. 1873:65)*

Another *gat* in *bhairavīn* has a series of *toḍās* representative of the full technical range found in the *"Qānūn-i sitār."* It even ends with a *toḍā jhārā*, showing how *jhālā* was worked into the framework of the Masitkhani *gat-toḍā* repertoire:

```
                       x (z)             (z)              o
S    | Ṇ̲ S G̲ M       | N̲ P P P         | D̲ P D̲ Ṡ         | Ṡ D̲ P
dir  | dā dir dā rā  | dā dā rā dir    | dā dir dā rā    | dā dā rā

       (z)                (z)             (z)              (z)
P    | N̲ D̲ G̲ M       | P N̲ D̲ P         | G̲ M N̲ P         | G̲ G̲ S
dir  | dā dir dā rā  | dā dā rā dir    | dā dir dā rā    | dā dā rā
```

toḍā 1 from sam

```
x                                  o ---(z)---
Ṇ̲ S G̲ M        | P D̲ N̲ Ṡ        | Ṙ̲ Ṙ̲ Ṙ̲ Ġ̲        | Ṙ̲ Ṡ N̲ D̲
dā dir dā rā   | dā dir dā rā   | dā dā rā dir   | dā dir dā rā
x  (z)                             o
P N̲ D̲ P        | G̲ M N̲ P        | G̲ G̲ S
dā dir dā rā   | dā dir dā rā   | dā dā rā
```

toḍā 3

```
x
Ṇ̲S̲R̲     S̲R̲G̲     R̲G̲M     G̲MP     | MPD̲     PD̲N̲     D̲N̲Ṡ     N̲ṠṘ̲     |
dir dir dir dir dir dir dir dir | dir dir dir dir dir dir dir dir |
```

o (z) (z) (z) (z)
Ġ̲ Ġ̲ Ṡ Ṙ̲ Ġ̲ N̲ | Ṡ Ṙ̲ D̲ N̲ Ṡ P |
dir dir dā dā dir dir dā dā | dir dir dā dā dir dir dā dā |

x - (z)- o
Ṩ Ṙ̲ N̲ Ṡ | D̲ N̲ P D̲ | D̲ P MG̲ S --
dā rā dā -- dā rā dā -- | dā rā dā -- dā rā dā -- | dā rā dā rā dā --

Ex. 11a. Gat-toḍā bhairavīn *(1a) (Khan, M. S. H. 1873:56-61)*

It is specified that the *"dir dir"* at the beginning of this *toḍā* should be distributed over the three notes, which are played using two fingers. In the second part of the *toḍā*, *zamzama* is described as to be played with two fingers, simultaneously with the *"dir dir"* strokes.

toḍā jhārā 9

x o
Ġ̲ Ṙ̲ Ġ̲ | Ṡ Ṙ̲ N̲ Ṡ | D̲ N̲ P D̲ | M P G̲ M
dā rārārā dā rārārā | dā rārārā dā rārārā | dā rārārā dā rārārā | dā rārārā dā rārārā

x o
ṠĠ̲ Ġ̲ Ṙ̲ Ṡ N̲ D̲ | N̲ Ṡ Ṙ̲ Ġ̲ Ṙ̲ Ṡ N̲ P | D̲ P M G̲ S
ddd d dā rā dā rā | dā rā dā rā dā rā dā rā | dā rā dā rā dā

Ex. 11b. Toḍā bhairavīn *(Khan, M. S. H. 1873:56-61)*

Here it is specified that the *jhālā* strokes are to be played not on the *cikārī* strings, but on the *kharaj*, the lowest, a brass or bronze string, with a reverse *mizrāb* stroke (Khan, M. S. H. 1873:61). This is a type of *jhālā* rarely heard today, but specifically described in several of the 19th-century books. Satya Kinkar Banerji of Vishnupur made use of it in a demonstration at Banaras Hindu University in December 1980.

The Later Masitkhani bāj

Rahimsen and Amrtsen and their relatives in Rajasthan and Gwalior were the leading exponents and innovators of the Masitkhani *gat-toḍā* style throughout the second half of the 19th century. The available notated *gats* do not begin to do justice to the playing style of these great *sitār* players. However, with careful imaginative reconstruction and descriptions by musicians who had contact with them in mind, we can gain some understanding of what their styles contributed to later *sitār* playing. Sudarsanacarya tells us that Rahimsen and Amrtsen put together the best elements of *dhrupad* and *bīn*, the best of *khyāl*, and the unique capabilities of the *sitār* to create his style. Mushtaq Ali Khan said that the Senias played different types of Masitkhani *gats*, short and long, *khyāl* and *dhrupad*-based, and that they used different techniques accordingly to fit the style of each *gat*.[168] We know that the Senias specialized in the subtle melodic definitions of each *rāga*. A *gat* of theirs in *rāga darbārī* specifies *gamak* (g), *mīḍ* of one note (m-1) and *sūt* (s), and together these techniques bring out the character of this *rāga*. The octave jump in the *toḍā* corresponding to the *antarā* seems to have a *dhrupad* quality:

			x	---(g)---		(m-1)	o	(s)
P̣	I	Ṃ P̣ N̲̣ S	I	G̲ G̲ G̲ MP	I	G̲ G̲ R S	I	N̲̣P̣N̲̣ S
ḍiṛ	I	ḍā ḍiṛ ḍā ṛā	I	ḍā ḍā ṛā ḍiṛ	I	ḍā ḍiṛ ḍā ṛā	I	ḍā ḍā ṛā

toḍā (1a)

			x				o	(m1)
R	I	R R N̲̣ S	I	S Ṡ Ṡ Ṡ	I	N̲ Ṙ Ṡ Ṙ	I	Ṙ Ṡ Ṡ
ḍiṛ	I	ḍā ḍiṛ ḍā ṛā	I	ḍā ḍā ṛā ḍiṛ	I	ḍā ḍiṛ ḍā ṛā	I	ḍā ḍā ṛā

Ex. 12. Gat-toḍā darbārī kānhaḍā *(1a) (Sastri 1916:103)*

A *gat* in *rāga bhīmpalāsī* also shows a dramatic octave jumping that seems to reflect a *dhrupad* style. Unlike modern *bhīmpalāsī* it has *komal* (flat) R̲ and D̲. The commentary says the *rāga* calls for the use of *mīḍ* from G̲ to M and P and from P to N̲ and that in descent, *śuddha* (natural) R is slightly touched. *Mīḍ* is called for from R to G̲:

x				o		
P̣ P M P	I	G̲ M P P	I	N̲ Ṡ Ṡ N̲	I	D̲ P M P
ḍā ḍiṛ ḍā ṛā	I	ḍā ḍiṛ ḍā ṛā	I	ḍā ḍā ṛā ḍiṛ	I	ḍā ḍiṛ ḍā ṛā

toḍā (3)

x ... Ṙ ... D ... o ... R

N N G G | Ṡ Ṡ N P | P M M S | S G M P

ḍā ḍiṛḍā ḍā | ḍā ḍiṛḍā ṛā | ḍā ḍā ṛā ḍiṛ | ḍā ḍiṛḍā ṛā

Ex. 13. Gat-toḍā bhīmpalāsī *(3) (Sastri 1916:73)*

A *gat* attributed by Rahim Beg to Rahimsen is unusual in that it is played almost entirely in the lower octave. It uses the second string for the low G. It is in *rāga sinda bhairavīn*. It calls for "a lot" of *zamzama* (z+) on certain notes. It also adds a natural, *śuddha*, G in the *toḍā*:

x ... -(z+)- ... o ... (z)

G M P P | D D P P | D P P G | P N D P

ḍā ḍiṛḍā ṛā | ḍā ḍiṛḍā ṛā | ḍā ḍā ṛā ḍiṛ | ḍā ḍiṛḍā ṛā

toḍā (3)

x ---(z+)- ... o -(z)- ---(z)--- (z)

P P P P | P M G M | P P M M | M G R R

ḍā ḍiṛḍā ṛā | ḍā ḍiṛḍā ṛā | ḍā ḍā ṛā ḍiṛ | ḍā ḍiṛḍā ṛā

x -(m)- ... o

M G M M | N S R G | R S N S | N D P P

ḍā ḍiṛḍā ṛā | ḍā ḍiṛḍā ṛā | ḍā ḍā ṛā ḍiṛ | ḍā ḍiṛḍā ṛā

Ex. 14. Gat-toḍā sinda bhairavīn *(3) (Beg 1876:112; 1884:76)*

Another of Rahimsen's *gats* was memorized by Beg from one of Rahimsen's disciples. It is in *rāginī mīyāṅ kī toḍī*. Although the author comments that this *rāginī* has a large scope and that *ālāp* is played in it by good players, no ornamentation is specified:

x ... o

R | S R S R | G G G 'M | P D P 'M | G R S

dir | dā dirdā rā | dā dā rā dir | dā dirdā rā | dā dā rā

toḍā (3)

		x		o
G	G 'M P D	N Ṡ N D	P Ṡ N Ṡ	N Ṡ Ṡ
dir	dā dir dā rā	dā dir dā rā	dā dir dā dir	dā dā rā

		x		o
Ġ	Ṙ Ṡ N D	D Ṙ Ṙ Ṙ	G 'M P D	G R S
dir	dā dir dā rā	dā dir dā rā	dā dir dir rā	dā dā rā

Ex. 15. Gat-toḍā mīyāṅ kī toḍī *(1a) (Beg 1876:63)*

A *gat* attributed to Amrtsen uses a two-note *mīḍ* from 'M to P and D. It is in *rāga deśkār* which here has *komal* R and *tīvra* 'M:

		(m-P-D)			x(m-G)				(m-PD)			o		
P	'M	'M'M	'M	G	R	P	P	P	'M	'M	'M	G	R	S	S
dir	dā	dir	dā	rā	dā	dā	rā	dā	dā	rā	dā	dir	dā	dā	rā

Ex. 16. Gat deśkār *(Sastri 1916:49)*

Umar Khan demonstrated a *gat* of Amrtsen's in *rāga gurjarī toḍī* which has delicate *dhrupad*-style *mīḍ* between D and N, high Ṡ and N and in the RG GR phrase. All the notes notated above the main melody line are to be played by *mīḍ*:

	'M	x N NN Ṡ		o (m) (m)
D	N D G 'M	D N Ṡ ṠṠ	N D 'M D	RG GR S
dir	dā dir dā rā	dā dā rā dir	dā dir dā rā	dā dā rā

Ex. 17. Gat gurjarī *(Umar Khan, Calcutta)*

Sitār players other than the Senias also played *dhrupad*-inspired *gats* through the late 19th century. An austere *gat* in *rāga bhairav* from Pannalal Gosvami's "*Nād vinod*" has an appeal for its *bīn*-like quality. It begins from the seventh *mātrā*. The *bol* syllables are unusual:

	o		x	
R SṆ	S R S SR	Ṇ S Ḍ Ṇ	S S S S	S S
ḍāu ḍiṇ	ḍā ḍā ṇāṃ ḍiṇ	ḍā ḍiṇ ḍā ṇāṃ	ḍā ḍā ṇāṃ ḍā	ḍā ṇāṃ

	o		x	
S G	G G G R	G G M P	G M G R	R S
ḍā ḍiṇ	ḍā ḍā ṇāṃ ḍiṇ	ḍā ḍiṇ ḍā ṇāṃ	ḍā ḍā ṇāṃ ḍā	ḍā ṇāṃ

antarā

	o		x	
P D	Ṡ Ṡ Ṡ D	N Ṡ Ṙ Ġ	Ṙ Ṡ N D	P M
ḍā ḍiṇ	ḍā ḍā ṇāṃ ḍiṇ	ḍā ḍiṇ ḍā ṇāṃ	ḍā ḍā ṇāṃ ḍā	ḍā ṇāṃ

	o		x	
N Ṡ	N D P N	D PD M P	G M G R	S S
ḍā ḍiṇ	ḍā ḍā ṇāṃ ḍiṇ	ḍā ḍiṇ ḍā ṇāṃ	ḍā ḍā ṇāṃ ḍā	ḍā ṇāṃ

Ex. 18. Gat bhairav *(Gosvami, P. 1895:5)*

All of the *gats* presented so far appear to take their inspiration from *dhrupad rāga* movement and *bīn* techniques. But *khyāl* elements in the Senias' playing probably helped a great deal in gaining them their fame and popularity. It is possible to find notated Masitkhani *gats* of the Senias and others that seem to illustrate a *khyāl* leaning. One *gat* in *sindh bhairavī* is heavily ornamented and, along with *sūt* (s), contains a new technique, *kaṭ*, "cut" (k), for which it is described that the second finger quickly touches and leaves the fret adjacent to the main note:

x		o (s) (k)RS R(k)	Ṇ(k) P̣(k)
P̣ G R G	S R Ṇ S	ṆG S Ṇ S	Ṇ Ḍ Ṃ P̣
ḍā ḍiṛ ḍā ṛā	ḍā ḍiṛ ḍā ṛā	ḍā ḍā ṛā ḍiṛ	ḍā ḍiṛ ḍā ṛā

x	Ṇ	o (k)RS R(k)	Ṇ(k) P̣(k)
Ḍ Ṃ P̣ Ṇ	P̣ P̣ Ṇ S	ṆG S S S	Ṇ Ḍ Ṃ P̣
ḍā ḍiṛ ḍā ṛā	ḍā ḍiṛ ḍā ṛā	ḍā ḍā ṛā ḍiṛ	ḍā ḍiṛ ḍā ṛā

Ex. 19. Gat sindh bhairavī *(3) (Sastri 1916:64)*

An attractive *gat* in *rāga "khamāc"* by Amrtsen's son Nihalsen even contains a *tān* movement in the *toḍā*:

```
x   (m-1)          D   P   (k)   o D   P
Ṡ   N̲    N̲   Ṡ  | N̲   D   Ṙ   N̲  | N̲   D   M   G   | M   M   P   D
ḍā  ṛā   ḍā  ṛā | ḍā  ṛā  ḍā  ḍiṛ | ḍā  ḍā  ṛā  ḍiṛ | ḍā  ḍiṛ ḍā  ṛā
```

toḍā

```
x                                 o
P   M   G   R  | S   G   M   P  | GM   ṖD   N̲Ṡ   ṘĠ   | ĠṘ   ṠN̲   DP   MG
ḍā  ḍiṛ ḍā  ṛā | ḍā  ḍiṛ ḍā  ṛā | ḍāṛā ḍāṛā ḍāṛā ḍāṛā | ḍāṛā ḍāṛā ḍāṛā ḍāṛā
```

Ex. 20. Gat-toḍā khamāc *(Sastri 1916:90)*

A *gat* in *rāga pīlū* is full of ornamentation. Sudarsanacarya comments that the *rāga* is a favorite of untrained musicians *(atāī)*, and that it calls for a generous amount of "*kāṭ katar:*"

```
RS    P      R      x               R     NSR       oR     R
Ṇ   | D  MP  S  R | S  S  S  Ṇ   | S  S  G̣̲  G̣̲   | S  Ṇ  S
ḍiṛ | ḍā ḍiṛ ḍā ṛā | ḍā ḍā ṛā ḍiṛ | ḍā ṛā ḍā ḍiṛ | ḍā ḍā ṛā
```

Ex. 21. Gat pīlū *(Sastri 1916:79)*

A long unattributed *gat* from the "*Sarmāya-i 'ishrat*" in *rāga bihāg* is full of a similar sort of ornamentation. It may represent a *khyāl*-influenced style of *sitār* music found in the later 19th century:

```
                   x                                      o
G   | G   M   P  Ṡ  | DNPDMPGM    | GMG   GMPM  M     | GR  SṆ  S
dir | dā  dir da rā | dā dā rā dir | dā  dir dir  dir   | dā  dā  rā

                   x                                      o  (m)
M   | G   S   Ṇ  Ṇ  | S  S  Ṇ  Ṇ   | S   S   G     GM    | G   G   S
dir | dā  dir dā rā | dā dir dā rā | dā  dir dā    rā    | dā  dā  rā

                   x           (g)                        o  (m) (m) (m)
G   | G   M   P  Ṡ  | N  Ṡ  Ṡ  Ṡ   | NṠN   P       PNPN  | N   D   N
dir | dā  dir da rā | dā dā rā dir | dā  dir dā    rā    | dā  dā  rā

                   x                                      o  (m) (m) (m)
N   | NDP P   D  Ṡ  | Ṡ  Ṡ  Ṡ  Ṡ   | N   D   P     PNPN  | N   N   N
dir | dā  dir da rā | dā dir da rā | dā  dir da    rā    | dā  dā  rā
```

```
(m)                          x   (m)                   (m)    (m)     o    (m)
N    I  ND  P   MG   I  P  P  G  G   I  S  S  G       G      I  G  R  S
dir  I  dā   dir da rā  I  dā dirda rā  I  dā dir da     rā     I  dā dā rā
```

Ex. 22. Gat bihāg *(Khan, Sadiq A. 1884:244)*

Finally, an intriguing *gat* in *rāga kāfī*, also from the same work and unattributed, shows a similarly high degree of elaboration. It starts from the seventh *mātrā*:

```
        o     ---(g)---          (g)                x          (m) (g,s)
SR  Ṡ   I  S  RG̲MG̲R  R  I  G̲M  G̲   MP  M   I  P  P  P  D  I  PD    M
dā  dir I  dā dā   rā  dir I  dā   dir dā  rā  I  dā dā rā dir I  dā    dir

(k)       o    (m)        (m)                       x  (m)
G̲MR  I  R   D    D    D  I  P   D   M   P   I  G̲  G̲  M  M  I  RG̲M  R
dā rā I  dā dir  dā   rā I  dā  dir dā  rā  I  dā dā rā dā I  dā    rā
```

Ex. 23. Gat kāfī *(Khan, Sadiq A. 1884:248)*

System and Development in Senia and Later Style

Performance traditions tracing themselves to the disciples of the Senias fill in some details about the types of *toḍās* played and the development of the *gat* in the Senia *sitār* style. Mushtaq Ali Khan spoke of five phases of *gat* development: *gatkārī*, *mukhḍā*, *fikrā*, *toḍā* and *laykārī*. In *gatkārī*, "working with the *gat*," the melody is elaborated upon while the *bol* pattern of the *gat* is maintained. "*Mukhḍā*" is the name of the five-*mātrā* portion of *gat* pattern 1a, which leads to *sam*. In the section of *gat* elaboration by that name, the *mukhḍā* portion of the *gat* is varied both melodically and rhythmically. This is the beginning of rhythmic variation, and is at first confined to this small portion of the *gat*. "*Fikrā*" is a word used in *khyāl*, sometimes heard as *fikrebandī*, and often refers to short, quick series of note permutations, normally included in types of *tāns*. Karam Imam speaks of it as a technique essential to the *ṭappā* vocal form (Khan, M. K. I. 1925:42). *Ṭappa* specializes in fast short *tān* sequences, and it is possible that this was *fikrā*'s source of entry into *khyāl*. Sudarsanacarya speaks of *fikrā* as an element of *khyāl* which Rahimsen and Amrtsen put into their *sitār* music (Sastri 1916:Introduction, 27).

Mushtaq Ali Khan defined it as short, spontaneously composed phrases inserted into the *gat*.[169] The *bols* of the *fikrā* should "cut" the pattern of the *gat*, ornamenting it rhythmically. The next section of *gat* development, according to Mushtaq Ali Khan's tradition, is *toḍā*, consisting of many longer composed or semi-composed melodic and rhythmic pieces which are more or less independent of the *gat* pattern. Mushtaq Ali Khan described *toḍās* as "bouquets of flowers, with each flower in its proper and beautiful place."[170] Essential to *toḍās*, he said, are complex and interesting *mizrāb* patterns. The last section in this system is *laykārī*, in which all sorts of difficult rhythms are displayed using the *gat* as the melodic base. *Dūn*, *caugun̩* (one fourth), *āṭhguṇ* (one eighth), *āḍ*, *kuāḍ*, *atīt* and *anāgat* (the intentional showing of *sam* after and before the actual *sam* position) are rhythms and techniques that make up the *laykārī*, "working with lay" section.[171]

Umar Khan, speaking of the Senia system of *gat* development, described a similar pattern, using, however, only the terms *fikrā*, *toḍā* and *tān*.[172] *Fikrās* are the first, short, progressive rhythmic and melodic variations within phrases of the *gat*. In the *gat* for *rāga gurjarī*, the first series of *fikrās* Umar Khan gave were:

fikrā 1

				x	
D	I	N D 'M G 'M		I	D
dir	I	dā dir dā dir dā dir dā rā		I	dā etc.

fikrā 2

			x				o	
D	I	N D G 'M	I	D N Ṡ ṠNṠN	I	N D 'M D	I	RG GR RS
dir	I	dā dir dā rā	I	dā dā rā dādirdārā	I	dā dir dā rā	I	dādir dārā dārā

fikrā 3

			x	
D	I	N -- D -- D N D N D -- 'M -- D 'M G 'M	I	D
dir	I	dā -- dā -- dā dir dā rā dā -- rā -- dā dir dā rā	I	dā etc.

After a series of *fikrās*, according to Umar Khan's description of Senia style, the entire *gat* was played at different speeds and fit into the *tāla* cycle in increasingly difficult displays of rhythmic skill. This is a technique derived from *dhrupad laykārī* work. These rhythmic transformations of the *gat* were followed by *toḍās* of all sorts which broke away from the *bol* pattern of the *gat*, and were characterized by complex *mizrāb bol* combinations. After a series of *toḍās*, according to Umar Khan, *tāns* of the *khyāl* variety were played in a higher speed, eventually covering the entire range of the instrument and the gamut of the *rāga*. In all these sections, the *gat* would be rejoined intermittantly at the *sam*, *mukhḍā*, or at different places displaying the rhythmic skill of the performer.[173]

Balkrsnapati Bajpeyi of Gwalior, in his "*Sitār kī tīsrī pustak*," represents a tradition learned from Amir Khan, Amrtsen's nephew. Immediately following the *gats* in Bajpeyi's book are *toḍās* in *ṭhā* within the *bol* pattern of the *gat*, as is standard throughout late 19th-century and early 20th-century notations. After these *toḍās* come a series of variations called "*gat kī sīdhī āḍī.*" These are, like the *toḍās*, played in *ṭhā*, the original rhythm of the *gat*, but they invert, extend and mix the *bols* of the *gat*. Following the "*gat kī sīdhī āḍī*" are *fikrās*, which are played in *dugun*, double the speed of the *gat*. They consist of long passages, often with repetitive melodic patterns and a large variety of *bol* combinations. Below are selections from each of the type in *rāga jaunpurī*. "*(k)*" indicates a *kaṭṭhā*, a left hand two-finger pluck and hammer technique on three frets, producing for R the notes G̲RSR; *mīḍ*, *gamak* and *sūt* are also specified

		x (k)	(m) (m)	o
M	P Ṡ D̲ PD̲	MP G̲M R M	P P ṘĠ̲ ṘĠ̲	Ṙ Ṡ Ṡ
diḍ	ḍā diḍ ḍā rā	ḍā ḍā rā diḍ	ḍā diḍ ḍā rā	ḍā ḍā rā
(g)	(g)	x (g) (g)		o (s)
Ṙ	Ṡ N̲ D̲ P	N̲ N̲ Ṡ Ṡ	Ṙ N̲ D̲ P	G̲ G̲SR
diḍ	ḍā diḍ ḍā rā	ḍā diḍ ḍā rā	ḍā diḍ ḍā rā	ḍā ḍā rā

toḍā

	(g) (g)	x (g)		o (g) (g)
M	P D̲ N̲ Ṡ	N̲ Ṡ Ṡ Ṙ	Ṡ N̲ D̲ P	M M P
diḍ	ḍā diḍ ḍā rā	ḍā ḍā rā diḍ	ḍā diḍ ḍā rā	ḍā ḍā rā
	(s)	x		o
D̲	P M G̲S R	Ṙ Ġ̲ Ġ̲ Ġ̲	Ṙ Ṙ Ṡ ṠṘ	D̲N̲ D̲N̲SṘ Ṡ
diḍ	ḍā diḍ ḍā rā	ḍā diḍ ḍā rā	ḍā diḍ ḍā rā	ḍā ḍā rā

gat kī sīdhī āḍī

(begins from the fourth *mātrā* and joins the *gat* at *mātrā* twelve)

M	P	P	ṘG̲	ṘG̲	Ṙ	Ṡ	Ṡ	
diḍ	ḍā	diḍ	ḍā	rā	ḍā	ḍā	rā	two times

Ṙ	Ṡ	N̲	D̲	P	
diḍ	ḍā	diḍ	ḍā	rā	two times

N̲	N̲	Ṡ	Ṡ	Ṙ	N̲	D̲	P	
ḍā	diḍ	ḍā	rā	ḍā	diḍ	ḍā	rā	two times

	(s)		
G̲	G̲S	R	
ḍā	ḍā	rā	two times

M	P	Ṡ	D̲	
diḍ	ḍā	diḍ	ḍā	two times

fikrā

(begins at *sam*, rejoins *gat* at fourth *mātrā*: *diḍ diḍ* = 1 *mātrā*)

diḍ	diḍ	diḍ	diḍ	diḍ	diḍ	ḍā	rā	ḍā	rā	repeated throughout
D̲	P	D̲	P	D̲	P	M	G̲	R	S	
N̲	D̲	N̲	D̲	N̲	D̲	P	M	G̲	R	
Ṡ	N̲	Ṡ	N̲	Ṡ	N̲	D̲	P	M	G̲	
Ṙ	Ṡ	Ṙ	Ṡ	Ṙ	Ṡ	N̲	D̲	P	M	
Ġ̲	Ṙ	Ġ̲	Ṙ	Ġ̲	Ṙ	Ṡ	N̲	D̲	P	
S	R	M	P	N̲	Ṡ	Ġ̲	Ṙ	Ṡ	Ṡ	
Ġ̲	Ṙ	Ṡ	N̲	D̲	P	M	G̲	R	S	

Ex. 24. Gat-toḍā jaunpurī *(1a-b) (Bajpeyi 1936:7-9)*

Bajpeyi gives us details on an aspect of Amir Khan's style which shows us that the Senias also played pieces in less conventional styles. Amir Khan, according to Bajpeyi, used to play something called a "*gat lahara.*" This would begin in the *rāga sarparda* and soon move to *fikrās*, in other *rāgas*, intermittantly returning to the original *mukhḍā* of *sarparda*. Gradually he would increase the speed of the *gat*, ending in a high speed with *jhālā*:

x										o								
													PD		-(z)- S			
PM	PM	P	G	I	MG	MG	M	R	I	GR	GR	RG	MM	I	M	R	R	R
dā	dā	rā	dir	I	dā	dā	rā	dir	I	dā	dā	rā	dir	I	dā	dir	dā	rā

Ex. 25. Gat lahara *(Bajpeyi 1936:58-9)*

The variety of *gats* and techniques found within the Masitkhani system at the end of the 19th century reveals that this was a dynamic and intricate genre. But it was to change a great deal in the 20th century before becoming what it is today.

9

The Firozkhani *bāj* and *gat* Forms of the *sarod*

Firozkhani gats

Although the *sarod* repertoire has been closely related to that of the *sitār* throughout its history, forms and techniques differ significantly enough to warrant separate discussion. The history of *sarod* music is traceable to the region of Rohilkhand in the period following Muhammad Shah's rule in Delhi. Firoz Khan and other Delhi musicians settled there, and under their influence *rāga* melodies began to be applied to the Afghani *rabāb*, which later became the *sarod*. Relatively little early written information is available on the history of the *sarod* and its music, but some points on technique and *gat* style can be extracted from oral and later written sources.

The free movement of the right hand and the percussive sound of the *rabāb* and *sarod* were conducive to fast rhythmic techniques. Strength and versatility characterize the right hand actions of the earliest *sarod* playing to which we have access. Melodically, long intervallic jumps are suited to the instrument because the gamut is distributed across several strings. The left hand "cutting" ornamentations of *kaṭ* or *kṛntan* are often especially associated with *sarod*.

The *gats* of the extant Firozkhani style show characteristics that would seem to suit the early *sarod*. Radhika Mohan Maitra demonstrated that Firozkhani *gats* are played at a middle speed, make use of a variety of interesting *bol* patterns and have long intervallic jumps. Notated Firozkhani *gats* as well often reflect these characteristics. If the Firozkhani style is indeed linked with the early *sarod*, a collection of Firozkhani *gats* in Bakhtavar Singh's "*Svar tāl samūh*" (c.1915) may be close to representing early *sarod* music. The author was a disciple of Ghulam Ali himself. The *gats* in his book are clearly old, differing in both *rāga* and *bol* patterns from later *gats*. The simplest is in *rāga* "*Īman:*"

x		o	
Ḍ S -- R	G -- -- 'M	P -- -- G	P G R S
dārā -- dā	rā -- -- dā	rā -- -- dir	dā dir dā rā

toḍā

x		o	
R G -- P	D N Ṡ D	P -'MP 'M	P GR -R S
dārā -- dir	dā dirdā rā	dā -r dā rā	dā rdā -r dā

Ex. 26. Firozkhani gat-toḍā īman *(Singh, B. c. 1915:75-6)*

The halting, percussive rhythm of this *gat* is striking. Another *gat* in *rāga megh* sounds almost like a march:

x		o	
M MD -D D	Ṡ -- -- Ṡ	D -- D P	M G̲ R S
dā rdā -r dir	da -- -- -d	dā -- dā rā	dā dir dirdir
x		o	
S SS -S S	M -MM M	D D D M	Ṡ ṠṠ -Ṡ Ṡ
dā rdā -r dā	dā -r dā rā	dā dir dir dir	dā rdā -r dā

toḍā

x		o	
G̲G̲ MM D DD	-D Ṡ Ṡ Ṡ	D DD DD G̲G̲	M MM -M D
dir dir dā rdā	-r dā dā rā	dā dir dir dir	dā rdā -r dā
D DṠ -Ṡ Ṡ	Ṡ -- N̲ Ṡ	Ṡ DD DD PP	M MG̲ -R S
dā rdā -r dā	dā -- dā rā	dā dir dir dir	dā rdā -r dā

Ex. 27. Firozkhani gat-toḍā megh *(Singh, B. c. 1915:93)*

A *gat* from the "*Sitār candrikā*" of 1893 Bombay is not labelled as Firozkhani, but it appears to have a character similar to those from the "*Svar tāl samūh.*" It is in *rāga gārā* and sounds like a simple march:

```
        x                                        o
G R   | G GGG S    | R RR R Ṇ    | S SS S S    | S S
ḍā ṛā | ḍā ḍiṛ ḍā ṛā | ḍā ḍiṛ ḍā ṛā | ḍā ḍiṛ ḍā ṛā | ḍā ṛā

        x                                        o
D D   | Ṇ -Ṇ S S   | R P PP PP   | M MG -G R   | S S
ḍā ḍā | ḍā -ṛ ḍā ṛā | ḍā ḍā ḍiṛ ḍiṛ | ḍā ṛḍā -ṛ ḍā | ḍā ṛā

        x                                        o
P M   | P PP P G   | M MMM R     | G GG G R    | S S
ḍā ḍā | ḍā ḍiṛ ḍā ṛā | ḍā ḍiṛ ḍā ṛā | ḍā ḍiṛ ḍā ṛā | ḍā ṛā
```

Ex. 28. Gat gārā *(Vastad 1893:5)*

The "*Saṅgīt kalādhar*" of Bhavnagar, Gujarat, contains some *gats* labelled as Firozkhani. One in *rāga bhūp kalyāṇ* has a march-like rhythmic quality that seems to group it with those above:

```
o                              x
P -P R G    | S Ḍ -- Ḍ     | S -- S R      | G G -G P
dā-r dā rā  | dā rā -- dā  | dā -- dirdir  | dā rdā -r dā

o                              x
G -- -- P   | G -- P D     | P D P G       | P PR -R G
dā-- -- rā  | rā -- dā rā  | dā dirdirdir  | dā rdā -r dā

[toḍā]
o                              x
P -P R G    | P D Ṡ P      | -D D P D      | Ṡ Ṙ -- Ṙ
dā-r dā rā  | dā dirdā dā  | -r dā dā dir  | dā rā -- dir

o                              x
Ġ -- Ṙ Ṡ    | D Ṡ -Ṡ D     | P D Ṙ Ṡ       | P PR -R G
dā-- dā rā  | dā dā -r dā  | dā dirdirdir  | dā rdā -r dā
```

Ex. 29. Firozkhani gat-toḍā bhūp kalyān *(Shivram 1938:315-6)*

Some Firozkhani *gats* show a *bol* pattern that has shades of the Masitkhani style, supporting the possibility that they stand historically between the Masitkhani and the Purab styles. Two Firozkhani *gats* from the "*Svar tāl samūh*" are examples:

		x		o
R	S N̲D DN̲ P	D S S S	R R -R M	G̲M RG̲ SR
dir	dā rā dā dir	dā rā dā dir	dā rdā -r dir	dā dā rā
M	G̲ G̲ M G̲	S S -- R	S N̲ D P	M G̲R -S
dir	dā dir dā rā	dā rā -- dā	dā rā dā rā	dā rdā -r

Ex. 30. Firozkhani gat jangla *(Singh, B. c. 1915:125)*

		x		o
D	Ṡ D P M	M -- -- -G̲	R -- S R	M G̲ -M
dir	dā dir dā rā	dā -- -- -r	dā -- dā rā	dā rdā -r
		x		o
	G̲ M D Ṡ	-Ṡ Ṡ Ṡ D	P M M M	G̲ R -S
	dā dir dā dā	-r dā dā rā	dā dir dir dir	dā rdā -r

Ex. 31. Firozkhani gat malār *(Singh, B. c. 1915:96)*

Notation does not make details of style clear. We must take the word of performance traditions that the style of presentation and elaboration distinguished these from the fast *gats* of the Purab *bāj*. Also, the best *gats* of any *bāj* are always found not in written collections but in performance tradition. Two Firozkhani *gats* demonstrated by Radhika Mohan Maitra are outstanding examples of a professional level of this style. He played them at a leasurely flowing pace. He attributed the *gat* in *rāga jaunpurī* to Abdullah Khan, grandson of Ghulam Ali. He thought that both *gats* dated to at least the last quarter of the 19th century and that they could be earlier:

x		o	
P M P Ṡ	-Ṡ Ṡ P M	P D̲ -- D̲N̲	D̲ P -M P
dā dir dā dā	-r dā dā dir	dā dā -- dir	dā rdā -r dā
x		o	
G̲ -- -- R	-- M P D̲	N̲ N̲ S R	N̲ N̲D̲-D̲ P
dā -- -- dā	-- dā dā rā	dā dir dir dir	dā rdā -r dā

x		o	
D̲ D̲ -D̲ N̲	Ṡ Ṙ Ġ̲ Ṙ	Ṡ Ṙ N̲ Ṡ	N̲Ṡ D̲ -D̲ P
dā rdā -r dir	dā dir dā rā	dā dir dir dir	dā rdā -r dā

Ex. 32. Firozkhani gat jaunpurī *(Radhika Mohan Maitra, Calcutta)*

o		x	
Ṇ R G Ḍ	-Ḍ Ṇ R G	P 'M G Ṇ	-Ṇ R G 'M
dā dir dā dā	-r dā dā rā	dā dir dā dā	-r dā dā rā
o		x	P(k)
D P 'M G	'M N -N D	P -P 'M G	M G R G
dā dir dā dā	rā dā -r dā	dā -r dā rā	dā rā dā rā
P(k)		x	
M G R G	R Ṇ -Ṇ S	Ḍ Ṇ Ḍ G	-G R S Ṇ
dā rā dir dir	dā rdā -r dā	dā dir dā dā	-r dā dā rā
o		x	
Ḍ Ṇ Ḍ S	Ṇ ṆḌ -Ḍ P̣	P 'M G M	R G Ṇ R
dā dir dir dir	dā rdā -r dā	dā dir dā rā	dā rā dā rā

Ex. 33. Firozkhani gat yaman kalyāṇ *(Radhika Mohan Maitra)*[174] *[(k) =* kaṇ, *a touch with the left hand second finger]*

Sarod gats *of the Purab* bāj

Besides the Firozkhani *gats* in which only some *sarod* lines continued to specialize, *sarod* players by the late 19th century played a repertoire of fast Purab *gats* that were of a distinctive and characteristic style. These *gats* often contain abrupt rhythmic patterns, not unlike some of the *gats* noted earlier above. One demonstrated by Radhika Mohan Maitra was attributed by him to Murad Ali Khan, a son of Ghulam Ali. It is in the *rāga kāfī khambāj*, and contains a number of *kṛntans (kṛ)* which are integral to the *gat*. He played it at a fast speed and emphasized its off-beat rhythms:

	o (kṛ)		x (kṛ)	
N̲̣ R	S N̲̣ḌP̣ -P̣Ṃ	-- Ḍ -Ḍ N̲̣	S -- -- G	-R G M P
dā dir	dir dā -r dā	-- dā -r dā	dā -- -- dā	-r dā dā dir

```
o                        (kṛ)  x          (kṛ)
| G M   -- M  | P M G GRS | -S G R SND  | -P D
| dā rā -- dā | dirdirdā dā | -r dirdā dā | -r dā
```

Ex. 34. Purbī gat kāfī khambāj *(Radhika Mohan Maitra)*[175]

One *gat* pattern appears again and again in older compositions played by both *sitār* and *sarod* players. Radhika Mohan Maitra attributed the following *gat*, which has this pattern, to Murad Ali Khan. It is tempting to think that it may be traceable to a 19th-century *sarod* tradition. It is suited to a very fast speed:

```
x                          o
N Ṡ N Ṡ     | -- Ṡ N Ṡ     | N Ṡ Ṙ Ṡ      | N ND -P D
dādir dā dā | -- dā dā dā  | dā dirdirdir | dā rdā -r dā

x                          o
P D P Ṡ     | -- Ṡ N D     | M P D P      | M MG -R G
dādir dā dā | -- dā dā dā  | dā dirdirdir | dā rdā -r dā

x                          o
S N S G     | -G M P D     | N Ṡ Ṙ Ṡ      | N ND -P D
dādir dā dā | -r dā dā dā  | dā dirdirdir | dā rdā -r dā

antarā

x                          o
M NN D N    | -N D P D     | N Ṡ N Ṙ      | Ṡ ṠN -N Ṡ
dādir dā dā | -r dā dā dā  | dā dirdirdir | dā rdā -r dā

x                          o
Ṡ Ġ Ṙ Ṁ     | -Ṁ Ġ Ṙ Ṡ     | N Ṡ Ṙ Ṡ      | N ND -D N
dādir dā dā | -r dā dā dā  | dā dirdirdir | dā rdā -r dā

x                          o
P D P Ṡ     | -Ṡ Ṡ N D     | M P D P      | M MG -R G
dādir dā dā | -r dā dā dā  | dā dirdirdir | dā rdā -r dā

x                          o
S N S G     | -G M P D     | N Ṡ Ṙ Ṡ      | N ND -P D
dādir dā dā | -r dā dā dā  | dā dirdirdir | dā rdā -r dā
```

Ex. 35. Gat khambāj *(Radhika Mohan Maitra)*[176]

Sakhawat Husain Khan played a *gat* on a 78 rpm recording which is nearly identical to this in its pattern, but is melodically transposed to fit *rāga gārā*:

x		o	(kṛ)
N̲ S N̲ S	-- S P D	N̲ S G̲ R	S N̲DP -PD
dādirdā dā	-- dā dā rā	dā rā dirdir	dā dā -r dā
x		o (k)	
S G G M	-- M G M	G M G PM	G̲ G̲R -R S
dādirdā dā	-- dā dā rā	dā rā dirdir	dā dā -r dā
x	--(m)--	o	(kṛ)
S R R M	G̲ M G̲ R	S R G̲ R	S N̲DP -PD
dādirdā dā	-- dā dā rā	dā rā dirdir	dā dā -r dā

Ex. 36. Purbī gat gārā [(kṛ) = kṛtan; (k) = kaṇ][177]

Still other *gats* of the same pattern shift the melody up a third and begin it from G M G M.

Murad Ali Khan's son was Abdullah Khan, and Radhika Mohan Maitra attributes the following *gat* in *rāga kāfī* to him. It became fairly widely played:

x		o	
P -- P D	M G M P	R G̲ M P	G̲ G̲R -S R
dā-- dā dā	dā dā dā dā	dā dirdirdir	dā rdā -r dā
x		o	
D N̲ D N̲	S G M P	N̲ D M P	G̲ G̲R -S R
dirdirdā dā	dā dā dā dā	dā dā dirdir	dā rdā -r dā
x		o	
R N̲ D N̲	P D N̲ Ṡ	Ṙ Ġ̲ Ṙ Ṡ	N̲ N̲D -D P
dādirdā rā	dā dā dā dā	dā dā dirdir	dā rdā -r dā
x		o	
G M R G	M P N̲ D	P M G M	G̲ G̲R -S R
dādirdā dā	dā dā dā dā	dā dā dirdir	dā rdā -r dā

Ex. 37. Gat kāfī *(Radhika Mohan Maitra)*[178]

The *sarod* players of Shahjahanpur in the 19th century and early 20th century, according to Umar Khan, would sit outside in the evenings on their cots, showing off, comparing and trading *gats* that they knew or had composed. Each would try to top the others, giving a new rhythmic or melodic twist to each *gat*. The friendly competition resulted in a great variety and a lively spirit in the *gats* of the time. The same process must have gone on among the *sitār* players who were creating their fast Purab *gats*.

A *gat* from the Shahjahanpur *sarod* players' repertoire begins at *sam*, but returns to *sam* only after two rounds. It is in the *rāga gārā*, or sometimes played as *zilā*. It is played at a fast speed:

		x		o
N	D M D N	S -- D N	S -- D N	R -- D N
dir	dā dir dā rā	dā -- dā rā	dā -- dā rā	dā -- dā rā
		x		o
	S R G M	G GR -R S	S R G M	-- G R S
	dā dir dir dir	dā rdā -r dā	dā dir dā dā	-- dā rā dā
		x		
	D N S R	S D -D		
	dā rā dir dir	dā dā -r		

Ex. 38. Purbī gat gārā *(Umar Khan, Calcutta)*

Another *gat* in *gārā* from the Shajahanpur *sarod* players is called *ṭhā-dūnī*, "single-double," because it combines single and double speed rhythms in one *gat*:

	x		o
D N D N	S -- -- --	SRG -- R S	D -- N --
dā dir dā rā	dā -- -- --	dā -- -- --	dā -- rā --
	x		o
M -- -- --	R G M P	R G R M	G GR -R S
dā -- -- --	dā rā dā rā	dā dir dir dir	dā rdā -r dā

Ex. 39. Ṭhā-dūnī gat gārā *(Umar Khan, Calcutta)*

A *gat* composed by Na'matullah Khan, also in *rāga gārā*, can be played either in *tīntāla*, or in *ektāla* of twelve *mātrās*:

x		o	
Ṃ Ḍ -- Ṇ̲	-- Ṇ̲ -Ḍ Ṇ̲	Ṃ Ḍ -Ḍ Ṇ̲	S Ṇ S --
dā dā -- rā	-- dā -r dā	dā dā -r dā	dā rā dā --
x		**o**	
S -- S S	Ḍ Ṇ̲ R R	R G̲ R M	G̲ G̲R -R S
dā -- dā rā	dā rā dā rā	dā rā dirdir	dā rdā -r dā
x		**o**	
S R G̲ M	-- G̲ R S	Ḍ Ṇ̲ S R	S Ṇ̲ -Ḍ Ṇ̲
dā dirdā dā	-- dā rā dā	dā rā dirdir	dā dā -r dā

Ex. 40. Purbī gat gārā *(Umar Khan, Calcutta)*

Na'matullah and his son Karamatullah Khan were active teachers, and a number of *gats* from their family tradition came into wide circulation, played on both *sarod* and *sitār*. This *gat* attributed to Na'matullah's son Kaukab Khan became popular:

x		o	
R -G̲ R S	R G̲ P M	G̲ R S R	S SḌ -D Ṇ̲
dā -r dā rā	dā rā dā rā	dā rā dirdir	dā rdā -r dā
x		**o**	
Ṃ Ṃ Ṃ P̣	P̣ P̣ Ḍ Ḍ	N̲ S -- R	S Ḍ -Ḍ Ṇ̲
dā rā dā dā	rā dā dā rā	dā rā -- dir	dā dā -r dā
x		**o**	
G M M G	M M G M	G M G P	M G̲ R --
dā dirdā dā	dirdā dā rā	dā dirdā rā	dā rā dā --
x		**o**	
R N̲ D N̲	P D M P	G M G̲ R	S Ṇ̲ Ḍ̲ Ṇ̲
dā dirdā rā	dā rā dā rā	dā dirdā rā	dā rā dā rā

Ex. 41. Purbī gat zila *(Jyotish Chandra Chaudhury, Varanasi)*

Waliullah Khan, *sitār* player and son of Kaukab Khan, N'amatullah Khan's other son, played the following well-known *gat* on an early 78 rpm recording. Its origins may be in his family line:

o		x	
S G̲ R G̲	-- S R Ṇ	S -- -- M	G̲ R S Ṇ
dā dirdā dā	-- dā rā dā	dā -- -- dā	dā rā dā rā
o		x	
S G̲ R G̲	-- S R Ṇ	S -- -- --	S R M P
dā dirdā dā	-- dā rā dā	dā -- -- --	dā rā dā rā
o		x	
N̲ D P M	G̲ G̲R-S R	R N̲ D P	-MM G M
dā dirdirdir	dā rdā -r dā	dā dirdā dā	-r dā dā rā
o		x	
G M G M	G̲ G̲R-S R	P -D P M	G̲ R S Ṇ
dā dirdirdir	dā rdā -r dā	dā -r dā rā	dā rā dā rā

Ex. 42. Purbī gat pīlū *(recording: Waliullah Khan)*

Another *gat* in *khamāj* which is well-known in slightly varying versions, was attributed by Jyotish Chandra Chaudhury to Waliullah Khan. In this, which may well be its original version, it is played largely in the lower register:

x		o	
Ṣ G̣ -G̣ G̣	Ṃ P̣ -P̣ P̣	G̣ Ṃ G̣ --	-- -- -- --
dā dā -r dā	dā dā -r dā	dā rā dā --	-- -- -- --
x		o	
S R -R S	N̲̣ Ḍ -Ḍ P̣	G̣ Ṃ P̣ Ḍ	G̣ Ṃ G̣ --
dā dā -r dā	dā dā -r dā	dā dirdā rā	dā rā dā --

Ex. 43. Gat khamāj *(Jyotish Chandra Chaudhury, Varanasi)*

Oral histories indicate that the Masitkhani *gat-toḍā* style did not enter *sarod* playing until after the mid-19th century, when *dhrupad* played an increasingly important role in *sarod* music.[179] Jyotish Chandra Chaudhury remembered that even in early 20th-century Bengal the *sarod* players he heard rarely played the Masitkhani style, but when they did, he said, they played it at a faster speed than *sitār* players, and filled the *gats* with many added strokes.[180] Radhika Mohan Maitra demonstrated a *ṭhā-dūnī gat* from a *sarod* tradition which combines Masitkhani and Purab *bols*. It is in *rāga naṭ malhār*, and is ornamented with *murkī (mu)* and *mīḍ (m)*:

(m) (m)	o (mu) (m)	-(m)-	x (m)	--(m)--
MD PD	M -- GR M	GR G Ṇ S	GR -- GR GR	G Ṃ
di r	dā -- di r	dā -- dā rā	dā -- dā --	dā rā
	o (mu) (m)	-(m)-	x	
MD PD	M -- GR M	GR G Ṇ S	R R R M	-- M
di r	dā -- di r	dā -- dā rā	dā dir dā dā	-- dā
	o		x	(m)
P D	M P D Ṡ	D N̲D -D D	P D G M	GR G
dā rā	dā rā dir dir	dā rdā -r dā	dā dir dā rā	dā rā

Ex. 44. Ṭhā-dūnī gat naṭ malhār *(Radhika Mohan Maitra)*[181]

Firozkhani *gats* which resemble Masitkhani closely were noted earlier. It is possible that these types of *gats* represent an early style of Masitkhani-related *sarod* playing.

A late 19th-century instructional book by *sitār* player-author Azharuddin who learned in Amroha near Rampur contains the *gat* types Masitkhani, Firozkhani and "Mizrāb." Mizrāb *gats* seem to have an affinity to Masitkhani, and might again represent a type of *gat* played by early *sarod* players. One is in *rāga jhinjhoṭī*:

		x		o
P̣	D S R G	R M G M	R M G R	S N̲ Ḍ
dir	dā dirdā dā	dā dirdā dir	dā dirdā dir	dā dirdā

Ex. 45. Mizrāb gat jhinjhoṭī *(Azharuddin 1898:n.p.)*

10

The Purab and Razakhani Styles

The fast *gats* of the Purab and Razakhani *bāj* probably had several sources of inspiration. History indicates that the Firozkhani *bāj* predated the Purab style, and that the creators of the Purab *bāj* might have received their original inspiration from Rampur musicians. Once begun in its eastern centers, however, the Purab *bāj* built its repertoire around the musical trends predominant at the time. That *ṭhumrī* was an important source of the fast speed *gats* of Ghulam Raza was pointed out with some disdain by Muhammad Karam Imam, who commented that they lacked scope in *rāga*, and were composed for the sake of the pleasure-loving Lucknow nobility. *Gats* ascribed to the *dhrupad* instrumentalists Pyar Khan and Basat Khan in performance and written traditions, on the other hand, show a high degree of sophistication with respect to *rāga*. Some may have had *dhrupad* music as their source. But it is clear from attributed compositions in performance tradition that disciples of the *dhrupad* instrumentalists also used *ṭhumrī* music as the basis for many of their *gats*. Other prevalent forms of the time, *tarānā*, *khyāl*, and even Masitkhani *gats*, were also probable inspirations for various Purab *gats*. It is often difficult to identify the musical sources of specific *gats*.

Purbī gats *of the* dhrupad *Instrumentalists*

The single most famous *gat* in *sitār* playing is probably one in *rāga kāfī*. It is to be found, with only minor variation, in virtually every collection of *sitār* music, oral and written. Karamatullah Khan attributed it to Pyar Khan of Lucknow. Radhika Mohan Maitra ascribed it to Pyar Khan "*Angulī Kaṭ*" of Banaras and called it a Firozkhani *gat*. Others say it is a Purab style or a Razakhani *gat*. Often *ṭhumrī* is pointed to as its musical source, but some performers think that it could have been inspired by *dhrupad*. The following notation is from the "*Saṅgīt kalādhar*" which assigns it no specific type, but says that it is to be played at a fast speed:

```
o                           x
S  R R G̲   |  -- M -G̲ M   |  P -- P M    |  G̲ R S Ṉ̣
dā dirdirdā |  -- dā -r dā |  dā -- dā rā |  dā rā dā rā

o                           x
S  R R G̲   |  -- M -G̲ M   |  P -- -- M   |  P D Ṉ --
dā dirdirdā |  -- dā -d rā |  dā -- -- dā |  dā dir dā --

o                           x
D  P -- M   |  G̲ -- R --   |  R Ṉ D Ṉ     |  P D M P
dā rā -- dā |  rā -- dā -- |  dā dirdā rā |  dā dir dā rā

o                           x
G̲  M -- P   |  M -- S Ṉ̣   |  S G̲ R M     |  G̲ G̲R -R Ṉ̣
dā rā -- dā |  dā -- dā rā |  dā dirdirdir |  dā rdā -r dā
```

Ex. 46. Gat kafī *(Shivram 1938:329)*

In many versions the G̲ at *khālī* in the last line is natural, perhaps indicating more of a *ṭhumrī* influence.

Pyar Khan's brother Basat Khan was an important Lucknow *dhrupadia* and was one of the founders of the Purab *bāj*. Ilyas Khan stated that Basat Khan's *gats* were always forty-eight or sixty-four *mātrās* long.[182] Karamatullah Khan gives us a *gat* which he ascribes to Basat Khan, who was his father's teacher. It is forty-eight *mātrās* long and is in *rāga bhūpālī*. It does not seem to be based on a *ṭhumrī* :

```
                   x                         o
S  |  Ḍ S -S R   |  G -- G R    |  G P P P         |  G GR -R R
dā |  rā dā -r dā |  dā -- dā rā |  dā dir dir dir  |  dā rdā -r dā

                   x                         o
   |  G P D Ṡ     |  Ṡ Ṙ Ṙ Ṙ       |  Ṡ ṠD -D P      |  Ṡ D G --
   |  dā dā dā rā |  dā dirdirdir  |  dā rda -r dā   |  dā rā dā --

                   x                         o
   |  D -- P D    |  P D D P       |  -- G P P       |  P PG -R
   |  dā -- dā rā |  dā dirdā rā   |  -- dir dir dā  |  dā rdā -r
```

Ex. 47. Purbī gat bhūpālī *(Khan, K. 1908:197)*

Radhika Mohan Maitra demonstrated a *gat* in *rāga bihāg* which he described as a type of *gat* in the *dhrupad* style (*aṅg*) taught by the Lucknow *dhrupad* instrumentalists. He played it at a medium tempo and used *kaṇ (k)* and a distinctive *murkī (mu)* at *sam*:

o		x (mu)	
P 'MG M	G RSṆ S	G -- -- --	-- -- P M
dā dirdā rā	dā dirdā rā	dā -- -- --	-- -- dā rā
o R(k)		x	
G -- -- S	S S Ṇ S	-- P Ṇ S	G GS -Ṇ S
dā -- -- rā	dā dirdā rā	-- dirdirdir	dā rdā -r dā

antarā

o		x	
P 'MP G	-- M P N	-- Ṡ Ṡ Ġ	Ġ ĠṘ -Ṙ Ṡ
dā dirdā rā	-- dā dā rā	-- dirdirdir	dā rdā -r dā
o	R(k)	x	
N -- -- Ṡ	-- Ṡ N --	-- D N Ṡ	N NP -P P
dā -- -- dā	-- rā dā --	-- dirdirdir	dā rdā -r dā
o R(k)		x	
G M G S	Ṇ S P̣ Ṇ	S G R S	Ṇ ṆS -Ṇ S
dā dirdā rā	dā dirdā rā	dā dirdirdir	dā rdā -r dā

Ex. 48. Purbī gat bihāg *(Radhika Mohan Maitra)*[183]

A Purbī *gat* in *rāga khamāj* in the "*Saṅgīt kalādhar*" is specified as to be played in a medium speed. It is full of ornamental techniques and may be, like the previous *gat*, representative of the non-*ṭhumrī* style *gats* taught by the *dhrupad* instrumentalists:

o		x	
G̣ Ḍ -Ḍ Ṇ	S Ṇ S --	R R -R R	S Ṇ̲ Ḍ --
dā dā -r dā	dā rā dā --	dā dā -r dā	dā rā dā --
o----(os)----		x	-(os)-
R R R R	S SṆ̲ -P̣ Ḍ	S M G M	GM -M R R
dirdir dirdir	dā rdā -r dā	dā dirdirdā	rdā -r dirdir
o-(os)-		x -(gh)-	
R RS -S S	Ṇ̲ Ṇ̲Ḍ -P̣ Ḍ	P̣ḌṆ̲ Ḍ P̣	Ḍ Ṃ G̣ --
dā rdā -r dir	dā rdā -r dā	dā -- dā rā	dā rā dā --

toḍā

		x (z)	(z)
		M -- -- --	M -- -- --
		dā -- -- --	dā -- -- --
o		x	
G P M M	G GR -RS	S M G M	R G S R
dādirdirdir	dā rdā -r dā	dā -- dā --	dā -- dā --
o		x -(gh)-	
Ṇ S -Ṇ R	S Ṉ D Ṉ	PDṈ D P	D M G --
dādā -r dā	dā rā dā rā	dā -- dā rā	dā rā dā --

Ex. 49. Purbī gat khamāj *(Shivram 1938:325)* [(m) = mīḍ; z = zamzama; gh = ghasīṭ; os = *oscillate the string* (tār hillānā)]

Muhammad Azharuddin gives us *gats* in the Purab style composed in an extrordinarily large number of *rāgas*. One in *rāga soraṭh malhār* may have come from the early *dhrupad*-influenced composers:

o		x	
R M R M	-- P -P P	Ṡ -- Ṙ Ṡ	N̲ -- D P
dā dirdā dā	-- dā -r dā	rā -- dā dā	rā -- dā rā
o		x	
-- P -P D	P M G R	-- R -R M	G R S S
-- dā -r dā	dā rā dā rā	-- dā -r dā	dā rā dā rā
o		x	
S N̲ D N̲	P D N̲ Ṡ	N̲ D P M	G R G S
dā dirdā rā	dā dirdā rā	dā dā rā dā	dā rā dā rā

Ex. 50. Gat soraṭh malhār *(Azharuddin 1898:n.p.)*

Purab style *gats* clearly traceable to the *dhrupad* instrumentalists of Lucknow are now very rarely to be found in performance practice.

The next generation of Purab composers produced shorter, faster and spirited *gats*. One of the most prominent Lucknow *sitār* players in the generation following Pyar Khan was Qutub ud-Daula. Karam Imam says that he learned from Pyar Khan, and comments that he "occupies a place of his own in sitar playing" (Khan, M. K. I. 1925:46). We remember that he was a friend of Ghulam Raza's. Interestingly, *gats* of his in both the Masitkhani and the Purbī styles are found in written notation. A *gat* in *rāga khamāj* attributed to him by Radhika Mohan Maitra is fairly well-known today in versions that differ slightly from player to player. Radhika Mohan Maitra calls it a Firozkhani *gat*:

x		o	
-- G R G	M -- -- G	R G S --	-- G R G
-- dā rā dā	dā -- -- dā	rā dā dā --	-- dā rā dā
x		o	
M -- -- G	R G S --	-- G R G	M P G M
dā -- -- dā	rā dā dā --	-- rā dā dā	dā dir dā dā
x		o	
P D P Ṡ	-Ṡ Ṡ N̲ D	M P D P	M MG -R G
dā dir dā dā	-r dā dā dā	dā dir dir dir	dā rdā -r dā

Ex. 51. Firozkhani gat khamāj *(Radhika Mohan Maitra)*

A Purbī *gat* in Rahim Beg's "*Tahsīl al-sitār*" is very similar to the one above and may have its origin in the same composition:

	x		o
-- G G --	M -- -- G	-G G S --	-- Ṇ -Ṇ N
-- dir dā --	dā -- -- dā	-r dā dā --	-- dā -r dā
	x		o
S -- S --	G -- G --	M P M M	G GR -R S
dā -- rā --	dā -- rā --	dā dir dir dir	dā rdā -r dā

Ex. 52. Purbī gat gārā *(Beg 1884:30)*

Another *gat* attributed to Qutub ud-Daula notated in the "*Naghmah-i sitār*" is similar in its *bol* pattern, except that its *bols* reduce to one half speed in the second half of the *gat*. This may be an example of a *gat* called *ṭhā dūnī*, "single double," one of the special *gat* types worked out by 19th-century composers:

x		o	
-- D -D D	-- N̲ -N̲ N̲	-- D -D D	-- P -P P
-- dā -r dā	-- dā -r dā	-- dā -r dā	-- dā -r dā

```
x                                 o
M -- -- --   | -- G  -G  G  | S  -- -- --  | -- S  -S  S
dā -- -- --  | -- dā -r  dā | dā -- -- --  | -- dā -r  dā

x                                 o
M  -- -- -M  | P  -- -- -P  | D  -- -- --  | -- -- N̲  N̲
dā -- -- -r  | dā -- -- -r  | dā -- -- --  | -- -- di r

x                                 o
Ṡ  Ṡ  Ṡ  Ṡ   | N̲  -- -- -N̲  | D  -- -- -D  | P  -- -- --
di r  di r   | dā -- -- -r  | dā -- -- -r  | dā -- -- --
```

Ex. 53. Purbī gat khamāc *(Beg 1876:49; 1884:45)*

Another disciple of Pyar Khan's was Hashmat Jang, to whom a number of Purbī *sitār gats*, some influenced by *ṭhumrī*, are traced. Ilyas Khan attributed the following *gat* in *rāga gārā* to him. It is a well-known *gat*, and has often been performed by *sarod* players. The version below is as taught to me by Raj Bhan Singh:

```
o                                   x
-- Ḍ  -Ḍ Ṇ̲   | S  R   G  M  | G  -- R  G̲   | S  R   Ṇ  S
-- dā -r dā  | dā dir dā rā | dā -- dā rā  | dā dir dā rā

o                                   x
Ṇ  S   Ṇ   R   | S  SṆ̲  -Ḍ S   | Ṇ̲  Ṇ̲Ḍ  -P̣ Ṇ̲   | Ḍ  P̣  M  --
dā dir dir dir | dā rdā -r dir | dā rdā -r dir | dā rā dā --

o                                   x
-- Ḍ  -Ḍ Ṇ̲   | Ḍ  Ṇ̲  S  --  | -- Ḍ  -Ḍ Ṇ̲   | S  R  G  --
-- dā -r dā  | dā rā dā --  | -- dā -r dā  | dā rā dā --
```

Ex. 54. Purbī gat gārā *(Raj Bhan Singh)*[184]

Ghulam and Ali Raza

The "*Saṅgīt kalādhar*" distinguishes Purab from Razakhani *bāj gats*, and Lucknow history has indicated that they were originally distinct. It is difficult, however, to find a significant difference between the two types in the "*Saṅgīt kalādhar*" or in performance tradition. Karam Imam indicates that Ghulam Raza's *gats* were fast, "incomplete" and showy. Ilyas Khan said that the *gats* of Ghulam Raza were long, of sixty-four *mātrās*, with the *antarā* as an integral part of them. Examples of Razakhani *bāj gats* in "*Saṅgīt kalādhar*" are found to be both of the short and simple type and the longer, more complex type. One *gat* in *rāga tilang* is played entirely in the low *mandra* range:

x		o	
M P M G	M N P M	G GR -R S	N S G G
dā dir dā rā	dā dir dir dir	dā rdā -r dā	dā rā dā rā

Ex. 55. Razakhani gat tilang *(Shivram 1938:323)*

Another in *rāga khamāj* is long and has a complete melodic development. It is also set in the *mandra* range:

x		o	
S G G M	-MP P P	D D -MG	M M P D
dā dir dir dā	-r dā dir dir	dā rdā -r dā	dā dir dā rā
x		o	
P S N S	-- D -DN	P D M D	P M G --
dā dir dā rā	-- dā -r dā	dā dir dā rā	dā dā rā --
x		o	
M P P S	-S N D D	D P -PM	G R S N
dā dir dir dā	-r dā dir dir	dā rdā -r dā	dā dir dā rā

Ex. 56. Razakhani gat khamāj *(Shivram 1938:325)*

Gats of Ali Raza, Ghulam Raza's son, are more available in oral and written collections than those of his father. They tend to be light in character. A *gat* in "*Qānūn-i sitār*" attributed to Ali Raza is in *rāga purbī jhinjhoṭī*. It is very close to the *gats* earlier attributed to Qutub ud-Daula. It is not possible to say who composed the original pattern:

	x		o
-- MGR -R G	S -- -- M	-MG R --	-- N -NN
-- dā -r dā	dā -- -- dā	-r dā dā --	-- dā -r dā

x o
S -- G -- | G -- G G | M -- P P | M -M G S
dā -- dā -- | dā -- dā rā | dā -- dirdir | dā -r dā dā

Ex.57a. Gat purbī jhinjihoṭī *(Khan, M. S. H. 1873:109)*

Two *toḍās* for the *gat* give us an idea of a simple development:

toḍā 1

x o
-- -- Ṡ Ṡ | N -Ṡ -Ṡ Ṡ | -- -- P P | 'M -P -P P
-- -- dirdir | dā -dā -d dā | -- -- dir dir | dā -dā -d dā

x o
-- -- M M | G -M -M M | -- -- G G | R G -G S
-- -- dirdir | dā -dā -d dā | -- -- dir dir | dā dā -d dā

toḍā 2

x o
Ġ Ġ Ṙ Ṙ | Ṡ Ṡ N N | D D P P | M M G G
dir dirdirdir | dirdir dir dir | dirdir dir dir | dirdir dir dir

x o
S -- G -- | M -- D D | M -G -- S
dā -- dā -- | dā -- dir dir | dā -dā -- dā

Ex.57b. Toḍa purbī jhinjihoṭī *(Khan, M. S. H. 1873:109)*

But Ali Raza composed musically detailed *gats* as well as short, light ones. Satya Kinkar Banerji demonstrated a beautiful slower and longer *gat* which he attributed to Ali Raza. He played it in a medium speed and used two delicate *sūts (s)* in the second line. It is reminiscent of the *gats* attributed to the earlier *dhrupad* instrumentalists:

o x
S G -R G | M M P M | P -- -- G | M -- D P
dā dā -r dā | dā dir dā rā | dā -- -- rā | dā -- dā rā

o x
$\underline{N}$ D P M | D P M G | M P G M | G M -R G
dā dirdā rā | dā rā dā rā | dā rā dirdir | dā rdā-r dir

o		x	
S G -R G	M M P M	Ṡ -- -- N̲	-- D P P
dā dā -r dā	dā dir dā rā	dā -- -- dā	-- rā dā dā
o		x	
P D N̲ D	P G -G M	G M P --	-- -- -- --
dā rā dir dir	dā rdā -r dā	dā rā dā --	-- -- -- --
o-(s)- -(s)-		x	
SRG RGM	G -- -- --	Ṡ N̲ D P	M G R G
dā -- dā --	dā -- -- --	dā rā dā rā	dā rā dā rā

Ex. 58. Gat khambāj *(Satya Kinkar Banerji)*[185]

Other Centers and Composers

The late 19th century saw a great deal of activity in the composing of Purab *gats* all across North India. Even the instructional books from the western centers contain Purab style *gats*, despite authors such as Safdar Husain Khan's expressed preference for the Masitkhani style. Many of the 19th-century notations are rhythmically difficult to decipher and others are very simple beginners' *gats*. A few are both intelligible and interesting. A *gat* from "*Nād vinod*" of Delhi in *rāga khamāj* has a spirited and unusual *bol* pattern:

x		o	
Ṡ N̲ -N̲ Ṡ	D -D Ṡ N̲	D P -- D	P M G M
dā dā -r dā	dā -r dā dā	dā rā -- dir	dā dir dā rā
x		o	
R G R M	G GR -R S	S G G M	M P D Ṡ
dā dir dir dir	dā rdā -r dā	dā dir dā rā	dā rā dā rā
x		o	
N̲ N̲ Ṡ --	P D Ṡ N̲	D DP -P G	M MP -P D
dā rā dā --	dā rā dā dir	dā rdā -r dir	dā rdā -r dā

Ex 59. Purbī gat khamāj *(Gosvami, P. 1895:276)*

A *gat* in the "*Sarmāya-i 'ishrat*" in *rāga pīlū* contains "*rā*" strokes which would seem to indicate strokes on the *cikārī* or the low bronze strings. There is a *mīḍ* in the second line, probably to G̲:

```
                    x                                       o
M    |  G R S R  |  N -- -- S  |  -- -- N S  |  R -G R
dā   |  dā rā dā rā  |  dā rā rā dā  |  rā rā dā rā  |  dā -r dā

                    x                                       o      (m)
M    |  G R S R  |  N -- -- S  |  -- -- N S  |  R R R
dā   |  dā rā dā rā  |  dā rā rā dā  |  rā rā dā rā  |  dā rā dā

        (m)
R    |  R -- S R
rā   |  dā -- dā rā
```

Ex. 60. Purbī gat pīlū *(Khan, Sadiq A. 1884:247)*

A number of *gats* from late 19th-century Gwalior are available in both written texts and in performance tradition. The vocal music for which Gwalior was famous in the 19th and early 20th centuries must have had a special impact on its instrumental music. A *gat* in *yaman* by Bhaiya Sahab Mavlankar (born about 1870) has a lively movement and a *bol* pattern in the second half that may have been influenced by the syncopated rhythm of a *tarāna*:

```
x                                  o
G -- G --  |  S R N S  |  D N S R  |  S N D P
dā -- dā --  |  dā dir dā rā  |  dā dir dā rā  |  dā dir dā rā

x                                  o
P P P D  |  D N D S  |  N R R G  |  R S N S
dā dir dā dā  |  rā dā rā dir  |  dā dā rā dir  |  dā dir dā rā
```

Ex. 61. Purbī gat yaman *(Bajpeyi 1936:94)*

A *gat* in *rāg kedār* also by Mavlankar has a distinctive last line leading to *sam*:

```
x                                  o
D -D D P  |  'MP D P  |  M -- -- M  |  P 'MD P
dā -r dā dā  |  rā dā dā rā  |  dā -- -- dā  |  dā rā dir dir
```

x		o	
G GM-M R	S Ṇ R S	-- P̣ -- Ṇ	S R Ṇ S
dā rdā -r dā	dā dir dir dā	-- dā -- dā	dā rā dā rā
x		o	
-- M -M M	P -P P Ṡ	-Ṡ Ṡ Ṙ --	M -- M P
-- dā -r dā	dā -r dā dā	-r dā dā --	dā -- dā rā

Ex. 62. Purbī gat kedar *(Bhaiya Sahab Mavlankar)*[186]

An entire Gwalior *tarāna* in *rāga bihāg* was modified into a *gat*, which became widely played and is still found in slightly varied form in different schools of *sitār* and *sarod* playing:

o		x	
S M G P	'M P Ṡ N	P -- -- D	G M G --
dā dir dā dā	rā dā dā rā	dā -- -- dā	dā rā dā --
o		x	
G M P D	M MG -R G	Ṇ S R R	Ṇ S G R
dā dir dir dir	dā rdā -r dā	dā dir dā rā	dā dir dā rā
o		x	
G M D P	M MG -R G	-- N -D N	Ṡ Ṁ Ġ Ṙ
dā rā dir dir	dā rdā -r dā	-- dā -r dā	dā dir dā rā
o		x	
Ṡ N 'M P	D G -R G	M D P M	G R S Ṇ
dā rā dā rā	dā dā -r dir	dā dir dā rā	dā rā dā rā

Ex. 63. Purbī gat bihāg *(S. R. Mavlankar, Allahabad)*

In later 19th-century Bengal, one of the instrumentalists who helped to create an intense interest in music was Sajjad Muhammad Khan, *sitār* and *surbahār* player, grandson of Lucknow's Ghulam Muhammad. Satya Kinkar Banerji demonstrated *gats* composed by Sajjad Muhammad which made prominent use of *zamzama (z)*, *kṛntan (kṛ)*, *kaṇ (k)* and *sūt (s)*, the first two of which Banerji said were specialties of Sajjad Muhammad's playing. Banerji played the one below in *rāga "khambāj"* in a medium tempo. It may represent the delicate and highly developed style of the best Purab *sitār* players:

o (z)		x	
G M G M	-G M P D	N -- -- Ṡ	N Ṡ N Ṡ
dā dir dā dā	-r dā dā rā	dā -- -- dir	dā dir dā rā
o(z)	--(s)-- (k) (k) (kṛ) (k)	x (k)	(z) (kṛ)
N D P D	NṘ ṠR N DN	PD M P D	P G -R G
dā rā dā dā	-- dā dā rā	dā rā dir dir	dā rdā -r dā

Ex. 64. Gat khambāj *(Satya Kinkar Banerji)*[187]

Another of Sajjad Muhammad's *gats*, which Satya Kinkar Banerji played in the same *rāga*, is also found in Tagore's "*Yantra Kshetra Dipika*" as *rāga jhijhiṭ khāmbāj*. The notation here is from Tagore:

--(kṛ)--	x		o
-- MG -R G	M -- -- P	M G R G	M P M P
-- dā -r dā	dā -- -- rā	dā dir dā rā	dā dir dir dā
--(kṛ)--	x		o
-- MG -R G	M P M G	R S Ṇ S	S S S D
-- dā -r dā	dā rā dā rā	dā rā dā rā	dā dir dā rā
(k)	x		o
PD D G M	P Ṡ -- G	M P R G	M P M P
dā dā dā dā	dā rā -- dā	-- dā dā rā	dā dir dir dā

Ex. 65. Gat jhijhi khāmbāj *(Tagore 1879:84-5)*

A late 19th- and early 20th-century *sitār* player of Bengal was Bhagvan Das Sitaria (Figure 37). A *gat* attributed to him in *rāga sindh bhairavī* is another of the delicate middle speed type characteristic of some of the Purab instrumentalists. It is almost entirely in the lower octave:

	x		o	
G̣ M	P̣ -- Ḍ M	P̣ -- -- --	Ṇ Ṇ Ḍ Ḍ	P̣ --
dā rā	dā -- dā rā	dā -- -- --	dā dir dā rā	dā --
	x		o	
G̣ M	P̣ Ṇ Ḍ Ṇ	P̣ Ḍ M P̣	G̣ R Ṣ Ṛ	Ṣ --
dā rā	dā dir dā rā	dā dir dā rā	dā rā dā rā	dā --

```
        x                              o
G M   | P -- S S   | N D N --   | P D N D     | P --
dā rā | dā -- dā rā | dā rā dā -- | dā dir dā rā | dā --

        x                              o
G M   | P N D N     | P D M P     | G R S R     | S --
dā rā | dā dir dā rā | dā dir dā rā | dā rā dā rā | dā --
```

Ex. 66. Gat sindh bhairavī *(Jyotish Chandra Chaudhury, Varanasi)*

Many of the *gats* notated by Tagore in his "*Yantra Kshetra Dipika*" are filled with techniques unique to the Bengali language books. Some of the *gats* seem to be the works of a non-traditional composer, probably Tagore himself, and others appear to be inspired by European music, perhaps by way of Bengali theater tunes. A *gat* in *rāga bhūpalī* makes use of "*svar saṃyog*," Tagore's term for a two-note chord. The chorded notes are in parentheses here. The lower of each of the paired notes is to be played on the *joḍī* string. In the second half of the *gat*, the P and D notes are also to be played on the *joḍī* string:

```
x-(m)-                           o  -(m)-
DS  DS  D   S  | D   S   R   G  | GP  GP  R --  | (RD)(RD)(SP) (RD)
dā  --  dā  rā | dā  dir dā  rā | dā  --  dā -- | dā   dā   dā   dā

x                                o
P   D   S   R  | D   PG  GR  G  | D   S   R  G  | PD  SR  S   --
dā  dir dā  rā | dir dir dir dir | dā  dir dā rā | dir dir dā  --
```

Ex. 67. Gat bhūpālī *(Tagore 1879:184)*

Another composition in *rāga bhūpālī* is an amusing experiment in parlor style. It uses the open lower strings as rhythmic filler, in a manner more akin to guitar than *sitār*:

```
(m) (m)          x                 (open) o  (m)(m)
NS  NS S  R    | G -- S R   | G S P P     | GPGP G R
dā  dā dā rā   | dā -- dā rā | dā dā dā dā | dā dā dā rā

      (open) x               (open str.) o
GR -- S   S  | R S S NS    | -- S P P     | S D -- D
dā -- dir dir | dir dā dā -- | -- dā dir dir | dā dā -- dir
```

```
                  x                              o
P    R   -- --  I  D S R G      I  P R G P     I  D Ṡ D P
dā   rā  -- --  I  dā dirdā rā  I  dā rā dā dir I  dā rā dā rā

                  x                              o
G    P   -- --  I  R P -- --    I  R P -- --   I  R P S R
dā   rā  -- --  I  dā dā -- --  I  dā dā -- -- I  dā dā dā rā

            (m) x  (m)             --k--         o
G    --  --  GP I  GPG R G      I  R -- -- D   I  P G R S
dā   --  --  rā I  dā dā rā dā  I  -- -- -- dir I  dirdirdirdā

-(cikarī)- (k)  x           (m)             (k)  o    (open)
P    P   P   SR I  G -- -- GP   I  G R S SNS   I  -- -- P P
rā   rā  rā  dā I  dā -- -- dā  I  dā rā dā dā I  -- -- dirdir
```

Ex. 68. Gat bhūpālī *(Tagore 1879:173-4)*

Among the large number of *gats* in performance traditions dating to the 19th and early 20th centuries are some defined by particular techniques that they use. The one below features a *capkā (c)*, a slap on the second and third strings with the left hand fingers to produce a percussive note. Here the slap is on the S fret to produce P̣. It is in *rāga tilak kāmod*, and Raj Bhan Singh, who got it from his father, attributes it to a late 19th-century Delhi *sitār* player named Ilahi Baksh:

```
(c)               x                              o
P N -N  S      I  R -- -- G      I  R G R G      I  S R G M
-- dā -r  dā   I  dā -- -- dir   I  dā dirdā rā  I  dā rā dirdir

G S -S  R      I  P P M M        I  G G P M      I  G S -S N
dā dā -r  dā   I  dirdirdirdir   I  dirdirdā rā  I  dā dā -r dā
```

Ex. 69. Gat tilak kāmod *(Raj Bhan Singh, Varanasi)*

Various other special types of *gats* such as *cakradār* ("cyclical"), *tappā aṅg* ("*tappa* style"), *ek hāth kā* ("one-handed") and *kulfidār* are mentioned in different performance traditions.

Elaboration in the Purab bāj

A number of three-minute 78 rpm recordings of early 20th-century *sitār* and *sarod* players give us a sketchy idea of the way in which the musicians elaborated their fast speed *gats*. Although not completely satisfactory because of their brevity, these performances may be the closest we can come to the style of the 19th century. Recordings of Kaukab Khan, Waliullah Khan, Shafiqullah Khan, Amir Khan and Sakhawat Husain show a fairly consistent system of development. In the beginning the *gat* is played several times in its entirety. Short interjections of double speed strokes then replace four or eight *mātrās* of the *gat*. Following this, longer *tāns* consisting of *"dir dir"* strokes in straight scalar runs or in simple melodic phrasing patterns of the *rāga* are inserted. *Tāns* sometimes end in a short *tihāī* (group of three), a phrase repeated three times ending at a juncture with the *gat*. It might be noted, however, that *tihāī*, a very important aspect of 20th-century playing, is not mentioned in any of the 19th-century written sources. The *gat* speed is then increased and *jhālā* is begun. *Jhālā* is interspersed with *"dir dir" tāns* played in a very fast speed. When the speed of *jhalā* has reached a certain level, a melodic section occurs that centers on a short melody line repeating itself up the scale. This section is called *naghma* (tune) in some traditions. *Naghma* is followed by a return to the *gat* at an extremely high speed, and an ending with an ascending *tān* and a single descending *tihāī*. *Naghma* is still used by modern traditional players, and the following one from Kaukab Khan's recording of *rāga zila* will be recognizable to many *sitār* players. Lines one and two are each played twice; three and four are played together and repeated:

x									o										
$\underset{.}{N}$	--	R	--	I	R	$\underline{G}$	M	--	I	$\underline{G}$	R	$\underline{G}$	--	I	--	S	--	S	
dā	--	rā	--	I	dā	rā	dā	--	I	dā	rā	dā	--	I	--	dā	--	rā	(twice)

x									o										
R	--	M	--	I	M	P	M	--	I	$\underline{G}$	R	$\underline{G}$	--	I	--	S	--	S	
dā	--	rā	--	I	dā	rā	dā	--	I	dā	rā	dā	--	I	--	dā	--	rā	(twice)

```
x                                o
D D D --  |  D D D --  |  D N N --  |  -- M -- M
dā rā dā -- | dā rā dā -- | dā rā dā -- | -- dā -- rā (continue)

x                                o
P N N --  |  -- D M --  |  G R G --  |  -- S -- S
dā rā dā -- | -- rā dā -- | dā rā dā -- | -- dā -- rā (twice)
```

Ex. 70. Naghma zila *(recording: Kaukab Khan)*[188]

Another *naghma*, from the tradition of Imdad and Inayat Khan, is set in *rāga pīlū*:

```
x                          o
P -MP G     | M -GM R     | G -RG N     | S -- G M
dā -r dā rā | dā -r dā rā | dā -r dā rā | dā -- dā rā

x                          o
M P -P P    | G M -MM     | R G -GG     | N S -S S
dā dā -r dā | dā dā -r dā | dā dā -r dā | dā dā -r dā

x                          o
M P P --    | G M M --    | R G G --    | N S S --
dā rā dā -- | dā rā dā -- | dā rā dā -- | dā rā dā --

x                          o
G -- P P    | -- G M M    | -- R G G    | -- N S S
rā -- rā dā | -- dā rā dā | -- dā rā dā | -- dā rā dā

x                          o
P P M M     | P P -- P    | M M G G     | M M -MM
rā dā rā dā | rā dā -- dā | rā dā rā dā | rā dā -r dā

x                          o
G G R R     | G G -- G    | R R S S     | R R -- R
rā dā rā dā | rā dā -- dā | rā dā rā dā | rā dā -- dā

x                          o
-- P M --   | -- P G --   | -- M R --   | -- G S --
-- dā dā -- | -- dā dā -- | -- dā dā -- | -- dā dā --

x                          o
P M -- P    | G -- M R    | -- G S --   | -- N -S S
dā rā -- dā | rā -- dā rā | -- dā rā -- | -- dā -r dā
```

Ex. 71. Naghma pīlū *(Jyotish Chandra Chaudhury, Varanasi)*

Purab *bāj* elaboration was not devoid of *bīn*-related elements. *Sitār* player Waliullah Khan played a fast section leading to *jhālā* that sounds very much like *ṭhonk*, each stroke a forceful "*rā*:"

G	--	--	G	|	G	G	G	G	|	G	--	--	S	|	S	S	S	S
N	--	--	Ṇ	|	D	P̣	Ṃ	P	|	P	P̣	N	Ṇ	|	N	--	--	Ṇ
Ṇ	--	Ṇ	--	|	Ṡ	--	--	S	|	Ṡ	--	Ṡ	--	|	Ṡ	--	--	--

Ex. 72. Ṭhonk *(recording: Waliullah Khan)*[189]

Besides *jhālā* and *ṭhonk*, *tār paran* was also sometimes played in connection with Purab *gats*. Satya Kinkar Banerji demonstrated several *tār parans* along with a fast *gat* in *rāga bhairavī*. *Tār paran* was a technique especially emphasized by *dhrupad rabāb* players, and was adapted from them for *sitār* and *sarod*. *Sitār* and *sarod* traded styles and techniques throughout this period, and emphasis on fast, percussive and flowing rhythms, fast right hand movements, and especially extended stroke patterns of "*dir dir*" may be influences of *sarod* in *sitār* style.

As instrumental music entered the 20th century, several great contemporaries gave new direction to *gat* style, elaboration and *ālāp*. In *sitār*, the brilliant Imdad Khan and his son Inayat Khan introduced striking new developments in high speed work and in melodic movements and ornaments imitative of sung *khyāl*. These two *sitār* players became phenomenally popular and influenced musicians all across North India. Other instrumentalists continued to blend tradition and innovation and contribute to the development of what we know as modern *sitār* style. The great Allauddin Khan was outstanding in helping to shape the form of 20th-century performance. The successors of this generation of instrumentalists are today's senior musicians, Ali Akbar Khan, Ravi Shankar, Vilayat Khan, Imrat Khan, Amjad Ali Khan and others, who have in their turn most dramatically changed performance style. Their successors are the newest innovators. It is clear that substantive changes since the end of the 19th century have expanded the techniques and styles of *sitār* playing, and that the instrument and its music have continued to thrive as they have adapted to the demands and challenges of the 20th century. It is now time that the 20th-century history of these instruments and their music be made the subject of thorough and systematic study.

Notes

1 Some of the available books on the *sitār* in English are Ghosh 1988, Bandyopadhyaya, S. 1988, Alford 1988 and 1973, Hamilton 1988, Slawek 1987, Chaudhuri 1981, Avtar 1980, Mishra 1979, Gupta, P. 1975, Junius 1974, Hansen 1973, Keesee 1968, Shankar 1968, Rao 1967.

2 The *sehtār* of Persian music, also transliterated "*setār*," dates from the same period or earlier but does not figure in this theory. It is considered to be a member of the Turkish and Persian *tambūr* family. The *setār* existed in Persia (accordi: ʒ to H. G. Farmer) as early as the 13th century, and was one of a series of instrum for which the Persian term *tār*, "string" with a prefix denoting number was used. C Farmer 1978:7-8, Sachs 1968:156-7. Also cf. During & Dick 1984:354.

3 *Tambūr*: Deva 1978:163. Kashmiri *setar*: Krishnaswami 1971:99. Uzbek *dutār*: Dick 1984:393.

4 There are a number of unrelated instruments that carry the name *tambūr* or a name closely related to it; cf. "The New Grove Dictionary of Musical Instruments" (1984) for discussions of these. The instruments under discussion here are long lutes, for which the terms "*tambūr*," "*tambūrah*" and "*tambūrā*" and "*tānpūrā*" are all found in Persian, Urdu and Hindi music literature. "*Tambūr*" or *Tunbūr* is the term found in Persian works to the 16th century, and it refers to the instrument capable of carrying a melody. Later Persian works in India use both the terms "*tambūr*" and "*tambūrah*" in contexts where the characteristics of the instruments are not always determinable. Hindi uses "*tambūrā*" or "*tānpūrā*," (a later term) and both of these terms refer to the drone instrument. Maharaja Pratap Singh in the 1799 "*Saṅgīt sār*" says the instrument's name is "*tambūr*" but it is popularly called *tambūrā* (Singh, S. P. 1910-II:6). Throughout this work "*tambūr*" will be the term used for the melody instrument and "*tambūrā*" the drone, unless a specific citation requires a different spelling because of its source.

5 Braj has its own history and literature but is normally considered a member of the larger Hindi language family.

6 The *rāgas* attributed to Amir Khusrau in the "*Tuḥfāt al-Hind*" and "*Rāg darpan*" are: *muhaiyar* or *mujir*, *sazgiri*, *yaman*, *ushaq*, *muafiq*, *ghanam* or *ghazan*, *zilaf*, *farghan*, *sarparda*, *bakharz*, *farodast*, *sanam* or *mu'nam* (cf. Ahmad 1984:53; Mirza 1962:238). These attributions are not confirmed in Khusrau's writings according to Askari 1972:113-5.

7 The "*Ain-i Akbarī*" gives Amir Khusrau credit for *qaul* and *tarānā* (cf. Gladwin 1965: 204). "*Rāg darpan*," "*Ma'dan al-mūsīqī*," "*Naghmāt al-Hind*" and "*Ma'ārif al-naghmāt*" give him credit for the *tarānā* (Ahmad 1984:125-6). *Tarānā* was a Persian term for a song form in general. Shahab Sarmadee believes that Amir Khusrau did make changes to earlier forms and introduce the new *qavvālī* and *tarānā* (Sarmadee 1975a:263); Mirza also says "there is no doubt that the popular melodies qual and ghazal were first introduced in Indian music by Khusrau ..." (Mirza 1962:238).

8 Sarmadee 1975a:265, Note 12. This contradicts others' understanding of Khusrau's use of the term *khyāl* (cf., for example, Wade 1984:1).

9 A *vīṇā* called *alābu* or *alāvanī* is mentioned in Sanskrit texts (*alābu* - Sanskrit: "gourd").

10 "*Prakṛtiḥ śrīsāvīṇānāmeṣā śrīśārṅgiṇoditā*" (Śārṅgadeva 1986-III [1950]:328). *Vīṇās* in the "*Saṅgītaratnākara*" are *ekatantrī*, *nakula*, *tritantrikā*, *citrā*, *vipañcī*, *mattakokilā*, *ālāpinī*, *kinnarī* (*laghavī*, *bṛhatī*, *madhyamā*), *pinākī* and *niḥśanka* (Śārṅgadeva 1986-III [1950]:342-3, 386-401, 425-9).

11 *Vīṇās* in the "*Saṅgītopaniṣatsāroddhāra*" are: *pinākī*, *kinnarī*, *ālambī*, *kacchapī*, *bṛhatī*, *mahatī*, *kalāvatī*, *prabhāvatī*, *ghoṣavatī*, *vipañcī*, *kaṇṭhakūṇikā*, *vallakī*, and *brahmavīṇā* (Sudhākalaśa 1961:75). Interestingly, there is mention of the *tabla*, described as a drum of the "foreigners" (Sudhākalaśa 1961:88). This is probably the Persian *ṭabl*.

12 Mirza 1962:239-40. Rashid Malik also gives a long list of authors who falsely attribute these inventions to Amir Khusrau (Malik, R. 1975:134-5).

13 Little is known about this important 19th-century writer. Joep Bor suggests that Willard was a Eurasian and the son of a British musician A. Willard, who died in 1825 in Kanpur according to India Office records (Bor 1988:59).

14 Sahasrabuddhe 1887:56-7. The Poona Gayan Samaj was a pioneering institution for musical education and publications founded in 1874.

15 Tansen, the prized musician of the court of Akbar, came from Gwalior. He died in 1589 and is considered to be the virtual founder of the *dhrupad* performance tradition that dominated North Indian music for the following two hundred years.

16 Umar Khan, interview, Calcutta, January 1979.

17 Muneshwar Dayal, interview, Brindavan, October 1979.

18 The two Urdu translations of the "*Muraqqa'-i Dehlī*" give significantly different readings of this section. The earlier translation by Hasan Nizami describes only one man, Na'mat Khan's brother, while Ansari's describes both a brother and a nephew. The Nizami version is "He, like his outstanding brother, is a master in music. And his specialization is that for hours he can play one instrument and one section of music in many ways. Probably no one exists anywhere around Delhi who can demonstrate such skill at playing various instruments at the same time with such technique and beauty. That is Na'mat Khan's brother's art. And his second excellence is this, which music experts can well understand, that on an instrument with three strings he plays hundreds of *rāgs* and *rāginīs*. This is really an impossible feat that even those who know music consider unfeasible. He has an instrument of three strings that is counted among the wonders of music ..." (Khan, D. Q. B. 1933:67. My English translation). One oral tradition comments on the three-stringed instrument. Muneshwar Dayal said that the instrument mentioned here was not the *sitār* but a piece of bamboo on which three strings were mounted and rough frets tied. Muneshwar Dayal, interview, Brindavan, October 1979.

19 Khan, D. Q. B. 1982:174. My English translation.

20 Tagore 1879:4, 1976:19. The *kacchapī* is a *vīṇā* listed in early and medieval Sanskrit texts. Tagore identifies this with the *kachuā sitār*, a *sitār* with a flat-cut gourd.

21 Collections are or were once held in Brussels (cf. Mahillon 1893-I:142-55); Leiden, the Ethnological Museum; London, the Victoria and Albert Museum; New York, the Metropolitan Museum (cf. anon. 1906); and Calcutta, the Indian Museum (cf. Meerwarth 1917). Joep Bor points out that Tagore's collections influenced (and misled) leading European scholars of the day including Curt Sachs (Bor 1988:64).

22 The *ekatantrī*, "one-stringed," which is described in detail, was a stick zither, and the relation of its name and its proximity in the text suggest a structural relationship with the *tritantrī* (Śārṅgadeva 1986-III:342; *Kalānidhi*, 248).

23 Abu al-Fazl 1983:268. Also cited in Gladwin 1965:205.

24 In other areas it exists in a different form: a *jantar* of Madhya Pradesh, also a stick zither but with only one gourd, is bowed (cf. Bor 1986-87:51, 52).

25 "This Citrā (vinā) probably developed later into Persian Sitar. It may be that the Greek kithara with seven strings is also connected with it" (Bharata 1961-II:45).

26 Alastair Dick suggests that the name *kacchapī* for the musical instrument does not relate to tortoise (Dick 1984:397). The popular understanding, however, is that it does.

27 Abhinavagupta in Bharata 1964-IV:122.

28 Also mentioned in the *divān* of Masud-i Sa'ad-i Salman are the *chang*, *barbat*, *nay*, *kamancha*, *rabab*, *anqa*, *'ud*, *sarod*, (shāhrūd?) and *rud* (Askari 1972:91-2, 95, 102). For *shāhrūd* cf. Farmer 1929:154, 209.

29 Also employed in the court were players of the *chang* and *qānūn* (Brhaspati 1974:62).

30 Adil Shah 1956 - *tambūrā*: 107; *tambūrkār*: 105; *tambūr*: 54.

31 In the Naprstek Museum, Prague, cf. Hajek & Forman 1960: Plate 10.

32 The importance of the *rāg darpan* for Karam Imam is evident in the extensive excerpts from it that he uses in his "*Ma'dan al-Mūsīqī*."

33 Khan, M. K. I. 1925:30, translation Vidyarthi 1959:17.

34 The *kinnarī, ekatantrī* and *ālāpinī vinas* are all described with bridges called *kakubha* which were probably flat (Śārṅgadeva 1986-III:328).

35 Ouseley 1965 [1797-1800]:170f. I have not been able to locate the manuscript from which this illustration was taken.

36 Ahmad 1984:73-7, Alam [1797] The "*Nādirāt-i shāhī*" has been edited by Imtiaz Ali Arshi and published by the Raza Library, Rampur, but I have been unable to locate this edition.

37 Dick points to an 18th-century reference in the "*Hammīr Rāso*" (Dick 1984:393). The c.1725 date given by Dick is not correct. The editors state that this Hindi epic poem by Kavi Jodhraj was completed in 1785 (Jodhraj 1979:2). David Roach refers to a mention of the *sitār* in an unnamed text of Farrukh Shah dated 1719-48, without naming his source (Roach 1971:16). The dates are those of Muhammad Shah's reign. Is this the "*Muraqqa'-i Dehlī*"?

38 A photograph can be seen in Welch 1985:Fig. 262.

39 "*Bīn rabāb tambūrā sitār kānūn damāme sāringī muhcang*
jhānjh manjīrā aur ḍholakī dairā bansarī karah aur hī cang
khaṭkarī aur kaṭṭār liye surnāī bhalī karnāī abapang
gāye gunī śāh ālam ko sab det mubārakī bajāye mirdang."
also
"... *gāvat rāg kanacan bājat bīn rabāb tambūr* ..."
(Ahmad 1984:76, 77).

40 Umar Khan, interview, Calcutta, January 1979.

41 Dick 1984:393. Dick cites the later *sitār*'s decorative collar and perceived imitations of carvel ribbing (a characteristic construction style for wooden-bodied instruments), and proposes that the Uzbek *dutār* was the model for the Indian *sitār*. But early *sitārs* did not necessarily have these characteristics, as the figures here show. The relationships of locality and cultural history needed to support ideas of direct Central Asian influence on the *sitār* have not yet been satisfactorily demonstrated. For the variety of instruments found in Northwest India, Pakistan, Afghanistan and Central Asia cf. Jenkins & Olsen 1976; Baloch 1966; Vertkov, Blagodatov & Yazovitskaya 1975.

42 Kindersley in Dyson 1978:336.

43 Singh 1910-II:6-7. My translation.

44 *Javārī* is the intentional light buzz of the metal strings as they vibrate on the surface of the wide bridge. It is probably related to *jīva*, "life," the term for the thread placed between the string and the bridge in the Sanskrit texts as early as the time of the "*Saṅgītaratnākara*." Later the *javārī* sound came to be produced only by the carefully worked slope of the bridge surface.

45 Khan, S. A. 1875/84:203. See Part Three for a discussion of the terms.

46 Parks 1850-I:29-30. Also cited in Dyson 1978:350.

47 Della Valle 1892-I:118. Cited in Bor 1988:52.

48 The term *mizrāb* was used for a plectrum from before the 9th century (Farmer 1978-II: 89).

49 See the later discussion of techniques.

50 Baden-Powell 1872-II:273. Excerpted in Mukharji 1888:78-9.

51 Sachs 1968:122. *Zir* is a term for the highest string on the Arabic lute, the *'ūd*.

52 In "*Muraqqa'-i Dehlī*," for example, musicians are called *arbāb-i ṭarab*.

53 Mushtaq Ali Khan, interview, Varanasi, January 1979.

54 *Sitār* maker Radhakrishna Sharma told me that as recently as 50 years ago more *kachuā sitārs* than ordinary *sitārs* were made. Personal communication, Varanasi November 1988.

55 *Ṭhok* or *ṭhonk*, Hindi, "hammer," "hit," is a technique associated with the faster movements of *ālāp* on *bīn* and *rabāb*, later on *sitār* and *sarod* (cf. Roy Chaudhury 1975:13).

56 The stick fiddle disappeared from Hindustani mainstream music but can still be found in various forms in regional North Indian music cultures (cf. Bor 1986/87).

57 Cf. Bor 1986/87 for an excellent pictorial history and appeal for the future of this neglected instrument.

58 Prajnanananda 1973:468; Ali Akbar Khan, interview, San Anselmo, California, June 1988.

59 Prajnanananda 1973:468; also Roy Chaudhury 1975:134.

60 Instruments mentioned by Masud-i Sa'ad-i Salman along with the *rabab* are the *chang*, *kamanche*, *barbat*, *tambur* and *nay* (Askari 1972:91-7).

61 Curt Sachs refers to the barb on these instruments but does not form a distinct category. The category "barbed lutes," is used in Dick *et al.* (1984-III:181).

62 Cf. Sachs 1968:160-1; Marcel-Dubois 1941:87-8.

63 For a painting of the Jahangir period allegedly showing Tansen playing the *rabāb*, cf. Brown 1981:plates 31 and 62.

64 Anon. 1967:59-61; Mansukhani 1982:54.

65 Abu al-Fazl 1894:254. Reprinted in Gladwin 1965:205.

66 Gosvami, O. 1957:299; Roy Chaudhury 1975:134.

67 The four strings of the Arabic lutes were *bamm*, *mathlath*, *mathnā* and *zīr* (Farmer 1964: 176; Farmer 1978-I:97-8).

68 I understand that someone in the Dagar family of musicians still has a *rabāb*.

69 The earliest mention of the *sarod* is allegedly in Prinsep 1833: Bor, personal communication. I have not had access to this work. Cf. also Perera 1985.

70 Cf. for example Greig 1987; Bor 1986/7.

71 Manucci 1907:6; Aurangzeb is stated to have banned music at the later date in Ikram & Spear 1955:52.

72 From Khafi Khan, cited in Elliot 1877-VII:283; also cited in Manucci 1907-II:5-6.

73 Khan, I. R. 1961:30-1; Rehman 1803-4:folio 466; also noted in Arshi 1978:20.

74 Smith, V. A. 1958:433; Lane-Poole 1964:289.

75 Shaikh Allahyar, "*Hadiqat-ul aqalim*," 131 and "*Dastur-ul insha*," 133, cited in Irvine 1971-I:180-1.

76 From the "*Tarikh-i Ahmad Shah*," in Elliot 1877-VIII:104-5.

77 Hijra 1151 = 1738-39, courtesy of G. D. Bhatnagar, in Khan, D. Q. B. 1933:5.

78 From the "*Tarikh-i Ahmad Shah*," in Elliot 1877-VIII:104-5.

79 See such works on *khyāl* as Desai 1969; Dhond 1980; Meer 1980:50-70; Wade 1984.

80 Panna Bai is depicted in a Kishangarh painting dated c1764, where she is labelled a singer of Shahjahanabad and said to be in the service of Sardar Singh of Kishangarh (d. 1766) (Dickenson & Khandalavala 1959:38-9).

81 Khan, D. Q. B. 1933:89-91; Khan, D. Q. B. 1982:200-1. There is some difference in the two versions.

82 The following sources give us the name Khushhal Khan: Nur ud din Faruqi Balkhi Dahlavi Multani, "*Jahandar Shah Nama*," (IOL 3988); Shafi Warid Tehrani, "*Mir'at-i Waridat*" or "*Tarikh-i Chughta'i Tarikh-i Muhammad Shahi*," (Bankipur vii 580), 222. One text says that Na'mat Khan is Lal Kunwar's uncle: Ghulam Husain, "*Siyar-ul Muta'akh khirin*," (litho, Lucknow, 3). All sources and their locations are cited from Chandra 1959:276. Muhammad Hashim, "*Muntakhāb-ul lubāb*," 2:688 says that Khushhal Khan was Lal Kunwar's brother, cited in Elliot 1877-VII:432-3.

There is an intriguing reference to a musician of Muhammad Shah's court named Khushhal son of Karim Khan who moved to the Deccan after Muhammad Shah's death. There he wrote a work on music entitled "*Rāg rāginī-e rūz u shab*" mentioned in the "Descriptive Catalogue of the Government Oriental Manuscript Library," Madras, 1939-54, i, 530, no, 515: Marshall 1985:260. Two famous musicians L'al Khan and Khushhal Khan of the 17th century are different figures.

83 Khasusiat Khan is mentioned in Shaikh Allahyar, "*Hadiqat-ul aqalim*," 131 and "*Dastur-ul insha*," 133, cited in Irvine 1971-I:180-1. Nirmol Khan is named as Na'mat Khan's father in Khan, Inayet (1961:30) and in Rehman 1803-4:folio 466. There is also

an oral tradition that gives Na'mat Khan's father's name as Lal Khan: Roy Chaudhury 1975:171, and Bandyopadhyaya, S. 1937:94; or as Lal Khansani: Josi 1935:36.

84 Rahim Sen and Tan Sen in Khan, D. Q. B. 1982:177.

85 Rehman 1803-4:folio 466. In this earliest named mention of Firoz Khan, he is called Na'mat Khan's son-in-law and disciple.

86 Radhika Mohan Maitra, interview, Calcutta, December 1977.

87 Umar Khan, interview, Calcutta, December 1977. This family does not consider Firozkhani to be authentic *gats*.

88 Sudarsanacarya Sastri was a disciple of Amrtsen, a descendent of Masit Khan; Sastri 1916:Introduction, 26; According to Josi (1935:250) Masit Khan was Firoz Khan's younger brother; in Roy Chaudhury (1975:168, 169) Masit Khan is not related to Firoz Khan, but shown as the son of Rajras or Ragras Khan, a descendant of Tansen's son. Here Amrtsen is five generations removed from Masit Khan.

89 Khan, D. Q. B. 1982:182, in connection with Husain Khan *ḍholak* player. *Gat paran* is a *pakhawaj* composition type probably predating this period.

90 A relationship with the common Hindi word *toḍnā*, "to break," is sometimes proposed (Powers 1980-IX:109), but this seems to be a less likely possibility.

91 Jyotish Chandra Chaudhury, interview, Varanasi, January 1980.

92 Mushtaq Ali Khan, interview, Varanasi, January 1979.

93 Bandyopadhyaya, K. 1866: Part 2, Introduction.

94 Brhaspati 1976:356. Sources, probably from the Rampur Raza Library, are unspecified.

95 Umar Khan, interview, Calcutta, January 1979.

96 Radhika Mohan Maitra, interview, Calcutta, December, 1977.

97 References to Firozkhani *gats* are found in the following books: Bhaju Lal 1873; Azharuddin 1898; Shivram 1901; Khan, Inayat 1912; Singh, B. c.1915.

98 Spear 1978:90. Rohilkhand was surrendered by Avadh to the British in 1801.

99 Sharma, B. R. 1980:105. The treatise is untraced.

100 *ibid*., also untraced.

101 Khan, M. K. I. 1925:32; translation Vidyarthi 1959:18. *Mārga* and *deśī* are terms from Sanskrit music literature, denoting respectively traditionally defined and regional *rāga* types. Here the implication might be a reference to *dhrupad* as opposed to non-*dhrupad* or regionally associated music. *Rāgas* having such regional names as *zila, pīlū, kāfī, gāḍā* and *beswāḍā* became especially prevalent in non-*dhrupad*-oriented instrumental music in Lucknow.

102 Roy Chaudhury 1975:171, also Umar Khan, interview, Calcutta, December 1978.

103 Tripathi 1977:314; also Gupta & Umadekar 1953:3.

104 Sastri 1916:Introduction, 26. Some sources say Dulha Khan was Bahadur Khan's nephew: Josi 1935:250 and Roy Chaudhury 1975:169.

105 *Gats* attributed to Bahadur Khan are found in Beg 1876 and Khan, Sadiq A. 1884.

106 Beg 1876:108, 132, 134; Khan, Sadiq A. 1884:222, 226.

107 Khan, M. K. I. 1925:43; Khan, Saiyyid A. 1964:687; Khan, Sadiq A. 1884:4.

108 Khan, M. K. I. 1925:43, translation Vidyarthi 1959:23.

109 Khan, M. K. I. 1925:34, translation Vidyarthi 1959:19.

110 Khan, M. K. I. 1925:34, translation Vidyarthi 1959:19.

111 According to Roy Chaudhury (1975:169) Sukhsen was Bahadur Khan's son, making Rahimsen Masit Khan's great-grandson. This, however, places Masit Khan too far back in time to agree with other evidence.

112 Mushtaq Ali Khan, interview, Varanasi, January 1979.

113 Mushtaq Ali Khan, interview, Varanasi, January 1979.

114 Knighton 1856:277, quoted from the "Calcutta Review."

115 *Dhārī, mirāsī* and *ḍom* are closely related classes of professional Muslim musicians. Crooke says they are "singers, minstrels and geneologists" and are also known as "Pakhawaji, Qawwal or Kalawant." He quotes proverbs illustrating their unfavored status "*ḍom baniyā postī tīnon beimān*" ("The Dom, Banya, and opium eater are all three

rogues") and "*bāp ḍom aur ḍom hī dādā, kahe mīyan main shurfa zāda*" ("His father was a bard, and so was his grandfather; but he says, 'Sir, my family is noble'") (Crooke 1896-III:496-7).

116 Khan, M. K. I. 1925:49-50, translation Vidyarthi 1959:26.

117 Anis ud-Daula is called a "fiddler" in Sleeman 1858-I:105, and a *tablā* player in Bhatnagar 1968:232.

118 Quoted from the "Englishman," January 2, 1855 in Knighton 1856:281-2. A charming account of the courtesan's life in *navābī* Lucknow is to be found in Mirza Ruswa's novel "*Umrao Jan Ada*," which has ben translated into English (Ruswa 1970).

119 Roy Chaudhury 1969:48-9. Roy Chaudhury was a disciple of Muhammad Ali Khan, Basat Khan's son.

120 Umar Khan, interview, Calcutta, December 1977. The book has not been located.

121 Khan, Sa'dat A. (1921:5) refers to him in connection with the reign of Muhammad Yusuf Ali Khan, 1854-1864.

122 From the tradition of Ilyas Khan, in Srivastav 1977:70.

123 *Atāī*, a term used for a musician without proper training.

124 Khan, M. K. I. 1925:44-5; also cf. Vidyarthi 1959:23.

125 Mushtaq Ali Kh n, interview, Varanasi, January 1979.

126 Satya Kinkar Banerji, interview, Varanasi, February 1981.

127 Asad Ali Khan, interview, Delhi, August 1979.

128 D. T. Joshi, interview, Shantiniketan, December 1977.

129 Gupta, N. 1978:36. An article on Ravi Shankar's series of articles in "Desh."

130 Pandit 1933. Eknath Pandit's photograph appears f. p. 86 in Fox-Strangways 1914.

131 Dilip Kumar Mukharji; cited in Gupta, N. 1978:37. Also see Mattoo 1967.

132 Umar Khan, interview, Calcutta, December 1978.

133 Shamsuddin Faridi, interview, Brindavan, March 1980.

134 Salamat Ali Khan, interview, Delhi, November 1980.

135 Umar Khan, interview, Calcutta, December 1978.

136 Umar Khan, interviews, Calcutta, December-January 1977-78.

137 Ilyas Khan, interview, Lucknow, February 1978.

138 Mushtaq Ali Khan, interview, Varanasi, January 1979.

139 Mushtaq Ali Khan, interview, Banaras, January 1979.

140 Satya Kinkar Banerji and Ilyas Khan both demonstrated *gats* by Bajpai.

141 "*Hārmoniyam sikhyā*" (Nandalal 1894) and Ali, Saiyyid I. n.d.

142 Umar Khan, interview, Calcutta, January 1978.

143 Satya Kinkar Banerji, interview, Varanasi, December 1980.

144 Included as an appendix in Tagore 1965:396.

145 D. T. Joshi, interview, Santiniketan, December 1977.

146 D. T. Joshi, interview, Santiniketan, December 1977.

147 Jyotish Chandra Chaudhury was one of his disciples.

148 Umar Khan, interview, Calcutta, December 1977.

149 Umar Khan, interview, Calcutta, December 1977.

150 Works providing details on Allauddin Khan and his family include: Shankar 1968; Das 1975; Bhattacharya 1979; Khan, Allauddin 1980.

151 For some details on his life, cf. Jong-Keesing 1974.

152 Sahasrabuddhe 1887:33-4, quoted from the "Times of India," October 25, 1876.

153 Pandit 1933:4. A photograph showing Eknath Pandit playing the *bīn* can be seen in Fox-Strangways 1970:f.p. 86.

154 Thanks to S. Gadgil for this reference. A photograph of a Rahmat Khan playing *sursingār* appears in Khan M. M. 1971:f.p. 68.

155 (1) *humphit*, (2) *khādit*, (3) *gaṇpat*, (4) *āhat*, (5) *anāhat*, (6) *āndolit*, (7) *prahat*, (8) *bruvāhat*, (9) *durāhat*, (10) *atharat*, (11) *sānt*, (12) *tirap*, (13) *khareśan*, (14) *okhareśan*, (15) *nisuthān*, (16) *okharasuthān*, (17) *kartarī*, (18) *syunt*, (19) *nimni*, (20) *dhāl*, (21) *suhān*, (22) *madarā* (Roy Chaudhury 1975:27).

156 Abul Majid Khan of Delhi taught his students *joḍ* on the *sarangi*. Joep Bor, personal communication, January 1989.

157 Zia Moiuddin Dagar, interview, Varanasi, August 1981.

158 Jyotish Chandra Chaudhury, representing the system taught by Dabir Khan, grandson of Wazir Khan, Varanasi, September 1980. Ilyas Khan, Lucknow, interview, February 1978.

159 Jyotish Chandra Chaudhury, Varanasi, September 1980.

160 (1) *ānīt*, (2) *jādat*, (3) *kampit*, (4) *āhaṭ*, (5) *āndolat*, (6) *purudā ānahat*, (7) *itarāhat* (?), (8) *paratāhat*, (9) *dorāhat*, (10) *astharat*, (11) *sāunt*, (12) *tarap*, (13) *kharsh*, (14) *avakharsh*, (15) *nisūthān*, (16) *akarsūthān*, (17) *kartarī*, (18) *sahansat*, (19) *nīmnī*, (20) *ḍhāl*, (21) *sudhān*, (22) *mudrā* (Khan, K. 1908:88-9).

161 D. T. Joshi, interview, Varanasi, April, 1980.

162 Mushtaq Ali Khan, interview, Varanasi, January 1979; Asad Ali Khan, interview, Delhi, August 1979; Platts 1960:400.

163 Umar Khan, interview, Calcutta, January 1979.

164 Salamat Husain Khan, interview, Delhi, December 1980.

165 Asad Ali Khan, interview, Delhi, August 1979.

166 Zia Moinuddin Dagar, interview, Varanasi, August 1981.

167 Beg 1894; Khan, Sadiq A. 1884.

168 Mushtaq Ali Khan, interview, Varanasi, January 1979.

169 Mushtaq Ali Khan, interview, Varanasi, January 1979.

170 Mushtaq Ali Khan, interview, Varanasi, January 1979.

171 Mushtaq Ali Khan, interview, Varanasi, January 1979.

172 Umar Khan, interview, Calcutta, January 1979.

173 Umar Khan, interview, Calcutta, January 1979.

174 Interview and recording: Calcutta, December 1978.

175 Lecture-demonstration, Banaras Hindu University, November 1979.

176 Notation courtesy of Michael Robins, Calcutta, December 1978.

177 Recording Sakhawat Husain Khan, thanks to Michael Robins, Calcutta, December 1978.

178 Notation courtesy of Michael Robins, Calcutta, December 1978.

179 Umar Khan, interview, Calcutta, December 1978.

180 Jyotish Chandra Chaudhury, Varanasi, August, 1980.

181 Lecture-demonstration, Banaras Hindu University, November 1979.

182 Ilyas Khan, interview, Lucknow, February 1977.

183 Lecture-demonstration, Banaras Hindu University, November 1979.

184 From *sarodia* Suprabhat Pal, a disciple of Allauddin Khan.

185 Lecture-demonstration, Banaras Hindu University, December 1980.

186 Unpublished notebook. Transcribed by Mahendra Singh.

187 Lecture-demonstration, Banaras Hindu University. December 1980.

188 Recording thanks to Michael Robins, Calcutta, December 1978.

189 Recording thanks to Michael Robins, Calcutta, December 1978.

Bibliography

anon.

1906 *Catalogue of the Crosby Brown Collection of Musical Instruments of All Nations.* Handbook no. 13. New York: The Metropolitan Museum.

1919 *Calendar of Persian Correspondence.* Vol. 3, 1770-72. Calcutta: Superintendent Government Printing, India.

1965 [1834] "Scientific Intelligence: Willard's Treatise on the Music of Hindustan." *Journal of the Asiatic Society* 25:n.p. Reprinted in: *Hindu Music from Various Authors.* S. M. Tagore, ed. Calcutta 1875. 2nd edition 1882. Reprint - Varanasi: Chowkhamba Sanskrit Series Office, 1965:235-9.

1967 *Sikh Sacred Music.* New Delhi: Sikh Sacred Music Society.

n.d. *Gulam Ali Sarode Gharana.* Calcutta. Unpublished.

Abu al-Fazl

1873 *Ain-i-Akbarī.* Vol. 1. H. Blochmann, transl. Calcutta: Asiatic Society of Bengal.

1891 *Ain-i-Akbarī.* Vol. 2. H. S. Jarrett, transl. Calcutta: Asiatic Society of Bengal.

1894 *Ain-i-Akbarī.* Vol. 3. H. S. Jarrett, transl. Calcutta: Asiatic Society of Bengal.

1983 Reprint of all three volumes: Bibliotheca Indica 61 (1-3). Osnabrück: Biblio Verlag.

Adil Shah, Ibrahim

1956 *Kitab-i Nauras.* Nazir Ahmad, ed./transl. New Delhi: Bharatiya Kala Kendra.

Ahmad, Najma Perveen

1984 *Hindustani Music: A Study of its Development in Seventeenth and Eighteenth Centuries* [sic]. New Delhi: Manohar Publications.

Ahobala

1879 *Saṅgītapārijāta.* Kalivara Vedantabagisa and Sarada Prasada Ghosha, eds. Calcutta: New Sanskrit Press.

1982 *Saṅgītapārijāta.* Edited from the published editions by Kamla Devi Nautiyal as *Saṅgītapārijāta kā vivecanātmak adhyayan.* Ph.D. dissertation, Banaras Hindu University.

Alam, Shah

[1797] *Nādirāt-i shāhī.* Handcopy from a manuscript in the Raza Library, Rampur. Department of Musicology, Banaras Hindu University.

Alford, Clem

1973 *The Sitar Manual for the Western Musician.* London: Keith Prowse Pub. Co.

1988 *The Sitar Book: a Practical Guide to Playing Sitar.* London: Asian Educational Resources Centre.

Ali, Meer Hassan, Mrs.

1832 *Observations on the Mussulmans of India Descriptive of their Manners, Customs, Habits, and Religious Opinions made During a Twelve Years' Residence in their Immediate Society.* London: Parbury, Allen and Co. 2nd edition: 1917. Reprint - Karachi: Oxford University Press, 1974.

Ali, Saiyyid Ibban

n.d. *Isrār-i hārmoniam.* Rampur: Munshi Gohar Ali Khan.

Ansari, Zoe (ed.)
1975 *Life, Times and Works of Amīr Khusrau Dehlavi*. Delhi: National Amir Khusrau Society.

Archer, Mildred
1960 "The Two Worlds of Colonel Skinner 1778-1841." *History Today* 10(9):608-15.
1969 *British Drawings in the India Office Library*, vol. 1. *Official and Professional Artists*, Vol. 2. London: Her Majesty's Stationery Office.
1972 *Company Drawings in the India Office Library*. London: Her Majesty's Stationery Office.

Arshi, Imtiaz Ali Khan
1978 "Hindustān ke chand mashhūr mūsīqīkār." *Rajat* 2(1):17-21.

Askari, S. H.
n.d. "Amir Khusrau aur Mūsīqī." In *Amir Khusro*. Nur Al Hassan Ansari, ed. Delhi: Urdu Bazar, 370-5.
1972 "Music in Early Indo-Persian Literature." In *Malik Ram Felicitation Volume*. New Delhi: Malik Ram Felicitation Committee, 89-120.

Avtar, Ram
1958 *Sitār śikṣā*. Delhi.
1980 *Learn to Play on Sitar*. New Delhi: Pankaj Publications.

Ayyangar, Ranganayaki Veeraswamy
1980 *Gamaka and vādanabheda, a Study of Somanātha's Rāgavibodha in Historical and Practical Context*. Ph.D. dissertation. University of Pennsylvania, Philadelphia.

Azharuddin, Muhammad
1898 *Risāla sitār va tabla*. Prog. no. 6415 H. L. no. 209. Patna: Khuda Bakhsh Public Library. Unpublished.

Baden-Powell, B. H.
1872 *Hand-Book of the Manufactures and Arts of the Punjab*. Vol. II. Vol. I: *Hand-Book of the Economic Products of the Punjab*. Roorkee 1868.

Bahadurji, K. N.
1887 "Indisches Saiteninstrument, genannt Taus." *Zeitschrift für Ethnologie* 19(5):418-9.

Baily, John
1988 *Music of Afghanistan: Professional Musicians in the City of Herat*. Cambridge Studies in Ethnomusicology. Cambridge: Cambridge University Press.

Bajpeyi, Balkrsnapati, "Bhimpure"
1936 *Sitār kī tīsrī pustak*. Lashkar, Gwalior: The author.

Baloch, N. A.
1966 *Musical Instruments of the Lower Indus Valley of Sind*. Hyderabad, Pakistan: Mehran Arts Council.

Bandyopadhyaya, Krishnadhan
1866 *Sitār śikṣā*. 2 Parts in 1 Vol. 2nd ed. Calcutta: Ārya citrālaya.
1885 *Gīta sūtra sār*. Cooch Behar: Rājakiya Yantrālaya. Reprint - Calcutta: A. Mukharji and Co., 1976.

Bandyopadhyaya, Sripada
1937 *Sitār mārg*. Lucknow: Sripad Banarji. 2nd edition: Delhi 1957.
1988 *Techniques of Sitār*. Delhi: B. R. Pub. Corp.

Beg, Rahim
1876 *Naghmah-i sitār*. Lahore: Babu Sarma Caran. 2nd edition - Delhi: Jivan Prakāś, 1894.
1884 *Tashīl al-sitār*. Lucknow: Naval Kishore. 1st edition: Kanpur, 1874.

Belnos, S. C.
1832 *Twenty-Four Plates Illustrative of Hindoo and European Manners in Bengal. Drawn on the stone by A. Colin from sketches by Mrs. Belnos*. London: Smith and Elder Cornhill.

Bhaju Lal, Ram
1873 *Guldastah-i mūsīqī*. Patna: Matba'-i Faiz-i 'Am.

Bharata

1926-64 *Nāṭyaśāstra of Bharatamuni with the Commentary of Abhinavagupta*. Vols. 1-3: Manavalli Ramakrishna Kavi, ed. Vol.4: M. R. Kavi and J. S. Pade, eds. Gaekwad's Oriental Series 36, 68, 124, 145. Baroda: Central Library (Vol. 1)/Oriental Institute (Vols. 2-4).

1961 *The Nāṭyaśāstra, a Treatise on Ancient Indian Dramaturgy and Histrionics, Ascribed to Bharata Muni* Rev. 2 Vols. Manomohan Ghosh, ed./transl. 2nd edition. Calcutta: Manisha Granthalaya.

Bhatkhande, Visnunarayan

1970-5 *Kramik pustak mālikā*. 6 Vols. Hathras: Sangeet Karyalaya.

Bhatnagar, G. D.

1968 *Awadh under Wajid Ali Shah*. Varanasi: Bharatiya Vidya Prakashan.

Bhatt, Madan Mohan

1880 *Sangit or The Rudiment of Hindustani Music*. Patna: Bihar Bandu.

Bhattacharya, Jotin

1979 *Ustad Allauddin Khan and His Music*. Ahmedabad: B. S. Shah Prakashan.

Blochmann, H.

1965 *The Ai'n-i Akbari*. Vol. 1. Calcutta: Asiatic Society of Bengal. 1873. Reprinted as "The Naqqarahkhanah and the Imperial Musicians." In *Hindu Music from Various Authors*. Sourindro Mohun Tagore, ed. Calcutta 1875. 2nd edition: 1882. Reprint - Varanasi: Chowkhamba Sanskrit Series Office, 1965:211-6.

Blumhardt, J. F.

1889 *Catalogue of Hindustani Printed Books in the Library of the British Museum* London: Longmans & Co.

Bor, Joep

1982 *De Roep van de Kokila: Historische en hedendaagse aspecten van de Indiase muziek*. 's Gravenhage: Martinus Nijhoff.

1986/7 *The Voice of the Sarangi: An Illustrated History of Bowing in India*. Bombay: National Centre for the Performing Arts. Quarterly Journal, 15(3-4)/16(1):1-183.

1988 "The Rise of Ethnomusicology: Sources on Indian Music c.1780-c.1890." *Yearbook for Traditional Music* 20:51-73.

Brhaspati, Kailas Candra

1974 *Musalmān aur Bhāratīya saṅgīt*. Delhi: Rājkamal Prakāśan.

1976 *Saṅgīt cintāmaṇi*. 2nd edition. Hathras: Sangeet Karyalaya.

Brown, Percy

1981 *Indian Painting under the Mughals: A.D. 1550 to A.D. 1750*. Reprint of 5th ed. New Delhi: Cosmo Publications.

Chandra, Satish

1959 *Parties and Politics at the Mughal Court, 1707-1740*. Publication No. 15. Aligarh: Aligarh Muslim University, Department of History.

Chaubey, S. K.

1958 *Musicians I Have Met*. Lucknow: Information Department, Uttar Pradesh.

Chaudhuri, Debu

1981 *Sitar and Its Techniques*. Delhi: Avon Book Co.

Coomaraswamy, Ananda K.

1930 "The Parts of a Vīṇā." *Journal of the American Oriental Society* 50:244-53.

Crooke, William

1896 *The Tribes and Castes of the North-Western Provinces and Oudh*. 4 Vols. Calcutta: Office of the Superintendant of Government Printing. Reprint - Delhi: Cosmo Publications, 1974-5.

Das, Bijan

1975 *Surer sandhāne* (On the Life and Work of Allauddin Khan). Calcutta: S. B. Publishers.

Datta, K. K.
1972 *Socio-Cultural Background of Modern India.* Delhi: Meenakshi Prakashan.
Davies, C. Collin
1959 *An Historical Atlas of the Indian Peninsula.* 2nd edition. Madras, New York: Oxford University Press.
Day, Charles Russell
1974 *The Music and Musical Instruments of Southern India and the Deccan.* Reprint - Delhi: B. R. Publishing Corporation. 1st edition: 1891.
Dayal, Muneshwar
n.d. *Biodata.* Unpublished manuscript.
Della Valle, Pietro
1892 [1664] *The Travels of Pietro Della Valle in India.* Vol. 1. G. Havers, transl. E. Grey, ed. London: The Hakluyt Society.
Desai, Chaitanya
1969 "The Origin and Development of Khyal." *Journal of the Music Academy* 40(1-4):142-82.
Deva, B. Chaitanya
1978 *Musical Instruments of India.* Calcutta: KLM Private Ltd.
1981 *An Introduction to Indian Music.* Rev. ed. New Delhi: Publications Division, Ministry of Information and Broadcasting, Government of India. 1st edition: 1973.
Dhond, M. V.
1980 *The Evolution of Khyāl.* New Delhi: Sangeet Natak Akademi.
Dick, Alastair
1984a "Sarod." In *The New Grove Dictionary of Musical Instruments.* Vol. 3. Stanley Sadie, ed. London: Macmillan Press, 298-9.
1984b "Sitar." In *The New Grove Dictionary of Musical Instruments.* Vol. 3. Stanley Sadie, ed. London: Macmillan Press, 392-400.
Dick, Alastair *et al.*
1984 "Rabab." In *The New Grove Dictionary of Musical Instruments.* Vol. 3. Stanley Sadie, ed. London: Macmillan Press, 177-83.
Dickenson, Eric & Karl Khandalavala
1959 *Lalit Kalā Series of Indian Art, Kishangarh Painting.* New Delhi: Lalit Kala Akademi.
During, Jean & Alastair Dick
1984 "Setar." In *The New Grove Dictionary of Musical Instruments.* Vol. 3. Stanley Sadie, ed. London: Macmillan Press, 353-4.
Dwivedi, Harihar Niwas
1953 *Mānsingh aur Mānakutuhala.* Gwalior: Vidyā mandir prakāśan.
Dyson, Ketaki Kushari
1978 *A Various Universe: A Study of the Journals and Memoirs of British Men and Women in the Indian Subcontinent, 1765-1856.* Delhi: Oxford University Press.
Elliot, H. M.
1877 *The History of India as Told by Its Own Historians: The Muhammedan Period.* 8 vols. Edited and continued by John Dowson. London: Trübner and Co. Reprint - New York: AMS Press. 1966. 1st Indian edition: Allahabad: Kitab Mahal, 1963-4.
Elphinstone, Mountstuart
1972 *An Account of the Kingdom of Caubul.* 2 Vols. Reprint of 3rd edition. Karachi: Oxford University Press. 1st edition: 1815.
Faqirullah
1953 [17th century] "Rāg darpan." In *Mansingh aur Manakutuhala.* Harihar Niwas Dwivedi, transl. Gwalior: Vidyā mandir prakāśan.
Farmer, Henry George
1926 "The Evolution of the ṭanbūr or Pandore." *Transactions of the Glasgow University Oriental Society* 26-27:26-8.
1929 *A History of Arabian Music to the XIIIth Century.* London: Luzac & Co.

1964 "Iranian Musical Instruments in the Ninth/Fifteenth Century." *Islamic Culture* 38(3):175-82.

1978 *Studies in Oriental Musical Instruments.* Reprint of the 1st and 2nd series. British Virgin Islands, Boston: Longwood Press. 1st edition: 1931 and 1939.

Fétis, F.-J.

1869 *Histoire générale de la musique: depuis les temps les plus anciens jusqu'à nos jours.* 5 vols Paris: Librarie de Firmin Didot Frères, Fils et Cie.

Forbes, James

1813 *Oriental Memoirs: Selected and Abridged from a Series of Familial Letters Written During Seventeen Years Residence in India.* 4 Vols. London: White, Cochrane and Co.

Fowke, Francis

1965 [1788] "On the Vina or Indian Lyre." *Asiatick Researches* 1:295-9. Reprinted in: *Hindu Music from Various Authors.* Sourindro Mohun Tagore, ed. Calcutta 1875. 2nd edition: 1882. Reprint - Varanasi: Chowkhamba Sanskrit Series Office, 1965:191-7.

Fox-Strangways, A. H.

1970 *The Music of Hindostan.* Reprint. Oxford: The Clarendon Press. 1st edition: 1914.

Francklin, W.

1798 *The History of the Reign of Shah Aulum, the Present Emperor of Hindostaun: containing the transactions of the court of Delhi, and the neighboring states, during a period of thirty-six years: interspersed with geographical and topographical observations on several of the principal cities of Hindostaun.* London: Printed for the author by Cooper and Graham. Reprint - Rare-India Series. Lucknow: Pustak Kendra. 1973.

Garg, Laksmi Narayan

1969 *Hamare Saṅgīt Ratna.* Vol. 1. Hathras: Sangeet Karyalaya.

Gazetteer

1911 *Gazetteer of the Rampur State.* Allahabad: Government Press.

Ghosh, Sharmistha

1988 *String Instruments (Plucked Variety) of North India.* Delhi: Eastern Book Linkers.

Gladwin, Francis

1965 "Sungeet." In *Ayeen Akbery.* Vol. 2. London: J. Sewell etc., 456ff. 1800. Reprinted in: *Hindu Music from Various Authors.* Sourindro Mohun Tagore, ed. Calcutta 1875. 2nd edition: 1882. Reprint - Varanasi: Chowkhamba Sanskrit Series Office, 1965:201-8.

Gosvami, Ksetra Mohan

1879 *Saṅgīt sār.* 2nd ed. Calcutta: Kally Prosonna Banerjea. 1st edition: 1870.

Gosvami, O.

1957 *The Story of Indian Music its Growth and Synthesis.* Bombay: Asia Publishing House.

Gosvami, Pannalal

1895 *Nād vinod.* Delhi: Narayandas Janglimal.

Greig, John Andrew

1987 *Tārīkh-i Saṅgīta: The Foundations of North Indian Music in the Sixteenth Century.* Ph. D. dissertation, University of California, Los Angeles.

Gupta, Babulal & Suman Umadekar

1953 *Madhya Bhārat men saṅgīt śailiyoṅ ka vikās, rāg rāginioṅ kī racnāyeṅ tathā sādhanā.* Gwalior.

Gupta, Nilaksha

1978 "One Man's Ego." *New Delhi* (4 September):32-7.

Gupta, Punita

1975 *Maintenance of the Sitar.* Southhall: The author.

Gutman, Judith Mara

1982 *Through Indian Eyes.* New York: Oxford University Press, International Center of Photography.

Hajek, Lubor & W. & B. Forman

1960 *Indian Miniatures of the Moghul School.* London: Spring Books.

Halim, Abdul Sharar
1971 *Purana Lucknow (Guzishta Lucknow)*. New Delhi: National Book Trust.
Hamilton, James Sadler
1988 *The Sitar Music of Calcutta*. Calgary: University of Calgary Press.
Hansen, Jan
1973 *A Simple Introduction to Indian Classical Music: a small collection of notes made to introduce non-Indian students of classical music to the sitar, its heritage and tradition, with lessons for beginners*. 2nd edition - Baroda: H. Jan.
Hardgrave, Robert L. & Stephen M. Slawek
1988-9 "Instruments and Music Culture in Eighteenth Century India: the Solvyns Portraits." *Asian Music* 20(1):1-92.
Hasan Rizvi, Saiyyad Mir
1876 *Tarjumā tālīm us-sitār*. Delhi.
Hay, Sidney
1939 *Historic Lucknow*. Lucknow: Pioneer Press.
Heber, Reginald
1829 *Narrative of a Journey Through the Upper Provinces of India from Calcutta to Bombay 1824-1825*. 3 Vols. 4th edition. London: John Murray.
Husain, Afzal (alias "Chunne Saheb")
1937 *Sitār mañjarī*. Allahabad: Central Art Press.
Ikram, S. M. & Percival Spear
1955 *The Cultural Heritage of Pakistan*. London, Karachi, New York: Oxford University Press.
Irvine, William
1971 *Later Mughals*. Edited and augmented by Jadunath Sarkar. New Delhi: Oriental Books Reprint Corporation.
Jan, Mir Yar Ali
1950 *Musaddas-i Benazīr*. Rampur: State Press.
Jenkins, Jean & Poul Rovsing Olsen
1976 *Music and Musical Instruments in the World of Islam*. London: Horniman Museum.
Jodhraj, Kavi
1979 *Hammīr Rāso*. 3rd edition. Nāgarī pracāriṇī granthmālā 11. Banaras: Nāgarī pracāriṇī sabhā, samvat 2006.
Jong-Keesing, Elisabeth de
1974 *Inayat Khan, a Biography*. The Hague Postbus 7617: East-West Publications Fonds/ London: in association with Luzac.
Josi, Laksman Dattatrey
1935 *Saṅgīt śāstrakār va kalāvant yāñcā itihās*. Pune: Laksman Dattatrey Josi, Arya Bhusan Press.
Junius, Manfred
1974 *The Sitar: the Instrument and its Technique*. International Institute for Comparative Music Studies and Documentation, Berlin. Wilhelmshaven: Heinrichshofen.
Keene, Henry George
1887 *The Fall of the Moghal Empire of Hindustan*. London: W. H. Allen. Reprint - Lahore: Al-Biruni, 1975.
Keesee, Allen
1968 *The Sitar Book: a beginning instruction method for playing the Indian sitar, with musical exercises, detailed explanation of Indian musical notation system, ten ragas, and a brief history of Indian music*. New York: Oak Publications.
Khan, Allauddin
1980 *Āmār kathā*. Calcutta: Ananda.
Khan, Amjad Ali
1973 "My Guru My Father." In *Ustad Hafiz Ali Khan Memorial Music Festival*. Prem Shankar Jha, ed. Calcutta: Ananda Press and Publications Pvt., [n.p.].

Khan, Dargah Quli, Bahadur

1933 *Purānī Dehlī ke ḥālāt*. Translation of the *Muraqqa'-i Dehlī* from Persian to Urdu by Khwaja Hasan Nizami. Delhi: Majūb-al ṭabi'a burqī Press. 2nd edition: 1949.

1982 *Muraqqa'-i Dehlī*. Edited with Persian text and Urdu translation by Nur al-Hasan Ansari. New Delhi: Department of Urdu, Delhi University.

1989 *Muraqqa'-i Dehli The Mughal Capital in Muhammad Shah's Time*. English translation, introduction and notes by Chander Shekhar and Shama Mitra Chenoy. Delhi: Deputy Publication.

Khan, Ilyas

1976 "Sitār vādan kā drut bāj." In *Golden Jubilee Souvenir*. Puru Dadhic, ed. Lucknow: Bhatkhande Music College, 93-4.

Khan, Inayat

1912 *Minqār mūsīqār*. Allahabad: Indian Press.

Khan, Inayet, Rasikh

1961 [18th century] *Risala-i-zikr-i mughannian-i Hindustan*. Arabic and Persian Re-search Institute Publication Series 7. Syed Ali Haider ed. Patna: Arabic and Persian Research Institute.

Khan, Karamatullah

1908 *Isrār-i karāmat urf naghmāt-i na'mat* and *Risāla sitār*. Allahabad: Janaki Press.

Khan, Mirza

n.d. [17th century] *Tuḥfāt al-Hind*. University of Pennsylvania Libraries. Microfilm 2948.

Khan, Muhammad Ashafaq Ali (alias Navab Jani Sahab)

[c.1925] *Naghmāt al-Hind*. Lucknow: Nizami Press.

Khan, Muhammad Karam Imam

1925 *Ma'dan al-mūsīqī*. Lucknow: Hindustani Press. 1st edition: 1856.

Khan, Muhammad Moulamia

1971 *Pages in the Life of a Sufi*. London: Sufi Publishing Co.

Khan, Muhammad Najm al-Ghani

1919 *Tārīkh-i Avadh*. 4 vols. Lucknow: Naval Kishore Press.

Khan, Muhammad Navab Ali

1927 *Maarifun naghmāt*. 3 vols. Lucknow: Naval Kishore Press.

Khan, Muhammad Safdar Husain

1873 *Qānūn-i sitār*. 2nd edition. Lucknow: Naval Kisore Press. 1st edition [Delhi?] 1871.

Khan, Navab Mardan Ali

1879 *Ghuncha-i rāg*. Lucknow: Naval Kishore Press.

Khan, Sa'dat Ali, Bahadur (alias Chamman Sahab)

1921 *Falsaf-i mūsīqī*. Rampur: Sarkari Press.

Khan, Sadiq Ali

1884 *Sarmāya-i 'ishrat* or *Qānūn-i mūsīqī*. Delhi: Munshi Muhammad Ibrahim. 1st edition: 1875.

Khan, Saiyyid Ahmad

1964 *Āsāru al-sannādīd*. 4th ed. Delhi: Central Book Depot, Jama' Masjid. 1st edition: 1847.

Khan, Saiyyid Muhammad Raza Ali

1956 "Darbar Rampur aur mūsīqī." *Ājkal, mūsīqī ank*:49-51.

Khan, Vilayat Husain

1957 "Fan mūsīqī ke kuch baḍe fankār." *Ājkal, mūsīqī ank*:28-30.

Khanna, Lalita

1973 "The Last Interview." In *Ustad Hafiz Ali Khan Memorial Music Festival*. Calcutta: Ananda Press and Publications Pvt., [n.p.].

Kindersley, Jemima

1978 *Letters from the Island of Teneriffe, Brazil, the Cape of Good Hope, and the East Indies*. London. Published London 1777. Excerpts in Dyson 1978:124, 336.

Kippen, James
1988 *The Tabla of Lucknow: a Cultural Analysis of a Musical Tradition*. Cambridge Studies in Ethnomusicology. Cambridge: Cambridge University Press.
Knighton, William
1856 *The Private Life of an Eastern King: Compiled for 'a member of the household' of his late Majesty, Nusseer-u-Deen, King of Oude*. London: G. Routledge & Co.
Kosar, Na'im
1956 "Ustad Hafiz Ali Khan." *Ājkal, mūsīqī ank*:120-1.
Krishnaswami, S.
1971 *Musical Instruments of India*. Boston: Crescendo Publishing Company. 1st edition: Publications Division, Ministry of Information and Broadcasting, Government of India, 1965.
Kunst, Jaap.
1968 *Hindu-Javanese Musical Instruments*. Koninklijk Institut voor Taal-, Land- en Volkenkunde Translation Series 12. The Hague: Martinus Nijhoff.
Lane-Poole, Stanley
1964 *Aurangzeb and the Decay of the Moghal Empire*. Delhi: S. Chand.
Limaye, Vinayak Mahadev (ed.)
1970 *Limaye-kul-vṛttānt*. Pune: Vinayak Mahadev Limaye.
Mahillon, Victor-Charles
1893 *Catalogue descriptif & analytique du Musée Instrumental de Conservatoire Royal de Musique de Bruxelles*. Vol. 1. Gand: Librarie Générale de A.D. Hoste, Ed. 1st edition: 1880.
Maitra, Radhika Mohan
n.d. "Sarod or the Indian Banjo." *Souvenir Jhankar*. Calcutta
Majumdar, R. C.; Raychaudhury, H. C.; & Kalikinkar Datta
1967 *An Advanced History of India*. 3rd edition. London: Macmillan.
Malik, Rashid
1975 *Hazrat Amir Khusrau ka 'ilm-i mūsīqī*. Lahore: Reference Reprints.
Malik, Zahiruddin
1977 *The Reign of Muhammad Shah 1719-1748*. New York: Asia Publishing House.
Mallik, Ram Chatur
n.d. *Life Sketch*. Unpublished manuscript.
Mansukhani, Gobind Singh
1982 *Indian Classical Music and Sikh Kirtan*. New Delhi: Oxford and IBH Publishing Co.
Manucci, Niccolao
1907 *Storia do Mogor or Mogul India*. 3 Vols. William Irvine, transl. London: Indian Text Series. Reprint - Calcutta: Editions Indian, 1965-66.
Marcel-Dubois, Claudie
1941 *Les instruments de musique de l'Inde ancienne*. Paris: Presses Universitaires de France.
Marcuse, Sibyl
1964 *Musical Instruments: a Comprehensive Dictionary*. New York: Doubleday and Company.
Marshall, D. N.
1985 *Mughals in India: a Bibliographical Survey of Manuscripts*. Reprint. London and New York: Mansell Publishing Ltd. 1st edition: London 1967.
Mattoo, Jiwan Lal
1967 "Bande Ali Khan." *Indian Music Journal* 8(4)II.
Mavlankar, Bhaiya Sahab
n.d. Unpublished notebook. Transcribed by Mahendra Singh.
Meer, Wim Van der
1980 *Hindustani Music in the Twentieth Century*. New Delhi: Allied Publishers.

Meerwarth, A. M.
1917 *A Guide to the Collection of Musical Instruments Exhibited in the Ethnographical Gallery of the Indian Museum, Calcutta.* Calcutta: Zoological Survey of India.

Mirza, Mohammad Wahid
1962 *The Life and Works of Amir Khusru.* Reprint. Panjab University Oriental Publications/Lahore: The University of the Panjab. 1st edition - Calcutta: Baptist Mission Press, 1935.

Mishra, Lalmani
1973 *Bhāratīya saṅgīt vādya.* Delhi: Bhāratīya jñānpīṭh prakāśan.
1979 *Tantrīnād.* Kanpur: Sahitya Ratnalaya.

Mukharji, T. N.
1888 *Art Manufactures of India.* Calcutta: Government of India.

Munib, Laksmandas (alias Munimji)
1925 *Saṅgīt samucay.* Banaras.

Nandalal
1894 *Hārmoniyam sikhyā.* Lahore.

Narada
1920 *Ṣaṅgītamakaranda,* Mangesh Ramakrishna Telang, ed. Gaekwad's Oriental Series 16. Baroda: Central Library.

Narayanadeva, Gajapati
1966 [18th century] *Saṅgītanārāyaṇa.* Bhubaneswar: The Orissa Sangeet Natak Akademi.

Neville, H. R.
1928 *Fyzabad, A Gazetteer.* Allahabad: Government Press.

Ouseley, William
1965 [1797-1800] "Anecdotes of Indian Music." In *Oriental Collections: Illustrating the History, Antiquity, Literature. &c., of Asia* 1. Reprinted in: *Hindu Music from Various Authors.* Sourindro Mohun Tagore, ed. Calcutta 1875. 2nd edition: 1882. Reprint - Varanasi: Chowkhamba Sanskrit Series Office, 1965:163-72.

Pacholczyk, Józef
1978 "Sufyana Kalam, the Classical Music of Kashmir." *Asian Music* 10(1):1-16.

Pandit, Krsnarao Sankar
1933 *Sitār va jaltarang.* Gwalior.

Parks, Fanny
1850 *Wanderings of a Pilgrim in Search of the Picturesque During Four-and twenty Years in the East with Revelations of Life in the Zenana.* 2 Vols. London: Pelham Richardson.

Perera, E. S.
1985 "A Brief Note on the Origin of the Sarode." *Journal of the Department of Instrumental Music, Rabindra Bharati University* 3:43-7.

Platts, John T.
1960 *A Dictionary of Urdu, Classical Hindi, and English.* Reprint of 5th edition. London: Oxford University Press. 1st edition: 1930.

Powers, Harold
1980 "India." In *The New Grove Dictionary of Music and Musicians.* Vol. 9. Stanley Sadie, ed. London: Macmillan, 69-166.

Prajnanananda, Swami
1973 *Historical Development of Indian Music.* Calcutta: Firma K. L. Mukhopadhyay.

Prinsep, James
1833 *Benares Illustrated in a Series of Drawings. Lithographed in England by Eminent Artists.* Calcutta: Baptist Mission Press.

Qureshi, Regula Burckhardt
1986 *Sufi Music of India and Pakistan: Sound, Context and Meaning in qawwali.* Cambridge Studies in Ethnomusicology. Cambridge: Cambridge University Press.

Rao, Harihar
1967 *Introduction to Sitar.* New York: Peer International.

Rehman, Abdul, Shah Nawaz Hashmi Burhani Dehlavi

[1803-04] *Mir'āt-i āftāb numā*. Khuda Bakhsh Oriental Public Library, Patna. Manuscript B 30 481.

Rennell, James

1793 *Memoir of a Map of Hindostan or the Mogul Empire*. 3rd edition. London: W. Bulmer and Co. for the author. Reprint - Calcutta: Editions Indian, 1976.

Roach, David

1971 *The Sitar: its Tradition, Technique, and Compositions*. M. A. thesis, Wesleyan University.

Rosenthal, Ethel

1928 *The Story of Indian Music and its Instruments*. London: William Reeves.

Rosse, Michael D.

1980 "Tagore, Sir Sourindro Mohun." In *The New Grove Dictionary of Music and Musicians*. Vol. 18. Stanley Sadie, ed. London: Macmillan Pub., 525-6.

Roy Chaudhury, Vimalakant

1969 "Svargīya Ustad Muhammad Ali Khan Rabābia." *Sangeet* 35(2):48-9..

1975 *Bharatiya Sangeet Kosh*. Hindi translation. New Delhi: Bharatiya Jnanpith.

Roy Choudhury, Birendra Kishore

1957 "The Veena Paddhati of Hindustani Music." *Journal of the Music Academy* 28(1-4):72-5.

1973 "My Ustad." In *Ustad Ali Khan Memorial Music Festival*. Prem Shankar Jha, ed. Calcutta: Ananda Press and Publications, n.p.

Roychowdhury, Harendra Kishore

1929 *The Musicians of India (Illustrated)*. Part 1. Ramgopalpur, Mymensingh: The author.

Ruswa, Mirza Mohammad Hadi

1970 *The Courtesan of Lucknow (Umrao Jan Ada)*. Khushwant Singh and M. A. Husaini, transl. Delhi: Hind Pocket Books.

Russell, R. V. & R. Bahadur Hira Lal

1916 *The Tribes and Castes of the Central Provinces of India*. 4 vols. London: Macmillan & Co. Reprint - Delhi: Cosmo Publications, 1975.

Sachs, Curt

1968 *The History of Musical Instruments*. New York, London: W. W. Norton. 1st edition: 1940.

Sadie, Stanley (ed.)

1980 *The New Grove Dictionary of Music and Musicians*. 20 vols. London: Macmillan.

1984 *The New Grove Dictionary of Musical Instruments*. 3 vols. London: Macmillan.

Sahasrabuddhe, B. T.

1887 *Hindu Music and the Gayun Samaj*. Pune, Madras: The Madras Gayan Samaj Offices.

Sakata, Hiromi Lorraine

1983 *Music in the Mind: the Concepts of Music and Musician in Afghanistan*. Ohio: Kent State University Press.

Sarkar, Jadunath

1966 *The Fall of the Mughal Empire*. 4 Vols. 3rd edition. Calcutta, Bombay: Orient Longman.

Sarmadee, Shahab (ed.)

1971 *Ghunyat al-munya*. New Delhi: Asia Publishing House.

1975a "Ameer Khusrau's own Writings on Music." In *Life, Times and Works of Amīr Khusrau Dehlavi*. Zoe Ansari, ed. Delhi: National Amir Khusrau Society, n.p.

1975b "Musical Genius of Amir Khusrau." In *Amir Khusrau*. New Delhi: Ministry of Information and Broadcasting, Government of India, 33-61.

Śārṅgadeva

1978 *Saṅgītaratnākara*. Vol. 1. R. K. Shringy and Prem Lata Sharma, transl. Delhi: Motilal Banarsidass.

1986 *Saṃgītaratnākara* with the *Kalānidhi of Kallinātha* and the *Sudhākara of Siṃhabhūpāla*. Vol. 3. 2nd edition. S. Subrahmanya Sastri, ed. Revised by S. Sarada. Madras: The Adyar Library and Research Centre. 1st edition: 1951.

1989 *Saṅgītaratnākara*. Vol. 2. R. K. Shringy and Prem Lata Sharma, transl. New Delhi: Munshiram Manoharlal Publishers Pvt.

Sastri, Sudarsanacarya

1916 *Saṅgīt sudarśan*. Varanasi: Chowkhambā Sanskrit Series Office.

Sen, Sharmishtha

1972 *String Instruments (Plucked Variety) of North India*. Ph.D dissertation, Visva-Bharati University, Santiniketan.

Shankar, Ravi

1968 *My Music, My Life*. New York: Simon and Schuster. Reprints: 1970, 1972.

Sharma, B. R.

1980 "Contribution of Rajasthan to Indian Music." In *Indian Music: a Perspective*. Gowry Kuppuswamy and M. Hariharan, eds. Delhi: Sundeep Prakashan, 104-21.

Sharma, Vinod Chandra

1959 *Lucknow*. Uttar Pradesh District Gazetteers. Lucknow.

Shivram, Dahyalal (comp.)

1938 *Śrī saṅgīt kalādhar*. 2nd edition. Bhavnagar: Chhanalal Dahyalal Nayak and Chandulal Dahyalal Nayak. 1st edition: Ahmedabad, 1901.

Singh, Bakhtavar

[c.1915] *Svar tāl samūh*. Bombay: Gangavisnu Sri Krsnadas "Laksmivenkalisvar" Publishing House.

Singh, Sawai Pratap, Maharaj

1910-2 *Rādhāgovind saṅgīt sār*. 7 Parts. Pune: Poona Gayan Samaj.

Slawek, Stephen

1987 *Sitār Technique in Nibaddh Forms*. Delhi: Motilal Banarsidass.

Sleeman, W. H.

1858 *A Journey Through the Kingdom of Oude in 1849-1850*. 2 Vols. London: Richard Bentley.

Slobin, Mark

1976 *Music in the Culture of Northern Afghanistan*. Published for the Werner-Gren Foundation for Anthropological Research: Tucson: Arizona Press.

Smith, Robert

[c.1833] *Pictorial Journey of Travels in Hindustan from 1828 to 1833*. Manuscript: Victoria and Albert Museum, London, I.M. 15-1915.

Smith, Vincent A.

1958 *The Oxford History of India*. 3rd edition. Edited by Percival Spear. Revised by A. L. Basham, J. B. Harrison, M. Wheeler and P. Spear. London: Oxford University Press.

Solis, Theodore

1970 *The Sarod*. M.A. thesis. University of Hawaii.

Solvyns, F. Baltazard

1799 *A Collection of Two Hundred and Fifty Coloured Etchings Descriptive of the Manners, Customs and Dresses of the Hindoos*. 2 vols. Calcutta: [Mirror Press ?].

1804 *The Costume of Hindostan Elucidated by Sixty Coloured Engravings with Descriptions in English and French Taken in the Years 1798 and 1799*. London: Edward Orme.

1808/10 *Les Hindous*. 4 vols. Paris: chez l'auteur.

Somanatha

1945 [17th century] *Rāgavibodha*. S. Subrahmanya Sastri Adyar Library Series 48. Madras: Adyar Library and Research Centre.

Spear, Percival

1951 *Twilight of the Mughals: Studies in Late Mughal Delhi*. Boston: Cambridge University Press.

1978 *A History of India* 2. Harmondsworth, England; New York: Penguin. 1st edition: 1965.

Srinivas Kini, K.& U. Bhavani Shankar Rao

1960 *Oxford Pictorial Atlas of Indian History*. 8th edition. Madras: Oxford University Press.

Srivastav, Rajni

1976 *Sitār vādan evaṃ uskī vibhinn śailiāṅ*. M.A. thesis Lucknow, Bhatkhande Music College.

1977 "Gayaki ke sandarbh men sitār vādan." *Chāyānaṭ* 1. Lucknow: Uttar Pradeś Saṅgīt Nāṭak Akademi.

Sudhakalasa

1961 *Saṅgītopaniṣatsāroddhāra*. Umakant Premanand Shah, ed. Gaekwad's Oriental Series 133. Baroda: Oriental Institute.

Tagore, Sourindro Mohun

1874 "Hindu Music." In *Hindoo Patriot*. Sept. 7, 1874. Reprinted as *Hindu Music*. Calcutta 1974: "Hindoo Patriot" Press. In *Hindu Music from Various Authors*. Part 2. Calcutta 1882. Reprint - Varanasi: Chowkhamba Sanskrit Series Office, 1965:339-87.

1879 *Yantra Kshetra Dipika*. 2nd edition. Calcutta: Sri Kally Prosonno Banerjea [1872, 1890].

1963 *Universal History of Music: Compiled from Diverse Sources, Together with Various Original Notes on Hindu Music*. Reprint - Varanasi: Chowkhamba Sanskrit Series Office. 1st edition: Calcutta 1896.

1965 *Hindu Music from Various Authors*. Reprint - Varanasi: Chowkhamba Sanskrit Series Office. 1st edition, Part 1: Calcutta 1875. Reprint with Part 2: Calcutta 1882.

1976 *Yantra Kosha or a Treasury of the Musical Instruments of Ancient and of Modern India, and of Various Other Countries*. Reprint. New York: AMS Press. 1st edition: 1875

Tarlekar, G. H. & Nalini

1972 *Musical Instruments in Indian Sculpture*. Pune: Pune Vidyarthi Griha Prakashan.

Taylor, Meadows

1965 [1864-66] "Catalogue of Indian Musical Instruments: Presented by Colonel P. T. French." *Proceedings of the Royal Irish Academy* 9(1). Reprinted in: *Hindu Music from Various Authors*. Sourindro Mohun Tagore, ed. Calcutta 1875. 2nd edition: 1882. Reprint - Varanasi: Chowkhamba Sanskrit Series Office, 1965:243ff.

Titley, Norah

1977 *Miniatures from Persian Manuscripts and Printed Books: a Catalogue and Subject Index of Paintings from Persia, India and Turkey in the British Library and the British Museum*. London: British Museum Publications.

Tod, James

1950 *Annals and Antiquities of Rajasthan or, the Central and Western Rajpoot States of India*. 2 Vols. 3rd edition. London: Routledge and Kegan Paul. 1st edition: London 1829-32.

Tripathi, Shivanandan Rao

1977 *Saṅgīt sādhan śāstra*. Kanpur: Saṅgīt sādhan samiti.

Varma, Raja Fatah Sinha

1899 *Rāg prakāśikā*. Shajahanpur.

Vastad, Maniram

1893 *Sitār candrikā*. Bombay: Ganga Vishnu Sri Krsnadas.

Velankar, H. D. (ed.)

1949 *Jayadāman*. Haritoṣamālā. 1. Bombay: Haritosha samiti.

Vertkov, K.; Blagodatov, G.; & E. Yazovitskaya

1975 *Atlas of Musical Instruments of the Peoples Inhabiting the U.S.S.R.* Moscow: State Publishers.

Vidyarthi, Govind

1959 "Melody Through the Centuries." (Translations of sections from the "*Ma'dan al-musīqī*" of M. K. I. Khan.) *Bulletin*, Sangeet Natak Akademi 11-12,13-26,33.

Vyas, Lakshmidas Aditram

1916 *Evolution of Indo-Aryan Music and its Present Needs with Hindi Musical Compositions.* Ahmedabad.

Wade, Bonnie

1984 *Khyāl: Creativity Within North India's Classical Music Tradition.* Cambridge Studies in Ethnomusicology. Cambridge: Cambridge University Press.

Welch, Stuart Cary

1978 *Room for Wonder: Indian Painting During the British Period 1760-1880.* New York: The American Federation of Arts.

1985 *India: Art and Culture 1300-1900.* New York: The Metropolitan Museum of Art.

Willard, N. Augustus

1965 [1834] *A Treatise on the Music of Hindoostan, Compromising a Detail of the Ancient Theory and Modern Practice.* Calcutta: Baptist Mission Press. Reprinted in: *Hindu Music from Various Authors.* Sourindro Mohun Tagore, ed. Calcutta 1875. 2nd edition 1882. Reprint - Varanasi: Chowkhamba Sanskrit Series Office, 1965:1-122.

INDEX

[Note: * refers to a musical notation.]

H

I